IT · WASN'T · ALL · VELVET

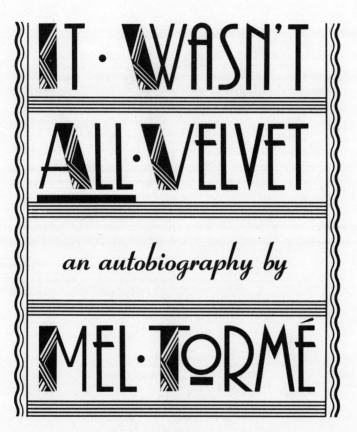

IT · WASN'T ALL · VELVET

an autobiography by

MEL · TORMÉ

viking

VIKING
Published by the Penguin Group
Viking Penguin Inc., 40 West 23rd Street, New York, New York 10010, U.S.A.
Penguin Books Ltd, 27 Wrights Lane, London W8 5TZ, England
Penguin Books Australia Ltd, Ringwood, Victoria, Australia
Penguin Books Canada Ltd, 2801 John Street, Markham, Ontario, Canada L3R 1B4
Penguin Books (N.Z.) Ltd, 182–190 Wairau Road, Auckland 10, New Zealand

Penguin Books Ltd, Registered Offices:
Harmondsworth, Middlesex, England

First published in 1988 by Viking Penguin Inc.
Published simultaneously in Canada

1   3   5   7   9   10   8   6   4   2

All photographs, unless otherwise credited, are from the author's collection.

LIBRARY OF CONGRESS CATALOGING IN PUBLICATION DATA
Tormé, Mel, 1925–
It wasn't all velvet.
1.Tormé, Mel, 1925–   .   2. Singers—United
States—Biography.   I. Title.
ML420.T69A3 1988   784.5′0092′4 [B]   88-14249
ISBN 0-670-82289-2

Printed in the United States of America by
Arcata Graphics, Fairfield, Pennsylvania
Set in Granjon
Designed by Liney Li

This book is dedicated to my parents,
William and Betty Tormé,
and to my wife, Ali

PREFACE

MORT SAHL once said to me, "By 1990, every man, woman, and child in America will have his or her own talk show and will have written an autobiography." He may be right. Exposing one's past via the written word has apparently become as much a national pastime as baseball watching and cheating on your income tax. Statesmen pen their memoirs in order to contribute to the long litany of history. Adventurers, inventors, scientists, military men, and the like leave their exploits in book form for posterity. Entertainment celebrities do it to ventilate, to expiate their real or imagined sins, to relive, vicariously, the good times and the bad by way of their own tape-recorded or handwritten words. And for the money.

When I wrote a book about my experiences with the late Judy Garland during her 1963–64 CBS television series (*The Other Side of the Rainbow,* William Morrow, 1970), I accidentally laid my hands on a critique, written by the president of that publishing house. It was very flattering with regard to the writing itself, but it ended with the observation: "Who cares?"

Who, indeed? Obviously, there is a willing market for the reminiscences of the famous and the infamous; the proud and the profane; the good, the bad, and the ugly. At the same time, it seems important to me to keep the value of these personal diaries in perspective. In the final analysis, they're probably not of any world-shaking significance.

My second published book was a novel, *Wynner* (Stein & Day,

1979). It was mildly successful and enjoyed fairly decent reviews. Many buyers of the book, however, told me they had purchased *Wynner* because, for some reason, they thought it was an auto-biography. I was at work on yet another new novel, but I put it aside when I realized a substantial number of people out there seemed interested in how I got started and how I came to the place in the road in which I now stand.

I have dragged my feet on this autobiography. It has taken me seven years to get it down on paper. Frankly, I felt no vicarious thrill in reliving the past and, be assured, there are no literary pretensions within these covers. The remembrance of things past was often hurtful, sometimes almost unbearable. Yet recalling certain times, certain places, people, events was, by turns, stimulating, euphoric, funny, and bittersweet.

At the outset, let me say I am a man splattered with luck. I am not about to dig my toe into the parquet, hang my head, and mutter, "Aw, shucks, it weren't nothin'." Talent has to be a factor in any career. I have some talent; I have more luck. I am lucky to have survived in a business shot through with the vagaries of an often forgetful, fickle public. As one critic put it, "Tormé hasn't merely survived; he has prevailed." That remark was supremely rewarding.

I am lucky to have had a succession of managers who believed in me, sometimes in defiance of other opinions, sometimes to the exclusion of all else.

I am lucky to have collaborated professionally with some of the greatest talents in show business.

I am lucky to have had a mainly affectionate relationship with the critics at large.

I am lucky to have been friends with many famous (and occasionally, infamous) people, who have enriched my life.

I am lucky to have five bright, wonderful kids and a pair of attractive, intelligent stepchildren, as well as the most supportive parents on the planet and the single finest lady I have ever known for a wife.

Enough already. I hope you will enjoy what you are about to read. I hope it answers some questions you might have wondered

about. Above all, I hope you won't put this down upon finishing
it, look up at the ceiling, and say, "Who cares?"

—MEL TORMÉ

Beverly Hills, California
February 1988

ACKNOWLEDGMENTS

*A*S in every book, there are a lot of people to thank. I want to express my gratitude to my friend writer/producer Rudy Behlmer for his suggestions and annotations during the earlier drafts of this book.

And: Pam Dorman, senior editor at Viking, for her keen eye, good judgment, and meticulous editing suggestions. Her contribution to the final draft is inestimable.

And: Sterling Lord, my literary agent, who has believed in and encouraged every writing project I have set out upon. This is the third book of mine he has represented and sold. "Gratitude" is not a strong enough word.

And: my wife, Ali, who patiently listened as I read the "work in progress," adding her own common-sense comments with regard to additions and deletions. An invaluable wife, lover, friend, and adviser.

And: Mary Williams for her tireless efforts in the clearance of songs and lyrics. She has long been the undisputed expert in this area and I am lucky to have had her working on my behalf.

And: Stacey Endres of The Academy of Motion Picture Arts and Sciences for not only supplying me with some archive photographs vital to this book, but for taking the time to track them down in the vast files of the Academy.

And: Will Friedwald, for his help and continuing interest in my recorded output.

And: all those people I met along the way—fans, fellow performers, agents, musicians, and friends, who expressed a desire to read this, the final product. I appreciate your interest, all of you.

Finally, my manager, Dale Sheets, deserves a ton of credit, along with Ali, for keeping me sane during those times when I became disenchanted with this project, when I felt that I had had enough of seeing "I—I—I" and "me—me—me" repeatedly on every single page. That, however, is part and parcel of an autobiography, so here it is, warts and all.

IT·WASN'T·ALL·VELVET

1.

BEGINNINGS

*E*THEL WATERS was once widely quoted as having said, "Mel Tormé is the only white man who sings with the soul of a black man." I never met that great lady, but if there is even a grain of truth in her words, it may have been because I was born in Chicago on September 13, 1925, in the heart of what was then called the "colored" neighborhood. My father owned a dry goods store at Thirty-third and Michigan, and we lived in a small apartment at the back of the store. My only friends for the first four or five years of my life were "colored" kids.

Just like a scene in some "socially conscious" Warner Bros. movie of the 1930s, I saw little kids tap-dancing on the corner for pennies. I marveled at the syncopated snap of the shoeshine man's rag as he swiped at a customer's shoes with a rhythmic tattoo. And I remember one scrawny little fellow who had gotten hold of a pair of drumsticks. They looked like Indian clubs permanently attached to his seven-year-old hands. He went rap-tap-tapping on everything in sight, including my dad's precious store window. Dad shooed him away on dozens of occasions. . . . God forbid the glass should shatter under the tiny drummer's enthusiastic blows.

Music seemed to be as constant in my life as traffic noises, the shouts of kids at play, or the incessant bargaining my dad went through daily with his customers.

My mother played the piano passably, and my dad had a real passion for singing. He knew reams of songs from the old country and sang them in that clear cantorial voice of his. I have always believed he could have been a great cantor.

Years before I was born, Dad's younger sister, Faye, had become famous in Chicago as the "Wonder Frisco Dancer" and had helped raise thousands of dollars for the war effort in 1917–18 through her dancing. My dad, in his youth, had been an amateur dancer in New York (as a child in Russia he had taken dancing lessons from the great Nijinsky) and had won dozens of contests. I am still surprised he didn't follow through and turn professional. In those days, one of his best friends was Sy Bartlett, who became a well-known screenwriter/producer, as well as the coauthor of the classic film *Twelve O'Clock High*. In the late fifties, I arranged a reunion for Sy and my dad. They greeted each other like long-lost brothers. Sy said to me: "Your dad here was the goddamnedest dancer I ever saw. All the girls wanted him for a dancing partner." Dad beamed. So did my mother.

She was remembering the first time she danced with my dad. It was in the summer of 1923. She had gone to a wedding at the Morrison Hotel in downtown Chicago. Bored stiff, she slipped away and went downstairs to where they were having an afternoon tea dance. There she spotted a young man doing his stuff on the dance floor with an attractive young lady. That young man, blessed with a keen eye for pretty girls, saw young Betty Sopkin walk into the ballroom and made a beeline toward her. Their first dance led to many dates, and those dates culminated in marriage in January 1924.

My parents came from Russian-Jewish backgrounds. My mother was born in America, but Dad came from Russia with his mother, father, and younger brothers when he was eleven. When the family reached Ellis Island, a harried, hurried immigration officer glanced at the name-tag card pinned to my grandfather's coat. It read "Torma" but the "a" was indistinct. The officer grunted and said: "Torme. Your name is Torme." He stamped the papers, handed them to my father's father, and the former Tormas stepped onto the ferry and into the New World as the "Tormes."

My father, William, always called Bill, grew up in New York City's Hell's Kitchen with his younger brothers, Arthur and Albert, and their baby sister, Faye. In 1917, the Tormes moved to Chicago to be near relatives who had settled there.

For people who never ventured into the world of professional entertainment, my family was inordinately musical, especially my dad and his brothers. Whenever the clans met for dinner, the Sopkins and the Tormes invariably punctuated the occasion with a rousing singing session. Old Hebrew songs, current tunes of the day, nostalgic musical memoirs of the past, all were fodder for these family get-togethers. My Uncle Al played the ukelele and the Albert-system clarinet and was my first and only music teacher.

I basked in the warmth of these evenings. The old-country songs were plaintive and touching. When the brothers sang, it was always in three-part harmony and perfectly in tune! I never understood how they managed that. Very early on, I began to sing with them, and I have no doubt that my later propensity for vocal group arranging was directly traceable to those early sing-alongs with my family.

My mother swears I sang my first complete song when I was ten months old. I have grilled her about that as ruthlessly as a Nuremberg war crimes prosecutor. She implacably sticks to her guns. While she did her housework or helped my father in the dry goods store, she used to sing to me as I sat in my high chair or crawled in my playpen:

> Pretty little baby,
> Everybody knows,
> Pretty little baby,
> I love you.

One day (so she says), she was astonished to hear me singing bits of it back to her. At ten months of age. Clearly. In tune. Go argue with my mother.

With so much music going on around me, it should come as no surprise that my favorite household item was a Stromberg-Carlson Cathedral model table radio. I particularly loved listening to the Coon-Sanders Orchestra from the Blackhawk Restaurant in Chicago's Loop. When I was four, I used to push my standard-gauge Lionels around the floor and sing, "You're Driving Me

Crazy" with their band, as the murmur of the Blackhawk patrons and the tinkle of silverware and glasses wafted their way through the speaker.

One Monday night in 1929, my parents dressed me up in a sailor suit and took me to dinner at the Blackhawk. I sat at a front table, my eyes glowing at the sight of the burnished horns, the ebony piano, the shiny massive bell of the tuba, the drums and cymbals. I knew every selection by heart, thanks to our faithful Stromberg, and I sang along with every number. Several dancers observed me and finally one of them went over to one of the band's co-leaders, Joe Sanders ("the Ol' Left Hander"), and pointed me out. At intermission, Sanders walked over to our table and asked my folks about me. When they told him how I loved his radio broadcasts, he smiled at me and went back to the stand.

Before beginning the next set, he had Carlton Coon, the drummer, and his co-leader play a drumroll. "Folks," he announced, "we have with us tonight our youngest and most devoted fan, little Melvin Howard Torme." (He pronounced it "Tormee," as did most people at that time.) "Little Melvin's parents tell me he listens to our broadcasts and knows every number we play. Well, whaddaya say we give him a chance to prove it, eh?"

Sanders led the applause and, while I would like to be able to paint a picture of a four-year-old gulping with fright at the thought of singing before all those people, this was simply not the case. I walked up to the bandstand. Joe Sanders reached down and shook my hand, went to his piano, asked me what I wanted to sing. I told him, he gave the band a downbeat, and my career began at that moment. I sang "You're Driving Me Crazy" and the patrons applauded long and loud. My memories of that evening are absolutely indelible. I particularly remember Carlton Coon lifting me up onto his lap behind the drums and my bouncing up and down each time he worked the bass drum pedal. I fell in love with drums that night.

Before we left, Sanders had a word with my mother and father. Believe it or not, he wanted me to come to the Blackhawk every Monday night and sing one or two songs with the band as a special feature. The offer was fifteen dollars an evening and dinner for the three of us. The folks asked me if I wanted to do it. They were not, nor have they ever been, "stage" parents. The experience had been exhilarating. The lights, the noise, the band, being downtown in a beautiful restaurant with such wonderful food. Did I want to? Please! Could I?

For nearly six months, little Melvin Howard Torme was featured on Monday nights at the Blackhawk, followed by engagements at the Oriental Gardens with Louis Panico's band, and at the College Inn of the Hotel Sherman with Frankie Masters's group and Buddy Rogers's orchestra. I think it is important to note that America was in the death throes of the Roaring Twenties. Black Tuesday had come and gone, but the wackiness of the Charleston era was clinging stubbornly to the national consciousness. Flagpole sitters were still doing their dizzying thing, daredevils walked tightropes between buildings twenty-five stories high, and ex–World War One aviators were flying surplus Jennies under the Brooklyn Bridge. Novelty was the key to success and a kid in short pants and a beret belting out pop tunes with a famous band fit right in with the nutty goings-on that attended the collapse of Wall Street and the subsequent Great Depression.

Just prior to the October debacle, my mother gave birth to my only sister, born August 26, 1929. She was named Myrna, after Myrna Loy. She was an especially pretty baby, and I can imagine the pain my mother and father must have felt when it was discovered that Myrna, at age ten months, had developed meningitis and needed to have a mastoid removed. The operation was successful, but it left my sister with an astigmatism from which she suffers to this day.

Myrna's misfortune seemed to be the prelude to several other setbacks in our family. By 1931, almost everyone in America was in financial trouble, and we were no exception. My dad lost his dry goods store and went to work as a salesman for Hart, Schaffner & Marx. My mother worked in a dress shop owned by distant relatives, and we all moved in with my maternal grandparents on the South Side. Money was extremely tight and the occasional few dollars I earned in kid vaudeville units in and around Chicago went into the family pot. I thank God now that we never starved during those early Depression days, and that I was able to help out, minuscule though my contributions were.

Grandma Sopkin hired a huge, light-skinned Negress to keep house for us and take care of me and my sister during the day while everyone was at work. The woman's name was Alberta, and she came to work for the family on one condition: that she be allowed to have Friday and Saturday nights off so she could play piano with a five-piece combo at the Savoy Ballroom at Forty-seventh and South Parkway, next door to the famed Regal Theatre. During the daytime, when her housework was finished, she would play the Kimball upright in the living room and sing with me. She had it all, the syncopation, the jazz conception, the deep feeling in her singing, the deliciously dissonant chords she played. She exposed me to all of it, and I ingested her musicality by some process of osmosis. (Are you listening, Ethel Waters?)

2.

RADIO

*B*ESIDES music, my family had one other obsession: the movies. It is no secret that during the bleak early thirties, people would go without food so they could go to the movies. Motion pictures (and radio, of course) were the national prescription against mass suicide. The false optimism of songs like "We're in the Money," and others featured in lavish musicals like *The Gold Diggers* and *Forty-Second Street,* was just what the country needed: rose-colored dreams within the gilded walls of movie palaces that blotted out the harsh reality of the daily struggle to survive.

My father and my uncles particularly were manic moviegoers, and I caught the bug from them. As a child performer, my favorite reward for doing a good show was a chocolate malted and a movie. In addition to the first-run houses in the Loop, the South Side boasted some genuinely beautiful theaters: the Avalon, with its Moorish motif, the Tivoli on Cottage Grove, and the Picadilly. All were lushly appointed, comfortable vessels, and we went to the movies three or four times a week, doing our bit toward single-handedly supporting Balaban and Katz theaters.

My Grandpa Sopkin and his brothers opened a dress factory on Wentworth Avenue, and my dad went to work for them as a cutter. The Sopkins and the Tormes were as different as chalk and cheese. The Sopkins ranged from semiaffluent to downright well-off. Grandpa's brother, Ben, was a rich man and took on the mien of patriarch. He dispensed largesse to all branches of the family with dogged frugality, but he was a kind and good man nonetheless.

My grandfather Harry had a great sense of humor and, during my life, came to my rescue financially on several occasions. He used to say he wasn't interested in leaving his money to his children and grandchildren when he died; he wanted to see them enjoy it while he lived. His wife, my grandma Dora, was completely devoted to her children. I always thought she felt Mom had married beneath her, but what my mother got in my father cannot be measured in monetary terms.

My mother and father have to be two of the best-matched people in the history of matrimony. Mom (she was named Sabina at birth, but changed her name to Betty early in her teens) was the strength of my family. Practical, sensible, slightly domineering, she possessed the connective tissue necessary to hold us together during severely trying times. She was a beautiful young woman and it's easy to see why Dad fell in love with her. Terribly popular with young men who had far better prospects than did my father, she opted for him, against the advice of her family. And I know why.

My father was a runaway optimist, a believer in the American Dream. He never intended to stay mired down in the Sopkin dress factory or to plod along selling men's clothing at Hart, Schaffner & Marx. He had ideas, not get-rich-quick plans, nothing like that. Ideas. The kind that have made men wealthy in this country. One of his (and his brother Art's) ideas did make a relative of ours rich. He cheated my dad and uncle out of something they invented and it nearly killed them both. That story I will tell in due course, but I remember how, when I saw the anguish on my father's face knowing his own relation had betrayed him, I fantasized for months about growing up, becoming impossibly wealthy, and hatching an elaborate scheme to ruin the traitor à la Monte Cristo. I told you movies were a way of life with me.

The Tormes—Grandma Rose, Grandpa Sam, Aunt Faye, and the brothers—were cut from totally different cloth than the Sopkins. Essentially poor from the time they landed on Ellis Island, they scratched out their existence. My father was the oldest child, so naturally he became, along with my grandfather, the prime laborer and cobreadwinner. Arthur, the middle son, went to law school with the help of the family. Albert, the youngest, was affable and bright and went on to hold a number of good jobs throughout his lifetime.

Grandma Torme kept a strictly kosher house, and Friday nights belonged to her. Dinner was a ritual, with the best gefilte fish ever, cold Russian borscht with hard-boiled eggs, boiled chicken (which I frankly hated), and her own honey-nut cake that I can still get mouth-watery about. The favorite table drink was seltzer with fresh raspberries mixed in it and something she called "mead" (she pronounced it "medd"), also mixed with seltzer, slightly reminiscent of weak ale and absolutely delicious.

After dinner we would go out on the back porch, Al would unlimber his uke and/or clarinet and we would sing. The neighbors, principally Jewish, seemed to love these little Friday night concerts.

They were happy but difficult times. My parents fought a lot (hell, they still do after sixty-four years!), and the subject was always the same: money. Or rather, the lack of it. No one had any money in those days and, despite their industriousness and my occasional little contributions, we seemed to exist on a day-to-day basis. We never starved, as did so many during that terrible decade, but it was touch and go, and, since we occasionally had to depend on Grandpa Sopkin to see us through, my mother naturally felt embarrassed, rankled, and hurt that Dad had to turn to her father to keep us from going under.

By the time I was eight, in 1933, I was becoming well known locally as one of a dozen or so kids who sang or danced or played a musical instrument in special little companies touring Chicago and the outskirts during the weekends. By now, it was clear to everyone that I wanted to pursue a career in show business. I was getting good experience on these weekend junkets. Things were progressing for me and an even bigger break was just about to present itself.

In June of 1933, the Chicago World's Fair, "A Century of Progress," opened on the lakefront. One of its many events was a contest called the "Radio Auditions Finals." Performers of all ages were invited to participate. The eliminations would be broadcast over one of the top Chicago stations, and, although there was no money involved for the winners, they would each receive a properly inscribed silver cup.

My parents entered me. The year was 1934. I got by the quarter-finals and the semifinals and finally won the children's division cup with a vocally dramatic rendering of Al Jolson's "Goin' to Heaven on a Mule" from *Wonder Bar*.

I got lucky. Two of the judges were Walter and Ireene Wicker. He was a radio producer for NBC. She was the famed "Singing Lady" whose fifteen-minute daily storybook show for children on NBC was one of the highest rated in the country. Chicago was, at that time, the virtual hub of radio, just as Broadway meant theater and Hollywood was the capital of the film industry. The Wickers were branching out, launching a new daytime "soap" called "Song of the City," in which Ireene would also star. A fine child actress, Lucy Gilman, had been signed to play her daughter. There was also a fat role for a young street-urchin orphan called "Jimmy the Newsboy." My reading of the "Mule" lyric won me that role. Suddenly, I was a radio actor.

The show was done from the nineteenth floor of the Merchandise Mart, hard by the Chicago River downtown. The Stineway Drugstore at the mart made great chocolate malts, and during the next few years I enjoyed many of them.

Nate Gross, a top Chicago columnist of the day, ran a big picture of Lucy and me in front of an old NBC ribbon microphone, and my whole family *kvelled*. It looked like Melvin was on his way. Like a chain reaction, other roles were offered to me, and in the next several years I became one of the busiest child actors in radio, appearing on "The Story of Mary Marlin," "Little Orphan Annie," "Jack Armstrong," "Captain Midnight," "Lightning Jim Whipple," "It Can Be Done" with Edgar A. Guest, "Lights Out," "In Chicago Tonight," and scores of others.

The main Chicago clearinghouse/agency for almost all child radio actors just then was a drama school called "The Jack and Jill Players." A tough old gal named Marie Agnes Foley ran the place with just the right amount of patience, understanding, and no-nonsense brittleness.

Since my folks could not afford acting lessons for me, Miss Foley offered me a scholarship. I became a classmate of Franklin

Adams, Jr.—radio's "Skippy" and "Corny" Peeples—who looked
a little like Willie Shoemaker and was an exceptional young actor;
Frankie Pacelli, who probably did more radio shows than any
other youthful thespian in the country; and another bright young
lad with the unusual name of Cleveland Towne.

I joined this select group of talented kids and, thanks to Marie
Agnes Foley, became one of Chicago's most in-demand child radio
actors.

I was still singing as well. Paul Ash, the famous bandleader
and "starmaker," chose me to appear in a Chicago-made movie
whose title happily escapes me. I was assigned an original song
called "Whose Sweet Patootie Are You?" When I saw the final
product, I became ill and vowed that, if I ever crashed the movies,
I would never look at myself on the screen again. I rarely have.

Myrna was now, in 1934, of kindergarten age, and my folks
had enrolled us in Shakespeare Grammar School at Forty-sixth
and Greenwood on the South Side. The school was inhabited by
some of the toughest young punks in the Windy City. One classmate of mine, John Lopez, became a prime mover in the hoodlum
element of the town and was later shot to death in a ninety-mile-
an-hour running gun battle pursuit along Lake Shore Drive in the
early fifties.

Now came this little squirt, Melvin, to school with the rough
monkeys. Melvin, the teacher's pet. Melvin, who, two or three
times a week, was excused from class at noon so he could go
downtown and act on the radio. Melvin, the sissy, who wouldn't
fight. My dad had warned me to stay out of trouble and not get
cut or have any teeth knocked out.

"Remember," he said sternly. "You want to be in the show
business. You can't afford to get into fights. You could get a scar
on your face. Or break a finger and not be able to play the uke."
(Thanks to my uncle Al's tutelage, my ukelele playing was coming
right along.) "Also," Dad continued, "someday, you may get into
the movies. You gotta look good for the movies. No fighting."

There was only one thing wrong with his advice: my school-
mates had other ideas. They beat me like a gong, especially a
scrappy little Irish kid named Steve.

My dad had quit the dress factory. He and my uncle Art were

working on the project I mentioned earlier, and Dad needed more free time. He bought a Model A two-door Ford, khaki-colored body with black fabric top, which he kept—as he has every car he has ever owned—in immaculate condition. He made contacts with several farmers outside of Chicago and, three or four days a week, he would pick up crocks of butter and cheese and cardboard cradles of eggs, which he would then resell to various grocery stores back in town.

One day, he came home from one of his trips early in the afternoon. I traipsed into the house with a bloody nose, having just taken another superb beating from Steve. My sister cried when she saw me, my mother put her hand over her mouth, and my dad marched me into the bedroom to find out what had happened. When I told him, he promptly slung me over his knee and whacked me soundly five or ten times.

"I told you to try and stay out of fights. I didn't tell you to be a sissy," he said.

"No, Pop," I corrected him. "Remember? You said—"

"Be quiet. I don't want you to be a sissy. No matter what."

I was having trouble following his line of reasoning. Still, that spanking (the only one he ever gave me) opened new vistas. His words were tantamount to waving a red flag in front of a bull.

Now Steve was one of the toughest guys in my school: no way to beat him fair and square. But when I recalled all the times he had used me for a punching bag, the derisive laughter at my expense, the humiliation suffered in front of giggling girls, I wasn't terribly concerned about the Marquis of Queensbery.

The next morning I ran all the way to school. I took the stairs to the second floor two at a time, turned a corner, and waited. It was five minutes to nine. Several kids looked at me quizzically. At two minutes to nine, Steve came bounding up the stairs, books in hand. As he reached the top stair, I turned the corner and hit him square in the nose, breaking it. Blood gushed from it like a broken red inkwell and he toppled backward all the way down to the first floor. God, that felt good.

I was suspended by the principal for one full week and had to bring my mother to school before I could get reinstated. My first day back I was wary as a cat, looking around, expecting to be jumped at any moment. Steve was nowhere to be seen. Strangely, my classmates acted as if nothing had happened, but no one picked a fight with me from that day on.

When Steve came back into school, amazingly, he gave me a wide berth. But four months later, coming out of drum-and-bugle corps practice, I was grabbed from behind by Steve's older brother, pinned to the ground by two of his pals, and forced to eat a tin of Mail Pouch tobacco. For the next two months or so, everything I ate, steak, potatoes, spinach, apples, cake, ice cream, *everything* tasted like tobacco. It was an instant cure, however. I have never smoked a cigarette, cigar, or pipe.

My dad certainly was no sissy, little guy that he was. The janitor of our apartment house was a big, ugly brute. His fourteen-year-old son was cast in his image. One day, as I turned into the walkway leading to the front door of our building, Sonny Boy grabbed me and began pounding on me. No reason. He simply had nothing else to do at that moment.

When my dad found out, he went right downstairs to brace the janitor. Ignatz (or whatever his name was) stood out front, watering the sparse little lawn in front of the place. I watched out the window as my brave little dad shook a finger in the face of the big oaf, shouting at him and warning him to tell his kid to lay off me.

"Ignatz" took it for a while. Then he casually turned and slammed my dad in the face. Blood spurted from Dad's nose and down he went, tripping over the little wire fence that separated the sidewalk from the grass. Dad got up. The bastard knocked him down again. It was David and Goliath, except this time, William David Torme was getting the worst of it. The janitor looked down at my dad, spit on the lawn, and walked unconcernedly away. Dad came back upstairs, holding a handkerchief to his nose. His eyes were tearing in humiliation. He walked into his bedroom and closed the door. I never felt so impotent in my life.

The next day, my beloved uncle Al put his two cents in. Al, my musical mentor, Al of the sweet disposition, Al, who became

a major in World War Two and saw active duty in the Pacific.
Al, with delightful simplicity, walked up to "Ignatz" during the
latter's daily grass-watering session and, without a word, decked
him. And decked him again. And again. The bum went to the
hospital. Al explained to the police, summoned by the janitor's
wife, what had happened. When they took a look at my dad, they
actually grinned at my uncle and drove away.

3.

SONGWRITER

*A*S I have mentioned, Mom was the pragmatist, Dad, the dreamer. Not content with his road trips, hawking wares of small farmers, my father put his active imagination to work. Along with his brother Art, a budding attorney but also a fine amateur artist, Dad improved on something that is still being produced today: the pop-up book.

First he would take semiheavy paper, cut and fold it into the shape of a scene from a fairy tale, such as "Puss 'n Boots"; then my uncle Art would illustrate the scene on the cut-out silhouette. Finally, they would take a book, any book, and paste the finished product between the pages. After several weeks of trial and error, the scene "popped up," an illustrated story come to life in front of your eyes.

Since they were ignorant of the ways and wiles of the publishing business, a relative by marriage offered to take the idea to the Whitman Publishing Company in Racine, Wisconsin. Whitman was one of the largest publishers of children's books and was currently having a field day with its "Big Little Books," small hard cardboard–covered reprints of all the popular Sunday and daily funnies with equal pages of text and panels. I devoured these little gems like some kids wolfed candy bars, and I recall fondly the numerous times my dad went up to Racine to talk with the Whitman people, returning with dozens of Big Little Books for me and my sister.

Dad and Art then plunged into a new idea for Whitman: the Mickey Mouse Waddle Book. They cut several pieces of heavy cardboard and fashioned them into a small, steep ramp. Next, they made Mickey's body from thick cardboard stock. His arms and legs were cut separately. At the base of the torso, Dad cut a deep groove into which he inserted a cleverly formed piece of steel spring. The legs were affixed to the bottom side of the spring, and when Mickey was placed at the top of the ramp, he would waddle right down to the bottom.

Whitman loved it and produced a handsome "Waddle" book, complete with Mickey and Minnie, and, of course, the ramp and the steel spring inserts, all made of high-quality materials and beautifully lithographed. The book sold extremely well. It was not inexpensive, and dollars during the Depression were at a premium. It looked as though my dad's dreaming had borne real financial fruit.

Neither he nor my uncle Art ever saw a dime of profit from either the pop-up books or the Waddle Book. Our relative made the deal with Whitman and reaped the rewards from the royalties. Dad had trusted him and was betrayed for that trust. Our relative died rich and Dad never again came close to a windfall, the experience having taken much wind out of his optimistic sails. (For the record, the Mickey Mouse Waddle Book is among the most coveted and hard-to-come-by of all the Mickey Mouse collectibles, and is currently worth, in mint condition, $15,000.)

Movies fostered my obsession with airplanes and bred what became my first hobby: model building. During the dark, cold wintry Chicago nights, I built World War One–scale models: Fokker D. VIIs, Spads, Nieuports. In our small apartment on Forty-sixth Street in the heat of a windless Windy City summer, I carved and shaped balsa-wood replicas of Albatri, Sopwith Camels, and SE5s. I won some prizes for my efforts at local hobby shops, and my interest in World War One aviation never waned. In 1959, along with eleven other enthusiasts, I started a club dedicated to the history of flying in the Great War. It is called the "Cross and Cockade," and today the society boasts hundreds of members.

Our family survived the Depression. Keep on keeping on was the way things worked and, somehow, the Tormes did. Between what I earned as a radio actor and in those kid-vaudeville units, and the combined efforts of Mom and Dad in their respective jobs, we never, really, wanted for anything. And, luckily, there was always Grandpa Sopkin to help out in emergencies.

I was enormously lucky as a kid, when I think about it. The Torme clan, lacking affluence of any sort, provided, well, clannishness—a protective, loving cocoon that included affection, attention, talents to be shared, and close family experiences.

The Sopkins were no less loving, albeit less demonstrative. My maternal grandparents, particularly Grandpa Sopkin, were supportive beyond belief. The Sopkins were proud of me, but they took it all in stride. Why shouldn't Melvin be musically talented? Isn't his second cousin George Sopkin, a great cellist who played with the world-famous Fine Arts String Quartet since its inception? Isn't his other second cousin Henry Sopkin, a great conductor who founded the Atlanta Symphony and conducted that organization from the mid-1950s until he retired in 1965?

Having been in the Shakespeare Grammar School Drum and Bugle Corps since I was eight, my interest in drums burgeoned. Record collecting had somewhat supplanted model building by 1937. Benny Goodman and Gene Krupa were haunting my dreams. I saw _Hollywood Hotel_ no less than five times, and Krupa's junglelike tom-tomming on "Sing, Sing, Sing" grabbed me where I lived. I discovered Chick Webb and had trouble deciding which had come first—the Chick or Krupa. It didn't matter. They were both great, my new heroes . . . along with Ray Bauduc of the Bob Crosby band. His drumming, so musical and inventive, simply put me away.

Uncle Art was coming into his own as a lawyer. His acquaintances ranged from highly placed city officials to many who lived on the darker side of the law. I remember one evening when Art took me to dinner at the home of a man whom I shall call "Spinelli." He was a tall, handsome gent, sporting an incongruously deep tan in wintertime Chicago. At one point during the meal, I asked to be excused to go to the bathroom. Spinelli pointed to the stairway and said, "Up the stairs, second door to your right."

I went up to the second floor of his luxurious house, turned right, and opened a door. It was dark inside, so I snapped on a light. It wasn't a bathroom; it was a closet. Inside, on pegs and in racks, was an arsenal: handguns of every description, rifles, and a pair of Thompson submachine guns. I gasped. The movies I attended so regularly, particularly westerns and gangster epics, had made me, along with hundreds of my peers, minor experts where firearms were concerned. All my young pals, especially my best friend, Vic Grenrock, knew the difference between an automatic in the hands of Jimmy Cagney and a six-gun wielded by Bob Steele. Now, here in front of me, were the real things.

I stood in the closet for the better part of ten minutes taking this revolver and that automatic from their respective pegs, examining them thoughtfully, then gingerly replacing them. I did not know whether or not those guns were loaded, but, being the proud owner of one of the finest cap-gun collections on the South Side, I simply had to handle the genuine articles. When I finally, quietly, closed that closet door and went back to the table, Art remarked that I had been gone a long time and asked if I had found the bathroom all right. I mumbled yes. I had forgotten to go and suffered all the way home.

Another of Art's acquaintances was a man named Danny Pulagi, a stocky, swarthy little guy with a gentle smile. Danny was a jukebox distributor, and, one day, Art brought me to his place of business, located on the near South Side at Twenty-second and Wabash, near Colosimo's, where Big Jim had been gunned down by Big Al. The place was swimming in records. I didn't know where to look first. Danny smiled. Art had told him about me, my growing interest in jazz, and my expanding record collection.

"Take," Pulagi said, grinning. "Go and look and find and take."

"Honest, Mr. Pulagi?" I asked, hoping to God he meant it.

"Certainly. Whatever you see that you want, take."

I took. Ellington and Barnet and Lunceford and Basie and much more. Like that onetime Big Little Book bonanza, I came away from Danny Pulagi's warehouse with arms full of 78s. Most of them had been used on jukeboxes and were slightly worn, but all were in good playing condition. I was allowed to visit and "take" many times over, and I will never forget Danny's kindness. I still have every single record he ever gave me. They were a basis for my ongoing musical education, the primers of my formative years.

The Duke's "Reminiscing in Tempo," poignant, dirgelike; Basie's "Every Tub," sheer exuberance appended by the "Pres," Lester Young; Charlie Barnet's "Lament for May" and his version of Ellington's "The Sergeant Was Shy"; all were among the first batch of goodies I appropriated from the Pulagi warehouse. I yearned for a set of drums with which to accompany those records. My grandpa Sopkin went to the Boston Store and bought me a set of Wm. F. Ludwig drums. They were white lacquer, labeled THE RAY BAUDUC BOB CAT COMBO (after Bob Crosby's Bob Cats), and I loved them. I proceeded to drive my family and our neighbors out of their collective minds every afternoon after school, playing along with Goodman's "Roll 'Em," Dorsey's "Song of India," and Bob Crosby's "Big Noise from Winnetka."

The "Bauduc" drum set did not, however, come with a floor tom-tom, nor did it sport a high-hat stand and cymbals. Within a year, impressed with the progress I was making, despite the headache-producing results, the Tormes and the Sopkins banded together and traded in my drums at Frank's Drum Shop for an incredibly beautiful pearl-and-chrome ensemble of drums and gleaming brass cymbals, the like of which would have gladdened the heart of any professional name-band drummer.

What a family.

≡

That I began writing songs when I was thirteen should surprise no one. I had been singing professionally since near-toddlerhood. Songs, by the time I had reached my first year of adolescence, were as much a part of my life as brushing my teeth. We had a piano in the living room of the flat we were once again sharing with Grandma and Grandpa Sopkin, and I began fooling with it, picking out chords, trying to shape sounds the way Duke Ellington did. It was pedestrian and awkward at first, but soon I was able to accompany myself with reasonable accuracy. The next step was songwriting.

By the time I was fourteen, my voice had changed and I wasn't getting as many offers to play kid parts on radio as I once had. As much as I enjoyed acting, music was my dominant interest now. By 1939, Duke Ellington was firmly entrenched as my musical hero. His arranging-composing-pianistic talents seemed to dwarf everyone else's by comparison, although I also admired the arranging efforts of Billy May; Jerry Gray; Billy Moore, Jr.; Jimmy Mundy; and Fletcher Henderson. Duke's compositions, however, stood alone, in a class by themselves.

The Ellington orchestra, bursting with originality, rich in its combined tonal quality, its individual soloists, and the peculiar, thickly voiced arrangements of its leader, stuck to my ribs like Irish stew. The ensemble work was not as precise as Glenn Miller's, or as easily digestible as Tommy Dorsey's, but Ellington's clustered chords, his moody ramblings and the utterly loose way his musicians interpreted his genius was more appealing to me than the tightest section work imaginable. I never thought of Duke's brood as a "swing" band. Sonny Greer's drumming alone was too stylized and somewhat rigid (although absolutely more right for that band than any other drummer would have been) actually to "swing" the orchestra. Rather, the band seemed to me to be a canvas upon which Duke painted; light sunshiny pastels, dark mosaics, and, on occasion, a masterwork such as "Black, Brown and Beige," his Tone Parallel to the American Negro.

With Duke as my inspiration, I began writing songs. They weren't very good, but it was a beginning. The family had a summit meeting. Should Mel (blessedly I had graduated from "Melvin" to "Mel" by that time) take piano lessons? To find out, they took me to the Kimball Building on Wabash Avenue in the Loop, where I met a small, talented crippled woman called Lucille Gould. She was one of Chicago's foremost piano teachers. She listened to me play what I had taught myself by ear and immediately offered me a scholarship. My parents were delirious. I studied with her for three weeks. One day I played some of the songs I had written. She listened thoughtfully. Finally, she said: "Mel, I think you ought to stop studying the piano."

I couldn't believe my ears. "Are you kidding, Miss Gould?"

"No, I'm absolutely serious," she replied. "You have a unique way of forming chords, of making sounds on the instrument. You told me how much you admire Duke Ellington. I can hear that in your songs. Now, think. Do you want to become a pianist? I mean simply that: a pianist. Or is songwriting and, perhaps, arranging your aim?"

"Well," I said haltingly, not quite knowing how to express myself at that point, "I kind of want to do it all, you know, Miss Gould? I mean, I want to sing and drum and write songs and, sure, maybe someday be an arranger. It all interests me."

"But do you want to be a pianist? To play the piano professionally?"

"Well . . ." I hesitated.

"Stop studying the piano," she said decisively. "You have a real gift for writing songs. It's original, fresh, and slightly amazing for your age. If you keep studying the piano formally with me, it's just possible that some of that freshness you have will get erased in favor of being a piano player. Do you understand?"

I didn't, and I'll never know whether Lucille Gould did me a great favor in arresting my piano lessons because she really believed I had a future as an inventive, original composer-arranger, or because, on second thought, she realized she had a klutz on her hands who would never get the hang of technique or sight reading or the discipline it takes to put away the drumsticks and practice the piano several hours a day if one planned to be good at it.

It was just around this time that "Torme" got changed to "Tormé." Who changed it or how it came to pass I simply can't remember. I vaguely recall my mother having something to do with it. At any rate, my name came to be pronounced "Tormay" early in 1940 and that's that. Frankly, the added accent *ague* over the "e" in my last name has been a headache. Most advertisers forget to print it, and the name looks naked without it.

I had graduated from grammar school and enrolled in Hyde Park High School at Sixty-third and Stony Island Avenue. It was a large, pale yellow edifice with Greek-style columns out in front. Five thousand students labored there and, oddly enough, we all seemed to meet each other at some point. Vic Grenrock, who was my best buddy at the time, also went to Hyde Park. Vic was a quiet kid who loved jazz and played damned good harmonica. Had he stayed with it, he might have graduated on to woodwinds and become a professional musician.

I will never forget one of our forays on a Saturday afternoon in pursuit of our main mutual interest: the big bands. We had eagerly awaited the release of a movie called *Some Like It Hot*. The 1939 version starred Bob Hope and Shirley Ross and, more importantly, it featured the newly formed Gene Krupa Orchestra. Having lived four blocks away from Krupa's old homestead on the South Side, and as obsessed with drums as I was, I was counting the days until Saturday, when I could go to the Tivoli Theatre and see the film.

Vic and I rode over to the Tivoli that day on my brand-new Roamer bike, a gorgeous red thing bought for me by my mother's sister Ruth, and her husband, Ben Baer. We dutifully chained the bike to a large light standard just outside the theater and made our way inside. The movie knocked us out, with Gene and the band performing "Wire Brush Stomp," and "Drum Fantasy," as well as a couple of fine Frank Loesser tunes, "The Lady's in Love with You" and, of course, "Some Like It Hot." When the picture ended, Vic and I made a decision: we had to stay and see it again. I walked outside to check the bicycle. Cottage Grove Avenue was not the safest place in the world. The Roamer was fine, right where we had left it. We sat through the movie one more time, singing the tunes as we walked out into the late afternoon sunlight.

The bicycle was gone.

I was in a high state of depression as I boarded the streetcar for home. I explained what had happened and my mother immediately called Aunt Ruth to see if the bike had been insured. It had not. I never again owned a bicycle. I had loved the Roamer. It was gone. At various times, different members of my family offered to replace it, but I refused. I suppose the shock of losing it was something I did not want to experience again.

Hyde Park High was bursting with talented students. A guy named Arch Pettigrew played good piano; a tall, olive-skinned kid named Larry Berlin was a surprisingly adept bass player, and I joined them on drums to form a trio that would win several prizes way over on the North Side at the Edgewater Beach Hotel. Every Friday, Ted Weems's famous band conducted talent nights, and we three South Siders would make the trek, do our particular thing, and walk away with cash prizes. The money came in handy. We were all courting girls at Hyde Park and, as I have learned along the way, girls cost money.

The Weems band boasted two good singers: Perry Como and Marvel (later Marilyn) Maxwell. They were kind and encouraging, as was Weems and his excellent drummer, Orme Downs. These little triumphs were giving the trio some small measure of celebrity at Hyde Park. We got together with some other school musicians and formed a band. Arch Pettigrew dropped out and was replaced by a lanky, bespectacled classmate named Steve Allen. A gaunt outsider, slightly older than the rest of us, held down the second trumpet chair. Niles Lishness almost became famous after Steve became famous and began mentioning Niles's name à la Durante's "Mrs. Calabash."

Me, I was in love. Her name was Sophie Kostak. She was Greek, blond, and gorgeous. She had eyes only for Hyde Park's reigning football star, Gordon Vaundry. He also was blond and gorgeous. Together, they were gorgeosity personified. Occasionally, Sophie graced me with a smile in the hallway and I would go slack-jawed. Once, I actually got her to go out with me. The date was a dud. I kept expecting her to put her hand in front of her beautiful mouth and go "ho-hum" throughout the evening.

I went home and did a lot of teeth-gritting and finally, at my dad's suggestion, wrote a song, a balm for my aching heart. I called it "Lament to Love."

Life wasn't too horrible, though. I joined yet two other bands as drummer and sometime singer. The Aristocrats (do you believe it?) were essentially a group of guys from neighboring Hirsch High School, and while I played with them, I met a beauty named Jean Plimpton. She went to Hirsch and lived farther to the west than I really liked to travel, but she was worth it. On home ground, I gave up pursuing the unattainable Sophie and settled for an equally lovely girl. Her name was Shirley Matthews. She was a slightly shy, somewhat insular young lady with the kind of arrestingly beautiful features that made the male population of H.P. stand stock still, turn in their tracks, and stare in open admiration. No one, however, had been able to get next to her. Why me is something I still cannot answer. Shirley and I "teamed up" with a girl named Dale Hershey and her boyfriend, John Poister, who was to become my closest friend at Hyde Park for the three and a half years I would spend there.

John Poister was tall, with straight dark hair, a perpetually red nose, and a great sense of humor. He came from old money and lived with his parents in a beautiful high-rise on South Shore Drive, drove his own car, a Buick coupe, and, while he played no instrument well (he toyed with drums once in a while), he was the single prime appreciator of music I have ever known.

On the weekends, unless I was playing with the Aristocrats or our Hyde Park orchestra or with a society-type band led by another affluent young South Sider, a piano player named Fritzy Freund, John, Dale, Shirley, and I would spend our evenings downtown, hearing Charlie Barnet's band at the Panther Room of the Hotel Sherman, catching T. Dorsey at the Chicago Theatre or J. Dorsey at the Oriental or Louis Armstrong's big band at the State-Lake.

I was up to my kneecaps in music. I was still acting on radio occasionally. I had good friends, a pretty girl who cared about me, a doting family, a happy existence at school and, though I couldn't have known it then, something very big was about to happen for me. Why can't we simply freeze life at times like that?

4.

HARRY

"**W**E'RE going to the State-Lake Theatre this afternoon," my dad said. "We're meeting Art there along with a friend of his, Henry Kalcheim."

Puzzled, I looked at him and waited for more.

"Mr. Kalcheim is an attorney, a big one. He's a friend of Art's. His brothers, Nat and Harry, are two of the biggest men at the William Morris Agency. Anyway, Art told Henry about your songs and Henry's arranged for you to play a couple for Harry James."

Harry James? I couldn't believe it! Only the day before I had been playing drums along with James's records of "Night Special," "Feet Draggin' Blues," "Back Beat Boogie," and "Flash." The relatively new Harry James band was gutty and swingy and one of my favorites. Young Frank Sinatra had sung with him but had gone on to the Tommy Dorsey Band. A robust baritone named Dick Haymes was James's current singer, and a diminutive little guy, Mickey Scrima, was the band's propeller on drums. My God . . . Harry James!

Dad and I caught the I-C (Illinois Central train) on that Saturday afternoon in early October of 1940 and were downtown in less than twenty-five minutes. Art and Henry Kalcheim met us at the stage door of the State-Lake Theatre. We were directed to stand in the wings while the James band finished their last number on stage. They closed with "Two O'Clock Jump" and I softly sang the final riffs along with them. The audience applauded vigorously, the screen came down, the movie began, and the musicians filed off the stage.

Speaking in that peculiarly high voice of his, Harry greeted
Henry Kalcheim warmly. Kalcheim, a dapper man who was something of a dandy with his Sulka ties and white-on-white shirts,
introduced us to the gangly trumpeter. Harry was charming and
effusive. I was a swift fifteen years old, but I will never forget his
total lack of condescension. He treated me as an adult, an equal.
We went downstairs, under the stage. An old white-enameled
piano, slightly out of tune, awaited us. I played and sang several
of my songs. One particular tune really interested James—"Lament
to Love," my minor-keyed torch song for Sophie.

James had shown a predilection for tunes in a minor key, an
almost Jewish musical leaning that I suspect had rubbed off on
him sitting next to Ziggy Elman for so long in the Benny Goodman
trumpet section. He had me play and sing "Lament to Love" three
times, commenting to Henry that he liked the song enormously.
He also liked my singing and said so to my dad and uncle. I was
grinning moronically, Alfred E. Neuman basking in the sunshine
of Harry James's compliments. My uncle Art, no shrinking violet,
then pulled a picture out of his briefcase: Mel at the drums. Harry's
eyes widened a bit. He was famous for his love of drums and
drummers. Like another great trumpeter, Roy Eldridge, he was
also quite an accomplished drummer himself. He had spent nearly
forty-five minutes with us. Now, he rubbed his nose thoughtfully.

"Listen," he said, "could you come back after our performance?
I hate to keep you so long, but I've got a few things to take care
of before we go on again. However, if you could come back, I'd
appreciate it."

"You mean you want to think about some of these tunes in the
meantime, Harry?" Kalcheim asked.

"Well, yes," James replied. "But what I really want to do is
hear Mel play drums."

My heartbeat became erratic. I'd never be able to do it. Two
hours later, I did, in front of Mickey Scrima, Dick Haymes, and
a half-dozen members of the band and, of course, Harry himself.
When I finished my solo, they applauded and James said one word:
"Neat."

His road manager, Don Reid, pulled him aside and they con-
ferred in hushed tones for a few minutes. Then they asked us to

go on up to Harry's dressing room. Once inside, Don closed the door and said, "Look, Harry likes Mel." He looked at me. "You've got a hell of a lot of talent, young man." He turned to my dad and uncle again. "We'd like to add Mel to the band. He could sing the rhythm things that Dick doesn't do, and we'd like to feature him on drums."

On drums? What about Mickey Scrima, I thought. Don read my thoughts. "We wouldn't want to replace Mickey. He's our drummer and one of the best in the business. No, I mean we would have Mel play a specialty number with the band and Harry. Sort of a featured attraction, you might say."

I piped up. "Yes, Mr. Reid, but wouldn't Mickey resent—"

"Not at all, Mel. Mickey's a sweetheart. Not a jealous bone in his body. You'll see. You'll become great friends."

He addressed my dad again. "Well, what do you think, Mr. Tormé?"

Dad was speechless for a moment. Then he said, "The thing is, Mr. Reid, Mel's right in the middle of a semester and, well, what about school?"

Don laughed. "Oh, I didn't mean we'd take him with us now, when we leave Chicago. We have details that would have to be worked out. Let him finish his current semester and we can plan for February. How's that?"

It was all I could do to contain myself from digging my elbow into my dad's ribs. To go with Harry James's band! Please, Dad, say yes.

My father smiled at me. He knew the kind of education I could get with a name band was more important to me than the curriculum at Hyde Park High. "Okay," he said, "we'll wait to hear from you."

Don wrote down our address in his little breast-pocket address book. They're not kidding, I thought breathlessly. They mean it.

My family cheered when they heard the news that night, and we celebrated (how else?) by having dinner out and going to a movie.

The next morning, Sunday, I made a mistake that was to cause me grief throughout the rest of my time at Hyde Park High.

I called my friend, John Poister, and told him what had happened. He was euphoric. Within fifteen minutes he showed up at our flat and insisted we pick up the girls and celebrate. Dale flushed with excitement when I told her about the offer. Shirley smiled wanly. She was happy for me, unquestionably, but my going away, leaving school (and her) did not sit well at all. I understood and loved her for it.

"One thing, you guys," I said later as we prepared to break it up for the evening, "not a word about this at school. It's a long time off, and—"

"Jesus, you're kidding!" John exploded. "The gang will go crazy when they hear this!"

"Okay, okay, Johnny," I said, smiling a little proudly, "but now isn't the time to talk about it. Let's wait a while."

"I think Mel's right," Shirley said.

"So do I," echoed Dale.

"Nuts!" said John impatiently.

Four days later, my knees buckled when I saw that week's issue of the school paper. The headline read: HYDE PARK PRODIGY TO PLAY WITH NAME BAND. John Poister, one of the editors of the paper, simply could not wait. As I walked through the halls that day, I was the recipient of much back slapping, glad handing, shouts of congratulations, and outright cheers. It felt damn good. But I was angry with my best friend. I found him, expecting a sheepish grin, but he imperiously waved away my objections.

"Hey, come on. It's a fact, isn't it? What's wrong with doing a little crowing, huh? How about out there in the halls? Chicks smiling at you, right? Guys wanting to shake your hand, right?"

"Well, yes, but—"

"Felt good, didn't it?" John asked, smiling broadly.

"Sure it felt good, but—"

"Felt *damn* good, didn't it?"

I smiled lamely. "Yeah, all right. It felt damn good."

"So, fine. So wallow in it."

I wallowed.

5.

HUMILIATION

$\mathcal{F}$OR the next few months, I was the most popular kid in that school. Girls who had never before given me a second look suddenly found me fascinating. Guys who had treated me with no more than perfunctory politeness now had this strange urge to be "best friends." I was invited to parties, picnics, and proms, and I was pledged to a popular fraternity, Phi Alpha Phi (illegal in high school, the frats flourished nonetheless).

I loved it. Who wouldn't? I weighed the danger of giving in to such celebrity and decided the risk was minimal. After all, hadn't Harry James offered me the job? No doubt about it. No doubt at all. Hadn't Don Reid promised to keep in touch right up until February, when I would finally join the band? As if by magic, a letter from him, on the Harry James Orchestra stationery, arrived in mid-November, reaffirming everything we had talked about. Reid even mentioned Dick Haymes as my possible roommate on the road.

Time marched on happily. New Year's Eve came and went. In January I began saying good-byes to friends. I had received two more letters from Don Reid, the last of which, written in late December 1940, contained a slightly disturbing phrase: "child labor laws." Reid assured us in that letter that he was working on the problem. Certain states in which the band appeared apparently had strict legislation with regard to adolescents appearing professionally on the stage. Schooling and environment played a large part in these state laws. "Don't worry, Mel. I'm sure we can solve it, and we are all looking forward to your becoming a member of our organization," Reid concluded.

An icy February 1941 blew in; the new semester began and I was part of it. February . . . the month I was to have joined the band. The days blew away, like one of those windswept calendars one sees in movies denoting the passage of time.

I waited for a letter from Don Reid.

Nothing.

By mid-March, I was nervous and slightly depressed. A few snide remarks had been passed by those who, just a couple of months back, had lionized me. I confessed my concern to my uncle Art and he, in turn, called Henry Kalcheim, who promised to contact Reid and get some kind of explanation.

During the first week in April a letter arrived, confirming my worst fears. In it, Don Reid explained: "We have gone back and forth on this situation, and I'm afraid it's simply unsolvable. In order to hire Mel, we would be forced, by several states, to also hire a full-time tutor, which, frankly, we cannot afford. I can't tell you how sorry I am, or how disappointed Harry is. Maybe we can still work things out sometime in the future, when Mel is older and out of school, but right now . . ."

I was sick. And now it came back to me: my warning to Poister *not* to leak the news. I had been in show business long enough to know how fragile a "deal" is until the papers are signed, but I had gone along with my best friend's enthusiasm. What to do now? Tell all my friends the James job had fallen through? Would they believe me? Why not? I had the letters to prove every word I had said.

I called John and told him the bad news. He was, if anything, sicker about it than I. I said I felt we had to tell people that I would not be joining Harry James, at least not right away. He agreed.

In school the next day, I glumly spread the news. Although I had never had a reputation as a liar, my "friends" chose to disbelieve me. It had all been a hoax, they decided, and they treated me accordingly.

None are so cruel as the young. When an adolescent puts his or her mind to it, nastiness can achieve world-class proportions. I now became the butt of countless jokes.

On a streetcar, going home from school: "Hey, look. There's Harry James's ex-drummer. Everybody rise."

In the halls of good old H.P.: "Well, if it isn't Fibber McGee. How's the band business these days?"

In a classroom, a challenge from Marvin Margolis, a hulking young brute who bore a startling resemblance to future star Dustin Hoffman: "Hey, Tormé. I'll be waiting for you in Jackson Park after school."

"Oh, yeah? What for?"

" 'Cause you're a goddamn liar, and I'm going to beat the shit out of you." Marvin could have mashed me to a pulp. I skulked away from the school grounds later that afternoon, avoiding an encounter and thereby adding "coward" to the growing list of epithets being hurled at me.

And then there was the matter of the fraternity. When "Hell Night" arrived, the temperature was a brisk 28 degrees, with the wind blowing its head off from the lake. The plan was to drive the pledges downtown and degrade them on the corners of State and Randolph. We were required to wear an undershirt and jockey shorts. Period.

My mother and father rebelled. I had a bad cold and they insisted I wear something warm. I conveyed the message to my future fraternity brothers. They didn't believe me. After all, wasn't I the jerk who had lied his behind off about going with Harry James? They refused to let me off the hook.

So, after eight weeks of severe paddlings and doing other guys' homework, I was kicked out, blackballed, and otherwise informed that I was definitely not Phi Alpha Phi material. It hurt.

All of the foregoing must seem inconsequential to anyone reading this right now; it seems so to me as I write it. Yet, back in 1941, when the center of my life was my school and my friends, the kind of treatment I was subjected to seemed catastrophic.

John Poister and his girl, Dale, Shirley, and perhaps a round dozen more stuck by me. It got so bad that, at one point, my parents and even Poister suggested that I transfer to the newly built South Shore High. It was much closer to where we lived, a bike ride really, and my aunt Ruth, God bless her, offered to replace the Roamer I had lost. I refused. Stubbornly. Stupidly, I suppose. Things would have been much easier had I taken their suggestion. Now that South Shore High was a reality, I was actually, legally, residing in its district. I was *supposed* to transfer to that school. But, damn it, Hyde Park was where I had started. To be sure, the erstwhile friends who had turned against me by the dozens made every day a painful experience. But there were still John and Dale and Shirley and Buddy Green and his girl, Betty Hope Heller, and Gil Kleinfelter and Larry Berlin and John Segal and a handful more who made me feel like a human being.

No, goddamn it! I was staying at Hyde Park. It was my school. The bastards were not going to drive me away.

"All right," said Poister resignedly, "then at least bring Don Reid's letters to school. Prove that everything you ever said about Harry James and you is true. Hell, nobody could fake those letters."

My mother piped in. "Fake them? We still have the envelopes they came in, for God's sake. With the postmarks. And they are all written on Harry James's own stationery."

"I know, I know," John said. "How about it, Torm? Bring 'em to school and shove 'em down their lousy throats." He brightened. "Hey! I just got a great idea. I'll print the damn things up in the school paper. Not just what's in them. The actual letters. We'll reproduce them, Harry James masthead and all. Oh, Jesus! They'll all swallow their rotten tongues!"

My parents were all for it and I will admit I seriously considered it. It would certainly have vindicated me. I called Shirley and we chewed it over for the better part of an hour.

The next day, at lunch, I told John my decision.

"I'm not going to do it, Johnny. Now wait a minute, hear me out. So I bring them in. And you publish them. And the kids all read them. And they say to themselves, 'My God, we've sure been unfair to poor little Mel. All the time he was telling the truth.' And suddenly we're all buddy-buddy again. The hell with that. Sure, you saw the letters every time they arrived. But Dale didn't. Shirley didn't. And neither did Gil or John or Buddy or any of the others who believed me. I treasure my friends. Screw the rest of them."

John shook his head and gave me the rueful grin I had expected months earlier. "I sure as hell opened a can of peas, didn't I?"

"A bucket, dummy." I smiled.

"Well." He sighed, rising and looking at his watch. "I'm late for Baumgartner's class." He looked at me once more. "Are you sure?"

I nodded. "I'm sure, pal."

He grinned broadly. "You're weird, Torm. But maybe that's why I like you."

6.

RETRIBUTION

*J*UST when I began to feel as though the scorn of my school-mates had become unbearable, something interesting happened. In June 1941, Harry James's recording of "Lament to Love" was released and immediately took off. A Chicago publishing house, Roe-Krippene, had bought the song and, because of my rather tender years, a great to-do was made over "America's Youngest Hit Songwriter." The BMI-ASCAP war was raging then. The two licensing organizations were slugging it out toe-to-toe, and BMI, in partcular, was looking for anything—*anything* promotable. I seemed to fit the bill, and suddenly I began receiving an avalanche of publicity.

In the *Chicago Tribune*:

> Love, unrequited,
> robs me of my rest.

Mel Tormé, the Hyde Park High School junior who composed "Lament To Love," the sweet-sing song now surging nasally through America, recently told 1400 high school girls and boys its origin. Sophie, a girl he liked, deserted him for a football player. "I loved her," the little blond boy, 15, and in the requisite baggy tweeds said. "She was cute but she just played around with me. Then she started going out with this big bruiser. I couldn't take it so one night I just went home and wrote that song."

In the *Herald and Examiner*:

A young high school stude, Mel Tormé, is the composer of
a new hitoon, tagged "Lament To Love." It was networked
last week and is definitely of hit caliber. Mel is only fifteen
years old. Boy, when he learns more about luv, then he'll
really pen a ditty.

On and on it went.

Soon there were five different recordings of the song, with
Sonny Dunham, Les Brown, Lanny Ross, and Roy Smeck following close on the heels of the James version. Nightly, "Lament" was
heard over the airwaves in the muscal hands of Larry Clinton,
Gene Krupa, Sammy Kaye, Fred Waring, Russ Morgan, and many
more. The top singers, Dinah Shore, Buddy Clark, and even Bing
were crooning:

> The moon was low
> You kissed me tenderly
> I loved you so
> We were in ecstasy
> I wished upon a star,
> but I reached too far
> This is my lament to love.

The little nickel-and-dime song sheets that everyone bought in
those days, monthly pulps that listed all the current popular songs
in lyric form, announced on their covers, in bold black type, that
"Lament to Love" was one of the top tunes to be found within.

My maternal grandparents had moved to a small town called
Shelbyville, Indiana, and in the late summer of 1941, I went to
visit them for a few weeks. The local malt-shop hangout was called
"The Hut," and Harry James's recording of my song was on the
jukebox. I basked in the warmth of Hoosier friendliness and congratulations. I met a pretty girl and dated her. The summer was

sweet and warm, and the country-fresh smells of Indiana were positively exhilarating. I hated to return to Chicago and Hyde Park.

By September, when the new semester began, "Lament to Love" had become number seven on radio's "Your Hit Parade." I walked up the steps and through the columns of Hyde Park High tentatively. As soon as I stepped into the main lower hallway, it was old home week. Students who had snubbed me for months slapped me on the back. Former friends decided that I had "told the truth all along." After all, hadn't Harry recorded my song and made it a huge hit? The president of Phi Alpha Phi put his arm around my shoulder, smiled his perfect-toothed smile, and exclaimed: "Mel, the guys are proud of you. We always believed in you, you know. Always. At least I certainly did. We'd be proud to have you come into Phi Alpha Phi, right now, as a full-fledged fraternity brother." I wanted to throw up.

Briefly, I thought about once and for all changing schools. Instead, I settled in. I kept close to my few friends. John, Dale, Shirley, and I ate lunch every day at Parker's, just south of the school. I smiled as genuinely as I could when someone came over to the table and tried to patch things up. I wanted to be magnanimous, forgiving, friendly. I simply could not. In my own immaturity, I remained stoic, immovable, inflexible, and, eventually, the former disbelievers stopped trying to mend the fences.

There was great ambivalence toward me. I was neither popular nor unpopular. It got cold in early November. The leaves turned and fell, argyle sweaters, crepe-soled saddle shoes, mufflers, and earmuffs were everywhere. I rode the streetcar home every day, usually careful to have some reading material in which to immerse myself.

Weekends, my friends and I haunted the Panther Room of the Sherman Hotel, the Club De Lisa on the South Side, or sat through three shows at the Chicago Theatre, where we tapped our feet to the big band sounds of Count Basie or Tommy Dorsey or Charlie Barnet.

I had a new drumming hero: Buddy Rich. The moment I had heard him play with Artie Shaw's great 1939 band, I somehow knew he was the real master of the drums. He was young, only twenty at the time, but I wore out several copies of Shaw's "Carioca," "Traffic Jam," and "Prosschai" studying his playing, drumming along with him, marveling at his speed, his strength, his uncanny control. One evening, in late November, when I found the courage, I phoned backstage to the Chicago Theatre and asked for him. He had joined Tommy Dorsey's band and was the rock that kept that orchestra together. I waited on the line while they went to find him.

Soon, a gruff, young voice on the other end said, "Yeah? Who is this?"

I cleared my throat. "Mr. Rich," I said falteringly, "you don't know me, but I'm a friend of Mickey Scrima's. [Just call me the Great Prevaricator.] He, uh, asked me to call you when you came to town and say hello."

"Oh, yeah?" came the flippant reply. "Solid. How is the Mick?"

"Who? Mickey? Oh, fine, fine. Saw him when he came through with Harry. [Well, that at least was true.] He sends you his best."

"How long ago was that?"

"Oh, a few months back."

"Well, I just saw him last week. And he didn't tell me anything about someone calling to say hello in Chicago."

He was on to me. "Well, I just wanted to tell you you're the greatest drummer in the world."

"I know. Anything else?"

"N-no. Oh, yeah. Just one thing. I'm going to come and see you on Saturday. Wonder if I could drop backstage and say hello?"

"Saturday, huh? What's your name, kid?"

"Mel Tormé. Hey, I think maybe your band's playing a song I wrote—'Lament to Love.'"

"You putting me on?"

"Beg pardon?"

"You wrote 'Lament to Love'?"

"Yes, I did."

"Stop the crap, kid. You sound like you're about twelve."

"No, no, really. I did write it. And I just turned sixteen."

"Hmm. That's a groovy tune, kid. Yeah, we play it."

I flushed with happiness. "Look, I also play drums. I'd sure like to meet you and say hello. Maybe get a picture."

He thought about it. "Okay, squirt. Come on back after the show."

"Great! I really appreciate it. By the way, can I bring my girl back with me?"

"Is she pretty?"

"Sure is."

"Okay. What'd you say your name was again?"

"Mel Tormé."

"Okay, Mel Tormé. I'm going to check on you. If you didn't really write that song, and you're putting me on, you better not show up backstage 'cause I'll hand you your head. Otherwise, I'll see you Saturday."

"Hey, thanks, Mr. Rich. I really appreciate it."

"Buddy."

"What?"

"Buddy. Call me Buddy." He hung up.

On Saturday, John, Dale, Shirley, and I got to the Chicago Theatre early. We wangled front row seats, the curtains opened, and the band came out roaring with "Hallelujah!" Then Rich and Ziggy Elman powered that gang of fine musicians in a T.D. magnum opus, "Hawaiian War Chant," and Buddy's tom-tom work was breathtaking. A former child star and a brilliant tap dancer in his early vaudeville days, he brought to the drums what no other percussionist had—a spellbinding coordination between hands and feet, originality, blinding speed, and power. He also infused the performance with a rough humor that was not appreciated by all the band members, and especially not by Tommy's popular singer, Frank Sinatra.

The lights dimmed, and as Frank, dressed in sports jacket and slacks, cardigan sweater, and bow tie, strode upon the stage, the young bobby-soxers screamed like banshees. When they quieted down, he began to sing "This Love of Mine." After the third line of the tune, Buddy loudly and sarcastically chirped, "Tell 'em all about it, Bon Bon." ("Bon Bon" was George Tunnell, a fine black scat-type singer with the Jan Savitt band.) Sinatra's jaw muscles visibly clenched. He continued, uninterruped through the first chorus, giving way to Tommy's trombone interlude. As Frank came in again, with the last few bars of the song, Buddy turned to Ziggy Elman, sitting next to him in the trumpet section, and noisily remarked, "Hey, Ziggy, let's go hear Ellington tonight at the Panther Room." Ziggy shrunk in his seat and Sinatra looked as though he would have liked to murder Rich. Enioying the clash of temperaments and personalities of his two star attractions, Dorsey stood to one side, grinning. A big joke.

I thought it best not to go backstage after that particular show. Consequently, I didn't meet Bobby for almost four years.

In early December, Henry Kalcheim and his wife were going to New York to see his brothers, Nat and Harry, both prominent executives with the William Morris Agency. Henry offered to take me along and introduce me to them with the idea of perhaps getting William Morris to sign me as a singer/songwriter. My parents agreed.

I had been in New York once before, in 1936. My father had taken me via Greyhound and I had never forgotten it. Joe Lilley, soon to become a fixture at Paramount in Hollywood writing special musical arrangements and material for Bing Crosy, Bob Hope, and Dorothy Lamour, among others, was then working as a piano arranger for Famous Music, Paramount's publishing outlet, based in New York. During our trip my dad had persuaded him to write a special arrangement for me. The tune was "Sing Me a Swing Song and Let Me Dance." The fee was sixty dollars—a bargain.

I had marveled at New York, spent a day at Coney Island and even gone to Radio City Music Hall to see the extravaganza stage show, the high-kicking precision of the Rockettes, and *Green Pastures* on the giant Magnascope screen. A trip to New York to meet the Kalcheim brothers? I couldn't wait.

This time we went by train, the Twentieth Century. I had a small compartment of my own, while the Kalcheims languished in an elegant drawing room. I read a lot, watched the towns go by in a blur, and listened to the crisscross clacking of the rails, the occasional moan of the engine whistle, and the ding-ding-ding of crossbuck bells at railroad crossings, E-flat as we passed them, dropping to D and D-flat as they faded in the distance. I loved that train: the dining-car food, the soft-spoken Pullman porters, and the gentle rocking of the sleeping cars.

We checked into the Essex House and occupied a two-bedroom suite. I eagerly looked forward to meeting Henry's brothers. "Lament to Love" was still being played, so I figured I might have some sort of entrée with the Morris office. It was Saturday night. The Kalcheims were having dinner with friends. I was invited to tag along but I didn't want to intrude, so I excused myself and strolled down Sixth Avenue to Radio City Music Hall. The film that was playing was one I had recently seen in Chicago, so I simply walked around. Several name bands were appearing on Broadway, at the Paramount, the Capitol, the Strand. I walked over to Fifty-second Street. Stuff Smith and Joe Marsala and John Kirby's elegant little octet were holding forth on the Street; but I was sixteen and unadmittable without an adult. No matter. I really wanted to amble and gawk that night. For the next hour and a half, I got acquainted with Manhattan, the beginning of a long-standing romance. The air was brisk, a clear cold December night. I found my way back to the hotel and went to bed happy.

The next day, Sunday, at around noon, I had a light room-service brunch. The Kalcheims were still asleep, having come in very late the night before. I took pains to move around the suite quietly, reading the Sunday *Mirror* and waiting for them to stir. I turned on the radio built into the nightstand next to my bed. I could hear a voice coming through, almost shouting. I didn't want to turn up the volume and disturb Henry and his wife, so I put my ear close to the speaker and listened.

"I repeat again," the man was saying excitedly. "Forces of the Japanese Empire have attacked Pearl Harbor in Hawaii. Scores of torpedo planes and dive bombers descended on Oahu early this morning, without warning, and caused great damage to the U.S. fleet. Hickam Field and Schofield Barracks came under the terrible wave of gunfire and bombs. Unconfirmed reports state that the U.S.S. *Arizona* has been sunk with a very large loss of life. Other badly damaged naval vessels include—"

I ran to Henry's bedroom door and knocked loudly. Mrs. Kalcheim opened the door. I told her the news. She blanched and turned to Henry, who had also heard what I had said. He turned his bedroom radio on and listened to the tragic news. After a half-hour, he turned the radio off and we sat in stunned silence.

We took the next train back to Chicago.

7.

POLLACK

*E*ARLY in 1942, Ben Pollack came to town. The former drummer/bandleader who had discovered and nurtured within his orchestra such heavyweights as Tommy and Jimmy Dorsey, Glenn Miller, and Benny Goodman had been acquainted with my father when Dad had done his amateur Charleston dancing in the twenties. Dad had gotten in touch with him and asked if he could get me an audience with Glenn Miller, whose band was currently playing the Panther Room. Object: to have Glenn listen to some of the other songs I had written. "Lament to Love" had provided me with a tiny bit of visibility, and Pollack graciously agreed to arrange such a meeting.

I had heard and read that Glenn Miller was a cold, businesslike person, with no time or patience for amateur songwriters or musicians. Pollack, a short, portly man, met my dad and me in the lobby of the Sherman and led us downstairs to the Panther Room, which was empty that afternoon, except for a pair of cleaning men tidying up the place for the evening.

After a few minutes, Glenn Miller joined us. That famous, soothing voice ("Try Chesterfields. Everybody who smokes 'em, likes 'em.") welcomed us and, after several minutes of reminiscing with his old boss Pollack, the bespectacled bandleader asked me about myself: what kind of music did I like, what bands did I follow, what instruments did I play, how long had I been writing songs? I answered as succinctly as possible and found myself relaxing. He smiled a lot and, contrary to what I had expected, he seemed patient and interested in me.

At his request, I went to the piano on the bandstand, the same bandstand before which I had thrilled on so many occasions to Krupa and Ellington and Barnet *et al,* and played a few of my songs for him.

"Mel," he said, after he had heard two or three tunes, "I would like to see you begin to think more carefully about the lyrics. They're what make great songs."

"Not the music, Mr. Miller?"

"Call me Glenn. No, not the music. Oh, of course, when we're talking about 'A String of Pearls' or 'In the Mood,' then the musical content is everything. They're instrumentals. But where popular songs are concerned, the words, the idea behind the song is what makes it work. Wait a minute."

Glenn reached into the piano bench and pulled out several sheets of music. Finding the lead sheet he wanted, he set it before me on the music board of the piano. I peered at it. I had never studied music and my reading was rudimentary at best. I began to fumble with the melody.

"No, no," Glenn said. "Never mind the melody. Just read the lyrics."

I read:

> That old black magic has me in its spell
> That old black magic that you weave so well
> Those icy fingers up and down my spine
> The same old witchcraft when your eyes meet mine.

"New tune by Harold Arlen and Johnny Mercer. Now do you see what I mean? Those lyrics make pictures in your head: 'Icy fingers up and down my spine'—'witchcraft when your eyes meet mine.' Mercer is the very best of 'em all." He spoke to me not as an adult to a kid, but as an older man to a younger one, and I was grateful for his unpatronizing attitude.

"What you want to do, Mel, is to avoid writing 'moon-June-tune' rhymes. Anyone can do that. Pick up every lead sheet you can lay your hands on with a Johnny Mercer lyric and study the hell out of it. Then write some new songs and bring 'em to me.

The tunes you played for me are okay. They show promise, but I don't think they're different enough to record and, after all, records are what my band *is* all about."

I was delighted with the prospect of learning how to write good lyrics and told him so. My dad and Ben and I thanked him and we all walked toward the front of the Panther Room. Glenn stopped us before we got there and said, "Just thought of something."

He went back to the piano bench and took out another lead sheet. He brought it to me and asked, "Know a tune of ours called 'Caribbean Clipper'?"

"Sure. I have the record."

"Okay, let's have some fun. Take this lead sheet of the melody and see what you can come up with in the way of a lyric. Get it back to me sometime next week, okay?"

Okay? Hell, yes, okay.

I went home three feet off the ground, mainly because I had met Glenn Miller and he had been kind and constructively critical. I wrote a lyric to "Clipper," which was so puerile I won't quote any of it here. When I brought it to Glenn, he was the soul of tact. The last thing he said to me was, "Don't forget. Johnny Mercer. Study him, Mel. And read. Read anything and everything you can get your hands on. All good lyric writers are great readers."

I had always loved to read, but now I went at it in earnest. Dickens, Stevenson, Twain, Agatha Christie, Luke Short, Emily Dickinson, Melville, S. J. Perelman, Ogden Nash, Hammett, Chandler, and the pulps—*Argosy, G-8 and His Battle Aces*—virtually everything, as Glenn had advised, that I could lay my hands on.

And Johnny Mercer.

Not *just* Johnny Mercer. Ira Gershwin and Lorenz Hart, Johnny Burke and Frank Loesser, Yip Harburg and Irving Berlin, Hoagie, Jimmy Monaco and Dorothy Fields, Hammerstein and Howard Dietz, Henry Nemo and dozens more.

Mercer, though, was, and still is, my role model as a lyric writer. His range absolutely astonished me. He was the master of "down-home" lyrics, his only competition in that genre being Willard Robison. When Johnny appeared as singer and house lyricist on the old Benny Goodman "Camel Caravan" radio show, he would buy the newspapers fifteen or twenty minutes before airtime and scan them thoroughly for topical news items. Hurriedly, he would scratch out some lyrics on a note pad and, within minutes, be singing those words over the air to the tune of the old standard, "Loveless Love." Those scribblings, which he called "newsie-bluesies," covered everything from F.D.R.'s latest fireside chat to the abdication of the Prince of Wales to current women's fashions to Dizzy Dean's feats on the mound. Gemlike couplets of wit and wisdom, perfect in their construction, they shone with originality.

Later, of course, came "Laura," "One for My Baby," "Atcheson, Topeka," "Ac-cent-tchu-ate the Positive," "This Time the Dream's on Me," "Moon River," "Days of Wine and Roses." And "Song of India." Song of India?

One day, in the mid-sixties, I was driving through Beverly Hills, listening idly to the radio. An announcer on this FM station was saying, "And now, here is Mario Lanza to sing 'Song of India.'" I liked Lanza's singing (some of it, the gentler, non-blood vessel–bursting variety), so I left the station on. Orchestral intro, followed by vocal. The singing was good; the lyrics were miraculous. I have never been to India, but, driving up Sunset Boulevard, I was transported there for three and one-half minutes that sunny afternoon. I pulled up beside a pay phone and called the station. Who wrote those glorious lyrics? Who else? Johnny Mercer.

On the day we had met Glenn Miller, my proud father had lost no time filling in Ben Pollack on my adolescent accomplishments. Ben had been very complimentary about my singing and piano playing. He told my father that he might just have something coming up for me. I hoped it was something that would get me out of Hyde Park High and Chicago. I dreamed of going on the road with a band—any band—and making something of myself.

On May 8, 1942, John Poister and I coproduced an ambitious show in Loomis Hall, Hyde Park High, called "Let's Face the Music." The school was packed with talented kids and, like something right out of a Rooney-Garland MGM musical, John and I got the best of them together and presented them to our fellow students and their parents and friends in a review that was actually covered by the big Chicago newspapers. The proceeds were used to erect a plaque in the foyer of Loomis Hall, honoring Hyde Parkers who had gone off to fight for their country. The famed clarinetist Jimmie Noone, along with his combo, featuring a legend named Baby Dodds on drums, consented to be our special musical guests (how we euchred them into it I will never know), and it became the biggest event of its kind up to that time at Hyde Park High.

June 1942. I was sixteen, restless, and one semester away from graduation. Finally, in mid-July, at the height of the suffocating Chicago summer, a cool breeze in the form of a long-distance phone call arrived. Not a moment too soon.

Ben Pollack said to my dad, "Bill, you know I organized a band some months ago for Chico Marx. Remember? The Marx brother who plays the piano?"

"Yes. Sure I remember."

"How old is Mel right now?"

"He's sixteen. He'll be seventeen in September."

"Hmm. That means he won't be eligible for the draft for over a year."

"Right."

"Well, I'd like Mel to come out to California and join the band."

"Doing what, Ben?"

"Singing, organizing a vocal group within the band, writing for the group, and who knows, playing drums with the band eventually, if our drummer, George Wettling, gets caught in the draft."

My dad told me the news that afternoon when I came home from summer school. I suffered a few palpitations of sheer joy. But only a few. The Harry James mess still lingered, and when Dad told me that Pollack said he would have to "work things out" before he actually made a firm offer, hope faded like a dying light bulb.

This time I kept my mouth shut. Even Poister didn't know. Days became weeks and I actually forgot about Pollack's phone call. Then one morning, the mailman rang our bell and handed my mother a special-delivery letter from Ben Pollack. In it was a firm written offer to join the Chico Marx orchestra. The salary would be seventy-five dollars a week. There was also a prepaid ticket included for passage aboard Santa Fe's El Capitan, Chicago to Los Angeles.

8.

BANDSTAND

*H*OLLYWOOD! I couldn't believe it. Never mind that I was finally joining a band. I was in *Hollywood*. They made movies here, and I was a movie junkie. My very first night in town, I met Chico Marx. He was a diminutive man, with a strange, secret smile that said he knew something the rest of the world did not. He was warm and invited me to have dinner at his brother Groucho's house.

Groucho lived in Beverly Hills, of course, in a home that seemed like the Taj Mahal to a Chicago apartment-dweller. He was, by turns, droll, mocking, hilarious, and at times unfathomable. At the dinner table, he looked at me, turned to his brother, and exclaimed, "Jesus, kid, I know there's a war on, but do you have to recruit your musicians from Singer's midgets?" He shot a quick look at me to see if I was laughing. I was and he beamed. My lack of tall has never been a problem for me.

The band was staying at the Bimini Apartments near Third and Vermont, where the famed Palomar Ballroom had stood for years before burning to the ground on October 2, 1939, taking Charlie Barnet's complete library and most of the band's instruments along in the conflagration. I met the band my second day in Hollywood at a rehearsal in a large room within the apartment building. Most of the musicians and particularly the girl singer, Elise Cooper, made me welcome. A few of them, however, eyed me suspiciously. Had Pollack lost his marbles? Who the hell was this punk kid anyway? Still wet behind the ears and he's supposed to form a vocal group out of the band members? And write for it, yet? Christ!

Chico rarely attended rehearsals, Pollack being the leader in fact if not in billing. He put me to work at once, having chosen John Frigo, the bass player; Bobby Clark, the jazz trumpeter; Elise Cooper; and, of course, myself to comprise the "Revellis." ("Revelli" was the name by which Chico had appeared in a Marx Brothers film.) Admiring the thick, rich sounds of Six Hits and a Miss and The Modernaires with Glenn Miller, I had dabbled in vocal-group writing in high school.

Now here I was, a sixteen-year-old kid, writing for and rehearsing a vocal group made up of adults. It was inevitable that I would be resented, not only by the "Revellis," but by several members of the band.

I must say that I deserved *some* of the enmity being dished out. Hindsight is easy, and I can see now that I was something of a pain in the ass. I wanted badly to fit in, to please my fellow bandsmen, to be one of the gang. Obsequiousness, however, has never been my strong suit. I had, after all, been a professional performer since the age of four, hadn't I? I wasn't just some dumb jerk kid fresh out of high school with no experience whatsoever, was I? I had appeared in vaudeville and on dramatic radio for years before joining the band, and didn't that count for something? Apparently not. And as the days became weeks and several rehearsals went by, hostility grew and I became more and more defensive.

My heart began to sink. I had wanted this job. The band was really good, not the kind of orchestra one would associate with the likes of a novelty performer like Chico Marx. Pollack, of course, was the reason for its excellence. He had amassed some fine musicians (Marty Marsala on trumpet, Marty Napoleon on piano, Wettling on drums) and two great arrangers (Freddy Norman and Paul Wetstein, later to be known as Paul Weston), and the band swung.

I loved listening and I worked hard. When we finally boarded a bus and headed east on a string of one-nighters, ballroom dates, and theater engagements, I began to feel, tentatively, that I was "fitting in."

There were holdouts. Many of the band members smoked grass. (It was never called "pot" in those days.) On the bus, heading for

Denver, I was challenged to try some. I wasn't interested and said so, forcefully. Not out of any goody-two-shoes convictions or horror of it being against the law. Quite simply, my memories of that day on the parade ground of Shakespeare Grammar School and the forced swallowing of a large lump of tobacco had provided an instant cure to smoking anything. My major vice, up to that time, was my insatiable sweet tooth, and my idea of a "fix" was a milk shake, a chocolate bar, or a piece of cake.

Naturally, my refusal to turn on was looked upon with disdain by the tea heads. Doesn't Tormé want to be one of the guys? Shit, what a jerk! Soon, I was branded with the nickname "Junior," and the only member of the band who said it with affection was fellow singer Skip Nelson, the romantic baritone of the vocal department. He and I roomed together until he replaced Ray Eberle with the Glenn Miller band. Skip was a wonderful character from Pittsburgh; he was a tall, good-looking lady-killer who also sang the total hell out of ballads. He possessed a vocal quality not unlike Dick Haymes's—deep, rich, and perfectly in tune.

Denver: Lakeside Park Ballroom. A two-week stand. Opening night. I am called to sing the first song ever with the Chico Marx band. Slightly nervous, I step up to the microphone. The band plays the intro and a half-chorus of Freddy Norman's appealing arrangement of "Abraham," a new Irving Berlin tune from a movie, *Holiday Inn*. Now it is my turn. I begin to sing:

> Upon a February morn
> A tiny baby boy was born
> A-bra-ham! A-bra-ham!

I am looking out over the crowd, concentrating on the lyric. I feel a sharp, stinging sensation in my right calf. I jerk my leg back and look down. Five or six very rough-looking young kids are standing directly in front of me. The ringleader is Cagney's double.

"Hey you," he yells up at me, as I struggle with the words of the song I have only just learned. "Sing 'Sweet Eloise.'"

I continue to try to sing "Abraham." My right calf is burning.

"Hey, cockhead," the kid yells at me. "I'm talking to you. I want to hear 'Sweet Eloise.' "

I look at him and shake my head helplessly. Can't he see I'm singing something else? Doesn't he know Skip sings that one?

He tugs at my pant leg. "Listen, jagoff, stop singing this crap and sing 'Sweet Eloise.' "

I look at him again and shrug my shoulders, my palms to heaven. What can I do, fella? This is the song they assigned me.

The kid reaches up and pinches my right calf so hard that I see stars. Reflexively, my right foot shoots forward and connects squarely with the young tough's mouth. He loses several teeth. Blood bursts from his mouth onto the stage. He goes down. Two of his pals bend down to help. Two others are attempting to climb onto the stage and kill me.

Security guards materialize out of the crowd. Everything stops. I look around. The band is amused. I have to be escorted to the bus by two burly Park guards, and I sit alone for the rest of the evening.

My job, I am sure, is over before it has barely begun. The band plays the closing theme, "Revelli's Serenade," packs up, and makes its way to the bus. I sit there as they all come aboard. Many of them look at me and shake their heads in disgust. A few, a very few, offer words of encouragement and sympathy. Ben Pollack smiles at me. I have gotten my baptism of fire. He likes that. It's good for me. Gotta be a man. You're on the road now. No bed of roses. Have to learn to cope. Relax, Junior, it's not the end of the world. You'll be all right.

I haven't lost my job.

9.

VIRGIN

*L*IFE on the road.

One night stands ... the Val Air Ballroom in Des Moines ... the Tune Town Ballroom in St. Louis ... cold, semi-sleepless nights on the bus ... long hauls without benefit of bladder relief ... writing to the folks ... reading incessantly ... listening to records of Shaw and Goodman and Duke and Lunceford and Basie on one of the band member's portable player ... theater dates, the Riverside in Milwaukee and that forgotten one in Rockford, Illinois ... assimilating, learning to cope with a variety of adult egos ... subordinating my own, not too successfully at times ... hurried meals, mainly junk food—stomach problems at a very early age ... cold dressing rooms in drafty movie houses ... going out front after the performance and watching the accompanying film *free*! ... playing the army camps with thousands of service men and women laughing uproariously at Chico's pianistic antics ... catch-as-catch-can dates with young girls along the way, girls not unlike my own Shirley Matthews ... talk sessions with Ben Pollack, traveling with us as band manager, reminiscing about the old days when he was king of the hill, leader of one of the great bands and the Krupa of his era ... the band's drummer, George Wettling, sturdy, steady, and as functional a drummer as one could wish for, the rock of the band ... a new, gangly kid, Barney Kessel, a chinless wonder on the guitar, a "country boy" far slicker than all the city slickers in the band, a Pollack discovery as I was, a neophyte who paralyzed the whole band with his brilliance on his instrument ... my seventeenth birthday present from the folks, a black-faced, white-strapped Gallet chronograph, suitably inscribed, just like the one I saw on Benny Goodman's wrist in a _Metronome_ article . . . going to hear other bands on our infrequent off-nights—Barnet's, Charlie Spivak's, and, as I recall, Duke's band somewhere near Minneapolis on an impossibly frigid November eve. . . .

Not a whole lot of sleep . . . small, cheap hotel rooms, where one night Skip Nelson and his lady of that particular evening, indifferent to my presence, went at it with a vengeance in the adjoining bed, while I watched, almost clinically, the act of sex for the first time . . . laundered shirts when time permitted, which was all too seldom . . . little pockets of loneliness for my friends, my girl, my folks, and yes, even Hyde Park and the gang there . . . fits of depression over my ineptness as a vocalist (nothing changes— I still have them), my status with the band, and my difficulty in getting along with several members of the Marx organization . . . not a terribly easy life for a teen-ager.

I loved every single minute of it.

December found the band playing an extended engagement at, of all places, my old alma mater, the Blackhawk in Chicago. The Roth family, owners of the place, got a kick out of the fact that little Melvin Torme of the Coon-Sanders era had returned years later with the Marx band. Naturally, Shirley and Poister and dozens of other Hyde Parkers showed up throughout the engagement.

Since I was a hometown boy, several stories about me appeared in the _Tribune_, the _Herald_, and the _Daily News_, and the attention I was getting made my parents, sister, uncles, aunts, and grandparents terribly proud. It was also very satisfying to Shirley and John Poister and the few friends who had stood by me during the dark days at Hyde Park. It served as a surface anesthetic for my lingering pride and helped to deaden the hurt I still nurtured over my rejection by my former classmates. It also tended to swell my head.

Recently, in New York, my old friend John Poister and I got together over a long lunch. He brought along a large envelope, containing several letters I had written to him from the road during my Chico Marx days. I read them and gagged. "Christ, John," I exclaimed with embarrassment, "I was certainly full of myself in those days."

Poister smiled with tolerant affection. "Torm, that's not all you were full of back then."

I smiled back. "Amen."

After nine weeks in Chicago, the band headed east. We played the Indiana Roof in Indianapolis and the Palace in Cincinnati and moved to the Ohio Theatre in Columbus for a split week (three or four out of seven days). I had been surprised, when we were at the Blackhawk, at the number of Hyde Parkers who had come to see me dressed in the service uniforms of our country. The hectic pace of life on the road was such that, sometimes, days or even a week would go by without my reading a paper or listening to the radio, and the war would almost be forgotten. It was, however, a fact of life, and it had been brought home graphically during our stint in Chicago. I had looked for certain faces of guys I had known at Hyde Park in the crowd of diners and dancers; many of them, I found out, had gone overseas to fight the Germans or the Japanese.

In Columbus, in the basement of the Ohio Theatre, on a beat-up, cigarette-burned upright piano that had been painted white back in 1917, I wrote a song called "A Stranger in Town." It was actually a torch song that owed a lot to Willard Robison's "A Cottage for Sale," but the *raison d'être* for the tune was my sense of having missed something and the change in my life and in the lives of young people I had known as schoolkids who were now tramping through the steaming jungles of the Philippines or toting BARs and Thompsons and M-1's in North Africa and Europe.

A few years later, "Stranger in Town" became the first record I ever made with the Mel-Tones on Decca. Martha Tilton also recorded it for Capitol, and the song made the "Hit Parade."

≡

Skip and most of the rest of the band ribbed me mercilessly about my status as a virgin. I had made the mistake of admitting my condition on one of the long, all-night gab sessions aboard the bus, and now my nickname, "Junior," took on a new meaning. Every time I dated some young girl during the tour, I would get lewd

winks, sharp nudges in the ribs, and knowing smiles. "How about
it, Junior? Finally tear off a piece last night?" "Hey, Junior, didja
get your ashes hauled?" "Hey, kid, that cute thing you dated last
night had a nice pair of jugs. Bet ya gave her a little poke in the
pants, right?" During a one-week run at the Stanley Theatre in
Pittsburgh, I finally made the big move, almost in self-defense.

Looking back on my first night of "going all the way," I remember it being coupled with great affection for the band. It was
almost as though they had met in secret and had firmly resolved
to get me "off the bubble." We were staying at the William Penn
Hotel. Every morning before the first show at the Stanley (we did
four a day, five on Saturday), most of the musicians would have
breakfast at the hotel coffee shop. A dark-haired, pretty woman
in her early thirties invariably took our orders and cheerfully served
us; she had a talent for returning my colleagues' suggestive banter
tit for tat. Her name was Dorothy and, little did I know, she had
been "recruited."

"She likes you, Junior," Skip said one morning at breakfast,
after Dorothy had brought us ham and eggs. "Why don't you ask
her to come and see the show?"

"Come on, man," I said, slightly uncomfortable, "I'm just a kid
as far as she's concerned."

"Naw, you're wrong," Gabe Gelinas assured me. He played
lead alto, lived with Elise Cooper, the girl vocalist, and was one
of the more mature members of the band. "I can tell the way she
looked at you, kid. She goes for you."

"Yeah," chimed in Marty Napoleon, sipping his coffee. "Don't
be a square. Ask her for a date."

"Well," I said hesitantly, "I don't know...." I thought of Shirley. We had never "done it." She was a "good" girl, strictly raised.
But I was in love with her (wasn't I?) and I always figured that
some day, just like in the movies, she and I would, well, you know,
get married and lose our respective virginities together.

George Wettling, the band's elder statesman, white-haired, dapper, and salty-tongued, settled it. "Shit, squirt, what the hell are
you waiting for? That little pecker of yours'll rust and fall off if
you don't start using it. Ask the dame for a date."

Orders from the Silver Fox! The guys seated around the table nodded in unison. It was settled. Junior was going to become a man. Dorothy came over to the table with a Silex full of steaming coffee.

"Anyone for a refill?" she asked brightly.

Marty Napoleon kicked me under the table.

I cleared my throat. "Uh, Dorothy, I was just wondering if, uh . . . if you'd, well, if you'd like to come over to the theater and see the show."

She poured coffee into Wettling's cup, smiled, and said quietly, "I've seen the show."

A wave of relief coupled with slight disappointment washed over me. She walked over to where I sat and stood next to me, filling my cup. She smelled of freshly starched uniform and sweet-scented cologne. I looked up at her. God, she looked a bit like another Dorothy—Dorothy Lamour. Prettier, maybe!

She looked down and smiled at me. "It was a great show, and you were terrific. I'd love to see it again."

Smiles all around. My throat kept clogging. I cleared it again and asked, "Well, how about tonight?"

She shook her head. "No, not tonight. Saturday night. I get off early."

Christ! This was only Wednesday. Now, suddenly, I was eager. Dorothy's proportions were ample. Fulsome, really. I looked at her as she moved to another table and tried to picture her naked. I felt myself growing under the table. The guys watched my face and laughed.

All day and all the next and most of Friday and Saturday, every single member of the band, including the girl singer, kept reminding me of the upcoming "big night." Unsolicited advice poured from every mouth, including admonitions about using a "rubber," and "washing it off" right after I "did it."

"Come on, you guys," I replied, blushing, "it's just a date, for God's sake. She's just coming over to see the show again. I mean, she has no eyes for a kid like me."

"Young meat," smiled Bobby Clark. "Gets these older chicks every time."

Even Chico and Pollack joined in. "Relax, kid, and enjoy it."

I kept expecting a wire from Roosevelt: "Good luck, Mel. Eleanor, Fala, and I are pulling for you."

Things went right on schedule, and Dorothy was gentle and fierce and patient and beautiful and practiced and I came in just under forty-five seconds.

Next morning, in the coffee shop, as I walked in, the band was waiting for me. They cheered. Dorothy was there. She joined in. I turned red and smiled sheepishly. Later, I was informed of Dorothy's recruitment and that she had, indeed, for several years, solved many a musician's "problem." I was a little peeved. You mean she didn't really dig me for _me_?

"Live and learn, Junior," smiled Skip.

I had been feeling my oats a little too much for my own good. More and more, I was being featured on the "jump" or "rhythm" vocals; I had formed the vocal group and written for it, and it had coalesced into a pretty good quartet. By God, I was learning and getting good at what I did, and the girls in the front rows of the theaters seemed to be eyeing me almost as much as they ogled Skip or tall, blond, good-looking Bobby Clark, who also did a few vocals with the band. Damn it, why wasn't I getting proper billing with the band? I mean, Jesus, I deserved it, didn't I? Weren't my vocals and my vocal-group arrangements contributing to the band's success? And how would all the little gals out front know how important I was to the Chico Marx orchestra unless they read my name out front in letters _at least_ as big as Skip's or Elise Cooper's replacement, Kim Kimberly?

"All right, Junior," Ben Pollack said, when I had braced him for the twentieth time on the subject, "I'll do something about it."

Because of the Pennsylvania "blue law" prohibiting performances in theaters or ballrooms on Sunday, the big bands of the day always crossed the Ohio River into Ohio and played a one-day Sunday date at a little theater in Steubenville. On a bright Sunday morning, we crossed the river, headed into Steubenville, and made our way to the theater. The approach to this little building was through a long stretch of open, empty lots, in the middle of which it stood. As was the custom, the complete length of the building was painted each week like a billboard, announcing Sunday's attraction. As we neared the structure, I was able to make out the hugely painted letters:

> Sunday—One Day Only—
> Chico Marx and his Orchestra
> Featuring Skip Nelson and Kim Kimberly
> and great new vocalist
> MEL TROME

The band saw it. I saw it. No one said a word, but the lesson was learned. That day, Chico introduced me on the stage as "Mel Trome" and, from that day forward, my nickname in the band was "Trome."

Not much of an improvement on "Junior."

10.

ROADIE

NEW YORK CITY and the Roxy. The band played there for four weeks. I stayed at the Plymouth Hotel, dated several of the Roxyettes, and moved around town every night. On Fifty-second Street, I haunted the Onyx, the Hickory House, and the Famous Door. In Harlem the choices were just as numerous. That month in Manhattan offered me the best musical schooling I have ever had. The practical aspect of simply *being there* and digesting the music, the ambiance of the clubs and theaters, the actual *feeling* of the town at the height of the popularity of the big bands, was far more beneficial to me than learning about the playing and writing of music within the limiting parameters of a schoolroom.

Chico was interesting. He was seeing a beautiful woman named Mary Dee, who, as I recall, was a ringer for a later beauty, Cyd Charisse—and who later became Mrs. Marx. He also had a passion for teen-age girls. They would come into his dressing room seeking an autograph. On more than one occasion, their mothers would have to intercede angrily and hustle their offspring out of there. Twice, as I recall, the situation almost became a matter for the police. Then there was the little man's proclivity for wagering. He was a world-class bridge player, an expert at gin, and an almost peerless horse handicapper. He was in constant communication with several bookmakers and he did very well betting on the bangtails. The band seemed, more than anything else, to be a hobby with him.

During our stay at the Roxy, an RKO talent scout named Arthur Willi happened to catch our show. He came backstage asking to see me and informed me that RKO was looking for someone to play a featured role in an upcoming musical called *Higher and Higher*. Would I be interested in testing for it?

"I certainly would, Mr. Willi. But where?"

Willi, a tall, gentle man, smiled. "Right upstairs, Mel. On the roof of the theater."

"Honestly? But how ... ?"

"We'll just set up a camera and shoot some sixteen-millimeter footage on you. Silent, naturally."

"Yes, but how will they know I can sing if—"

"They don't have to know. I know. That's what they pay me for, to use my own judgment. All they have to see is what you look like on film."

Two days later, we went up to the roof of the Roxy Theatre building and made the test. Arthur Willi said he would be in touch. I did not allow myself to get excited, even when he told me that, in addition to *Higher and Higher* being my first possible movie role, it would also be Frank Sinatra's first starring vehicle.

Sinatra was, to me, the ultimate singer's singer. His breath control, phrasing, intonation, and enunciation—the very look of the man on the stage was so *right*. I permitted myself the smallest glimmer of hope regarding *Higher and Higher*; if it happened, what a kick to meet and work with the best singer in the world.

After the Roxy, the band headed back west. We played the Oriental Theatre in Chicago and, once again, I was able to spend time with Shirley and with Poister. One night, after the last show at the theater, we went to the Club De Lisa on the South Side. Red Saunders had held forth there for years. Next to Gene Krupa, he was Chicago's most famous drummer. We sat and listened and then Red got up in front of the band and said, "Hey, folks, the Chico Marx orchestra is playin' up a storm at the Oriental this week, and some of the cats in the band are in to hear us tonight." I looked around. Sure enough, Bobby Clark, Marty Marsala, and Pollack himself were seated at a table nearby. "Now, with a little encouragement..." Red continued. He nodded his head toward their table and began to clap his hands. The audience joined in, and the two trumpet players as well as the former bandleader stood up and took a bow.

The applause got stronger, and soon all three of them headed toward the bandstand. Marty and Bobby were known quantities to me, but— Ben Pollack? Somehow, in my admiration for scores of drummers, I had missed out on Ben. He laid down a rocking beat that lifted up the whole room. Pollack had a specialty: he would play with brushes, with the left hand caressing the snare drum and the right-hand brush pressed against the bass-drum head while moving in a circular motion. Nothing fancy, mind you. Merely keeping perfect time, which, after all, is the basic function of the drummer. Where Red Saunders's playing had been flashy and flamboyant, Pollack's was subtle and insinuating, felt rather than heard, and simply unforgettable.

A bit later I was asked to sit in and play drums. Afterward, Ben commented favorably on my playing and said that if Wettling got drafted, I could replace him.

Chico suddenly became ill (or bored?) and, for a few beautiful weeks, Harpo assumed leadership of the band. He was one of the sweetest, kindest men I have ever come across in show business. Diffident, almost shy, he had every member of the band loving him after the first few days. He was a serious student of the harp; he had taken lessons back in Hollywood every week from a well-known harpist/teacher. The band admired his musicianship and, in particular, his rendition of "East Meets West," an old, minor-keyed piece that sounded bittersweet, albeit undemanding. His wordless humor on the stage convulsed audience and orchestra alike, and I remember that brief interlude as being the happiest time ever with the Marx organization.

We paused in Denver, to play Lakeside Park once again. I was nervous for a pair of reasons: would the Cagney look-alike show up again with his motley crew and cause trouble, and would I be up to filling Wettling's shoes, now that he had been separated from the band by a letter that began: "Greetings."

"Cagney" never showed his face. I took over on drums and held my own without making percussion history. Chico was absent again. Pollack set up his own Leedy drums in front of the band, and so we became, for a time, the Ben Pollack orchestra, with "double" rhythm.

It was fun for those few weeks. I sat perched up at the top of the bandstand and behind the blue-pearl set of WFL drums that the whole Tormé-Sopkin clan had pitched in to buy for me. I played too loudly at times and too softly on other occasions, when strength was needed. It was good experience, though, and I learned from it. I had been promised a bump up in salary to $125 when I took over the drum chair, but Chico resisted the raise. I did not know at the time that the band's days were numbered. Chico had had enough. Perhaps the band was losing money, or more precisely, wasn't making enough to keep Chico's bookmakers happy. At any rate, I relinquished the drummer's throne to Hershey Kay, who took over at the Golden Gate Theatre in San Francisco. One week later, in July 1943, he was out of a job, along with the rest of us.

I didn't mind. Ben Pollack had talked about becoming a personal manager, with me as his first client. Also, I had finally heard from Arthur Willi. I had gotten the part in *Higher and Higher*. To say I was thrilled would be to put it mildly. I was out-of-my-mind, superdelirious, over the prospect of being in an honest-to-God Hollywood movie.

The band had a farewell party in San Francisco at the Olympic Hotel, where we all were staying. Chico did not attend, but Ben did, and there was a lot of drinking, smoking of grass, and promises to "keep in touch." Then Ben and I headed for Los Angeles. I called my folks and asked them to come out to the Coast. I was sure my future lay in Hollywood, in the movies or in front of a big band. Those were my twin dreams: to be either a movie star or a bandleader. Now, with *Higher and Higher* looming, it looked as though one of those dreams might be coming true.

The folks agreed to pull up stakes and, together with my sister, head out west. During the course of their packing, they threw away every template my dad had fashioned for his pop-up-books, as well as all the material on the Mickey Mouse Waddle Book he and Uncle Art had created. What a pity! Mom also dumped all my Big Little Books and all my aviation "pulps." "Mel's a man, now. What would he want with this junk?" Little did she (or I) realize I could have retired on that "junk," had I known what they would bring from collectors almost forty years later!

At the time, I couldn't have cared less. I was going to live in Hollywood. And make a film. With Frank Sinatra!

11.

MOVIE

I SETTLED into the Hollywood Plaza Hotel for a few weeks, awaiting the arrival of my family. Foremost in my mind was meeting Frank Sinatra at last.

Frank, even at that early stage, was a corporate entity. Hordes of agents, publicity men, women, studio officials, record executives, employees, and just plain hangers-on swarmed around him constantly. His initial introduction to the cast, including me, was perfunctory. He was perfectly polite, mind you, but rather remote. Marcy McGuire, an RKO contract player and my "girl friend" in the film, was crushed. She idolized Sinatra (what girl didn't?) and had hoped for a warmer reception.

When we began shooting *Higher and Higher*, with Michele Morgan, Jack Haley, Leon Errol, Paul and Grace Hartman, Victor Borge, and Barbara Hale, we were scheduled to do a number written by McHugh and Adamson (the original score by Rodgers and Hart was almost entirely broomed) called "I Saw You First." Marcy, Sinatra, and I were to perform the song in a kind of round-robin fashion. We shot the number, after several rehearsals, but, as Marcy later commented, "It was so strange. The minute the director, Tim Whelan, yelled 'cut,' Frank turned on his heel and, without a word, made for his dressing room."

In fairness, the demands on his time in a given twenty-four-hour period were staggering, and I feel he looked upon this first film, being shot at a lesser studio, as a mere stepping-stone to a much greater screen career just over the horizon.

I was hoping to become friends with him, but that wish died

aborning, and I contented myself thereafter with the affections of other cast members. Elizabeth Risdon and Mary Wickes were terrific ladies, Barbara Hale was beautiful and outgoing, Leon Errol was a pixie of a man, and Jack Haley was supportive and understanding. Ethel Griffies, a great old gal who played my mother in the movie, was everyone's favorite, a fine English pro who could teach us all something about acting; Victor Borge, just getting started in this country, was a bit cold, but perhaps that was an ingrained shyness; and lovely Michele Morgan, who was about to marry actor William Marshall, was the first Frenchwoman I had ever met. Her charm and subtle sophistication were pervasive around that company of players.

If I may be permitted to leap out of continuity for a moment, I must say that, for someone who worshiped Frank Sinatra and was deeply influenced by his singing, I have had an unhappy history with him. After *Higher and Higher*, I did not see him again for six years. On the occasion of a party at my parents' house to announce my engagement to Candy Toxton (about whom more later), Frank, uninvited, showed up, along with Jimmy Van Heusen and a third guy I can't remember. They were all well away in the Jack Daniel's department, and Frank started looking around for Candy and calling for her.

The moment Candy saw him walk in, she rushed up the stairs to my bedroom and locked herself in. My mother looked at me, and I bit my lip and headed up the stairs on the heels of Sinatra, who announced that he wanted to "wash up." He went into my bathroom, tried the door to my bedroom, found it locked, and began to bang on the door. Invited or not, he was a guest in my home, so I tried to reason with him.

"Hey, Frank, I don't know what this is all about, but Candy and I are going to be married and—".

He tossed an expletive at me and continued to pound on the door. I heard Candy, inside my bedroom, say, in a small, rather sad voice, "Go away, Frank, please." Van Heusen, a true gent, shamefacedly came up the stairs and pried Frank away from the bedroom door.

"Come on, Frank. Let's go," he pleaded.

"No," Sinatra said sullenly. "Wanna see Candy."

I gritted my teeth. I could now hear Candy crying in the bedroom. "Frank, I think you'd better get out of here," I said.

Van Heusen tugged at his arm. "Yeah, he's right, pal. Let's go." Frank hesitated at the top of the stairs and gave me one hard look. Buddy Rich told me that Sinatra was able to handle himself pretty well, and I sure as hell did not want to tangle with him.

Frank stormed out of the house and I suppose his famous "long memory" took over. For years I did not lay eyes on him. Then, strangely, I began to hear stories that, on his recent concert tours, he would talk to his audiences about the "few real saloon singers left." "There's me," he would say, "and Tony Bennett and Mel Tormé."

Finally, at Christmastime, 1986, in one of the nicest confrontations I have ever had, Frank and I met at his daughter Nancy's annual Christmas party and talked and talked. I was literally mesmerized by his comments on singing, his attention to lyrics and choice of musical material. One of the things about him that night that I really appreciated was his courtly attention to my wife, Ali, through all this conversation. The wives of celebrities often get nothing more than a passing nod from other celebrity guests at a party. Sinatra was charm itself, and it was easy to see why so many talented and respected people love and admire him. In subsequent months, he called me often, merely to chat or talk music or to commiserate, finally, over Buddy Rich's worsening health.

I have learned more from listening, over the years, to Frank Sinatra than I can possibly catalogue. I have always felt the need for closer contact with him; I'm that way about people I admire. Now, we are speaking on a more or less regular basis and I am all the happier for it.

All right. Back to *Higher and Higher*.

During the filming, Marcy McGuire, a temperamental, peppery little redhead, invited me to escort her to Donald O'Connor's sixteenth birthday party. It was held out in the San Fernando Valley in a huge barn. The motif was "country," the dress code western or farmer costume. I was excited—my first Hollywood party! Virtually every young player I had ever seen was there that night: Marcia Mae Jones, Cora Sue Collins, Ann Gillis, Peggy Ryan, Sidney Miller, David Holt, and a somewhat forlorn-looking Judy Garland. I was, of course, a total unknown, and felt slightly out-of-place in such fast company.

It was one of those events I had read about in movie-fan magazines but did not really believe took place. Well, they took place—this one, with a vengeance. There were square-dancing, games, prizes, and impromptu performances. Mickey Rooney and Donald were the best, along with their mutual sidekick, Sid Miller. Judy Garland, quiet and insular, remained in the background.

The young Hollywood players at that party were a part of an age that has long since departed the Hollywood scene. There seemed to be a genuine spirit of fun, mutual admiration, and youthful hijinks that was sweet and infectious. No one seemed to be draining anything more potent than Coca-Cola, and in those days, drugs were unheard of. I never forgot that party: the girls, in jeans or dirndl dresses and pigtails, fresh scrubbed and budding with sex appeal; the guys, exuberant, playful, and show-offish in the nicest, most appealing manner.

When *Higher* was finally completed, I had a few weeks of panic. My folks and Myrna had arrived on the Coast just a week or so after we began shooting. We had found a nice apartment at 617 South Detroit Street near the Wilshire Miracle Mile. My father now had to find work in a strange town. I had made one movie, for unspectacular money, and was now out of a job. Would I ever stand in front of a camera again? Was I any good at all in *Higher and Higher?*

Ben Pollack called. Universal was making a Gloria Jean opus called *Pardon My Rhythm*. He had told them about me and they wanted to test me.

"You've got the edge on this part, Trome," Ben assured me. "Kid in the picture has to play drums—really play them. The whole movie's built around him and his high school band."

I brightened. It sounded made to order for me. Ben wasn't through. "Listen," he continued, "I've found a group of talented kids at LACC."

"L.A. which?"

"Los Angeles City College. They're an organized vocal group who call themselves 'The Schoolkids.' Two girls, two boys. But they need an arranger. They need direction. A leader. What do you think?"

"About what?"

"Jesus, you're dense today. About taking them over. Writing the arrangements, being the leader, the solo featured singer."

"Gee, Benj, I don't know. I thought we were going to concentrate on a solo career for me?"

"We are, we are. But that can come later. Look, vocal groups are popular right now. The Pied Pipers, the Modernaires, all of 'em. And the stuff you wrote for the Revellis was damn good, Junior. Really fine. So?"

"Well, when can we hear them?"

"Tomorrow. My office. Four o'clock."

"And what about this Gloria Jean thing?"

"I'll find out and call you back."

The next afternoon, I heard the Schoolkids. They sang well enough and looked good, but their arrangements were little more than "head" charts, unwritten, "made up" as they went along, with very little originality. They seemed eager to team up with me and understood going in that I would be the featured singer with the group and principal arranger. Now that I had heard them, I felt good about it. I felt even better when, after they had left Ben's office at Crossroads of the World on Sunset, he advised me that I was to test for *Pardon My Rhythm* the following day.

As instructed, I brought my drums out to Universal Studios in the Valley. There was one other candidate for the role—an extremely handsome young man, tall and confident-looking. Mentally, I prepared myself for rejection by the director, Felix Feist. I tested first with a few pages of dialogue and a drum solo. They seemed unimpressed. Then the other young man tested. He was good. He had natural acting talent, straight teeth, crooked smile, and was at least three inches taller than I. But when it came time to sit behind a set of drums, he was hopeless. He had obviously never played drums in his life, and, while he made a valiant attempt to fake it, he was bereft of any rhythmic sense. I got the part.

Pollack went to work on the producer, Del Lord, and all of a sudden my new vocal group won parts in the movie as part of my "band." Patric Knowles, Evelyn Ankers, Marjorie Weaver, Walter Catlett, and Bob Crosby and his orchestra rounded out the cast. I wrote two songs for the little programmer, played my first lead opposite an established movie star, and began feeling minimally comfortable about my career again.

Gloria Jean was the most unaffected, unspoiled teen-age star I ever met. She had a clear piping voice and a somewhat tremulous vibrato, which did not, however, detract from the pleasant quality of her singing. Years later, when I had become well-known, I walked into a restaurant out in the Valley, and a nice-looking, somewhat matronly hostess led me and my date to a table. She handed us menus, smiled at me, and extended her hand.

"Hi, Mel." She smiled. "Remember me? I'm Gloria Jean."

My jaw dropped a quarter inch. I stood and hugged her and, at that moment, felt more hatred for this business than I ever had before or would afterward. When Gloria Jean's usefulness to the studio was over, she was thrown out unceremoniously among the civilians to make of her life what she could.

Other young players (Scotty Beckett, Bobby Driscoll, Doug MacPhail, and Ray McDonald come to mind) fared even worse. I have heard people remark cynically, "Well, hell, why didn't they save their money? Nothing is forever, for Christ's sake. They should have known that what they had couldn't last." Not true. Most of those young people were just that: young people. Their careers were managed by mothers, agents, and studio heads. Even the grown-up stars, at the height of their celebrity, give very little thought to a future in anything other than the picture business.

One night, at a party at Jack Lemmon's house, Gene Kelly walked over to me and inquired if I knew where he could get a print of *Singin' in the Rain*. He wanted to run the film for one of his kids who had never seen it.

"Gene," I said, "Films Incorporated has a rental print listed in their catalogue. But I simply can't believe you're asking me about this. You were the king of the MGM lot. You mean to tell me you don't have a print of every movie you ever made?"

He smiled sadly. "No, I don't. Not one of them. You see, Mel, in those days, I would call for a projection room, invite thirty–forty people, and run anything I pleased. Seven nights a week. Any movie I wanted to see. From any studio. And you know," he concluded, with a catch in his voice, "we thought it would never end."

That shook me. When you are as big as Gene Kelly, anything down the road other than high-visibility stardom _would_ be unthinkable. I'm sure Gloria Jean, her mother, and her agents felt the same way. Her films made a fortune for Universal during the war years. The kids in the movie business are the saddest members of our profession as far as I am concerned.

≡

A postscript: When Evelyn Ankers died in 1985, the Los Angeles _Times_'s obituary quoted her as having said the best film she had ever appeared in and the most fun she'd had making movies was _Pardon My Rhythm_.

12.

MEL-TONES

I NOW entered the most carefree, busy, exciting, and, in many ways, happiest time of my life. I began working seriously with the Schoolkids: Sheldon Disruhd, Betty Beveridge, Ginny O'Connor, and Bernie Parke. They were amazingly quick studies, with an almost extrasensory perception of what their individual notes should be in any given song. I soon realized they were able to sing at least the first chorus of any tune in near-perfect four-part harmony without benefit of a formal, written arrangement. They really were adroit at "head"-chart singing.

With the addition of a fifth voice (mine), I was able to expand the scope of the group. As I have previously said, I had long been a fan of the Modernaires as well as the Six Hits and a Miss, who had pioneered open-voiced harmonies, a process of inverting the notes in chords so that the range of the four or five singers is extended beyond the limits of close harmony. My concept in writing for the Schoolkids was to pattern the group after a saxophone section: two altos (the girls), two tenors (Bernie and myself), and a baritone (Sheldon). The principal inspiration was the Six Hits. Vince Deegan had fashioned arrangements for that great group of singers that sounded like a vocal band. They knocked me out, as did Kay Thompson and her choir of swinging singers, another group who employed the vocal-band sound.

Shelley Disruhd, who had been the organizer of the Schoolkids, was suddenly army-bound. I replaced him with a singer/arranger named Les Baxter, who was not only draft-exempt but who brought a high degree of professionalism, musical knowledge, and taste to the group.

On the heels of *Pardon My Rhythm*, I was offered a little Columbia picture called *Let's Go Steady*, with the Schoolkids as part
of the cast. Right about this time, Bernie Parke suggested the name
"Mel-Tones" as a replacement for "Schoolkids," and, for the first
time, in *Let's Go Steady*, we were billed as Mel Tormé and His
Mel-Tones. *Steady* was a minor epic about amateur songwriters. I
wrote three songs for this "B" movie and played one of the leads,
opposite that cute, blond gymnast June Preisser. We did the film
and I promptly forgot about it, but upon its release some months
later, it jumped up and bit me in the behind when Columbia made
me an offer I *could* and *did* refuse. But more on that later.

We were paged by the Armed Forces Radio Service to become
regulars on a show called "Swingtime," starring Martha Raye and
Murray McEachern's Army Orchestra. I was writing arrangements
for the Mel-Tones nonstop and loving it. I was also in demand as
a drummer and played many gigs at the old Radio Room on Vine
Street with musicians like Milt Raskin, Phil Stephens, Herbie Haymer, Shorty Sherock, and King Guion. When I wasn't playing
drums for money, I played for fun. The Mel-Tones were becoming
popular, so I had some entrée at the Palladium, where I was a
nightly visitor-cum-guest/drummer with Charlie Spivak, the Gene
Krupa band, and Stan Kenton's roarers.

Krupa and Kenton ultimately offered me the drum chair with
their respective organizations. Gene, at that time, was playing a
maximum of two tunes per set on drums and had a regular percussionist play for the majority of the evening. Kenton had always
had drummer troubles. The band was top heavy with brass; the
rhythm section, which tended to be soggy, dragged the whole
orchestra down with it. I would sit in with an imaginary set of
blinders in place and force the bassist and Stan, on piano, to follow
my lead. Understand, in those day I was very dedicated to drums
and drumming. I worked at my playing and was certain that,
somehow, drums were a big part of my future. The sit-in sessions
with Kenton worked, somehow, and Stan really pushed to have
me join the band. I was tempted, but what would I do with the
Mel-Tones?

I was gaining invaluable writing experience working with them.
The intermittent jobs on drums fulfilled my desire to play and

kept me in a "practiced" condition. Believe it or not, I was also going to Los Angeles High. My mother was obsessed with my graduating from high school. Further, I was eighteen and eligible for the draft—but was exempt until I finished my high school education. I felt out of place at L.A. High, but I persevered and got my diploma.

Once I graduated, the Mel-Tones got nervous. We were all prospering. Now the draft board was knocking on their leader's door. We knew it was inevitable that I would be inducted. To say I was champing at the bit to go get shot at would be something short of the truth. Still, in those times, just about everyone was imbued with some sense of resignation to military service, as well as a feeling of both duty and pride in wearing a uniform. I braced for the letter I knew had to come.

≡

It is was very early morning in the spring of 1944. In a large building in downtown Los Angeles, I stood, along with hundreds of other potential inductees, waiting to be examined by a plethora of doctors and a psychiatrist. My stomach rumbled, partly from hunger, partly from anxiety.

The physical went along without incident until one doctor got a look at my feet. "Hmm," he observed, "third-degree flat feet. Do you wear any kind of arch support?"

"No, sir."

"Do your feet hurt when you take long walks or run a lot?"

"Well, that's hard to say, sir. I rarely walk for long distances, and I run only when someone's chasing me."

"Don't try to be funny."

"I'm not, sir."

"Hmmm." He wrote something on my chart and ushered me out of his cubicle.

The final group of doctors, army, navy, and civilian, looked me over. Glancing at my chart, an army medico peered at my feet. He grunted. "Not a trace of an arch." He turned to his fellow practitioners. "He won't be able to march worth a damn."

A chunky navy doctor wearing a perpetual smirk looked at all five foot seven, 129 pounds of me, standing in my shorts and undershirt, and sneered: "What's the matter, bud? Don't you want to fight for your country?"

I was cold, tired, and nervous, and now I got angry and feisty. I told him to commit an impossible act upon himself. His fat face purpled. I was 1-A.

≡

Within a week, I found myself reporting to Fort MacArthur, near the San Pedro area. Fort Mac was an induction center where new draftees were given aptitude tests to determine where each man would be best suited to serve his country.

I made two mistakes. No, three.

First, I had already been approached by an officer named Tommy Jones, who led a fine air force band and vocal group. The band was stationed at the plush Miramar Hotel on the beach in Santa Monica, California. Tommy had become a rabid Mel-Tones fan; he expressed admiration for my arranging and offered me a berth with the band as singer/arranger. As soon as I finished my mandatory basic training, he promised, I would be requisitioned by the Air Corps, and orders would be cut to transfer me to the Miramar. My first mistake was mentioning this possible assignment to the examining officer at MacArthur. Distaste was evident on his overworked kisser, and I'll bet he had something to do with diverting my energies into other channels.

Second, I mentioned on my questionnaire that I had been a gun collector for the past couple of years. As a kid, I had sported the best cap-gun collection on the South Side of Chicago—when we moved to California, I began putting together a collection of the genuine articles. They were real-life extensions of my childhood fantasies, my enjoyment of "Terry and the Pirates" ("Pat Ryan," Terry's older sidekick, always brandished a long-nosed model 1907 Colt .45 automatic), and my fascination with the sidearms of the movie cowboys (Hoppy's twin-nickeled .45 single-action Colts were beautifully engraved and pearl-handled). I was also fascinated by the wicked, coldly functional appearance of the enemies' pistols: the cheaply made but efficient Japanese Nambu automatic, the ubiquitous German Luger, the broom-handled Mauser, and the compact, modern-looking Walther PPK.

During the war years, these were in cheap abundance in gun shops, pawn shops, and through classified ads in the *Times* and the *Examiner*. I became immersed in gun collecting. My dad and I built a cabinet, backed with green felt, mounted it on my bedroom wall, and I displayed my burgeoning collection behind glass and three locks. I began taking the guns apart and putting them back together. I soon became adept at it, particularly in field-stripping the Colt .45 automatic. After a while, I attempted to detail-strip the gun—which means that every single part was eventually spread on the floor, challenging me to reassemble the puzzle. I failed the first four times and had to take the bits and pieces in a bag to a gunsmith who, chuckling at me, completed the job in a matter of minutes.

Eventually, I mastered the task myself. Unfortunately, I made the mistake of mentioning that accomplishment on my army questionnaire.

Toward the end of my first week at Fort MacArthur, an army sergeant walked into my barracks, threw a service-issue .45 auto onto my bed, and said, "Field-strip it."

I did, quickly and efficiently.

"Okay. Put it back together."

I complied.

He threw the gun back on my bunk. "Now, let's see you detail-strip that piece."

I proceeded to obey the order and, then, without waiting, put the Colt back together again.

The sergeant picked up the gun, reholstered it, wrote something on a small spiral pad and left. My fellow inductees gathered round, speculating on what the outcome of the sergeant's unexpected visit might be. The consensus was that I might be assigned to teach the field-stripping and detail-stripping of the Colt .45 automatic to future G.I.s.

"That's impossible," I said. "First of all, only noncoms and officers use sidearms. I'm sure there are plenty of people around to teach them what I just showed the sergeant. Naw, there's not a chance of them doing that with me."

Within two days, a lieutenant asked me whether I would like to teach and demonstrate the nomenclature of the .45 automatic. He couldn't guarantee which camp I would be sent to, but an immediate PFC rating went with the job. Jesus, I thought, there goes the Air Corps band assignment. I asked if my accepting was mandatory. The lieutenant said no, but suggested I think about it for a few days.

My third drastic mistake, unwitting though it was, had to do with the Morse code test. Several draftees were seated in a room and given a piece of paper that looked like a laundry list. From top to bottom, that paper had thirty pairs of boxes, with "Yes" and "No" appearing alongside each pair. The officer in charge of this group then proceeded to play a record from which Morse code signals emanated in pairs. We were to listen to them, and then mark the boxes "Yes," if both signals were exactly alike, or "No," if they weren't.

I sailed through that test, because the signals were like drumbeats to my ears. They were played with great rapidity, with only a second or two between each pair of dots and dashes.

I got busy with my pencil, and, when it was over, I scored one hundred on the test. Only three other inductees had ever accomplished that, I was told. The guy in charge said I was a prime candidate for the Signal Corps. (Damn it, Trome, why do you have to be such a show-off? There goes the Air Corps band!)

Sure enough, I was quickly shipped to Camp Roberts, near San Luis Obispo, California, 87th Infantry Training Battalion, Company B, for the obligatory basic training course, after which, I was told, I would enter the Signal Corps. Swell! Just swell! In the end neither the Signal Corps nor the Air Corps was to claim my carcass.

Five days after I arrived at Camp Roberts, my bunkies and I were invited to participate in a nine-mile hike with full packs over rough country, "and no one had better report to sick bay beforehand." Now, get the picture. I have my mother's long, narrow, and unglamorously flat feet. My shoe size is 9AA. The army boots I was issued measured approximately 8C. My feet swam in them, but I had seen enough movies like *Caught in the Draft* with Bob Hope to know better than to complain about shoe sizes.

The hike was tough, especially for a bunch of mushy civilians.

I was proud to make it, all the way out and back, but my feet were killing me by the time we returned to camp at around 11:00 P.M., and my socks felt squishy and soggy. Were my feet perspiring as profusely as the rest of me?

I sat down heavily on the barracks steps and gingerly removed my boots and socks.

"Holy shit!" exclaimed one of my fellow sufferers when he saw my feet.

The absence of an arch, the oversized boots, and the rumpled, loose khaki socks had cut my soles to ribbons. Blood poured out of the cut strips of raw skin, and the pain, now that the night air made contact, was indescribable. The company lieutenant stopped, looked, grimaced, and sent me to the hospital.

First stop: psycho ward. Standard operating procedure. Any goldbricking G.I. who thinks he can get away with murder gets a taste of a few days behind barred doors. After seventy-two hours of boredom, he is usually anxious to return to his outfit and his buddies. My feet were doctored with salve, bandages, and a whole lot of whistling and head shaking by the medic in charge.

In a day or so, I was released from the ward and put in a recuperative barracks. I was having trouble walking, so I got assigned to the kitchen, where I could sit on a stool and put together crates of oranges and apples for the various hospital wards.

One day, the commanding officer of the hospital, Colonel Curdy, summoned me to his office. He asked me to remove my slippers (shoes were out of the question at the moment), and he examined my feet. They were healing slowly but surely. He shook his head and asked, "How did you ever get to be 1-A?"

I told him of the incident with the abrasive navy doctor in Los Angeles.

"Well," he said, "this is ridiculous. It's obvious you can't march with feet like that."

I waited. He reached into a drawer and pulled out an official-looking envelope. "Your company commander sent this over. It's a requisition for you to join an Air Corps band in Santa Monica. After," he added pointedly, "you complete your basic training."

I flushed happily.

"Melvin," the doctor continued, "the question is: how are you going to finish basic, with several more marches scheduled, with a pair of feet like yours?"

"Colonel," I offered, "if I could only get a pair of boots that fit, or even _nearly_ fit, I think I'd be okay."

The colonel shook his head. "That won't make any difference. You have third-degree flat feet. Third-degree! That's as flat as feet get."

"Well, is there any way at all I can get around the marching but still—"

"No, I'm afraid not, private."

Ten days later, I was processed and discharged.

≡

The Mel-Tones greeted me with open arms. I was feeling no small amount of guilt. Two months of military service was certainly nothing to crow about. I resisted wearing the "ruptured duck" I had been given upon discharge from Camp Roberts. I simply did not feel I was entitled to wear it in my lapel along with the thousands who had really earned theirs.

Now, out of equal parts of misplaced guilt and embarrassment, I set about making the Mel-Tones the most available-to-the-services vocal group in the business. We became regulars at the Hollywood Canteen; played virtually every Army, Navy, Marine, and Air Corps installation in California; and appeared, not only on our old standby, "Swingtime," but on numerous other service-oriented radio shows. We sang at bond rallies and veterans' hospitals the length and breadth of the state. It was little enough to do.

Let's Go Steady was released; it opened at the bottom half of a double bill at the Pantages Theatre on Hollywood Boulevard. The reviews for this silly little piece of celluloid were amazingly good, and my personal notices, in particular, drew a fair amount of attention. Ben Pollack called with some interesting news.

"Hey, Trome, have you seen the _Hollywood Reporter?_"

"No, not yet, Benj."

"There's a review on _Let's Go Steady_. Get a load of this." He began to read an excerpt: " 'Newcomer Mel Tormé stands out in this excellent cast of youngsters like Whirlaway in a livery stable.' How do you like that?"

"My God! I like it. I like it."

"So does Harry Cohn. His second-in-command, Max Arnow, called me this morning. They want to build a series around you at Columbia."

"You're kidding."

"But we got a problem."

"Problem? What do you mean?"

"Warner Brothers read the same review. Solly Biano, the main talent scout out there, also called me. They want to test you, and, if they like what they see, they'd like to sign you to a seven-year contract."

My head spun. "Ben, I don't believe this. All at once. It's happening all at once."

"That's the way it works sometimes, kid."

I took a breath. "Well, what do you think?"

"I think Warner Brothers," Ben said. "First of all, that cheap schmuck Cohn is offering one hundred dollars a week, seven-year contract, with pay raises up to seven-fifty at the end of the seven years. What a putz! Warners will start you off at three hundred per, if they sign you."

"Jesus, Warner Brothers. I'd sure like to—"

"Me too, Trome. Me too!"

"Listen, what about the kids?"

"The Mel-Tones? What about 'em? Nothing changes. You still work with them like always. I'm working on a record contract for all of you. If the Warner Brothers thing happens, you'll have a hell of a lot going for you on several fronts."

"Yeah," I answered in a slight daze, "that would really be something."

Harry Cohn hit the roof when he heard Warners was interested in signing me. He insisted that he had an option on my services (untrue) and that the brothers from Burbank had no right to test me. When Warner Bros. did finally test and sign me, Harry bad-mouthed both Pollack and me and swore I would never work on the Columbia lot again. A few years later, his anger trebled when

I filched one of his newer starlets from under his covetous nose and married her.

I seemed to be everywhere at once, suddenly. Days at Warners, doing improvs in acting class with Dick Erdman, Wanda Hendrix, and other acting hopefuls, tutored by the most beautiful ugly woman I've ever known, Sophie Rosenstein; late afternoons rehearsing the Mel-Tones or working on new arrangements for them; evenings at the Hollywood Canteen, singing for the service men and women and rubbing elbows with Dinah Shore, Eddie Cantor, Humphrey Bogart, Joan Leslie, Phil Harris, and the rest of the endless parade of stars doing their "bit" for the war effort; then, later in the evening, over to Mickey Scrima's new jazz club, a downstairs *boîte* on Ivar, off Hollywood Boulevard, where the Harry James drummer always greeted me warmly and invited me to sit in on drums with some of the jazz world's best.

I was appearing in the Cole Porter bio-film, *Night and Day*, in which I played drums on camera in a sideline band at the beautiful Lewis estate, a double for Porter's New England country estate. As much as I love drumming, I was upset at being relegated to the background as a band drummer, while Cary Grant, as Cole Porter, and Ginny Simms warbled their way through "You're the Top." I twirled my drumsticks in the background in a shamefully unprofessional move to call some attention to myself. It didn't matter. I was mainly seen in long shots behind the drums, the size of a pin on the big silver screen.

13.

BUDDY

V-E DAY. Hiroshima. Nagasaki. Then it was over. The studio welcomed back many of its contract actors whose careers had been interrupted by the Big Fracas. Many young, new contractees were terminated. I was one of them.

I had done the "lead" in a Warner Bros. two-reeler called *Movieland Magic*, in which I played a studio page conducting visitors on a tour of the lot. In *Janie Gets Married*, I was part of a group of G.I.s who sing a song about being overseas, away from their girl friends. And, of course, there was my appearance as a speck in *Night and Day*. That's all she wrote.

I gave in to slight depression, followed by great depression. I had been dating MGM starlet Jean Porter for several months. Suddenly we broke up; she moved on to greener fields; I, at the suggestion of the Mel-Tones, jumped into my Plymouth and headed for Yosemite. None of us had ever been there, but it was Christmastime and, since we weren't working at the moment, we all felt a change of scene was in order. We arrived up north safe but nearly broke. The lodge reluctantly rented us a single, large cabin-style room with five beds in it. Since none of the Mel-Tones were ever romantically involved with one another, we hung a blanket on a clothesline to bisect the room in *It Happened One Night* style, boys on one side, girls on the other.

I was gloomy and miserable and a flaming bore. The kids wanted to have fun, skate, hike, and I was a large tureen of ice-cold water dashed upon their plans. But they hung in there with me, trying to cheer me up.

Our combined budget was tight and, on the second evening, we sat in the spacious main room of the lodge itself, eating sandwiches as our main dinner course and watching young people ice-skate on the frozen lake, which we could see through the large bay windows. At around eleven, the skating ceased and a stream of exuberant, attractive young people, faces flushed from the cold, chatting, laughing, and joking, invaded the lodge. Soon a makeshift choir was formed and everyone began singing Christmas carols. The Mel-Tones remained at the far end of the room, away from the merry tumult.

After a while, one strapping youth in a ski sweater waved. "Hey, you guys," he called to us. "Come on over and join the gang." We looked at each other, rose, and moved toward the crowd. The friendly young man smiled (mainly at Ginny and Betty) and introduced himself. We did likewise, but, of course, our names meant nothing at all to him.

"We're singing Christmas carols," he said brightly.

"So we heard," smiled Les Baxter.

"Come on. Sing along. You all know them."

Now. Les had an extremely puckish sense of humor. He instantly grasped the possibilities of the situation. Among ourselves, we Mel-Tones used to make fun of movies in which a group of college football stars, out for a night on the town, suddenly burst into song in perfect five-part harmony. Les smiled at the young man. "Oh, yes. We know some Christmas carols, don't we, kids?" he asked, turning toward us.

"Um hmmm," said Bernie, barely containing a knowing smile.

Without prompting, we launched into a Christmas medley I had recently arranged for the group. The harmonies were modern and the singing close-knit and professional. When we finished, there was, in addition to wildly enthusiastic applause and shrill whistles, a profusion of open mouths and heads shaking in disbelief. An older man approached us.

"Who the hell are you folks?" he asked.

"We're Mel Tormé and the Mel-Tones," piped Ginny.

"Oh, yeah. Seems like I've heard something about you."

He introduced himself and added, "I'm the manager of the

lodge. Listen, how about coming in every night while you're here, just about this time, and singing. Like you did just now. Sing anything you like. What'd it take?"

The kids looked at me. "Well," I said slowly. "I guess we could sing for the few nights we're going to be staying. But——"

"Tell you what. Separate rooms for all of you and all meals and lodge facilities complimentary." He looked at all of us expectantly. "Whaddaya say?"

For the next four days we had the run of the place, comfortable rooms and great food. We walked, talked, sang, rehearsed, confided, and socialized; and, miraculously, I found, as we headed the Plymouth south, that I could face life without Jean Porter.

I continued to work, both with the Mel-Tones on the Hires Root Beer radio show, and on drums with varying jazz groups around town. I worked hard and partied a lot. John Carroll, a tall, handsome actor and singer, threw a number of bashes in honor of the Mel-Tones. We would happily sing our heads off at these soirées. It was at this time that I got to know Johnny Mercer. I had never forgotten Glenn Miller's good advice: if you want to write really fine lyrics, emulate Mercer. We became good friends right up to his untimely death in 1976. He was and is my favorite lyricist. I miss him.

I also met a budding lyric writer named Bob Wells during an evening at John Carroll's. We compared notes and decided to team up. We began meeting daily, and our output was predictably hit-and-miss. When we "hit," though, the results were gratifying. At the same time, Ben Pollack arranged a contract for the Mel-Tones with Decca and we made our first record, backing Bing Crosby.

A recent biography of Bing painted him as a cold, thoughtless, sometimes cruel man. I can only say that every encounter I ever had with this idol of mine was memorable, warm, instructive, and above all, filled with fun, banter, and great good humor. He treated me and the group as equals, helped us, even took suggestions, and in general was the perfect pro.

We made a few records for Decca, including the song "A Stranger in Town," which I had written while I had been with the Chico Marx band. Meanwhile, Bob and I were hard at work, writing our heads off, and, upon hearing two of our songs, "Willow Road" and "Born to Be Blue," a mutual friend, Carlos Gastel (who managed Nat Cole, Peggy Lee, and Stan Kenton), recommended us as a contract team to the firm of Burke and Van Heusen.

Johnny Burke and Jimmy Van Heusen were, of course, protean songwriters in Hollywood. Multiple Oscar winners, mainly for tunes they had written for Bing, they listened to our songs with interest and valuable criticism. They also signed us to a writing-publishing contract. Bob and I each received seventy-five dollars a week, advance salary against future royalties. The money really came in handy. In addition, Johnny and Jimmy secured for us motion picture title-song assignments, offers they had that they were too busy to handle. Consequently, we wrote the title songs for _Abie's Irish Rose_ and the Jimmy Stewart–Jane Wyman picture _Magic Town_. They also placed us with Walt Disney, and we wrote a long piece of material called "Country Fair" for a Disney film called _So Dear to My Heart_.

Bob, I should point out, was a great favorite with the ladies. Good-looking and well-built, he was an impeccably groomed young man-about-town, the possessor of a meticulously kept cherry-red '41 Buick convertible (for which I envied him no end), and the single most natural athlete I have ever known. While we were a team, he took an interest in golf; although he had never played the game in his life, within a few months he became a scratch golfer!

He then turned to skeet shooting and, one day, we went into Kerr's Sporting Goods Store in Beverly Hills. He pondered over this shotgun and that one. Very carefully, he chose two fine specimens, and began to practice daily. A few weeks (I said _weeks_!) later, he was challenging that supreme trapshooter, Bob Stack, and more than holding his own. Truly amazing.

One excessively hot afternoon, I drove out to Bob's house in Toluca Lake for a work session. The San Fernando Valley, always at least ten degrees warmer than the rest of the town, blistered in the July sun. Bob lived with his parents in a beautiful Colonial-type home, but even it was oppressive in those pre-air-conditioned days. I opened the front door and walked in. (Before Charles

Manson, some people left their front doors unlocked.) I called for Bob. No answer. I walked over to the piano. A writing pad rested on the music board. Written in pencil on the open page were four lines of verse:

> Chestnuts roasting on an open fire
> Jack Frost nipping at your nose
> Yuletide carols being sung by a choir
> And folks dressed up like Eskimos

When Bob finally appeared, I asked him about the little poem. He was dressed sensibly in tennis shorts and a white T-shirt, but he still looked uncomfortably warm.

"It was so damn hot today," he said, "I thought I'd write something to cool myself off. All I could think of was Christmas and cold weather."

I took another look at his handiwork. "You know," I said, "this just might make a song."

We sat down together at the piano, and, improbable though it may sound, "The Christmas Song" was completed about forty-five minutes later. Excitedly, we called Carlos Gastel, sped into Hollywood, played it for him, then for Johnny Burke, and then for Nat Cole, who fell in love with the tune. It took a full year for Nat to get into a studio to record it, but his record finally came out in the late fall of 1946; and the rest could be called our financial pleasure.

A humorous footnote: when Nat initially recorded "The Christmas Song," he sang the last line of the bridge: "To see if *reindeers* really know/How to fly." After the first pressings were released, and the song became a hit, we pointed out his grammatical error. Nat, a true gentleman, and a dogged perfectionist, stewed over this mistake, and, sure enough, at the end of another recording session of his, with the same-sized orchestra at hand, he rerecorded our song, properly singing "reindeer." The second version is virtually identical to the first, but those early first pressings have become collectors' items.

≣

One evening, late in 1945, I wandered into the Palladium to hear the Charlie Spivak band. A nice guy named Bobby Rickey was Charlie's drummer and he graciously would allow me to sit in with the band at some point during the second set. That night was the exception. A familiar-looking young man in a marine uniform was talking to Charlie at intermission after the first set. I didn't want to disturb their conversation backstage so I refrained from walking up and saying hello to Spivak.

At the very end of the second set, Charlie quieted the huge Saturday night audience and said: "Ladies and gentlemen, boys and girls, we have with us tonight a man we all consider to be the world's greatest drummer. Uncle Sam's been keeping him busy for a while, but he's fresh out of the marines and I am going to ask him to play one with us. A big hand, please, for the one and only Buddy Rich!" The crowd roared, and Buddy sauntered onto the stage, a cocky grin spreading over his features. Bobby Rickey handed him the drumsticks, and the band launched into Spivak's special arrangement of "Hawaiian War Chant," a tune that had featured Buddy and Ziggy Elman with the Tommy Dorsey band several years before.

Although Rich had never heard Spivak's arrangement before, he played it as if it were an old friend, and when the band taceted and Rich soloed, we were treated to eight or ten minutes of pure percussion genius. When the tune was finished and the cheers died away, I made my way backstage and suddenly there I was, face to face with my idol.

"My name's Mel Tormé," I said, extending my hand. "I have a vocal group called the Mel-Tones."

"Oh, yeah," he said gruffly, not accepting the proffered handshake. "I think I've heard of them." My phone call to him at the Chicago Theatre a few years earlier, naturally, had made no impression on him.

"Well, I just want to add my two cents. That was incredible. I play drums and I've always wanted to meet you."

"Figures," he said and turned away to talk to someone else.

I was slightly crestfallen. I had hoped to engage him in a somewhat longer chat. Still, I had met the Great One, and, after all, he was the man of the moment. I got out of there and rejoined my date in the main ballroom.

Soon the third set of the evening got under way. My date asked me if I was going to play drums that night. I laughed and told her that, after what we had just seen, I didn't want to be within a city block of a set of drums. We were leaning over toward each other, trying to speak above the band, when I felt a hand on my shoulder.

"Hey, kid. Mind if I sit down?"

I looked up. It was Buddy.

"Please do," I managed.

We spent the rest of the evening talking, or rather listening to him. Not that he tried to dominate the conversation. I wanted to hear him talk—about the Shaw band, Dorsey, his well-publicized beefs with Sinatra, the marines . . . hell, *any*thing!

Before we left that night, he said supercasually, "Hey, wanna hang out?"

"Try and stop me." I grinned.

Just like that, Buddy and I became inseparable. Once he got back into "civvies," I realized he was one of the sharpest dressers I had ever known. Tasteful. Contemporary. Sometimes innovative. When the collarless, lapel-free cardigan jackets came into vogue in early 1946, Rich led the way, wearing them long before anyone else did. He seemed to sense approaching trends and he had an almost eerie way of anticipating them and beating everyone to the sartorial punch.

He was obsessed with grooming. His nails were always polished and clean, his pants defied bagginess, his minimal bow to jewelry conservative, never flashy. Once he showed me an elegant, extremely expensive Patek Philippe watch encased in a gold mesh bracelet. On the back was engraved "Time for you always. L."

"Lana gave it to me," he told me, with a quaver of hurt. "We came that close to getting married." He told me about that love affair and several others. I confided in him. The one thing he had really missed during his tenure in the service was his beloved

Lincoln Continental. He had pictures of himself and Sinatra, parked in front of the New York Paramount Theatre with hundreds of girls clustered around the two Dorsey stars.

Now, he replaced his old blue Lincoln with a spanking new yellow copy. That car, with its steel-encased, exposed spare tire, and its protruding luggage compartment, was the complete end. Early in 1946, Buddy rejoined the Tommy Dorsey Orchestra, by virtue of his prewar contract with the trombonist. The setting was the newly refurbished Casino Gardens Ballroom out at the beach, now owned by none other than Dorsey himself. Night after night, Buddy (or "B," as his friends called him) would pick me up at my folks' apartment on Detroit Street, and we would glide out to the ballroom in the Lincoln, usually singing our favorite current tunes, "Some Other Time" or "Sure Thing." Every once in a while, he would ask me to sing his favorite song of them all, and I would lean back while he drove, and sing:

> When you shall see flowers
> That lie on the plain
> Lying there sighing for one
> Touch of rain
> Then you may borrow,
> Some glimpse of my sorrow
> And you'll understand
> How I long
> For the touch of your hand

I would smile to myself, thinking how extraordinary it was that this guy sitting next to me, with a reputation for pugnaciousness, a hot temper, abrasive vocabulary, two-fisted exploits, and the like, should love, of all songs, this tender, sentimental expression of caring, "The Touch of Your Hand." A truly complex man, BR.

14.

AVA

*J*UST when the Mel-Tones and I felt we had reached some sort of career dead end, two wonderful things happened: we became regulars on the famous "Fitch Bandwagon" radio show, along with host Dick Powell and actor Andy Devine, and we signed with a brand-new record company called Musicraft. Albert Marx, a music fan turned record executive, started the new label with an incredible roster that included Duke Ellington, Artie Shaw, Sarah Vaughan, Kitty Kallen, Teddy Walters, Dizzy Gillespie, and me and my Mel-Tones.

I believe it was Marx who came up with the concept of having the first Musicraft album be a multiartist affair. Perhaps it was Artie Shaw. I honestly don't remember. It was to be called *Artie Shaw Plays Cole Porter*. I was summoned to a meeting at Artie's home on Bedford Drive, and the door to his neo–English Tudor house was opened by his current wife, the gloriously beautiful Ava Gardner. She smiled warmly and led me into the music room where Artie was seated at a piano, going over prospective tunes for the album with arranger Sonny Burke.

I had been in awe of Shaw for years. Back at Hyde Park High, the controversy had raged daily: who is the better clarinetist, Goodman or Shaw? I was firmly entrenched in the Shavian camp. The 1939 Shaw band was my favorite of that era. If I felt like showing off in front of my schoolmates, I could rattle off the names of every single member of that band. I still can. Now, here I was, about to work with one of my musical heroes.

Artie was everything I had hoped he would be: friendly, helpful, thoroughly professional, full of great ideas, hugely intelligent, a voluble talker, and all in all, someone worth looking up to. At that initial session, we decided that the Mel-Tones would do "What Is This Thing Called Love?" and I would sing "Get Out of Town" in the album. Sonny and Artie would collaborate on the arrangements for the orchestra, a large studio aggregation complete with strings, horns, and the like. I would write the vocal arrangement for the Mel-Tones.

Ava sat quietly reading a book in a corner of the comfortably appointed music room. Sometimes she would put the book down and watch us. Occasionally, I would glance in her direction. I would have to have been superhuman to have been able to avoid looking at her. How could I know that by the end of the year, I would be dating her on a steady basis.

By mid-1946, Buddy had had enough of the Dorsey band. He had always hated the addition of strings and now he wanted to strike out on his own with a band bearing his imprimatur. Dorsey resisted the idea but finally promised B he would release him if Rich could find a suitable replacement. Who, I ask you, could have suitably replaced Buddy Rich?

A week came in August of '46 when the Dorsey crew was the Band of the Week on "The Fitch Bandwagon." We were all in rehearsal on the Saturday prior to the Sunday broadcast. The band had played a few numbers and were on a break. When they returned and settled into place, there was no sign of Buddy. Tommy glared at his watch and yelled, "Where the hell is Rich?" A unison shrugging of shoulders. More nervous waiting. Still no Buddy. Finally, Sandy Block, the bass player, said to Tommy, "Hey, Tom. Mel Tormé plays drums. Why not have him keep some time until Buddy shows up?"

Dorsey glanced at his watch again. He walked over to where I was standing, talking to Dick Powell. "Hey, Mel," he said. "Would you mind sitting in until your pal decides to return and play with the rest of us peasants?"

"Sure. Love to, Tommy," I replied.

We played "Chicago," "Sunny Side of the Street," and "Opus No. 1," three arrangements I knew as well as my birthmark. While

I never was in the same universe with The Master, I was currently playing drums a great deal of the time, and my style was similar to Buddy's. Tommy, apparently surprised and obviously delighted, began a campaign that was both flattering and embarrassing to hire me as his drummer.

I still lived with my parents in a pseudo-European edifice up on Kings Road, above the Sunset Strip. Tommy took to calling me at all hours, several times in the dead of night, waking my sister, my folks, and our dog. He would list the perks of being a Dorsey band member again and again. Blandishments would roll off his tongue like peas off a knife. Tommy was drinking with both fists in those days.

Needless to say, I was honored to think he considered me a passable replacement for Buddy Rich. I was also sorely tempted, since I loved playing drums and had committed to memory virtually the entire Dorsey library. Yet, I had a vocal group, a record contract, and I simply couldn't run away and join a band, *any* band. I kept trying to explain to Tommy and he let my explanations float over his head like so many Texas Leaguers, dropping in between short and center field. He called one Sunday and insisted that I come "for a drink" to his apartment on Sunset Plaza Drive. I said that it would really serve no purpose, but he insisted and, after all, we're talking about Tommy Dorsey. I arrived at his apartment a little after noon. It was the same apartment in which, during a drunken brawl with actor Jon Hall over Tommy's wife, MGM starlet Pat Dane, Tommy had taken a knife and sliced off the tip of Hall's nose.

I knocked on the door and Tommy greeted me, inviting me in. The place was beautifully furnished with white sofas and chairs, white tables, with throw pillows and paintings lending touches of colors. I was offered a drink. I was twenty-one years old and did not drink. I thanked Tommy and settled for a Coke, while he poured himself a large tumblerful of Scotch. We sat and he launched into what can only be described as a harangue regarding my stubbornness. Lamely, I kept trying to explain how impractical the whole situation was for me.

He waved aside my excuses and kept on, full bore. Suddenly,

the kitchen door opened and in walked Pat Dane Dorsey. Made in the mold of Ava Gardner, she wore white shorts and a halter tied in a bow at the back of her neck. She carried a tray of Danish pastries. Tommy regarded her, bleary-eyed, turned to me, and asked, in slurred tones, "You know my wife, Pat?"

"Uh—no. I've never had the pleasure."

"Say hello to Mel Tormé, honey," Tommy said.

Pat put the tray down, walked over, and extended her hand. I rose to my feet and shook it. She removed her hand from mine, picked up the tray, and started toward the dining-room table.

"Greatest tits in town. Show 'im, hon," ordered Tommy.

Pat stopped. With a slightly exasperated shrug of her shoulders, she put the tray down once again, faced us, reached with both hands toward the back of her neck, untied the bow, and let the halter fall, revealing, indeed, a gloriously formed pair of breasts. Tommy chuckled. "How about those, huh, kid?" he demanded.

My eyes were riveted. I couldn't take them off the undisputed focal point in that room at that moment. I stammered, "Very nice," while my eyes bored holes in the lady's chest. Calmly, she retied the halter, and went about her business. I never joined the Dorsey band but that's one incident that's indelible.

The Artie Shaw album with the Mel-Tones and myself was released and caused quite a stir. I began making some solo vocal records with Artie, as well as several more with the Mel-Tones and Artie's orchestra.

I had grown friendly with Donald O'Connor through his press agent, Glenn Rose, a soft-spoken young man who owned a house on Fountain Avenue between La Cienega and Crescent Heights Boulevard. Bob Wells and I spent some great, fun "men only" evenings in that house with Glenn, Donald, Sidney Miller, Warren Cowan (later of Rogers and Cowan, the famous publicists), and sundry other guys who shared our wild sense of humor.

At least once a week we gathered at Glenn's to drink beer and run sixteen-millimeter prints of old classic movies. One particularly hilarious evening early in 1945, the feature film of the evening was preceded by a two-reel March Of Time short subject called *Inside Nazi Germany*. There were dozens of shots of thousands of people shouting *"Sieg Heil,"* and every time one of them flashed on the screen, we would all jump to our feet and yell *"Sieg Heil"* along with the sound track. Donald found a black pocket comb, stuck it under his nose, and at the top of his voice, began to do a great impression of Hitler. He screamed at us in double-talk German and we would shout back, *"Sieg Heil, Sieg Heil."*

One day, in late 1946, Glenn opened his front door to get the morning paper. His next door neighbor, a sweet old lady, was watering her lawn. She smiled at him and he smiled back. She started to walk toward him, hesitated, thought about it, and then approached him.

"Mr. Rose," she said timidly. "I—I've never asked you, but I assume, now that the war is over this long, that everything worked out all right?"

"Excuse me?" said Glenn. "I'm sorry. I don't follow you, dear."

"Well, you know. With the FBI and all."

"The FBI?"

"Yes. You know. All that commotion about your house and—"

"Pardon me, dear, I don't understand what you're talking about."

"Well," she continued, not knowing whether she should or not, "of course I thought you knew about it. Some men from the FBI knocked on my door, oh, about a year ago, during the war. They said there had been reports from some of our neighbors, that you were holding German Bund meetings in your house, and—"

"German Bund meetings?"

"Well, yes. I thought you knew about this. They questioned everyone on the block. I thought you knew about—"

"For God's sake, no! I don't know anything about this. My God! I don't believe...I mean...why would...Jesus Christ! *Bund* meetings? I'm Jewish, for Christ's sake! Why would I—"

"Oh, I'm so sorry, Mr. Rose. I wouldn't have upset you for the world. I mean, I thought you knew about—"

"Oh, my God! I've got to call my lawyer right away."

The mystery went on for a week or so, until Sid Miller finally remembered that wild and crazy night of Donald's shrieking impersonation of *Der Führer* and our cheering replies. Needless to say, Glenn checked his phone. It was not tapped, and after careful consideration, decided to let the whole bizarre incident fade away.

≡

The phone rang at two in the morning. I ran downstairs and grabbed it on the third ring, hoping it wouldn't wake the folks or Myrna. I half-expected to hear Tommy Dorsey's Scotch-slurred voice on the other end, even though I had put the question of my joining his band to bed weeks before.

It was Carlos Gastel.

"Torment?" he roared into the phone, using his pet nickname for me.

"Carlos," I answered his question with a question, "I hate to say 'Do you know what time it is?' but, do you know what time it is?"

"Of course I do," said Carlos, who had been known to take a drink or twelve. "I am looking at my beautiful gold Universal chronograph on my beautiful wrist, and the big hand is on the—"

"Carlos, you whacko Honduran, it's two-forty in the morning."

"Shank of the evening, Torment. Shank of the evening."

I shut up and waited through a pause of heavy breathing on his part. When Carlos drank, heavy breathing was the norm, as well as huge beads of sweat, which rolled off his enormous head. Carlos weighed not a tad less than 300 pounds.

"Listen," he began again. "I hate to say, 'I suppose you're wondering why I called you,' but I suppose you're wondering why I called you."

I yawned. My mother appeared at the top of the stairs, a questioning look on her face. I waved her back to bed.

"Yes, as a matter of fact, that thought had crossed my mind. Fleetingly."

"Well, keep your pajama pants on, I'm coming to that. Les Brown and Woody Herman and I have been sitting here in my office, playing some of those things you made with Artie Shaw."

"Well, that's nice, Carlos, but this is a hell of a time of night to tell me how much you like my group."

"Not your group, you dumb little shit. You! Les and Woody think you ought to go out on your own as a solo singer. I agree. You've gone as far as you can go with the Mel-Tones. Let 'em be on their own. They're great! But singers, solo singers—that's what

the kids want right now. And, against my better judgment, Torment, I think you could make it. With my impossibly sensational
help, of course."

All of a sudden, I was wide awake.

"Look, Carloso, I know you guys are having a few drinks, and
I—"

"Oh, shit!" he roared disgustedly. "I'll put Les on."

"Mel, this is Les Brown."

"Hi, Les."

"Sorry to call so late, but you know Carlos. When he gets hot
about something..."

"So it's really on the level? He really wants to do something
with me?"

"I told him he's crazy if he doesn't. So did Woody. Here's
Woody."

"How you doin', Melvin?"

"I don't know, Woody. I'm in a mild daze."

"Yeah, I can imagine. It's a hell of a time of night to get good
news. Or any kind of news, for that matter."

"Yeah. Well..."

"Torment? This is Gastel again. Get your little ass into my
office tomorrow around one o'clock and we'll talk about it."

≡

In November of 1946, the Mel-Tones and I completed our farewell
engagement at, of all places, the Golden Gate Theatre in San
Francisco, the scene of the breakup of the Chico Marx orchestra.
The kids were sad about dissolving the group. Still, they understood
my desire to try the solo route. Ben Pollack graciously released me
from all manager-artist obligations. I took a deep breath and fas-
tened my mental seatbelt.

Carlos was quite excited about my prospects and felt that a trip
to New York to investigate the potential market for me was a
good idea. In early December, we traveled by train to the Big Town.
After arriving at Pennsylvania Station, we walked the length
of the train toward the station itself. I could see a cluster of young
girls at the far end, holding placards. They began running toward

us, and I could make out the printing on the placards: WELCOME, FOG! NEW YORK LOVES THE VELVET FOG!

I looked behind me to see whom they were meeting. There was no one there. The bobby-soxers, about twenty of them, gathered around shrieking, clapping, and laughing. Flashbulbs went off. I looked around and a photographer had mysteriously appeared. I glanced at Carlos uncomprehendingly. He was smiling the enigmatic smile of someone who knows something.

When we finally shook free of the small mob and found a cab, I looked at my new manager and asked, "Okay, what was that all about?"

"Never mind, Torment. You'll find out."

We checked into the Essex House, had lunch, met the president of General Artists Corporation Talent Agency, Tom Rockwell, with whom Carlos wished me to sign, and then made our way to a radio station, where I was introduced to a bright-eyed guy named Fred Robbins. His radio show, "Robbins' Nest," was the single most popular DJ program in New York.

Robbins, along with Art Ford, the helmsman of a rival program called "Milkman's Matinee," dominated the airwaves, and their endorsement and support practically ensured the success of a given recording. Luckily, they had been playing my solo sides with Artie Shaw for months. They had both chosen to champion my singing, with the pleasant result that they were friendly competitors over the right to claim Mel Tormé as their exclusive discovery. What a nice problem for me.

Now here I was, on the air with Robbins, a glib, fast-talking citizen with a talent for catchphrases and nicknames.

"Here he is, gang," Fred warbled into the mike. "First time ever in Gotham, just like I promised you, the kid with the gauze in his jaws. Mr. Butterscotch. The Velvet Fog himself, Mel Tormé!"

I made my way through the interview. Now, at least, I understood all that "Velvet Fog" hullabaloo at Penn Station, information Carlos had doggedly withheld all day.

Heading for the Art Ford show in a cab through the slushy winter streets, I turned to Carlos and said, "Listen, about this 'Velvet Fog' stuff—"

"Don't knock it, Torment," he cut me off. "That could become a household name."

"You're kidding?"

"I never kid about success."

Art Ford was a tall, thin man, much more laid back than Fred Robbins. His approach was cooler, quieter, far more subdued. We did a fairly sane interview with no mention by him, naturally, of the Velvet Fog thing. He said he was glad I had forsaken the Mel-Tones, since remaining a vocal group singer/arranger might have been a career wrecker for me. He was prepared to back me to the hilt in my solo vocal endeavors.

That night, Gastel and I went to the famous Copacabana nightclub where Joe E. Lewis was appearing. Long the prime watering place of New York's sporting set, mob figures and garment-center types, the Copa's parade of cabaret stars included Sophie Tucker, Jimmy Durante, Tony Martin, and other heavyweight saloon attractions.

Carlos introduced me to Monte Proser, a gruff little man who was the operator of the club. Proser, a vulgarian with a keen sense of business, was aware of the Ford and Robbins competition over me.

Proser was looking ahead toward high school prom season, 1947. Carlos, I now discovered, had talked with him about me before. Proser had agreed to try something highly innovative for the Copa. He would present me for the first time in New York as a special added attraction on a bill that starred Mitzi Green, the former child movie star and established nightclub comedienne. A twenty-one-year-old performing in the hallowed environs of the Copacabana was unheard of, but with the help of the two biggest DJs in Manhattan, the prospects for a successful solo debut looked promising. In addition, Gastel had made a new deal with Albert Marx to record me as a solo Musicraft artist. I was beginning to get excited.

We flew back to California where the pre-Christmas parties were in full swing. At one of them I ran into Marilyn Maxwell. The beautiful blonde had signed with MGM in 1942 and was doing well in films. I reminded her of the first time we had met, back in Chicago at the Edgewater Beach Hotel, when she had been Marvel Maxwell, Ted Weems's girl singer, and I had been a high school student, winning weekend contests at the hotel with my trio. I was between girl friends that Christmas season and was enjoying some attention, thanks to Nat Cole's just-released recording of "The Christmas Song." Marilyn and I made a date.

Later in the week, at yet another festivity, I was asked to sing. I sat at the piano, with the likes of Margaret Whiting, Van Heflin, Bob Mitchum, Esther Williams, and Barbara Britton gathered around, and sang "The Christmas Song" followed by "Have Yourself a Merry Little Christmas." The applause was enthusiastic and afterward, as I poured myself a weak Moscow Mule (vodka and ginger beer in a mandatory copper mug), a husky voice at my side whispered, "That was nice, Melvin."

I turned and found Ava Gardner standing there. She had separated from Artie Shaw and seemed to be on her own at the party.

"Melvin?" I grinned at her.

"Yeah, yeah, yeah." She smiled. "Melvin. It's a grand old name."

"No, that's 'Mary.' "

"Don't contradict me. 'Melvin.' It has a certain . . ." She paused.

"Don't say it. Think it but don't say it."

She was slightly tipsy. She smiled, her eyes half-lidded, and I thought I might just need the Pulmotor squad.

"Well, I don't care what you say. I like 'Melvin.' "

"I certainly hope so—"

"I like 'Melvin,' and that's what I'm going to call you."

"Which might indicate that you intend to see me frequently enough to call me that."

She took a drink from her glass of wine. "Run that by me again?"

"What I meant was, I think I could get used to your calling me 'Melvin,' if I saw you often enough."

She took another sip, and said into her glass, "Well, that's up to you, isn't it? When do you suggest we start this thing?"

I swallowed hard. "I don't think I can make it before tomorrow night."

She laughed that famous throaty laugh. "Hah! No, no, sorry,

no can do. I'm having dinner with my lawyer tomorrow night."

Dummy that I am, I thought she was signaling me that the game was over. I made a small grimace and shrugged.

"Monday," she said. "Dinner Monday."

This was Saturday night and I had made a previous date with Marilyn Maxwell for Monday evening.

"Sorry." I grinned bravely. "No can do. I'm having dinner with a blonde Monday night."

"Is she a lawyer?"

"Not so you'd notice."

"A blonde, eh? Brunettes are better, didn't your mother ever teach you that?"

"Oh, yeah. My momma done tole me."

"Well, then," she said imperiously. "Break the date."

"It's a party. She invited me. I couldn't do that to her."

She looked at me, a long, speculative look. Then she reached out and touched my face with her hand. It was to die.

"That's nice, Melvin. You're not a rat after all."

" 'After all?' " I said. "Does that mean you thought I was one to begin with?"

"No, no, no. Just a little test."

"Uh huh. How'd I do?"

"Passed. With flying colors."

"Whoopee," I said quietly. There was another pause. I felt I was losing the advantage.

"Listen," I said finally. "Enough of this snappy dialogue. I'd like to see you. Possible or not?"

She sipped at her wine and nodded her head. "Oh, possible. Very possible. I would even say probable."

"Try 'definite.' "

"Try asking me."

"I just did."

"No. Specific night."

"All right. Next week, New Year's Eve. I'm having a party at my house. I'd like you to be with me on that specific night."

She shook her head. "Uh uh. Already have a date. Lawford. He's taking me to several parties." She grinned at me. "I couldn't do that to him."

"That's nice, Ava. You're not a rat after all."

She threw her head back and laughed. "Jesus, Melvin. You're funny. I like you."

"There you go," I said, laughing happily myself.

"Tell you what," she said. "New Year's Eve is over a week away. How about dinner on Tuesday and we'll talk about it."

"About—what?"

"It. Life. Love. All that crap."

"I think you just made a date. Where does this philosophical discussion take place?"

She looked at me seductively. "Would you like to have dinner at my place?" she said huskily.

"I can think of worse places," I replied, trembling a bit.

"Yeah, well, that comes later. Maybe. Tuesday night you can buy me dinner and wine at Villa Nova."

I snapped my finger in mock disappointment and said to a nearby empty chair, "Damn it! Blew my chance! I thought I had her cornered."

She laughed again, kissed me on the cheek, and said, "I'm at the Wilshire Palms. Beverly Glen and Wilshire. Apartment 4C, upstairs." She took a piece of paper from her purse and wrote down her telephone number, shoving it into my hand. "I better go find my date now," she said, the first time I realized she had not arrived alone.

"Tuesday," I said.

"Why not?" she answered, walking away. I put my copper mug down and rejoined the party in the living room. It was in full swing, noisy with yuletide cheer, but I was oblivious to all of it. Dinner with Ava on Tuesday! How the hell was I going to get through Sunday and Monday? I looked around to catch another glimpse of the goddess, but she was nowhere to be seen. Probably left by now, I thought, and I felt a foolish twinge of jealousy over her unnamed escort of the evening.

After a while, the party began breaking up. I made my good nights and went to the closet to get my trench coat. I started putting it on and found that someone was helping me into it. A soft cheek and fragrant hair pressed very close to my face from behind.

"By the way, Melvin," Ava said, "who's the blonde?"

Startled, I stammered, "The blon—? Oh, the blonde. Marilyn Maxwell."

"Hmm. My fellow factory worker." Ava was also an MGM contract player. "Wait till I see her in the commissary Monday. I'll fix her for beating my time." She kissed my cheek and was out the front door before I could reply.

I didn't sleep that night.

Right through the Christmas holidays, Ava and I spent virtually every evening and portions of several days together. Love? I doubt it. We liked each other, laughed a lot, and I think she appreciated the fact that I was one of the few guys she had met in a long while whose prime interest was not to jump on her bones as quickly as possible.

As New Year's Eve approached, I found myself feeling very lost and unhappy. Here was this lovely creature who seemed to prefer my company at that moment more than anyone else's, and she would be spending the last, most significant night of the year with someone else. I was hosting a large party at my house, dateless. Marilyn Maxwell was coming, escorted by one of her beaus, arranger Dean Elliott. Nat Cole was coming, as were Carlos, Donald O'Connor, and Bob Wells.

The party, predictably, was boisterous and music-filled, funny and sentimental, and damn near perfect except for one minor detail: no Ava.

Shortly after we had celebrated the arrival of the new year, I was seated at the piano in the living room. Nat, Donald, Sid Miller, and Marilyn were singing and the party was in full swing. The front door bell rang and my sister Myrna opened the door. I glanced toward the foyer. There stood Peter Lawford, tuxedoed and already impatient to be gone and, beside him, the party's missing element. She was radiant in a full-skirted white ball gown, trimmed with fine gold threading throughout and emerald green tulle. Strapless and sleeveless, Ava's fine physical configuration was shown off to pulse-quickening advantage.

She and Lawford stayed for no more than fifteen minutes. She smiled sweetly at me several times. Soon the two of them were out the door, on their way to several other parties, I supposed. I

was miserable. Marilyn noticed, smiled at me, and nodded knowingly. By two-thirty in the morning, everyone had gone home
except Marilyn and Dean Elliott. We sat in the downstairs den,
playing records, and once, Marilyn looked at me, made a little kiss
with her lips, and mouthed the words "Poor baby." I managed a
weak smile. I wanted to go to bed, and be done with New Year's
Eve.

The phone rang.

"Hello?"

"Melvin?"

My heart thudded. "Hi, there," I said, trying to sound casual
in front of Marilyn and Dean.

"Lawford's still here, but he's leaving any second. I want to see
you. Come on over."

"Uh—sounds good. I'll—uh—do just that."

Click.

Now then, how to politely get my two remaining guests to go
home? Marilyn got the message. "Come on, Dean," she said to
her date. "Time to hit the road to Dreamland."

No sooner had their car faded from view than I hopped into
mine and drove straight to the Wilshire Palms. I killed the engine
and looked at my watch—3:00 A.M. Lawford had to be gone by
now. I ran up the stairs and knocked on the door. Peter opened
it and handed me my first embarrassment of the new year. He
handled the thorny situation with typical English aplomb. "Come
on in," he said cordially. "I'm just leaving."

I walked by him, into Ava's apartment, and sat down quietly.
Ava went to the door, kissed him on the cheek, and he was gone.

She walked right over to the couch and kissed me. Not on the
cheek. "Got a great idea, Melvin. Let me change and I'll be right
with you." She went into the bedroom and closed the door. Gracious me, I wondered, is this a replay of the Jean Harlow *Hell's
Angels* bit "Would you be shocked if I put on something more
comfortable?"

In a few minutes, Ava appeared. She was dressed in a three-
quarter-length dark green suede coat, with a matching green silk
scarf tied around her thoroughly desirable neck.

"Come on, come on, Melvin," she exhorted. "On your feet. Let's go."

"You're kidding? Another party?"

"No, you silly man. Just have faith."

We went down to her garage and got into a dark green convertible Cadillac. She drove it out, paused at the end of the driveway, and looked to her left. Parked under a streetlight stood a blue Chevrolet. She snorted and said to me: "One of Hughes's henchmen. That car is parked there twenty-four hours a day."

"Hughes? Howard?"

"Oh, yeah. Howard. He gave me this car. Now he thinks he owns me."

"He—bought you this car? Is it permitted to ask why?"

"Certainly. He does things like that, that's all."

"Gotcha."

"No, really, Melvin. That *is* all. Howard keeps tabs on about a dozen ladies in this town. I guess he gets his kicks that way."

She pulled out of the driveway and onto Wilshire Boulevard, heading toward Santa Monica. I looked back. The blue Chevy stayed put. When we got to Pacific Coast Highway, she turned north. It was 4:00 A.M., and the New Year's Eve traffic had dissipated. I was tired but happy. I asked her where we were headed. She looked at me, smiled, and said, "You'll see."

I dozed.

When I woke up, she had put the top down. I looked at the dashboard clock—5:20. I looked at Ava. She was wide awake with the wind blowing her hair, the lapels of her suede coat flapping, and the scarf trailing behind her. A faint rim of dawn light appeared at the edge of the Pacific, way beyond the breakers, halfway to Hawaii. Ava's classic profile stood out in relief against the faint twilight of the winter morning. God, this woman is astonishingly beautiful, was my highly unoriginal appraisal.

She drove to a pancake house in Santa Barbara. We had breakfast, turned right around, and drove back to her apartment, where we stayed until 7:00, New Year's night.

As I drove back to my folks' house, I couldn't help grinning contentedly and thinking, What a way to start the new year.

15.

SOLO

*I*N 1947, Carlos Gastel was the hottest personal manager in the music business. He guided the destinies of Stan Kenton, Peggy Lee, Nellie Lutcher, and Nat "King" Cole, and now I had become part of his stable of performers. He moved very quickly on my behalf, booking me, in early January, into an intimate nightclub just east of Vine on Sunset called the "Bocage."

Glen Billingsley, brother of famed New York Stork Club owner Sherman Billingsley, was the proprietor. The Bocage sat on the second story of a smallish, neatly kept building. Opening night, Ava, Peggy Lee, Nat, Johnny Burke, and Jimmy Van Heusen and others turned out for my solo vocal debut. The Page Cavanaugh Trio accompanied me and the repertoire ranged from Johnny Mercer's "Jamboree Jones" to Alec Wilder's "Trouble Is a Girl" (originally written as "Trouble Is a Man").

The reviews were more than encouraging and business was brisk. Bob Wells and I worked almost every day writing new songs. I was seeing Ava constantly. The nightly clientele at the Bocage was celebrity-studded. Howard Hawks, one of my favorite directors, was a frequent patron, always accompanied by a beautiful girl. Linda Darnell, Marilyn Maxwell, John Carroll, and Yvonne De Carlo were among the nightly contingent of celebrities.

One evening, Arthur Freed, the songwriter-turned-MGM-producer, came in, and the next morning Carlos called to tell me that Freed had been impressed with my singing and had offered me a featured role in his upcoming MGM musical, *Good News,* with Peter Lawford and June Allyson. Filming was to commence in late February with a shooting schedule of twelve to fourteen weeks. Freed also wanted an option on my services for two pictures a year, should my work in *Good News* prove satisfactory.

Excitedly, I called Ava. She sounded happy to hear the news. Marilyn Maxwell, too, had somehow heard about the offer; she called to congratulate me.

MGM was huge and intimidating. The cavernous sets, the sheer size of the property, the constant awareness that I was on the Rolls-Royce of movie lots was seldom far from my mind. In *Good News* I was assigned "The Best Things in Life Are Free," "Lucky in Love," "Be a Ladies Man," and "Just Imagine," the last of which was cut from the final print.

Considering the touchy incident at Ava's apartment scant weeks before we began working on *Good News,* Lawford's attitude was very decent and friendly. He even joined Bob Wells and me one Thursday evening at the Gilmore Stadium midget auto races, a sport my partner and I had gone bonkers for. Ray McDonald, Patricia Marshall, Joan McCracken, and hordes of singing and dancing young hopefuls rounded out the cast of *Good News,* a college picture set in the 1920s. The set was full of beautiful young girls and collegiate-looking guys, and the prevailing atmosphere throughout the shooting schedule was like that of the university I had never attended but had always wanted to, good old fictitious Tait College.

In "Be a Ladies Man," one of the voices heard on the sound track, dubbing for one of the five participants in the number, was a very young Andy Williams.

Ava was making *The Hucksters* and we shared many lunches together in the commissary. One day, I picked her up on her set and there I was, being introduced to Gable, big as life (no, bigger), who gave me a strong, warm handshake and a dazzling smile. That particular day was memorable for meeting The King and for another little scene that took place in the MGM commissary about twenty minutes later.

I was eating lunch with Gardner and her friend Peggy Maley, when I felt a tap on the shoulder. I looked up and saw a handsome young Englishman, newly under contract to the studio. He was towering over me, beaming like a long lost buddy.

"Mel," he cried in his strong English accent. "How marvelous to see you. How are you? How's _Good News_ going? I've been meaning to drop by the set and say hello."

Peggy looked at him curiously.

Ave sipped at her soup, staring into the bowl.

I was nonplussed. I barely knew him, although I would have to have been a total idiot not to understand why he had come over. He wanted to meet the ladies, especially Ava.

I obliged. Rising, I said, "Do you know Peggy Maley?"

"How do you do," he said, charming but disinterested.

"And this is Ava Gardner," I said.

He took Ava's hand, bowed, and kissed it.

"Miss Gardner," he said, lowering his voice a minor third, "this is a pleasure I've looked forward to for some time. The studio has more gorgeous creatures than one should honestly hope to meet in a lifetime. But you . . . the first time I saw you on the lot, oh, weeks ago, I told myself that such perfection was virtually impossible. Perhaps that's because I saw you from afar on that occasion, but now—here—up close, your loveliness exceeds even my original estimation of you!"

Ava looked up, put her spoon down, and said to him, quite conversationally, "Do you suck?"

Peggy Maley spit her food into the table and burst out laughing. Ava smiled sweetly at the crimsoning Englishman, who was looking around to see if anyone had heard her. I imagine he wanted to die. So did I. He made his apologies, excused himself, and was gone. Peggy was still laughing uncontrollably. Ava resumed her soup sipping. I sat there, mortified, and shook my head in disbelief.

I completed almost all my work on _Good News_ by the end of April. There remained only the "Varsity Drag" finale, in which, of course, I was scheduled to perform along with the other principals in the cast. The problem was, I was opening momentarily at the Copa in New York, a commitment I had made the previous December and to which I was signed and sealed, if not yet delivered. Carlos had one hell of a time with Arthur Freed, who was furious at my being unavailable for the final production number, but there was nothing he or I could do. Again and again, I have been asked why I was not in the "Varsity Drag," as well as the final shot of the film. Now you know.

One sad footnote to *Good News* and its cast: Ray McDonald, one of the most talented people I have ever worked with, was one of the stars of the film. We became good friends and spent a lot of time together. Eventually, his film career began to fade until he was virtually unemployed for long periods of time. I hadn't seen him for a while, and one night someone called to tell me he had killed himself. I went sleepless several nights after that phone call, thinking about Ray. He had one of the most lovable personalities I have ever encountered and a blazing talent. What a waste.

Bob Wells and I were busily writing music all during this period. Because we were intense about our work and what was happening in the songwriting community generally, I found myself in a situation that led to the breakup of my brief romance with Ava. I was still working on *Good News*. Ava had finished filming *The Hucksters*. One nonshooting day for me, I called to find she had a bad cold and was keeping to her bed.

"Tell you what, Melvin," she sniffled. "How about going over to Will Wright's." Will Wright's was the prime ice-cream connection in those days. "Pick up a quart of maple walnut, bring it over, and we'll spend a nice, quiet evening here, listening to music and stuff."

"I've heard worse suggestions, Avala. I just can't remember when. What time?"

"I dunno. How about sevenish?"

"There you go."

Wells and I worked most of that afternoon. Around five o'clock the phone rang. It was Marilyn Maxwell.

"Mel," she said, in a conspiratorial tone of voice, "I'm not supposed to tell anyone, but they're sneaking *Summer Holiday* tonight at the Alex in Glendale." (*Summer Holiday* was an MGM musical remake of Eugene O'Neill's *Ah, Wilderness*.) The Alex was a prime testing movie house for MGM, but Metro frowned vigorously on their contract players showing up at the theater to catch the latest MGM product. A "sneak" was a "sneak": an opportunity to expose a brand-new movie to an unsuspecting audience. In those days, sneak previews were rarely, if ever, announced in the papers. You went to a movie to see a film and suddenly at eight-thirty or so, a clip would appear on the screen: "This theater is proud to present a preview of a forthcoming MGM picture. Your comments on preview cards will be appreciated."

There would always be a gasp of surprise and delight from the audience and the film would begin. Marilyn's call to Bob and me was a no-no, but Wells and I found it irresistible. Everyone was talking about _Summer Holiday_. Mickey Rooney, Gloria De Haven, and Marilyn were the stars, but the main interest for Bob and myself was the highly touted score by Ralph Blane and Harry Warren. We simply had to see the movie.

"Oh-oh," I said to Bob, stopped in my tracks. "I promised Ava I'd come over and spend the evening with her."

"Come on." Bob laughed. "You're joking. We've been hearing about this one for months. Blane and Warren, Torm. Blane and Warren. We gotta go, that's all there is to it."

"What the hell will I tell her?"

Bob smiled. "Lie," he advised me. Damn fool that I was, that's exactly what I did.

"Ava," I said, crossing my fingers when she answered the phone, "I've hit a snag regarding tonight."

"Oh, no kidding?" she replied, sneezing, making me feel guilty as hell, which, after all, I was. "What happened?"

"Bob and I just got a call from the Burke and Van Heusen office. We've got an assignment. Title song for a new picture. At RKO. We've got to get right on it. They need to hear something tomorrow morning."

I heard the sound of my own voice, trying to be glib. There is no way, Melvin, I told myself, that she's going to buy this. You hate liars, you are not a liar, and you are stupid to try and lie to her.

Surprisingly, she said, "Damn it, that's a shame. I really looked forward to some ice cream and your presence around the old homestead."

I weakened visibly and was about to spill out the truth, but Wells was there, shaking his head, encouraging my perfidy.

"Aw, gee, beauty, I feel terrible," I said. "Look, I'm going to pop over to Wright's and pick up some maple walnut for you. I'll bring it by, give you a quick kiss, and—"

"For God's sake, Melvin, don't be silly. I'm in the business too, remember? I understand. I'm just disappointed, that's all."

"So am I." I meant it.

"Listen, don't work too hard, and if you finish early, call me."

Fat chance, Ava. I had spewed enough lies for one night. I said I would if I could and hung up. I felt terrible. Bob, man of the world that he was, shook his head and grinned. We went to the preview, liked the film, had a bite with Marilyn afterward, and called it a night.

I phoned Ava the next day. Her service picked up the call and said she was out. I called again. Same answer. Late in the afternoon, she called me.

"Hi," she said sweetly. "What're you doing?"

"Uh, nothing, really. I was just about to give you a ring and—"

"Come on over."

"When?"

"Now."

"Well, all right. I'll be there shortly."

When I walked into her apartment, her attorney was there, finishing up some business. She nodded at me and indicated a chair. I sat. Soon, her lawyer departed and she came over to me. She was wearing a black sheath, a rather formal dress for that time of day, and I asked her about it.

"I was at the studio today, doing some stills for *Hucksters*. I ran into Marilyn in the commissary."

I froze.

She smiled. "We're through, Melvin. Finished. Kaput. You lied to me and I won't take that from anyone. Out!"

To try and weasel out would have been foolish. I got up and left, a sadder but wiser twenty-two-year-old. We still had one more date in our future, but it wouldn't occur for almost two years.

Bob and I had become friends with a budding young actor/writer/producer named Blake Edwards. Together with his then-partner, John Champion, Blake was producing a low-budget western with Rod Cameron called *Panhandle*. He was looking for a leading lady but the film was still in preproduction. He had time. Meanwhile, we all buddied up and were having one hell of a good time.

I was dating, among others, a raven-haired young starlet named, appropriately, Raven McBride. Raven (her real name was Evelyn) had spectacularly good looks, the kind Milton Caniff used to draw in "Terry and the Pirates"—prominent cheekbones, pouty, full lips, impressive breastworks. Oh yeah, Raven was an authentic Irish beauty, if somewhat limited in the conversation department.

One weekend, my parents were out of town, and it was party time at my house. Blake, Bob, John Champion, and their respective ladies gathered to exchange views on life, movies, music, and other related subjects. Raven was my date for this debauched weekend. She sat quietly, saying little, looking eminently desirable. I couldn't take my covetous eyes off her.

Later, when the party began to break up, the other ladies inexplicably said their good nights. Only Raven remained, to share my bed, while my buddies looked forward to a bleak, barren night sans bed partners. Too bad, gents, I said airily, as the beauteous McBride and I ascended the stairs to my room.

Raven and I were really getting to know each other when suddenly the distinct sound of marbles—hundreds of them—being rolled under my bedroom door across my uncarpeted wooden floor nearly knocked us out of bed. The clatter was indescribable. I quickly got the message: if we're to be celibate tonight, Tormé, so are you. The Great Marble Caper lasted for twenty minutes or so.

Raven and I settled for an unsettling night's sleep.

Blake was opting for an acting career in those days, perhaps even more than a producer or director. We were constantly doing "improvs," improvising scenes out of typical westerns, musicals, and gangster movies. We would lapse into dialogue over dinner, at the auto races, anywhere. Sometimes the scenes would really work as we got caught up in the theme, and Blake would grab a pencil and write down snippets of dialogue, usable goodies for future productions.

One late afternoon when once again my family was out, Bob

and I were working on a song. Blake was on the way over. Wells and I rubbed our hands together expectantly. I went to my gun case and selected a Colt .32 automatic. I shoved a Luger into Bob's hands and we proceeded to load the magazines with blanks. The doorbell rang.

Bob and I secreted our guns in our waistbands. I answered the door. There stood Blake Edwards. "Hi," he greeted me cheerily.

"Hello, Johnny," I said grimly. "We been expecting you. Come in."

Blake picked it up immediately. The smile faded from his face. He walked into the foyer, looking around nervously, his mouth twitching slightly.

"Look, Joe," he said, a tremor of fear in his voice. "If—if you're busy right now, I can come back later. I—"

"No, no, no," I said expansively. "When is Johnny D'Amico not welcome in my house? Who could I be happier to see? Right, Carmine?"

Bob Wells, seated on a couch in the living room, looked up slowly at Blake. "Sure, Joe. Right. Come on in, Johnny. Take a load off your feet."

"Well, okay, if I'm not intruding. I know how busy you guys are and—"

"Busy?" I laughed. "Whaddya mean, 'busy'? How can I be busy? Last week I pushed two thousand barrels of beer. Two thousand, Johnny boy. This week? You know how many my boys moved this week, kiddo?"

"Uh—no. No, Joe, I got no idea."

I looked at Bob and jerked my thumb in Blake's direction. "He's got no idea. You hear that, Carmine?"

"Yeah, Joe. I hear it and I'm laughin'."

I looked back at Blake, who seemed to be sweating.

"Would it surprise you to know, Johnny boy, that I got rid of less than seven hundred barrels? Huh? Would that surprise you?"

Quietly, Blake said, "No, as a matter of fact, it wouldn't."

I shot Blake a look that could kill. "You double-crossing punk! You're hungry, ain'tya? Hungry for what's mine, for what I built up over the last six years. It ain't enough to be walkin' around in

two hunnerd buck suits, drivin' a flashy Buick, and sleepin' around
with some of the best-looking dames in town, all thanks to me.
No, you want it all, don't ya? You even want Poppy, I'll bet."

Blake impassively picked up the reference to Karen Morley's
name in *Scarface*. Without so much as a raised eyebrow he said,
"I've had Poppy, Joe. I *got* Poppy."

"What?" I sputtered. "I don't believe you, you sneakin', low-
down—"

"I'll tell you somethin' else," he continued. "You're washed up
in this town. The boys are with me. I'm running it all from now
on. Forget about Chicago, 'cause in a few weeks, Chicago will
forget there ever was a Joe Capelli."

Bob stood up and I turned to face Blake squarely. "You're
dumb, kid. You should never have screwed with me. And you
should know what's mine is mine. I'm talkin' about Poppy. Her,
I'll take care of later. You? Well, Johnny boy, your number's on
the board right now."

Bob and I drew our guns and blasted away at Blake, whose
look of stunned surprise was genuine. The gunshots reverberated
in that old house up on Kings Road like so many cannon going
off. The look of shock froze on Blake's face, and he did one of
the great dying scenes, worthy of Cagney or Robinson at their best,
so realistic that Bob and I were tempted to check our pistols to be
sure we had loaded them with blanks.

Gun-powder smoke hung in the living room like a gray drape.
Blake lay sprawled on the floor, half on his face, his left arm
twisted grotesquely outward and his hand upturned toward the
ceiling. The hand twitched once, twice, and was still. It was perfect.

There had to be an epitaph. Bob provided it. He bent down,
examined the "dead man," looked up at me, and said, "Does this
mean Johnny's out of the organization?"

We all cracked up, rolling on the floor. Blake kept pointing to
us, yelling, "Jesus! The guns! What a touch! Jesus! Terrific!"

We carried on like that for the next five minutes, congratulating
each other on not breaking up and sticking with the concept. We
were sitting in the breakfast room, laughing and drinking Cokes,
when we heard the sirens. We ran to the front windows, and

barreling up the hill were four black-and-whites. They screeched to a stop in front of our house and several blue uniforms erupted from the cars. Feet pounded on the outside stairs, there was loud knocking on the door, and the door bell shrilled repeatedly.

Wisely, Bob motioned us to duck under the front windows. The three of us stayed huddled like that, while police officers peered through the curtains just above us, and walked around the seemingly empty house. Why they never actually forced their way in is something I have never figured out. Undoubtedly, one of our neighbors had heard the gunfire and called the police. There were cars, Bob's and Blake's, parked out in front. We simply could not believe they hadn't broken down the front door. But they didn't.

They stuck around for fifteen agonizing minutes or so and left. We three play-actors were sweating profusely by the time they took off. I quickly took the Colt and the Luger, cleaned them, and put them back in the gun case. Our mood was decidedly subdued. Later in the day, after Bob and Blake had gone and the folks had returned, the police came back, to question my folks about the reported gunfire. Mom and Dad looked blankly at the inquiring officers. Guns? Fired in the house? *Our* house? That's crazy. Mel, do you know anything about any guns going off?

Gee, Mom, not a thing.

They never came back and, from then on, we restricted our "improvs" to tamer subjects.

≡

Through Blake, I became friendly with Mickey Rooney. Long a rabid admirer of the "Mick," I was delighted to find him an outgoing, genuinely friendly human being, witty and extremely bright. One night, in early April of 1947, Mickey invited Blake, Bob, and me to his apartment for dinner and a movie. Rooney was among the first to own a sixteen-millimeter projector and run films at his place. Over dinner, he produced a little black book. He thumbed through it, favoring us with comments and ratings on the various ladies contained therein. At one point he stopped, his finger lingering on an unseen name. He rolled his eyes to heaven, and did some of his famous mugging.

"Oh," he cried, in mock ecstasy. "Oh! Now then! Whooo!

Here's one. Oh, lordy, lordy! I hear this gal is out-of-her-mind de-lovely."

"Who is it, Mick?" Blake asked, interested.

"Oh, please," Mick said, covering his face with his hands, the imagined vision of loveliness too much for him. "Oh, God! I can't stand it. Nobody—nobody should be this gorgeous."

"What's her name, Mick?" I ventured.

He grabbed my wrist and squeezed it till it actually hurt. He was currently in training for a remake of an MGM Robert Taylor fight film, _The Crowd Roars_. Mickey's version was to be called _Killer McCoy_ and the diminutive actor was in top physical condition. I mean, he was strong as hell, and cutting off the circulation to my wrist.

"Aw, Mellie, Mellie, I don't dare tell you. Do you want sleepless nights? Do you want to go home and pull your pud till all hours?" He looked at all of us with sincere concern. "You guys, you're my friends. I care deeply for you. Gosh, fellahs, you're all I have in this cruel old world and I just can't—"

"Mick, you son of a bitch! Her name!" Bob commanded.

Rooney, with a mere flick of his talent switch, said matter-of-factly, "Oh, her name? That's what you want? Her name? Oh, sure. It's Cathy Downs. She's under contract to Fox and doing the lead with Fonda in something called _My Darling Clementine_." He handed over the black book. "Here's her number, just in case any of you guys—"

We grabbed the book.

Blake noted the number.

"Call her," he said to Bob.

Bob looked at the number.

"Call her, Blake," he said.

They both looked at me.

I picked up the phone, read the number in the book, and dialed it. A few nights later, Cathy and I had our first date.

≡

My first record for Musicraft as a solo artist was "You're Driving Me Crazy." Sonny Burke wrote an exquisite arrangement, treating the song as a lush ballad, and Fred Robbins and Art Ford in New

York went to work cramming it down the East Coast's throat with multiple plays daily. Carlos was overjoyed.

I was overjoyed.

Cathy was overjoyed. She was a tall, willowy young woman with more than a touch of class. She looked exactly like her name: Cathy Downs. Soft and sweet. The girl next door. I think she liked me a lot. We never had a big love thing going, just a considerable "like." Our mothers became friends. It was like that.

New arrangements were being written for my Copa debut. The day finally came when I said good-bye to the folks, to Cathy, and to my friends. Carlos and Bob and I got on a train and headed east.

I was off to take New York.

16.

DEBACLE

*H*ERE he is," declared Mike Levin, in a *Down Beat* magazine review of my Musicraft single, "Sinatra's successor!"
I cringed.

Why in hell anyone had to be regarded as someone else's "successor" rankled me no end. I chastised Levin for the Sinatra comparison. Although Frank was not at the peak of his popularity at that moment, no one would or could replace or succeed him, and I said so in no uncertain terms.

Bob and I took an apartment at the Sutton on Fifty-fifth Street prior to my Copa opening. We had been contacted by a rich, young Texan named Jimmy Gardner, a would-be producer/actor with a tiny speck of talent in both departments. He commissioned us to write a Broadway show for Gertrude Niesen and himself. Charlie Peck, Jr., had already written the book, something called *Break It Up,* having to do with the antique furniture business. Wells and I liked it and set to work.

In mid-May, I opened at the Copacabana. Mitzi Green, as I have mentioned, was the star. She was a warm, talented lady, married to an up-and-coming actor/director, Joe Pevney. They were both very encouraging and friendly. Monte Proser, manager of the Copa, was a nice guy with a rough cob exterior. Jules Podell, one of the owners, was a rough cob.

The Copacabana on East Sixtieth Street was the prime hangout for a broad spectrum of assorted Broadway types. Garment moguls, mob figures, and questionable ladies in gifted minks were the standard patrons. Their show-business heroes were Jimmy Durante, Joe E. Lewis, and Tony Martin. Heroines ranged from Sophie Tucker to Martha Raye. Mitzi, although younger than the afore-mentioned stars, was welcome at the Copa. New Yorkers had loved her as a child performer in movies, she was a comedienne of the first rank, and a former New Yorker.

I, on the other hand, was a young upstart from California, who had been inundating the airwaves with his vocal mewlings and pukings. This kid, this—this Velvet Fog jerk who was being force-fed to the Manhattan public by Ford and Robbins, has the *gall* to stand on the same stage in the hallowed environs of the Copa, where we have cheered the true greats of show biz? Some nerve!

The press was also less than enthralled with me. They preferred discovering new talents, not being told by the radio shouters that Mel Tormé was a new, hot musical commodity.

The real problem, though, was me. I enthusiastically had pre-pared what I thought was a sophisticated package of songs, just right for discerning Gothamites. The Copa audience didn't know from discerning. The people who frequented the smaller, chicer Versailles, the Martinique, the Blue Angel, or the Little Club might have enjoyed my repertoire, but not the Copa crowd. Consequently, opening night was a major disaster.

As I walked onto the stage in a powder-blue tux with a darker blue satin "string" bow tie, I spotted a huge blond lady in a white dress with red roses imprinted all over it. She sat ringside, and, as I was announced and made my way onto the tiny Copa floor, the woman turned to her companion and, in a perfectly audible tone of voice, said, "That's Mel Tormé?" She shrugged, turned her back on me, and stayed that way all through my performance. I never had any use for Sophie Tucker after that unpardonable, unprofes-sional slight.

I began to sing: "Trouble Is a Girl," "Jamboree Jones," and the production song Bob and I had written for Disney, "The County Fair." At one point, I said, "Here is a song made famous by the great Al Jolson that I hope you'll remember." A voice right out of a gangster movie came at me from the back of the room.

"You hope *we'll* remember? We hope *you'll* remember it!" Gales of raucous laughter.

Through the entire performance, the noise in the room was

nearly deafening. I got the message and mentally gritted my teeth to get through that deadly performance.

The Copa audiences were uniformly rude, crude, and cruel. Nowadays, any sixteen-year-old with a guitar, terminal acne, and a hit record is welcome at the once-glorious nightclub. But in May of 1947, I was definitely an unwelcome interloper.

I was in shock when I got off the stage, chased by scant applause. Carlos was already in my dressing room. He tried to soothe me, to reassure me that it hadn't been so terrible, but I wanted to cut my throat. Proser came in. "Listen," he said, "Podell doesn't want any jitterbug shit like that 'Country Fair' thing in the show."

" 'County Fair,' Monte *'Coun*ty Fair,' " corrected Carlos.

"Whatever," said Proser.

"Mr. Proser," I said, fighting to control my emotions, "Bob Wells and I wrote that song for a Disney movie. It's—it's about a yearly fair that rural people go to. There's not a single thing in the whole song that has anything to do with jazz or jitterbugs."

"Take it out," said Proser impassively.

Of course, he was right. If the rest of my act had gone over like the proverbial lead balloon, "County Fair" had been the cast-iron bomb. I looked around the dressing room for a knife to stick in my throat.

"Relax, Torment," counseled Carlos. "Wait till the second show."

Second show: hundreds of prom kids in tuxes and gowns overflowed the room. They sat on the floor of the Copa, at my feet, crowding out the disgruntled "regulars" and cheering for their new favorite of the moment—me. Those kids didn't care what I sang. Fred Robbins and Art Ford had told them I was the new Messiah of Song, and there they were, listening, clapping wildly, even cheering. The Copa patrons hated every minute of it; I loved it. "My kids," as I began to call them, were restless during Mitzi's portion of the show. Her adult humor went over their heads. The Copa was faced with a true dichotomy: a skinny crooner named Tormé who drew hundreds of teen-agers and a seasoned lady pro who appealed to the standard Copa-goer.

On one particular Friday night in June 1947, the club was overflowing with adolescent girls in mom-made formals and boys with heads slicked with Brylcreem, ill-at-ease in rented dinner jackets slightly too big for them. The weekdays belonged to the regulars, a diverse assortment of wise guys and dolls. The weekends belonged to me and the Prom Gang.

Now, as I stood center stage in that refrigerated cellar, I saw my manager, Carlos Gastel, motion to me from the back of the room. I made my way through the smiling, backslapping young people and collapsed into a chair in my dressing room. It had been the third show of the evening. Three shows—my God!

Carlos cleared his throat.

"Something to discuss with you, Mel." (He always called me by his favorite nickname, "Torment." What was this "Mel" business? Must be something serious.)

"The, uh, bosses here have had a talk with me."

"Yeah?"

"About you. About your, uh, future."

"Listen, Carlos, they can't be unhappy about business. I mean—"

"No, no, no. Not at all. That's just it. They think you've got one hell of a future ahead of you, based on what's going on out there in the showroom."

"So? What's the problem?"

"There's really no problem. It's just—they would like to buy a piece of your contract with me. A very big piece."

"Do I have anything to say about this?"

"Of course. You have everything to say. I mean ... it's up to you." I had never seen Carlos look so uncomfortable.

Yet, this was something to think about. Serious business, giving yourself over to "the Boys." Admittedly, my main knowledge about the Mob had been gained through my passion for movies. Joe E. Lewis, who had come to the Copa to see me a few nights earlier, had long ago defied a Mob edict and had had his throat cut in the bargain. Lesser show-business lights had suffered physical and/or mental abuse via their enslavement to syndicate characters. That the "connected" wise guys could make a difference in a singer's professional life went without saying. Their power in the entertainment field was indisputable. The price a performer would have to pay, however, was almost certainly unacceptable to a young hardhead like me.

"Do you want to sell part of our deal to them?"

Gastel cleared his throat. "Well, I think you ought to examine this carefully. I mean, they control a hell of a lot of nightclubs all over the country. Plus jukeboxes. Plus, someday, Las Vegas is going to be an important place—maybe *the* important place to play, and they'll be running the town. They've also got their paws into the recording industry. If they decide one of your records should be a hit, they have ways to make it a hit."

I got up and began unbuttoning my shirt. My piano player walked in with a note from a Copa girl I had been dating: Meet me at Lindy's. I told my pianist to tell her "Not tonight," and he left.

"Carlos," I said quietly, "I know I'm pretty young, but I'm not blind. I know the Mob owns and runs this place. You've told me all the good things that could happen if they get involved in my career. How about the bad things?"

He took a deep breath, and when he took a deep breath, he took a deep breath. "Well, frankly, they'd be in a position to tell you where to work, what to sing, maybe even who to date. In all honesty, they would literally run your life and—"

"Why are we wasting our time with this? You know my answer already."

"Well, I just thought I ought to—"

"You know my answer already."

He took another deep breath, this time in obvious relief. "Thanks, Torment." He smiled.

Torment. That was more like it.

When you come right down to it, the name of the game is business. Between Mitzi's crowd and my kids, we were doing land-office business at the East Side saloon. The three-week engagement was extended to nine weeks. My salary was $600 weekly, and I was spending every penny of it just keeping my head above water in that expensive big town. Bob and I were working our heads off writing our Broadway score. We worked in the mornings, after the last show at the club—whenever we could get to a piano. Life was hectic. Weekends at the club were heaven for me; weeknights, pure hell.

One night, as I was singing, some guy began to throw ice cubes at me. George Jessel, in the audience that night, stood up, looked at the slob, and said, "Hey, you goddamn *schlemiel,* cut that out. Give the kid a chance."

Gary Cooper and his wife, Rocky, came to see me. Years later on the Goldwyn lot, Coop informed me that he had seen me one night at the Bocage, and that their visit to the Copa had been prompted by my Bocage appearance. "My God, Mel," he said, referring to the Copa crowd. "Those people were sure mean to you."

Jules Podell, a squat, ugly little man, rarely said a word to me. He was famous for a garish pinkie ring he wore. When he wanted to make a point, he would turn his hand upside down and bang the ring loudly on a table or desk, punctuating his bellicose edicts. One night, unexpectedly, I was a victim of "the ring."

"Hey, you," he barked at me, in a gravel voice that sounded like the screeching of brakes. "You ain't taken that jitterbug number out of your act." He began to bang the table. "I—WANT—THAT—FUCKING—JITTERBUG—NUMBER—OUT—OF—MY—SHOW!"

"Gee, Mr. Podell," I answered timidly, "the kids seem to like it."

Without another word, he turned back to the people he had been talking to and resumed the conversation. "County Fair" stayed in.

And then there were the reviews. God in heaven, those reviews!

EARL WILSON: "I'll take Mitzi; to hell with Mel."

DOROTHY KILGALLEN: "His only claim to fame are his dates with Ava Gardner. Obviously, her taste in men hasn't improved since Mickey Rooney and Artie Shaw."

GEORGE FRAZIER: "An untalented little amateur in a Little Lord Fauntleroy outfit." (I guess he meant my powder-blue tux and string tie.)

Even my booster at *Down Beat,* Mike Levin, headlined his feature piece: COPA NOT ALL COPA-SETIC FOR MEL.

The reviews hurt. Having had seventeen years of professional performing behind me before opening in New York, I resented being called an "amateur." I thought Kilgallen's personal remarks were unnecessary and insulting; and I wasn't laughing about Wilson's "to hell with Mel" crack.

Bob and Carlos and I had long sessions about the Copa fiasco. "Goddamn it, Carlos," I would demand, pacing back and forth in my Sutton Hotel living room, "why do they hate me so much? What the hell have I done to deserve such hatred?"

Patiently, Carlos would reply, "They don't hate you, Torment. For Christ's sake, you're brand new and you're drawing thousands of kids, and older people resent that."

"But, Jesus, Gastel, I'm not in there singing 'Three Little Fishies in an Itty-Bitty Pool.' I'm singing good songs. Damn good songs."

"That's one of the reasons they're on your ass," offered Bob. "You look like you just got out of high school and you're singing all the great old tunes, tunes they associate with Tucker and Martin and Jolson. They figure: how dare you?"

"Bob, that's stupid. It's just stupid, if they really feel that way."

"That's people, Melvin."

"He's right," Carlos agreed. "That's people. Don't take it so personally."

I looked longingly at the open window. Four stories up. I wouldn't make much of a mess.

In one of the strangest turnabouts in my career, both Dorothy Kilgallen and George Frazier became good friends within a few years of my Copa debut. They both championed me, and before he died in the mid-1970s, Frazier wrote a long, extremely flattering feature about me in the *Boston Globe*. Even Earl Wilson eventually changed his early opinion of me and my singing.

A bizarre footnote to the Copa stint: while I appeared there I met an attractive young girl whose name was Lorry Hamilton. I dated her a few times during the Copa run, but she seemed unstable. One morning, I saw an article in the *Daily News* that chilled me. Lorry had jumped from the eleventh story of an apartment building. She had been depressed and under a psychiatrist's care for months because of her troubled background. Her father, reported the *News,* had been John Hamilton, a notorious henchman of John Dillinger, who, on April 29, 1934, had died of bullet wounds received in the famous "Little Bohemia" gun battle with the FBI in the woods of Wisconsin. I guess Lorry ultimately couldn't live with that.

17.

ATTRITION

ON it went, the disc jockeys versus the press; Tormé the
Terrific, insisted the jocks; Tormé the Terrible railed the
Fourth Estate. I was hurt, angry, and defensive. I grew a nearly
perceptible twenty-two-pound chip on my shoulder and dared
anyone to knock it off. The words "temperamental," "cocky" and
"hard-nosed" were common comments on my personal attitude in
almost any newspaper one read.

Because we had become part of the New York scene, and
because of the success of our "Christmas Song," as well as my
dubious triumph at the Copa, Bob Wells and I were sought-after
guests at parties, openings, premieres, and the like. At a glitzy
gathering one evening, we met E. Y. "Yip" Harburg, who had
heard about our songs and who graciously invited us to call at his
elegant Manhattan apartment the next afternoon and play some of
them for him.

We were excited. I mean, after all, he was one of our songwriting heroes, a genuine role-model lyricist, the giant who had
written "Over the Rainbow" for the ages, as well as the glorious
rhymes for Ella Logan in *Finian's Rainbow,* plus many other songs
that had gained immortality.

I didn't sleep that night. Next day, promptly at 1:30, we presented ourselves at his flat. After offering us drinks—my throat
was dry; I gulped a Coke—he motioned toward the piano and I
sat on the stool. Harburg towered over us. He was a tall man,
slim, gray-haired, with piercing eyes, and his face exhibited an
aristocrat's hauteur.

Which of our songs to play? Bob suggested "Willow Road," the first we had written together. It had been published by Burke and Van Heusen and those two wonderful tunesmiths had expressed delight and admiration over it. So had Nat Cole and Frankie Laine, both of whom wanted to record it.

I played an arpeggio and began to sing:

> At dawn you hear the rooster crowin'
> And he says it's time to rise
> So all the flowers open their eyes
> And when they stretch their petals
> You'd swear a rainbow growed
> All along the Willow Road
>
> I know the weeds sure need a-pullin'
> And I oughta paint my shack

Harburg slammed his hand down hard on the music rack of the piano.

"You young punks!" he bellowed. "You call yourselves songwriters! You don't know what the hell you're doing or what the hell you're writing about!"

I was dumbfounded. What had suddenly happened to the charming man we had met at the previous night's party? I shot a look at Bob. He had gone white, his lips compressed, his facial muscles taut.

Harburg raved on. " 'Willow Road,' f'chrissakes! How the hell do you come to write about somewhere you've never been or seen?"

Again, he brought his fist down on the music stand.

"First rule—*cardinal* rule—in songwriting: write what you know about from your personal experiences. Never, ever write about places you've never seen or been to."

Bob cleared his throat, looked Harburg directly in the eye, and said, with a slight, angry quaver in his voice: "I see. So you've been 'over the rainbow,' right?"

That stopped old Yip, and we made our way to his front door, out into the blessed taxi and bus fumes of upper Fifth Avenue.

Still, Harburg taught us a great lesson that day. Most—not all, but *most*—songwriters don't really want to hear the competition's output, whether from neophytes like Bob and myself in 1947, or from triple-A ASCAP heavyweights.

Johnny Burke and Jimmy Van Heusen were the exceptions. They encouraged new, young talent and genuinely enjoyed listening to other people's musical brainchildren. So did my personal lyric-writing hero, Johnny Mercer. But many other creators of great popular songs exhibited an attitude that seemed to say, "Well, I suppose your song is all right but I could have written it better" (which is probably true in certain instances).

That posture, nonetheless, was depressing and discouraging to us, since subsequently we allowed ourselves to be seduced into playing some of our songs for a pair of composers we worshiped— Richard Rodgers and Frank Loesser. You would have thought we'd have learned our lesson that day in Yip Harburg's digs. Ah, the follies of youth!

Loesser and Rodgers were only slightly less rude than Harburg had been. Bob and I began to wonder if we had any talent at all for songwriting. Mercer, Burke and Van Heusen, Duke Ellington, and Johnny Green assured us we had.

Still, Bob and I entered into a blood pact. No more testing our tunes on anyone except prospective publishers or recording artists. We kept that pact until we dissolved our partnership in the late 1940s.

The Copa run ended in something less than a blaze of glory, and I prepared to fulfill some engagements on the road. Carlos had secured two weeks for me at the New York Paramount Theatre, but first I had a few nightclub dates to play. One of them was at a downstairs den called, ironically enough, The Copa Club in Pittsburgh, Pennsylvania. The owner, Lenny Littman, was a hulking specimen who occasionally spit the juice from the wad of tobacco he was chewing onto the Copa's well-worn carpet. Nonetheless, I liked him.

The engagement went well and, one night, in walked José Ferrer, the Broadway *wunderkind*. He was a jazz buff, and after my last performance of the evening, he suggested that we slip across the street to the Carousel, where Stan Getz was fronting a quartet. Getz was his usual miraculous self on tenor, and late in his set he invited me up to play drums with the group. As I rose, Joe Ferrer whispered to me, almost pleadingly, "Ask him if I could sit in on piano. Please!"

As I settled behind the drums, I asked Stan if "my friend" could join us. Getz nodded, and Joe practically leapt onto the small bandstand. We decided on "Indiana," and when Joe's solo turn came, he knocked us all out with his playing. I was only minimally surprised. Joe Ferrer could—and can—do anything. At the end of the final chorus, there was a roar from the crowd, and Joe had earned his share of it. We went back to our table, and when Ferrer excused himself to go to the men's room, Getz came over.

"Hey, man," he asked, "who's the old cat?"

" 'Old cat'?" I laughed. "Stanley, that's José Ferrer. He pulls down about ten grand a week on Broadway."

Getz shrugged, looked around, and said offhandedly, "Makes no difference to me. If he wants to work with my group, he'll have to work for scale!" Getz was dead serious. Ferrer told his publicity people about the remark. It was hilariously reported in all the trade papers as well as the *Pittsburgh Press* next morning.

I played a few more eastern dates before going to the New York Paramount. They were unremarkable for the most part, except for a week at the Hippodrome Theatre in Baltimore, with my new accompanist/conductor, the inestimable Walter Gross. He was an angry genius who played brilliantly and wrote the lovely waltz "Tenderly."

I faced the upcoming Paramount stand with ambivalence. I was still shaken and angry over the barbed criticism I had received at the Copacabana. Still, the Paramount was the Paramount. Benny Goodman had had them dancing in the aisles a decade before. More recently, Sinatra had set the large theater on fire with his solo bow, striving to be heard above the endless screaming of his idolators, grinning bravely through it all. I wanted, despite everything, to play the Paramount. But how would I fare?

My Musicraft singles were being played almost incessantly by Freddie Robbins and Art Ford, as well as by several other D.J.s

in Mother Gotham, as S. J. Perelman called it. Yet, those first
Musicraft efforts of mine were not selling well, in spite of the fact
that several fan clubs in my honor had suddenly sprung up. "Mel's
Belles," they called themselves. And "Mel's Angels," "The Fog-
ettes," and, ultimately, the more austere and dignified "Official
Mel Tormé Fan Club."

They put out journals, sported sweaters with the club logos
prominently displayed, and, generally, were a lively bunch of young
ladies, whose conglomerate voice helped a lot in offsetting the sneers
of my detractors. I'm also proud to say that my fan clubs were
uniformly well-behaved gals (and a few guys) who seemed to come
to listen rather than to yell themselves hoarse.

My first engagement at the Paramount headlined Charlie Spivak and his orchestra with me as the extra added attraction. It was
one of the few times I ever questioned Carlos's judgment. I felt
we should have waited until I attained headline status before going
into the famous theater, just as Sinatra had. Carlos was adamant.
He wanted me to play the house then and there.

In fairness, Carlos's intentions were understandable. He was
proud of me and as disturbed as I was over the unnecessary cruelty
of the New York critics. He thought the Paramount engagement
would be something of a cure-all. He was wrong. And he was
wrong on yet another count where the Paramount was concerned.

Wiser heads than mine cautioned Carlos to wait until I could
command important money at the Forty-fourth Street showplace.
It's a crazy fact of life that when you make noise in show business,
when you're "hot," full advantage must be taken of what you are
worth to theater owners, nightclub operators, and concert promoters. The toughest thing to accomplish is getting your price to
go up once you are undersold. I was perfectly willing to wait as
long as it took to ensure a strong, initial financial return. I couldn't
budge Carlos. Nor could anyone else, including his friend and close
associate, Tom Rockwell. Consequently, I opened at the Paramount
at $1,750 a week. Of course, to many, that would seem a fortune,
but by the entertainment industry's superinflated standards, it was
lousy. Keeping up with the Joneses (and the Damones and the
Fishers and the Bill Farrells and the Alan Dales and on and on

ad infinitum) is a stupid yet vital way of professional life. Thereafter, the struggle to increase my income was endless and terribly difficult.

Because of my newfound visibility, I was offered a half-hour twice-weekly radio show, sponsored by a fast-rising company called Toni Home Permanents. The show was overseen musically by my friend Walter Gross, who put together a small, chamber music–like group, including a harpist, a flutist, and the redoubtable Tony Mattola on guitar. My kids descended on NBC in droves. So did the song pluggers. For a while, the pluggers were the bane of my existence. I suppose I should have been flattered by their attention, and, in certain cases, I was. Marty Mills, for example, was the working son of Jack Mills of the enormous publishing firm, Mills Music. He understood what I was all about musically and never brought trash along for consideration. Most of the rest of them, however, would have sold their sisters for a plug on my (or any other) network show.

I'm afraid I was not very tolerant of them, and I feel, in retrospect, that I was wrong. "Plug" was what their jobs were all about, and, when getting results is your bread and butter, I guess you will go to any lengths to get a song performed. I was offered everything from watches to hookers to put certain tunes on the show. I don't know, maybe I should have succumbed to such perks. I never did, and my attitude bemused and angered many of those guys. Sorry, fellas.

Bob Wells and I were having our problems with Jimmy Gardner, the would-be producer of our Broadway show, *Break It Up*. His desire to play one of the leading roles was complicated by one incontrovertible fact: he had no real talent other than his ability to fund the production. Bob and I had been paid a retainer and had written the complete score. Suddenly, two weeks into rehearsal, Gardner had decided to chuck it all and go to Europe for R & R. Good-bye, *Break It Up*. Several people had heard the songs, read the book, and months later, it was produced at Matunick, Rhode Island's famous Theatre by the Sea, with Nancy Andrews, David Burns, and Lew Parker, and directed by former Twentieth Century-Fox contract player, William Eythe. The production got excellent reviews, and, for twenty seconds there, we considered trying to get it to Broadway. That hope died, and *Break It Up* died for good. Too bad, I think. It had possibilities.

Bob Wells and I had a lot of other writing irons in the fire, so we decided to take an apartment at the Westover Hotel at Seventy-second Street and West End Avenue in Manhattan. It wasn't the choicest address in town, but it was affordable and we settled in, wrote a lot of songs and dated a number of pretty ladies.

One day, having had lunch at Al and Dick's Restaurant on Fifty-fourth Street west of Sixth Avenue, Bob and I were walking by a garage called Zumbach Motors. We happened to glance inside for a moment, and there, gleaming in new coats of paint, were five tiny, wire-wheeled sports cars, the like of which I had never seen before. The right-hand-drive steering wheels marked them as British, and my heart began to beat faster. We walked inside and introduced ourselves to the owner of the garage, Mr. Zumbach, a crusty old German who had worked during the First World War at the Zeppelin factory on Maybach engines.

"Em Chee," he said, in his thick guttural accent. "These are called Em Chees. Dot stands for Morris Garage, vere zay make zem in England." We decoded his identification as "MG," and they were, in fact, the first five M.G.-TC Midgets off the assembly line since before the war. I looked at Bob.

"Gotta have one, Robert. I simply have to."

"Do it," he advised.

"Mr. Zumbach," I began, "how much—"

"Iss not possible," the old man interrupted. "Those have been on order since before ze war. Maybe next year...." It was November of 1947.

"Next year?" I moaned. "Oh, no!" For the next hour or so, I pleaded, wheedled, cajoled, and practically stood on my head trying to convince him to sell me the lone red one, and damned if I didn't wear him down! The very next morning, I took delivery of that rakish little beauty, and Bob and I went for a long shakedown cruise. I took to the right-hand drive very quickly, and, every time we came to a red light, someone would inspect the car and ask the predictable questions:

"Say, what the hell is that thing?"

"Steering wheel's on the wrong side, ain't it?"

"Where do you get parts for somethin' like that?"

It got to the point where I printed up answers to those questions and Scotch-taped them to the windscreen. I never minded the questions, however. I loved that little vehicle. It cost (wait for it!) $1,750, in 1947. Today, if you can find a decent one, the M.G.-TC brings between $15,000 and $17,500. I wish I hadn't sold it. My love affair with automobiles began in earnest with the M.G.

A few weeks after I purchased the M.G., Buddy Rich saw me riding along Broadway. I stopped to say hello, and his eyes began to whirl in much the same manner as Mr. Toad's had in *Wind in the Willows,* when he spies his first automobile.

"Where . . . how . . . what?" Buddy almost stammered. I told him about Zumbach's garage.

Almost in a frenzy, B yelled, "I gotta have one! Gotta. Gotta! Show me where."

He got in and we drove over to Zumbach Motors. I warned him all the way over that it would do him no good, that the other four were firmly on order and not available. He wouldn't listen, and, to my total amazement, Buddy charmed Old Man Zumbach out of one of the black ones. Two nights later, in a driving rainstorm, we caravaned across the George Washington Bridge to catch Nat Cole at the Meadowbrook in New Jersey. We parked our British babies nose to nose, and a photographer took pictures of us in our rain-spattered cars. In 1978, when B and I did our album *Together Again for the First Time,* I dug out that picture of the two of us in our cars, and we used it on the back cover.

Good News opened in New York and the reviews were thrilling. After the slings and arrows, it was nice to be applauded by movie critics. Carlos added to my euphoria by calling me to say that Irving Berlin had gone to the West Coast opening with Arthur Freed and had also been highly enthusiastic about my work in the film. MGM, Carlos advised, was taking up its option on my services for two pictures a year at $30,000 per film! I had been feeling a bit guilty about buying the M.G. After all, I still had a car, a beautiful yellow Buick Roadmaster convertible, sitting in my parents' garage in California. Prior to the purchase of the M.G., I had been tooling around New York City in a surplus navy Jeep, purchased for a modest $400. Buying the M.G. had been a grunt beyond my means, but with Metro picking up its option, I breathed a lot easier.

Bob Wells and I had a great time during the final weeks of 1947. The Ebony Club (later to become Birdland) was in full swing, with a line of sumptuous girls and Billy Daniels coming into his own as a full-fledged singing star. We were regular customers there as well as the many other New York jazz emporiums and we met all kinds of people making the rounds. One of them was a debonair gent who ranked high on the social register. He had enjoyed my show at the Copa. "Come to a party at my place," he said, "next Thursday evening."

When Wells and I got there at least thirty people had already arrived, and the noise, the laughter, the cigarette smoke curling toward the ceiling presented quite a tableau of a typical Manhattan High Society shindig. Things were going along swimmingly for the better part of an hour when I noticed the butler sliding a huge wooden bar across the front door. Our host rapped a glass for silence.

"Right, everybody," he cried cheerfully, "let's have at it!"

There was a chorus of assents from the guests, and then everyone—*every*one—began to remove his or her clothes. Very soon there was a huge pile of clothing and a few dozen totally naked men and women. Wells and I looked at each other and shrugged; what the hell could we do? We stripped and I proceeded to participate in the single orgy of my entire lifetime.

What made that evening memorable was not so much our surprise at discovering that our socialite pal was far from the goody-two-shoes he was reputed to be, as our astonishment over one of the participants in the festivities, a famous blond British movie star, who threw herself into the evening's agenda with abandon and no little amount of joyous zeal.

If there is anything better than sex (well, maybe music), I doubt God has invented it yet; but I'm a square where group scenes are concerned. One-on-one is perfectly fine with me.

18.

CANDY

C ANDY and I never should have married. This dark-haired, good-looking girl from East St. Louis, Illinois, had an acting career on her mind. At twenty-three, I was a slightly disillusioned pop singer who had been the object of media hype, some positive, mostly negative, who was trying to put his career in perspective. I was also busy sowing my share of wild oats. So was Candy.

I first met Candy Toxton (a German-Irish girl—real name: Florence Ann Gertrude Tockstein) in Boston. I was appearing at the RKO Boston Theatre. One evening, I got a call from Tino Barzi, Tommy Dorsey's road manager. TD was in town, playing a one-nighter, and invited me to join a late-night supper party he was hosting for his band at a well-known Italian restaurant in downtown Beantown.

I did not carry an entourage around with me—no road manager, valet, piano player, conductor, advisers, well-wishers; sycophants, groupies—no nobody. I was unfettered by hangers-on. I was also lonely as hell. Four or five shows a day at a theater, grabbed-at naps, catch-as-catch-can meals, and virtually no social life was not my idea of a balanced existence. I've always responded best to familiar surroundings. Being away from home for weeks at a time, separated from friends, parents, and toys (my record library, the expanding gun collection, the Buick convertible, not to mention the handful of Hollywood ladies I had been dating), made me feel like I was in limbo. The only really happy moments came when I was performing on stage. I looked forward all that day to Tommy's bash.

When I arrived at the restaurant, I was greeted by a lovely young woman, green-eyed and dark-haired.

"Hi." She smiled. "I'm Candy. Tommy's waiting for you." She led the way inside. Tommy greeted me warmly, dead sober. I had heard that, following his divorce from Pat Dane, he had given up alcohol. The reports were true.

"C'mere, drummer boy." He grinned and gave me a bear hug. He introduced me to the guys in the band, many of whom were seated at a long table, slurping endless strands of linguine topped with red clam sauce. Other musicians, drinks in hand, were gathered around a jukebox. Tommy Dorsey music rumbled from the booming Wurlitzer speaker. It was a nice evening, full of music, off-color jokes, and lots of laughs. Candy bustled around, refreshing drinks, offering seconds of pasta to the hungry bandsmen, and generally making like a den mother. It didn't take a genius to figure out whose girl she was. Every few minutes or so she would solicitously drift back to Tommy, smiling at him with genuine affection.

The next time I saw her was months later, in mid-1948, on the MGM lot. I was appearing in the first of my new two-picture-contract movies, *Words and Music,* the highly fictionalized life stories of the songwriting team of Rodgers and Hart. Originally, I had been scheduled to sing "Mountain Greenery" with June Allyson. Somehow that tune went to Perry Como, and I was assigned "Blue Moon." Good song, I thought. Terrific. I would shortly regret my initial enthusiasm.

Mickey Rooney, playing Lorenz Hart, was shooting a night scene on one of the stages and had invited me to stop by. I walked onto the set just as the assistant director, Al Jennings, yelled, "Quiet! Going for a take!"

Norman Taurog, the director, calls for "action," and into camera range comes the Mick, a good-looking girl in a smart blue-trimmed white suit beside him.

They are walking on a sidewalk. Hart/Rooney looks sick, disturbed, vacant-eyed. They stop in front of a café. Music wafts through the open door. It is a Rodgers and Hart song. Mickey recognizes it. Absently, he recites the words, more to himself than the girl.

> Spring is here.
> Why doesn't my heart go dancing?
> Spring is here.
> Why isn't the waltz entrancing?
> Maybe it's because nobody needs me . . .

He stops, seems to understand something. He flags a passing cab and is whisked away, leaving the young lady standing there, shaking her head in disbelief.

Taurog yells "Cut!" and inquires, "Okay for sound?" He gets the nod from his sound man, and the normal hubbub of conversation and equipment moving resumes.

Mickey spots me. "Mellie! Hiya, babe!" He grins, pinching my cheek Jewish-mother style. The "stranded" girl drifts by. "Hey," he asks me, "do you know—?"

"We've met." I smile. "Hello, Candy."

We started dating casually. Shortly, it got to be exclusive. She had broken with Tommy. No future there, she explained. She had come to California and secured a studio-player contract with MGM. The scene with Mickey was her first before the cameras. She was a typical MGM starlet, indistinguishable from a dozen other young studio hopefuls.

I was pretty happy at that time. I was in a major MGM movie, with my social life restored and a fine-looking girl devoting all her free time to me. My big moment in _Words and Music_ was now at hand: first, recording the vocal, arranged by the brilliant Lennie Hayton, at that time married to Lena Horne; then filming the scene itself, lip-syncing the words.

About "Blue Moon." The song had had a somewhat checkered career, having first been written in 1934 by Rodgers and Hart as "The Prayer" to be sung by Jean Harlow in a terrible _pastiche_ called _Hollywood Party,_ an all-star mess vaguely starring Jimmy Durante. It is one of the few MGM films on which you will find no director's credit. Figure that one out for yourself.

Anyway, the song, which began

> Oh, Lord,
> I know how busy you are,

If I'm not going too far,
I wish you'd make me a star...

never saw the light of day. Harlow wisely stayed out of this cin-
ematic turkey, and the tune was tucked away on the MGM music-
library shelves to gather dust.

Richard Rodgers and Lorenz Hart, however, were nothing if
not determined. Imbued with ironclad belief in the melody, they
refashioned it into "The Bad in Every Man." Shirley Ross, an-
nointed in mulatto makeup, sang it in front of a "colored" combo
in *Manhattan Melodrama,* famed for being the last movie Dillinger
saw (at the Biograph Theatre in Chicago) before walking out of
the lobby and being gunned down in the street by Melvin Purvis
and sundry other G-men.

Once again, the song was "retired," only to reemerge a few years
later as "Blue Moon." Although it had never achieved "hit" status,
it was a much-played tune that couples liked dancing to in ballrooms
and cafés. Now, it was to receive the large-screen MGM treatment.

On the appointed day, I arrived at the huge recording stage,
brimming with anticipation. Mr. Rodgers was there, tall, slightly
imperious, and daunting. He smiled hello to me as I climbed onto
the riser in the isolated booth in front of the orchestra. I adjusted
the earphones onto my head. Lennie Hayton grinned at me, tapped
his baton (a pencil, actually) on his music stand. The orchestra
played the introduction. I began to sing. I got as far as

Blue Moon
You knew just what I was there for
You heard me saying a prayer...
For someone I really could care for.

Richard Rodgers let out a shout that startled everyone. "No,
no, no, no, no! Not like that, Mel! Not like that!" I stood frozen.
What the hell had I done? "Sing it like this," commanded Mr. R.

You heard me saying a prayer for
Someone I really could care for.

Now, how in the world could I handle this one? I did not agree
with the composer. I have always felt that the "reading" of a lyric
by a singer is concomitant with the reading of good poetry. One
doesn't rattle off the lines, singsong style, merely to serve the
rhyming. The "reason," the natural sense of the lyric lines, are of
paramount importance, as far as I'm concerned.

"Mr. Rodgers," I began, somewhat timorously, "I try to sing
the words as though I were saying them. I wouldn't say

> You heard me saying a prayer for (pause)
> Someone I really could care for.

It feels more natural to sing

> You heard me saying a prayer (pause)
> For someone I really could care for.

Rodgers would have none of it. Who was this Johnny-come-
lately to tell the master how to sing one of his songs? He stormed
off the stage in a nickel-plated huff. I was crimson with embarrassment.

Lennie walked over to me, put his hand on my shoulder, and
said, "You are fucking-A right!"

I stared at him. "Honest to God, Len?"

"Honest to goddamn God. He's wrong and a pompous ass to
boot!"

We recorded the song in two takes. When the second take was
found acceptable, the orchestra applauded, more, I think, for my
courage in standing up to Richard Rodgers than for my rendition
of "Blue Moon." I was gloomy, nonetheless. Rodgers was (and still
is) one of my genuine musical heroes, and to be out of favor with
him was extremely disturbing. He never forgave me "Blue Moon,"
and, later in life, exacted a small piece of vengeance, which I will
relate presently.

My problems with "Blue Moon" were just beginning. In the
film, I portray a bandleader at a lavish party being given by Larry
Hart. We spent five days on that set, Mickey, myself, 400 dress-

extras waiting for a tardy Judy Garland to present herself and sing "Johnny One Note" as well as duet with Mickey on "I Wish I Were in Love Again." When she finally showed and completed her numbers (beautifully, I might add), it was my turn.

≡

In the film, the party's over, the guests have departed and, just as the band prepares to pack up, "Larry Hart" asks for just one more song. "Sing anything, Mel," he says. "As long as it's Rodgers and Hart."

As "Hart" settles into a chair near the bandstand, I give the resettled bandsmen a downbeat and sing "Blue Moon." A few setups later, the filming is completed on the song.

That was a Wednesday. Thursday, I caught cold. Friday, I had one helluva virus going. Saturday morning at 7:30, the phone rang. It was Norman Taurog. "Mel, we want to shoot close-ups on you this morning for the 'Blue Moon' number."

"Oh, my God, Mr. Taurog. I'm in bed with a one hundred and three fever. I'm sick."

"Well, all I can say is we've got to get the shots today. They strike this set Monday and then we're simply out of luck."

"Gee, that's a shame, but—"

"It's for your benefit, Mel. It's your number. Important close-ups."

What can I tell you? I got out of bed over the protests of my parents, Candy, and my doctor and went to the studio. A company physician stood by while we shot close-ups the entire day. How could I know that, in the final cut of the film, Mickey would dominate the overwhelming bulk of the footage, listening to me sing while he toyed with an unlit cigar, looking desolate, vulnerable, and unhappy. It was a genuine case of, "If you blinked your eyes, you missed me altogether."

Unaccountably, when *Words and Music* was released, two interesting things happened. First, the one-sheet theater poster displayed yours truly prominently, and, second, "Blue Moon" became my first big hit record, reaching the number-two position on the *Billboard* and *Cash Box* charts. Crazy, no?

Candy's option was dropped at Metro and she was signed by Harry Cohn at Columbia. He changed her name to Susan Perry, the latter half being his wife's maiden name. Candy was cast as Humphrey Bogart's wife in _Knock on Any Door_ (1949), the picture that introduced John Derek to the world.

She shared a small apartment on Reeves Drive in Beverly Hills with another young actress. One night, I phoned Candy, and her roommate nervously told me she had "gone out for a while." Candy had told me she was going to bed early. I got in my car and drove over to her place, parked, and waited. In about an hour, a black limousine pulled up in front of her door. No one got out. I opened my car door, walked over, and peered inside. Candy was in the car talking with Harry Cohn. I stood there until she spotted me, surprise and agitation marking her features. She rolled down the window. "I'll—I'll be out in a minute, Mel."

"I'll wait," I said, not budging.

She rolled the window back up and talked to Cohn for a few more minutes. Then she opened the door and got out. The limo sped away. Candy was furious. And embarrassed. We stood there in front of her apartment. She berated me for "spying" on her.

"I am not," I told her, "going to put up with that kind of crap."

"Look," she countered, "I'm a working lady. We're not married, for God's sake. Cohn is my boss. He drove over to talk about my part in this picture as well as future plans. What do you want from me?"

"What I don't want is the naïve garbage you're coming on with. Cohn wants to bang you, Candy. You know it. I know it. Now either we're together or we're not, goddamn it!"

She collapsed in tears. I held her, comforted her, and we made up.

Looking back, I must say I was selfish and insensitive. We _weren't_ married, she _had_ to earn a living, she was one of thousands of would-be actresses trying to gain a foothold in pictures, and after all, this was her first leading role. Most of the bachelors in town were trying to date her, not the least interested of whom was Peter Lawford. One weekend, while we were supposedly going steady, she called to announce she was taking off with him for

Catalina. I broke with her then and there, facing an unhappy Friday night. I called Ava, who was free that evening, and proceeded to get swacked with her at Villa Nova. That weekend was terrible.

Monday, Candy called, contrite, tearful, and apologetic. She said she had had a rotten time, that she realized once and for all how much she loved me, that nothing had happened between her and Lawford, and that she wanted us back together. I stubbornly held out. For twelve minutes or so. Once we got together again, the proverbial handwriting was on the wall.

Christmas 1948. I was playing the Chicago Theatre. I wanted Candy to join me for the holidays. Harry Cohn said no. She had no assignments upcoming, nothing to do at the studio. Cohn was simply exercising his right as resident despot of Columbia Pictures to run her life.

"No," he thundered.

"Yes," she countered. "Go screw yourself, Mr. Cohn."

She came to Chicago. We bought each other expensive Christmas presents. Cohn had warned her that, if she defied him, he would suspend her. She went back to the Coast on January 1. He suspended, then dropped her. She had nowhere to turn. She feared the mighty Harry had blackballed her with the other studios. Maybe. Maybe not.

Her meager bank account began to run out. My folks, fully aware of her plight, recommended that she give up her apartment and move into Myrna's room in our house, since my sister had emigrated to New York to try her luck in the art and/or modeling world.

Candy moved in. My folks told me the news while I was on the road. I came home in a few weeks. Candy and I decided— what the hell, let's get married. By that time, the breathlessness had gone out of our relationship. There was love between us, no doubt about that. Enough for a lifetime marriage?

Who knew?

19.

RECORD ROOMS

*A*FTER our marriage ceremony in Chicago, in early February of 1949, with our parents, sisters, and brothers in attendance, Candy and I had our honeymoon on the Twentieth Century Limited, racing for New York. That was a Sunday. On Monday, I was opening at the Paramount Theatre with Buddy Rich and his orchestra. Candy and I checked into the Astor Hotel, across the street from the Paramount, and walked over to the theater. As we entered the rehearsal hall, I noticed several extra bass drum cases. I walked over to Buddy, said hello, and asked about the cases. Buddy explained tersely, "Louis Bellson better learn to play one bass drum before he screws around with two!" I knew Buddy was fond of Louis, who is one of the nicest human beings in our business. I also knew what was on Rich's mind.

Louis Bellson had electrified the drum world by performing on a drum set that, in addition to the standard snare drum, tom-toms, and cymbal impedimenta, sported twin bass drums. Louis had very effectively created some nice patterns with the double bass drum setup. Some of Louis's fans had thrown up that fact to Buddy. They had also, unwittingly, thrown down the gauntlet. Buddy now planned to pick it up.

We opened the next day at the Paramount. Just before my closing spot in the show, Buddy Rich uncorked a breakneck arrangement of "Ol' Man River." Perched above the band at his standard drum set, he played the arrangement to its midway point. Then, during a brief band interlude, he made his way down to the very front of the elevated Paramount stage. Awaiting him there were two bass drums. Nothing else. He settled behind them, his hands gripping his drum throne for support, and proceeded to play the damnedest drum solo I've ever heard. With his feet. When he finished, the Paramount audience erupted in cheers, tears, bravos, and like that. Even with my fan clubs and well-wishers in attendance, it took me a good ten minutes to make any impression on the crowd. And so it went throughout the entire engagement.

Thanks to Carlos's influence, Capitol Records had signed me. My first record, "Careless Hands," came out and took off. It was followed by "Blue Moon," which, as I have said, became my first big record hit. Candy and I were settling into this strange new state called married life. She traveled with me everywhere and, while that certainly took the bite out of the lonely road life, being together constantly wasn't easy. I think a law ought to be passed: minimum legal age for marriage—thirty years old. We had our first major fight driving back from Baltimore in Woody Herman's station wagon. I had just finished a week with Woody and his band at the Hippodrome Theatre and we were on our way to Hartford, by way of Manhattan, for a weekend stint along with the Herman Herd at the State Theatre.

Candy and I got into a major row along the way. At one point, she tearfully pulled off the sapphire-encircled wedding ring I had bought her and tried to throw it out of the car window. I stopped her in time, but the incident shook us and we wondered if her rashness was an omen. Were we really meant for each other? Had getting married been a giant mistake? Woody kindly lent us the station wagon. "You kids need a little time away from music and theaters and publicity men. You never really had a honeymoon. You've got three days before we open in Hartford. Why don't you check into the Astor and have some fun? Go to a couple of Broadway shows, see a movie or two, go dancing maybe."

"I'm a lousy dancer," I mumbled.

"So learn, Torment," he counseled.

We took his advice, and the three days we spent in New York City relieved a lot of tension. Late afternoon on Thursday, we checked out of the Astor, loaded up the station wagon with our suitcases, as well as Woody's bags, and set out for Connecticut.

When I got to the nineties on Broadway, I spotted a small movie house playing *Corridor of Mirrors,* a British film I'd been wanting to see. Nodding toward the theater, I said to Candy, "What do you think? Huh? How about it? Shall we ... ?"

"Yes, all right," Candy agreed patiently.

We parked the car on the side street opposite the theater and went in. When we came out, the broken car window told the story: every single piece of luggage was gone. I was sick, not so much for our loss, but because Woody had entrusted me with his things and now they were gone, too. I asked someone where the nearest police station was, got into the car in what can only be described as high dudgeon, and promptly bashed in the right front fender on a light pole. We reported the theft to the police and disconsolately made our way to Hartford, the March wind blowing through the broken wing window, freezing our faces. Next morning, shamefacedly, I broke the news to Woody. He took it like the champ he was, laughing it off and assuring me this had happened to him many times before. Some people have class.

Words and Music opened at the Loews State in Manhattan. I got surprisingly good notices considering my minuscule participation in the movie. Things were going fairly well as far as my career was concerned. Life with Candy settled into a set routine of road trips, theaters, nightclub engagements, airline terminals, train stations, hotel suites, packing and unpacking.

When we finally got back to the Coast, we bought a nice little house on a brand-new street called Thurston Circle, near Sunset Boulevard in west Los Angeles. I was assigned by MGM to Joe Pasternak, one of Metro's three major producers of musicals, the others being Jack Cummings and my mentor, Arthur Freed. I felt safe in Freed's talented and tasteful hands. For me, Pasternak was an unknown quantity. His movies were aimed at a less sophisticated market than Freed's, and I was concerned that I might get lost in a big shuffle. I was right. The Pasternak film titled *The Duchess of Idaho* starred Esther Williams and Van Johnson. Also in the film were Connie Haines, Tommy Dorsey's one-time vocalist, and even Bullets Durgom, an ersthile Glenn Miller bandboy turned personal manager. When the film finally came out in 1950, both of my musical numbers were cut, and I was relegated to nine lines of dialogue in the movie, for which I was paid $30,000. But don't get me wrong; I love Hollywood.

Happily, the Philip Morris Company had elected to sponsor a new radio program on NBC called "The Mel Tormé Show." It was a half-hour comedy-with-music format utilizing a college setting and employing the talents of some of the finest actors in Hollywood. My old pal, Sidney Miller, played my sidekick; Janet Waldo, famed in radio as "Corliss Archer," was my girl friend in the series. She was later replaced by an equally talented actress, Barbara Eiler. John Brown, a highly respected character actor, produced the show and also played the dean of "Fairmont College." Longtime friend Dean Elliott conducted and arranged the music for the largish orchestra, and the Mel-Tones, minus Betty Beveridge, were reconvened to help in the proceedings. The show ran for a year and was great fun. I wrote all the special material, using a creative muscle I hadn't flexed in quite a while.

Consequently, I began to think about a large-scale work that might serve as a West Coast alter ego to Gordon Jenkins's exciting *Manhattan Tower*. I started work on this project in early 1949. Toward the end of the year, Carlos had convinced Capitol's head honcho, Jim Conkling, to record the piece. A huge studio orchestra was assembled as well as a complement of chorus singers. The Mel-Tones were hired to offset the large choir, and several of Hollywood's finest arrangers were engaged to orchestrate the music. Paul Villipigue, Neal Hefti, Billy May, Dick Jones, and Hal Mooney all contributed mightily with their excellent arrangements to make my *California Suite* something to be proud of. An added surprise was the participation of one "Susan Melton," who sang the role of "the Easterner." "Miss Melton" was actually that enormously popular singer Peggy Lee.

Capitol did a fine job of promoting the *Suite,* and, while it did not initially make musical history, it was well-reviewed and well-received. It was also Capitol Records' first long-play album, a nice distinction in itself.

When the Philip Morris show faded, Candy and I went back on the road. This time we had company. I had long felt the need of a permanent accompanist. Al Pellegrini fit the bill admirably. A fine musician with a droll sense of humor, he became an asset in more ways than one. He also arranged music and played clarinet in the Benny Goodman manner (and damn near as well!). He not only played and conducted for me, he served up some tasteful charts for my act, joined me in a Krupa-Goodman salute on "Sing, Sing, Sing" and added an element of fun to the performances. He and his wife, Norma, became lifelong friends.

My agents, General Artists Corporation, had come up with a new wrinkle. The ploy was a then-current phenomenon called "record rooms." In most cases, these were unlovely joints that flourished by virtue of the "hot" recording artists who were willing to take the money and run. Most of these rooms looked like small warehouses into which someone had thrown some tables and chairs.

One such venue was a charming spot in Cleveland, aptly named Moe's Main Street. The proprietor, whose name the club bore, was a thick little man whose entire wardrobe seemed to consist of a navy pea jacket and a woolen watch cap—with a pom-pom, yet! The club itself was out on Euclid Avenue in a "neighborhood." Definitely not the Mocambo.

"Moe's Main Street?" I queried.

"Mel, baby, kiddie, it's a 'record room,'" my GAC agent explained. "They're all playing it. Joni and Gogi and Frankie and the Four Aces. I'm almost sure Bill Farrell and Don Cherry are signed to play the room. And the money's pretty good. Not great, but pretty good."

I joined the "club" and played the club. Two things I recall about the engagement: the top critic in Cleveland was a Clifton Webb–like individual named Winsor French. (Coincidentally, Webb was a close friend of his.) French caught my opening night performance and took me apart the next morning in the *Cleveland Press,* the town's major newspaper. He roasted me up one side and down the other. Brilliantly. I had never been slammed with such panache, wit, and style. After I read the review, I found out that he lived at the Hollenden Hotel. I called him, wondering whether he would take the call. To my surprise, he answered the phone.

"Yes?" came a distinctly effeminate question.

"Mr. French, this is Mel Tormé."

"I know. Your call was announced. What can I do for you, Mr. Tormé?"

"I just wanted to say that I've read your review this morning. I assure you, I haven't called to berate you or question your judgment about my performance. It's just that no one has ever written a negative critique on me before that I found myself reading again and again. Look, I'm not crazy, Mr. French. I don't like the content of the review, but I love the writing, and several times I laughed out loud. It's obvious you're a fine writer and I called to ask if perhaps you've written a book or two. If so, I'd like to read them."

French was flabbergasted. "My God," he cried, "I have gotten some nasty calls from wounded performers in the past, but no one has *ever* called to compliment me on a bad review." He paused. "Is this some sort of trick on your part, Mr. Tormé? Trying to butter me up? Because if it is—"

"Mr. French," I interrupted, "isn't this call 'after the fact'? The review is out and it stands. Nothing can change that. No axe is being ground here. I simply think you're one hell of a writer and I wanted to say so. Let's leave it at that and I thank you for your courtesy in accepting my call."

For the record, my motives were genuine. Having long been a devoted follower of S. J. Perelman, Robert Benchley, Max Shulman, and H. L. Mencken, the cleverly written vitriol of Winsor's column appealed to me. A few days later, he called and said he would like to do an interview piece on me for the *Press*. We met for lunch and I found him to be an endearing little man with a wistful countenance, a crew cut, and elegant taste in clothes. He lived alone at a suite at the Hollenden, and I guessed correctly that he was a terribly lonely, unhappy individual.

He wrote a fine piece on me—funny, revealing, and carefully wrought so as not to seem apologetic for the previous review. Winsor and I became friends. He did a 180 on me, became a staunch supporter, and was responsible for getting me booked into the class room in town, the Vogue Room at the Hollenden Hotel.

I am sure many Clevelandites "suspected" me because of my friendship with Winsor French. He was gay, and that fact, plus

Mel, looking the way he did
when he sang with the
Coon-Sanders Orchestra.

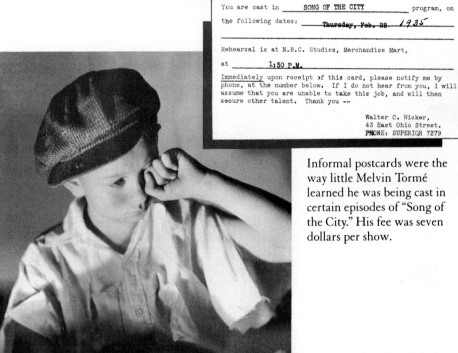

You are cast in _____ SONG OF THE CITY _____ program, on
the following dates: _____ Thursday, Feb. 28 _1935_ _____

Rehearsal is at N.B.C. Studios, Merchandise Mart,
at _____ 1:30 P.M. _____
Immediately upon receipt of this card, please notify me by
phone, at the number below. If I do not hear from you, I will
assume that you are unable to take this job, and will then
secure other talent. Thank you --

Walter C. Wicker,
43 East Ohio Street.
PHONE: SUPERIOR 7279

Informal postcards were the
way little Melvin Tormé
learned he was being cast in
certain episodes of "Song of
the City." His fee was seven
dollars per show.

Mel as "Jimmy the Newsboy"
on NBC radio soap, "Song of
the City," 1934. Newspaper
headline may refer to
Lindbergh kidnapping.

Mel at the mike, where he was one of the busiest young actors
in Chicago radio. Note the Gruen-Curvex watch, which he
won on a talent show.

Mel, a budding young songwriter, at a studio piano.

His first set of drums, "the Ray Bauduc Bob Cat outfit," a present from Grandpa Sopkin.

Mel behind his second drum set, playing with the Chico Marx Orchestra, Lakeside Ballroom, Denver, Colorado, June 1943. Other band members included guitarist Barney Kessel, pianist Marty Napoleon, and jazz trumpeter Marty Marsala.

Mel with Chico Marx and "the Revellis," the vocal group for which he wrote arrangements in 1942.

Silly time at the Donald O'Connor residence.

Mel Tormé and his Mel-Tones—(CLOCKWISE FROM BOTTOM) Bernie Parke, Betty Beveridge, Mel, Ginny O'Connor, and Les Baxter.

Mel does his first engagement at the Paramount Theater in New York in 1947.

Mel and Artie Shaw huddling over one of the tunes Mel sang on record with the Shaw Orchestra. Artie gave Mel his first chance at solo singing on record.

Mel with one of his all-time favorite singers, Miss Billie Holliday.

Mel's date, singer-actress
Marilyn Maxwell, on the night
of his solo vocal debut at the
Bocage in Hollywood, January 1947.

Ray McDonald, Peter Lawford, and
Mel Tormé perform in the MGM
movie musical *Good News*, 1947.

Mel and Buddy Rich in their beloved twin MG-TC Midgets
on a rainy night outside Frank Dailey's Meadowbrook off the
Pompton Turnpike in New Jersey in 1947.

At Mel and Candy's engagement party—Nat Cole lives it up
at the piano, Patsy O'Connor (Donald's niece), and
Dean Elliott look on. An unexpected guest later on was Frank Sinatra.

Mel and Candy, married at the Ambassador Hotel in Chicago
February 1949. Mel's sister, Myrna (AT FAR RIGHT), Mel's
parents, Bill and Betty (CENTER).

Mel, Candy, and baby Steven having a family sing-along in
their New York apartment. Spooky, the springer spaniel, sang bass.

his advanced age and lack of any steady, meaningful companionship in his life, eventually broke his spirit. During one of our early conversations, he carefully inquired if I had ever experienced any homosexual tendencies. As tactfully as possible, I explained that from earliest memory, I had always been, purely and simply, a girl lover. He died some years ago, mourned by many admirers and friends in the state of Ohio and beyond.

My other memory of Moe's occurred a few nights after I had opened. That night, I encountered one of the noisiest tables it has ever been my misfortune to try to entertain. I said nothing about this pair of couples, two brassy blondes and their escorts, ill-dressed and mean-looking, during my first few songs. But while I was singing "Blue Moon," the four of them were talking at the tops of their voices. I halted the performance and fell back on a stale old comic's bit.

"Folks," I announced, "years ago, I accidentally ran over a mule and killed it. I was warned that mule would come back to haunt me and, sure enough, that jackass"—I paused, indicating the louder of the two rough customers—"is with us tonight." The audience laughed. Moe, standing at the front door, waved his arms and shook his head vigorously from side to side.

"Apparently, these four people don't get out much."

Moe: frantically signaling me.

"You see, fella, this is a nightclub, not a football stadium. Cool it, will ya?"

Moe: jumping out of his skin.

"I mean, relax. You'll make out with the broad later. Right now, I'm trying to do a show for these people and I think they paid to hear me, not you."

Moe: slumping in a chair, head down, shaking it despairingly.

For the rest of the performance, I was treated to glaring looks and stony silence from the table in question. When I had finished and gone to what was laughingly called a dressing room, Moe came running back.

"My God," he screamed, "didn't you get my high sign?"

"I got it, but since you obviously weren't going to do anything about those noisy bastards, I figured it was up to me."

Moe took off his watch cap and wiped his sweating forehead. "J-Jesus," he stammered, "you got any idea who those guys are?"

"Nope, not a clue."

"Well, for openers, you were throwing wise-ass remarks at Julius Petrie. He's been in the can for shooting the mother of one of his own hoods. Petrie took a bullet in return and he got indicted. He's out on bail while his lawyers appeal. They're having a helluva time convicting him, 'cause he won't let them operate to remove the bullet. Get it? The bullet would prove he was there when this other hood's mother was shot." He paused for a breath. "Meantime, while he's out on bail, Petrie gets picked up for allegedly committing a seventy-thousand-dollar armored car robbery. He's out on bail for that one, too. And you're standing on that stage calling him and his party jackasses!"

"Whoops!" I said. "You're right, Moe. That was dumb. Well, what do I do now? Go up and apologize?"

"Too late. Minute you finished, they all left. Petrie looked mad. Listen, I'm not trying to scare ya, kid, but I think you ought to touch base with the police."

"Yeah, maybe you're right. First thing tomorrow, okay?"

"Okay, but watch yourself goin' back to the hotel tonight."

Candy had not joined me on that trip, so Pellegrini and I went to a popular late-night restaurant in Shaker Heights to have a bite. As we were being shown to our table, we passed right by Julius Petrie and friends. Petrie stared at me for a moment, then continued talking to his girl. I had a nervous snack, glancing furtively over toward Petrie's table every few minutes. He never looked at me again. I guess he had a few things on his mind. I forgot about it the next day. So, apparently, did Petrie. I never heard from him, but I read about him in the best-selling *The Last Mafioso*. I'm a very lucky guy.

A couple of months later, coincidentally, a few miles away in Akron, Ohio, a far more serious incident occurred. I got sandbagged by GAC into playing yet another record room. This time it was a dump called the "Yankee Inn." The owner, George Senior, wasn't exactly a quiche eater. Al and I had driven there from another engagement, barely arriving in time to make the first show.

We parked the car, took our luggage downstairs into the dressing room, washed and shaved, and went right on stage.

The room was a wide one, with the long bar very close to the stage. I began to sing. A huge, mean-looking, red-haired guy, wearing a leather Eisenhower-type jacket, stood at the center of the bar, towering over everyone, flipping coins on the polished surface. They clattered with annoying clarity, disturbing the rhythm songs, destroying the ballads. George Senior stood toward the front door, arms folded, apparently amused. After the Petrie incident, I was gun-shy about opening my big mouth to a noisy customer. I grinned and bore it, finishing the first show, certain the bum would leave before my second performance of the evening.

No such luck. He remained and was even more impossible, yelling to the bartender for beer, shouting hellos to acquaintances all over the room. At one point, I looked to Senior for help. He shrugged. Finally, I couldn't contain myself.

"Look, friend," I practically pleaded, "I'm really not on all that long. Be a pal and give it a rest until I finish, will you?"

Several people who had apparently come to hear me sing yelled in support. Redhead merely increased his activities. I walked off the stage in disgust. Down to the dressing room came the wonderful Mr. Senior.

"Thanks a million for your help, George," I said angrily.

"Hey," he countered, "I ain't gonna screw around with Big Red. He's a steady customer here. I just thought I'd come down and tell you he's threatening to wipe the walls with you. He's an ex-marine M.P. and a son of a bitch. He's broken more jaws in this town than you could count on your fingers. Better take care."

I looked at Al. "Christ," I said, "not again."

We purposely waited an extra half-hour for the club to clear out, so we could drag our luggage over to the hotel, check in, and get a decent night's sleep. Having driven all day and done two shows under difficult conditions, we were exhausted.

We lugged our bags to the top of the stairs. The club was empty. Except for Big Red. He stood in the aisleway, blocking the front door. George Senior stood close to the bandstand. He looked worried. Finally, I walked toward the door, Al trailing me. The ex-M.P. blocked my way, drunk as a skunk.

"I'm gonna mash you," he announced in slurred tones.

I pulled a Colt .38 Detective Special out of my overcoat pocket, jammed it into his stomach, and cocked the gun.

"Shit!" Senior's breath exploded.

Big Red looked down at the revolver rammed into his gut. He sucked in his stomach to break contact with the muzzle of the little snub nose, backed away, turned without a word, and stumbled out the front door. I began to shake and couldn't stop. I carefully let the hammer of the gun ease back into its normal position and sat down, before I fell down.

From the beginning of my gun-collecting days, I had never pointed a weapon at a living thing. Most of the guns I have owned are pure collector's items, beautifully engraved specimens and historical firearms of the Old West. In those days, however, Al and I did a great deal of traveling by car. Sometimes night trips were necessary, long drives on lonely roads, and more than once we had been close to thorny situations because of our schedule. I had taken to keeping a gun with me for self-protection, never believing for one moment that, one night in Akron, I would actually have to exhibit it to keep from being broken in half by a drunken slob of an ex-marine M.P.

Nowadays, thank God, I do all my traveling by plane. I haven't felt the need to have a weapon on hand for years. That night in Akron, though, I'm grateful I was prepared. Would I have used it? To this day, it's a question I can't answer. I have had an ongoing daydream of a nightmare: the cops show up at the Yankee Inn. I am lying on the floor, bloody, maimed, injured, perhaps dead. One of the cops remarks, "Well, you gotta say this for Tormé: He didn't break the law. Didn't pull a gun. Good citizen!"

I've hated that night with a vengeance, hated George Senior for not putting a stop much earlier to what was obviously a dangerous situation, hated having to threaten someone's life like that. Still, I feel I had no choice. What would you have done?

20.

TELEVISION

*I*N 1951 I played the Paramount again, headlining this time with Ella Fitzgerald and the Sam Donahue band. I started writing articles in earnest for *Speed Age* magazine, *Car Life, Guns, Metronome,* and *Down Beat.* I was resisting "record rooms" and, in the process, being offered better places in which to perform. Candy and I were getting along well. I sold my beloved M.G.-TC and bought a new XK 120 Jaguar, fitted with Borani wire wheels. White with blue interior, it was a dream car. And suddenly, an important break came my way.

Carlos called to say that Peggy Lee and I had been offered the summer replacement slot for the Perry Como fifteen-minute Chesterfield show. The show was called "TV's Top Tunes." It was produced by Como's helmsman, Lee Cooley, music was provided by Como's conductor/arranger, Mitch Ayres. It went on all through the summer of 1951. I must have done something right because, when the summer ended, CBS offered me a show of my own, to commence almost immediately. It was to be a half-hour show. I was free to hire the talent. It was to air daily. There was only one problem—no one would see it.

CBS and NBC were locked in a struggle over compatible color systems. The coming of color was imminent, and the industry standard for transmitting the new process had not yet been settled. In September 1951, I began telecasting the very first CBS color show. Unfortunately, it was a closed-circuit affair that only CBS executives could monitor and evaluate. I had hired a couple of fine performers, Peggy King and Kaye Ballard. I wrote a theme song that ended with the plaintive lament: "Hey, Mr. Paley, we're here daily . . ."

CBS Kingpin William Paley must have heard our cry for attention. Or perhaps it was the sudden decision on the part of all the networks to adopt NBC's color process. At any rate, "The Mel Tormé Closed-Circuit CBS Color Show" was terminated and instantly replaced by "The Mel Tormé Show" on the regular CBS network in glorious black and white. It was seen from 3:00 to 3:30 every weekday and sported an enlarged complement of performers. In addition to Peggy and Kaye, a fine vocal group called "The Mellowlarks" were signed.

Several excellent musicians augmented the trio that had provided music for the color show. Al Pellegrini headed a group of outstanding players that included my all-time favorite trombonist, Bill Harris; as well as Hal McKusick; Mickey McMickle (from the old Glenn Miller band); George Berg (late of the Buddy Rich roster) on tenor sax; and, as an added treat, Red Norvo and his talented cohort, Tal Farlow, on guitar. Norvo was later fired for two reasons, one of them logical, one of them stupid. I was not only hosting the show, I was playing drums for all the acts we booked, an unwieldy situation at best. I was ordered by the CBS brass to find a replacement for Norvo who could also double as house drummer. "Besides," one executive complained, "Norvo looks too old for the show. It's a young-looking program. Let's keep it that way." It was difficult having to let one of my musical favorites go, tougher still when Red began bruiting it about town that "That son-of-a-bitch Tormé fired me because he said I look too damn old for his lousy show." Bum rap, Red. Bum rap.

"The Mel Tormé Show" on CBS predated all the afternoon talk shows. In addition to plenty of music, the show adopted an interview format, and I chatted at length with such diverse personalities as Jackie Cooper; Duke Ellington; my old nemesis-turned-friend, Dorothy Kilgallen; and (wait for it) the son of the famous Apache chief, Geronimo. We were unsponsored and, unfortunately, stayed that way. The ratings were good, and CBS hung in there with us. Candy and I, anticipating a long stay in New York, took an apartment in Sutton Terrace on York Avenue and Sixty-first Street.

While our house in Los Angeles was furnished in traditional Early American, Candy made the new apartment in Manhattan into something quite different. Modern furnishings graced the large, airy flat, along with some attractive prints hanging on the walls. In a sense, I think Candy was happier in the cosmopolitan environs of New York than among the hills and valleys of the more rustic California.

Candy, I must say, was a stunning gal. Tallish, she looked great in either tailored suits or elegant dresses. She had an infectious way about her and a good sense of humor.

Weekends, Al and I would get into the Jag and fulfill engagements in and around New York to supplement our respective incomes. Weekdays, we had fun on the show with frequent guests Eddie Mayehoff and Wally Cox.

I was in a slight state of shock when the CBS "Mel Tormé Show" was canceled in the spring of 1953. The shock was somewhat softened when I was offered the summer replacement slot for the then-popular Jane Froman TV show. I took the job (prime time, after all), costarring with Teresa Brewer. When that came to a halt in September of '53, I headlined at the Roxy. Then there was a quick trip out to the Coast to fulfill a two-week engagement at the Mocambo. The gig itself was mildly successful, memorable only for two incidents, both involving superstars.

One night, as I crooned my little songs in the famous Sunset Strip supper club, who should walk in but John Wayne, well into his cups. Hosting a half-dozen equally inebriated cronies, he plunked down at a ringside table, and they proceeded to make my life miserable. Near the closing moments of my performance, I pleaded with the box-office giant, "Give me a break, John. After all, I don't talk through your movies." The Mocambo was an expensive watering hole, and, admire him or not, the audience was on my side. They applauded my entreaty. "I'd like to sing a fine Kurt Weill song from *Knickerbocker Holiday*," I announced. "Here's 'September Song.'"

Wayne's voice boomed in that pause between announcement and musical introduction: "Oh, boy," he slurringly informed his party and the rest of the patrons, "he's gonna get me with this one!" There was a burst of laughter from the audience and one from me as well. I began to sing the tune, forcing myself to keep a straight face. On almost every line of the lyric, the hushed audience could hear huge stage whispers of "Shh-h-h-h" from the big fella, his forefinger vertically pressed to his lips—like a kid in school, exhorting his classmates to hush up and pay attention to the teacher.

I learned something that night. The Duke and his pals were totally unmalicious in their revelry. They came to the Mocambo to continue the good time that had evidently begun earlier in the evening. But the main point is: their noisy participation in that night's performance was not calculated; it was never meant to degrade or humiliate. On those singular evenings throughout the years when happy drunks have attended my shows, the memory of that John Wayne incident has helped me keep my cool.

The second incident involved Betty Grable. For a few years I had been hearing that she was especially partial to my singing. Dan Dailey had once told me, "Kid, she has all your records in her dressing room. Matter of fact, she's trying to get you the second lead in this thing we're currently doing together."

"What? *Call Me Mister?*"

"Yeah. Look, she wants to meet you. Come out to Fox for lunch tomorrow, will you? I promised her."

Candy had been amused by Grable's desire to meet me. "What do you think, Cand?" I asked.

"For heaven's sake, go out and have lunch with her. It'll be fun."

When I walked onto the *Mister* set, the cast and crew were between takes. I asked a grip where Betty's dressing room was, and as I approached it, my record of "Again" was clearly audible from within her trailer. Dan suddenly appeared and knocked on her door. When she opened it, he introduced me. She smiled that dazzler that had inspired hundreds of thousands of G.I.s to fight for their country.

She offered me her hand and said, "It's about time." We had a delightful lunch. She astonished me by knowledgeably discussing not only my records but the output of several jazz artists, as well as the selective personnel of many name bands we both admired. I realized then it made good sense; she was married to one of the premiere bandleaders, Harry James. She was a vastly underrated tap-dancer (her turn with the Dunhills in *Call Me Mister* amply demonstrates that fact), and she sang in a plaintive, fetching manner, just slightly, although not unpleasantly, under pitch.

She mentioned that she had pressed her bosses to cast me in *Mister,* but they had gone with Danny Thomas. She seemed genuinely disappointed. I thanked her, told her it was enough of a pleasure just to have lunch with her, and went away understanding why everyone had nothing but good things to say about this beautiful, immensely likable lady. That was in 1951.

Now, one night during my 1953 Mocambo run, in walked Betty, chaperoned by her closest friends, Betty and Harry Ritz, of Ritz Brothers fame. Grable, a touch heavier than when we had last met at Fox, but still terrific looking, sat through two shows and then insisted the Ritzes and I stop by her house on Doheny Road for a drink. "Harry's out of town," she informed me. "It's lonely in that damn haunted house." She insisted her house was haunted, and the Ritzes confirmed this. (Years later, Joe Hyams and Elke Sommer bought the place, had several disturbing experiences there, and eventually moved.)

Candy was pregnant with our first child and had elected to stay in New York for those two weeks. Since I, too, was headed for our empty house on Thurston Circle, I detoured slightly and accepted Betty's invitation.

The James-Grable residence was impressive. The Ritzes kept trying to discourage Grable from drinking any more that night. She was getting sloshed and unhappier by the minute. "Nobody loves a fat lady," she kept repeating. Betty Ritz shook her head sorrowfully. Harry took me aside and told me there was big trouble in the James household.

Betty began to make noises like wasn't it time for the Ritzes to take their leave. Betty Ritz shot me a look that shrieked: for God's sake, Mel, Betty's drunk—she doesn't know what she's saying. The look was unnecessary. Plainly, Grable was miserable, feeling deserted and unloved, and being doggedly predatory. I made my good nights and left the three of them to the haunted house. Who says movie stars' lives are fun?

≡

Candy gave birth to our son, Steven Michael, on January 29, 1953. Work was medium-slow in the East, so we gave up our Sutton Terrace apartment and moved back to Thurston Circle. We decided we needed a larger house. We found a beauty of a Connecticut-type farmhouse, complete with shake roof, dormer windows, and flagstone facade, on Fontenelle Way, off Stone Canyon Road in Bel Air. It was a large financial chunk to bite off, but we fell in love with the property and took the plunge.

Our home at 10650 Fontenelle was situated directly across the street from Sharley and Keenan Wynn's pretty house. Predictably, we became good friends. Keenan's love of motorcycles gave me ideas that, later in life, became realities.

By that time, I had lost any illusions about becoming an important musical movie star. I was happy to be working, earning decent money, settled back in California, and enjoying my new house and my new son. Stevie was a joy, cute as hell, and as active as an erupting volcano. We hired a marvelous young black woman named Mary, who babied us all and became the fourth member of the family.

Of course, maintaining that house meant almost constant road trips for me. Al Pellegrini and I covered the length and breadth of the North American continent. I turned in my XK 120 and bought one of the prototype all-aluminum Austin-Healys that had just been introduced in America. *Car Life* magazine commissioned me to write the road report on the new, hot sports car. I decided to drive the A-H from New York City to Hollywood. Poor Pellegrini! He hated driving and wistfully eyed airports and train terminals. The trip was a good shakedown test for the little metallic-blue roadster, with stops to sing in Cleveland at the Hollenden, Dayton at the Esquire Red Room, and Indianapolis, where I got the thrill of my life tooling the Healy around the famous, deserted speedway for several laps at 93 mph-indicated. Then, Indy winner Sam Hanks got into the driver's seat and, with me holding on to the handgrip for dear life, "put his foot in it," goosing the machine up to 112-indicated. My heart finally dropped out of my throat a few hours later.

The longest stretch of driving was a run from St. Louis to Dallas, and we were fighting the clock. Since I had to be in Dallas posthaste, I drove all of one day and all that night, with Al napping restlessly in the cramped passenger seat. A rosy Texas morning dawned as we sped on a straight, empty ribbon of road toward Big D. Pellegrini opened his tired eyes. I glanced in the rearview mirror. I looked like hell. So did Al. He straightened up, yawned, and looked out the window at the countryside flashing by.

"So these are the kicks you promised me," he said. His message received five-by-five.

≡

Time spent at home was precious to me. Candy and I were fairly social animals, and we were invited to and gave numerous dinner parties. I divided my home time between my wife, my son, my folks, my friends, my piano (composing), and typewriter (article writing).

I built a playroom, complete with projection booth and recessed gun cases. It became my pride and joy. One night, I invited our neighbors, the Keenan Wynns, for dinner. Keenan and I had known each other slightly from a few years back at MGM. He called late in the afternoon to ask if he could bring a couple of guests. "Of course," I said, and, at around seven-thirty that evening, in walked the Keenan Wynns and the Lee Marvins. I was a runaway admirer of Lee's work, although I had never met him before. He turned out to be one hell of a guy and we got along famously; later on, though, the evening turned into a minor nightmare.

When I took our guests into the playroom, Lee gravitated right over to the gun cases. A Colt .45 automatic caught his eye. "I used one of those mothers in the service," he informed me. "Know that baby like the back of my hand! Inside and out. Used to be able to take the sucker apart and put it together blindfolded. Hell of a weapon." Lee looked at me. He had put away a few. "Hey, Mel," he said, "pull that thing outta there, will you?"

Considerate host that I was, I complied. That was my first mistake. Lee quickly and expertly tore the .45 down to its finite components. That was around 10:30. He cleared his throat, waved his hands over the disassembled parts like Mandrake the Magician, grinned, and set about making the gun whole again. He failed in his first attempt. And second. And fifth. And twelfth.

12.05 A.M. The women are getting restless. Lee, an open bottle of Scotch beside him, is grimly working on the Colt. Keenan, nursing his own bottle, is cheering him on.

12:55. The end is not in sight. Lee shakes his head, gulps a little Scotch, and tries again. The women have gone back into the living room.

1:30. Lee has made his twenty-fourth attempt to reconstruct the pistol. Almost, but not quite. He and Keenan are feeling absolutely no pain whatsoever. Our little Springer spaniel, Spooky, is kibitzing the charade. She gets too frisky with Keenan and he gently swipes her aside. She yelps and nips his hand, not quite breaking the skin.

2:45. Success! The gun is a gun again. Lee grins. "Told you I could do it. Nothing to it." He has been sitting cross-legged on the floor for hours. He rises painfully, raises his wristwatch to within an inch of his eyes, blinks, and says, "Late. Better go home." Keenan mumbles his agreement. The women, upon seeing us, raise a chorus of hallelujahs. We say our good nights.

The house is quiet. We check on Steven. He is fast asleep. It is ten after three. I laugh. "Time for decent people to be in bed." Candy says amen. We get into our nightclothes, turn out the lights, and lay our weary bones down.

The phone rings. It's Keenan. "Tormé," he rasps into my ear, "your goddamn dog bit me. I don't know what the hell he might have—"

"She."

"Huh?"

"She. Spooky is a she."

"Okay, okay. 'She.' The little bitch bit me and—"

"Are you bleeding, Keenan?"

"No, but she broke the skin and—"

"Keenan, you'll live, believe me. She barely nipped you. I was there, remember?"

"Listen, I could die from this. You hear me? Die! I could get rabies or something. What the hell would happen to my family? How would they get along without me?"

"All right, so what do you want from me?"

"I want you to take me to the hospital."

"Fine. Okay. In the morning, we'll—"

"Now. I want to go to the hospital right now."

I turned on the light. "You've got to be kidding. For God's sake, it's three-thirty in the morning."

"I don't give a shit. We go now or I'll call my lawyer in the morning and I'll sue you."

In my long singing career in saloons. I have learned not to argue with someone who is swacked. I got dressed, collected my swaying neighbor, and drove him to St. John's Hospital in Santa Monica. The doctor in Emergency looked at Keenan's finger. "What the hell is this? Are you joking?" he asked the actor.

Keenan shrugged and muttered, "Never can tell. Could die from something like this."

Keenan fell asleep in the car on the way home.

Candy and I saw less and less of each other. I was traveling, she was pregnant again, and had wisely chosen to stay put in our Bel-Air house.

On July 9, 1955, Candy gave birth to our second child. We named her Melissa. She was a beautiful little thing, and I felt equal feelings of pride in her and concern about the condition of my marriage to her mother, which had been disintegrating for well over a year.

I couldn't blame Candy for being unhappy and dissatisfied due to my constant traveling. We loved sharing the joys of having a new baby in the house, but Candy seemed distracted and distant, and there was no sexual activity of any kind between us.

One night, she tearfully told me she had met someone, fallen in love, and that she wanted a divorce. Her new love was Hal

March, actor and game-show host, whose "$64,000 Question" was the hottest program on TV at that time. I had known Hal for years and had recently seen him at a party. He and Candy had obviously been attracted to each other that night, and one thing had led to another. I wasn't angry; as a matter of fact, I was somewhat relieved, since I had known for some time that the marriage was not working. If I was having a bout with melancholia at all, it was because of the children. Steven was two years old; Melissa was a babe in swaddling clothes. The thought of another man raising my kids ("The $64,000 Question" was based in New York) was grinding my guts. On the credit side of the ledger, Hal was a decent man who would love my children and take good care of them. I counted myself lucky that Candy had fallen in love with someone like Hal March.

21.

MARILYN

[The] newspaper circuit . . . had her fighting with her studio again—and in new romances with Milton Greene, Jacques Sernas, Mel Tormé, Marlon Brando and Sammy Davis, Jr.

in *Marilyn*
by Norman Mailer

O N one of his final shows, Merv Griffin mentioned the above quote and asked me, point-blank, if I had had an affair with Marilyn Monroe.

I realized it is titillating to the reader to imagine this actor and that producer and those singers and politicians and even a U.S. president in bed with the likes of Marilyn Monroe. I am also told it sells books. But the last time I looked in a mirror, I bore little or no resemblance to Shelley Winters and this is not going to be another "tell-all" autobiography.

I liked Marilyn Monroe. We first met in New York City when I was playing the Roxy Theatre in 1952. . . .

≡

There is a knock on the dressing-room door. I holler, "Come in," and in walks this collegiate-looking guy, complete with Brooks Brothers suit, button-down shirt, rep tie.

"Hi, Mel," he says, extending his hand. His smile is open, friendly. "I'm Fred Kelman [not his real name]. I'm in the publicity department at Twentieth."

This was back in the pre-antitrust days when the major studios also owned theater chains. Twentieth Century-Fox owned the Roxy. "Look," Fred explains, "we need a favor. I understand you're a movie buff."

"Well, let's see," I laugh, "I've gone out in front to look at *What Price Glory* three times, and it's really not a terribly good picture. Yeah, I guess you could say I like movies."

He nods. "Well, then, you've seen Marilyn Monroe in some of our stuff."

"Everything she's done for you, as well as outside the studio on loan-out."

"Good, good. Look, the picture following you in here is called *Monkey Business*. It has Cary Grant and . . . oh, a lot of other people. But it's going to be especially important for Marilyn. I've seen it and she's marvelous in it."

I begin getting dressed for the next show. "So?" I ask, applying some pancake makeup. "What's the favor?"

"Mel, how would you feel about bringing her out on the stage with you next Thursday night? We're running a 'sneak' of *Monkey Business* here at the theater right after your seven o'clock show, and what we'd like is for you to introduce her, chat with her a little, let her talk about *Monkey Business* for a few minutes, and then—don't laugh—have her sing a duet with you to close the show." He takes a deep breath. "Well, what do you think?"

"Can she sing?"

"Yes, I think she can. She says she can."

"Hmmm. Frankly, it concerns me. That kind of impromptu appearance can fall flat on its face. I like ending the show with strength."

"Oh, not impromptu! Not at all. Rehearsed. Written. She'll be here Monday. You can get together with her between shows at the Sherry—or here, if you like."

I think some more about it. "All right," I say finally. "Call me when she gets in and I'll meet her and see."

≡

The following Tuesday, between afternoon performances, I went over to the Sherry-Netherland to meet Marilyn Monroe. She was heart-staggeringly gorgeous, eager to work with me, terribly nervous, and possessed of a breathy little singing voice that seemed incapable of rising to more than a whisper.

We worked. I had written a parody on "Oh, Do It Again" for the two of us. She liked it and learned it.

The Fox guy delivered a script with dialogue to precede the duet. It wasn't very good. I threw it away and wrote some light, bantering material, six minutes' worth, to be exact, which Marilyn felt comfortable with and was able to perform credibly.

We rehearsed Tuesday, Wednesday, and Thursday afternoons. We had sandwiches together, shared some personal confidences, and laughed a lot. And when that lady laughed, she was Lionel Hampton, sliding a mallet up and down your ribcage, tickling your funnybone, and raising little bumps on your arm with the pure, joyous abandon of her giggles, her guffaws, her full, open-throated explosions of laughter. She told me she was trying to better herself. Reading was the key, she earnestly informed me, and she was into all kinds of books.

She was then going with Joe DiMaggio. He wasn't much on reading, she said, but he was one hell of a man and they were very serious about one another. I thought to myself: Perfect! A movie star and a national hero. What could be better? Only in America!

I had long admired Joltin' Joe and I told her so. Her eyes shone. Would I like to meet him? Hell, yes! Well, then, come to dinner with us Thursday night, right after we do our bit on the stage. Love to, Marilyn, but there's so little time between shows to dress, get over to Toots Shor's (Joe's favorite hangout), and get back for the last show. Another time, okay?

She seemed genuinely disappointed. I had heard stories about this girl, unflattering gossip about her sexual exploits, her temperament, her flightiness, her undependability. Yet I had worked intensively with her for three solid days. She had been, with me at least, a consummate pro, practicing the duet again and again, trying the dialogue I had written this way and that, for maximum effect. She had been outgoing, easy, affectionate, complimentary, diligent—in short, terrific. Thursday evening, however, was something else.

At approximately 6:45, Marilyn walked into my dressing room. She was surrounded by a phalanx of Fox publicity men. As she came into the room, so help me, a woman walked directly behind her, arms extended, curling Marilyn's hair with a hot iron. Monroe had a glass of red wine in her hand and a wild look in her eyes, and my quiet dressing room suddenly erupted into chaos.

I looked at M.M. She was petrified. Her eyes were slightly glazed, and I had trouble associating this somewhat disheveled, slightly tipsy, thoroughly terrified young woman with the laughing, happy gal I had left at the Sherry only a few hours before.

The hubbub increased. I felt I was in one of those climactic scenes from a Capra film, where everybody talks at once and there is a feeling of controlled madness in the air. I clapped my hands several times and the room quieted.

"All right, gang. Everybody out, please. Just Marilyn and myself in here. Gotta run the skit and the song." There were protests, but they all filed out of the room.

"Mr. Tormé, I'll need time to finish her hair," warned the hairdresser.

"There'll be time," I promised, and she followed the Fox people out. I closed the door. Monroe was trembling. She tried smiling at me and her lips quivered.

"Jesus, babe," I said. "That was World War Three."

She grinned nervously. "I like that—'Babe.' Nobody ever called me 'babe.' "

"You all right?"

She looked away. "Of course not. I'm scared shitless."

"Come on. You're kidding."

She shook her blond head vigorously. Bobby pins flew in all directions. "No, I'm not. I can't go out there on that stage."

This scene was beginning to sound like something out of a "B" movie musical. I grinned and gave her my Gable imitation from *Dancing Lady:* "Now look, kiddo, you're going out there and knock 'em dead. This is the chance you've been waiting for." I switched gears to Warner Baxter's dialogue from *Forty-Second Street:* "You're going out there an unknown, but you're coming back a star!"

She ignored my attempt at humor. "I can't, Mel. I just can't. Every woman out there in that audience hates me."

"What?"

"It's the truth. They only came here tonight to sit and hate my guts."

"Yeah, well, the thing is: they came! Get it? They came. I've been doing good business here, but nothing like tonight. The house is jammed, and they all paid to see you. Believe me, Marilyn, they would all—every one of those females out there—love to be Marilyn Monroe. Where the hell did you ever get the idea that women hate you?"

"Oh, you know. All this 'sex-bomb' crap. It's got to make other women—"

"Screw other women! You've got to learn the difference between hatred and jealousy, enmity and envy."

She chuckled—finally! "What's 'enmity'?"

"Look it up. Hey, listen. What can I tell you? What we do on that stage out there isn't really important. It'll probably only affect my whole career."

She picked at an eyelash, laughed out loud, and mock-slapped at me. "You nut! Okay, enough of this pep talk. Let's go over the skit and the song one more time."

"Aw, to hell with that, Norma."

"Oh, Christ! Norma?"

"Yeah. Norma. A good meat-and-potatoes name."

"Norma," she murmured and raised the wineglass. I intercepted it on the way to her lips and put it on the dressing table.

"Look. You know the jokes and the duet. Sideways. What're you reading?"

"Huh?" she blinked. Her speech was slightly fuzzy. She didn't need any more wine.

"You told me you were reading a lot. What?"

Off balance, she muttered something about Jung and Proust.

"Oh, boy. Tough sledding, right?"

"No," she barked, archly defiant. "Yes!" she giggled immediately thereafter. "Boy, half the time I don't know what the hell I'm reading."

"Who put you on to Jung and Proust?"

"Oh, different people. You know, I'm trying to improve myself. I told you—"

"Don't you ever read anything for fun?"

"Well, certainly."

"What?"

"What 'what'?"

"What I mean is, what? What do you read for enjoyment?"

"Oh, lots of things."

"Bullshit, babe. Listen, Jung and Proust are fine; but you'll go blind reading those guys exclusively. Oh, Jesus, here I go sounding like a pontiff..."

"What's a 'pontiff'?"

"... You've got to stagger those mind-bogglers you're struggling through with lighter stuff. Now, come on. You *are* struggling with Jung, aren't you?"

She gave me her full-throated number and goblins walked the length of my spine. "Yes." She paused and laughed louder. "Yes, yes, yes, yes, yes, yes, Yes!" she roared uncontrollably. "Holy shit, *yes!*"

We laughed for two straight minutes, and the hairdresser reappeared and finished doing M.M.'s hair; and, all the while, America's newest Sex Goddess held my hand, giggled, and asked me for a list of "fun" books to read, which I promised to get her. She went out on that huge Roxy stage to cheers, whistles, and big applause and killed the people, as she stood there pressed against me and cooed sexily, "Oh, do it again, I may say, No, no, no, no, no/But do it again..." Afterwards, she came back to my dressing room and sat for fifteen minutes, despite repeated reminders from her entourage that DiMaggio was waiting for her at Toots Shor's. Finally she rose, kissed me on the cheek, and walked out into the hallway. Halfway down the hall, she turned, looked at me, standing in the doorway of my dressing room, and said, "I love you, Mel."

I smiled and made a small wave at her. "I love you too, babe. You were simply great."

She walked to the end of the hallway. The elevator came. She turned toward me again and said, "I mean it. I love you." Then she was gone.

I knew she did not mean "I love you" in any literal sense. She was in love with DiMaggio. She "loved" me for treating her like something more than a glossily packaged piece of meat. For taking the time to help make her look good in front of a large audience. For caring about what she read and thought and felt.

≣

Two years passed before we met again. By then, Marilyn had married and divorced Joe and had been in seclusion for quite a while. I was playing the Crescendo on the Sunset Strip and my marriage to Candy was in serious trouble. One night there, two significant events took place.

For his first appearance in public after losing an eye in an automobile accident, Sammy Davis, Jr., came to see me. With him, first time out in public after her grossly publicized divorce, was Marilyn Monroe, escorted by photographer Milton Greene. A photograph, now reprinted many times (and included here), was taken of the four of us.

Marilyn began to call me at the club. I was slightly uneasy about her attention, but I was also flattered by her calls.

She never announced herself as Marilyn Monroe, of course. She would ask for me, saying, "Tell him it's Sadie." I had gotten into the habit of calling her that, and, years later, it was also my nickname for Judy Garland.

We began to meet late at night. She loved Dolores' Drive-In hamburgers. Several nights we sat in my car, recklessly, in plain sight, eating those tasty burgers and talking—about everything. I am still surprised that our not-so-clandestine rendezvous were never discovered by the press.

We went to the movies. A few times we met at the home of a friend, who has asked to remain anonymous. This went on for the better part of two months or so. She told me she liked me because I made her laugh. (Shades of Ava.)

When we stopped, we stopped. She had things to do with her life. I had a marriage in disrepair that I thought I should try to salvage. We both got a little misty, that final night we saw each other. She assured me of her unbounded affection. I promised her if she ever needed me for anything—anything at all—she could send up a flare and I would come running. I kissed her and that was that.

The "slovenly," not-very-bright, temperamental, profligate woman described by so many writers was a Marilyn Monroe I never met.

The woman-child I knew for an all-too-brief period of time was a nice, reasonably intelligent, eager-to-better-herself individual. She was also insecure, slightly cynical, and opinionated. Her face was always scrubbed, her hair attractively windblown or set. Her language could be salty, but, like Ava Gardner's, her beauty and impishness allowed her to spew forth the most outrageous expletives and get away with them. She was, far and away, the sexiest-looking lady I ever knew.

22.

ARLENE

*A*FTER my breakup with Candy, I moved out of the house and into an apartment on Crescent Heights Avenue in Hollywood. My old songwriting partner, Bob Wells, lived in the same complex, so I didn't feel too isolated. I was preparing to go back east to appear at a new club called "the Cameo." At the same time, something wonderful happened to my singing career.

A feisty little man named Red Clyde was heading a new record company called Bethlehem Records. Out of the blue, he offered me a contract. Bethlehem was a pure jazz label; I was delighted to become part of a roster of artists that included some of the finest talents in jazz. For years I had wanted to shake my "Velvet Fog" crooner image. Now, here was my golden opportunity. I got a release from Capitol Records and joined the new, young company.

Funnily enough, Red suggested that my first LP for Bethlehem be a ballad effort. "Pick your own tunes, choose your own arrangers. I want you to make a great two-in-the-morning type album." I indulged myself. Friend André Previn agreed to write a couple of the charts. So did Russ Garcia and Sandy Courage. Al Pellegrini contributed one. And then there was Marty Paich.

I had heard some arrangements Marty had written for Shelly Manne's small group. They were jazz charts for horns, admittedly, but rich in content and ideas. I had a strong hunch that Paich would be a masterful writer for strings and woodwinds. Red fought me briefly, then capitulated. Marty Paich created four of the most beautiful pieces of orchestra work I had ever heard. The album was called *It's a Blue World*. Its release coincided with my thirtieth

birthday, September 1955. Thirty! My God, I thought, where did
my twenties go? I went back east, played the Cameo, and dated
some nifty ladies in Manhattan.

One night, back in Hollywood, as I fulfilled a return engagement at the Crescendo on the Sunset Strip, a young man invited
me over to his table. His date was a striking blond girl who seemed
impatient to leave.

"I'm James Dean," he said, rising and offering me his hand. I
shook it and sat. He was in a fit of passion for bongo drums.
Having just seen me play drums in my act, he asked me if I played
bongos. I told him I had been fooling with them a bit.

"I'd sure like to be able to play 'em. Really play 'em, you know?"

"Well, Jim, when you have some time, I'll be glad to show you
what I know. It's not much, but—"

"Jimmy," the blonde nagged, "let's go." Her name was Lily
and I recall her strong Swedish accent.

Dean ignored her. "When?" he asked me. "When could you
teach me?"

"Hold it, Jim. I wouldn't presume to teach anyone. I said I'd
show you what I've learned."

"Okay, fine. When?"

"Well, I'm off to Australia next week. How about right after
I get back?"

"Great." He smiled. He wrote his phone number on a piece of
paper and handed it to me. "You won't forget, will you, Mel?"

"Absolutely not. Call you when I get back."

I had gotten an offer to go to Sydney, Australia, to play the
Tivoli Theatre. It made great sense at that moment, and I grabbed
the opportunity. I went a little bananas in Sydney. Everywhere
you looked, there went the most beautiful women imaginable. I
began to realize how much I had missed being single. The Aussie
audiences were enthusiastic and warm and I made some great new
friends.

On my supporting bill was another American, a birdlike little
red-haired woman with a perpetual quaver in her voice and a
fluttery, Zasu Pitts sort of comic delivery. I thought she was wonderful, but the Australian audiences didn't react well to her brand

of humor. The managing director of the Tivoli, David Martin, was a rather cold man with zero tolerance for failure. He was cruel and rude to this poor little comedienne and the reason soon became evident: he wanted to push her into quitting so he could save a few weeks' salary. During the first week we played the theater, she came into my dressing room on several occasions, crying her eyes out over the rotten treatment she was getting from Martin.

"Why doesn't he like me, Mel?" she wailed pitifully. "What have I done to deserve such meanness?"

"Absolutely nothing," I tried comforting her. "Don't take it personally, dear. He's just a very irascible man. Tough it out."

She shook her head forlornly. "I can't. I simply can't." She quit, to David Martin's great satisfaction, and went back to the States, her tail between her legs. A couple of years later, Irene Ryan became world-famous on "The Beverly Hillbillies." The show ran and ran, and she made money hand over fist. When it was all over, she could have bought and sold David Martin. Once, when I saw her at a press party, she came over to me and smiled. That's all, she just smiled. I knew what she was thinking: *sometimes* there *is* such a thing as justice.

When I got off the plane back in the States on October 1, 1955, I spotted a newspaper headline and my stomach turned: FILM STAR DIES IN FIERY CRASH was the banner in bold black print. James Dean would never get those bongo lessons from me now. What a great talent to die so young.

More bad news. Al Pellegrini had decided to quit the road. His daughter was beginning to call him "Uncle Daddy," and his marriage was suffering. Reluctantly, I shook hands with him and said good-bye. He would be sorely missed. I made my second LP at that moment for Bethlehem. Marty Paich and I put together something we called the "Dektette," a ten-man combo patterned after the Gerry Mulligan Tentet and those early Miles Davis nonet sides. "Lulu's Back in Town" was among the tunes we cut in that album, and the song stuck to me in the same gluelike manner as had "Blue Moon."

I hated the idea of being alone on the road, so I prevailed upon a friend, Paul Blane, to join me as a sort of road manager/valet/

driver. I had just bought a Buick station wagon and, with a longish road tour facing me, it seemed like a good idea at the time. Candy was in Las Vegas, awaiting her final decree so she could marry Hal. Heading east in the Buick, I stopped to see my kids at the El Rancho Vegas. Candy was civil and sympathetic. We had sold the Fontenelle house (how I would miss that beautiful playroom!) and split the proceeds. Hal was doing extremely well, thanks to his TV show, and, to Candy's everlasting credit, she voluntarily returned half the divorce settlement to me. I give her full marks for that and a lot more. A good lady.

I kissed the kids good-bye in Vegas, assured them I would see them often in New York, and headed east. Happily, Paul was as fanatical about movies as I, and we stopped along the way at several theaters and drive-in movies to indulge our mutual passion for the flickers.

One of the first eastern dates I played was the good old Copa Club in Pittsburgh. Lenny Littman seemed glad to see me, and I was not especially unhappy. The divorce had been fairly painless and not particularly expensive. Candy and I had agreed to use the same attorney, a quiet little gentleman named Harry Fain. He was compassionate and understanding, and he expedited the proceedings with as little trauma as possible. I'll always be grateful to him for that, especially in view of future events in my life.

As I finished my first night at the Copa, I was called to the phone. A well-modulated, feminine voice greeted me. "Mel, we've never met and that's surprising. We know an awful lot of the same people in L.A. My name's Arlene Miles."

"Nice to talk to you, Arlene. What can I do for you?"

"Well, I'm in Pittsburgh visiting my mother. I'm going to New York day after tomorrow and I thought I'd like to come and see your show, but . . ."

"Yes?"

"Well, I'm not too happy about coming down there alone. Doesn't look good."

I paused. Was she asking me to invite her? Did I want to? I was in a strangely passive state of mind, at that time, where the opposite sex was concerned, and I hesitated a moment before answering her. Finally, I said, "Well, look, I understand how you feel. If you have no one to bring you, why not come and be my guest? I'll leave your name with the maître d', and he'll seat you when you come in."

"How kind of you. Can I say hello after the show?"

"Certainly. Just come backstage."

When Arlene Miles walked into the Copa Club that night, she was just about the best-looking girl I had ever seen, with small, high breasts and a perfect pair of legs. Every single male eye in the club did pirouettes, and she loved every minute of it. When she walked into my dressing room after the show, I couldn't decide if she more resembled Jean Simmons or a raven-haired Grace Kelly. Admittedly, I was smitten.

I took her out for a late bite and was delighted to discover she had a respectable knowledge of good poetry, literature, and music, classical, pop, and jazz. This girl's too good to be true, I thought. I was right. She explained that she was leaving for New York to see one of her two extremely rich boyfriends. Purpose of her trip: to make up her mind whom to marry, her Manhattan millionaire or his Bel-Air counterpart. As I walked her to her car, we paused for a moment under a street lamp. We kissed suddenly and then again, and that one lasted a long time.

In the morning, she asked me where I was going after Pittsburgh. I told her I had a few more dates to play in the East before heading for my first London engagement; for some unfathomable reason, one cut of a live album I had recorded ("Mountain Greenery") had caught fire in England, and I was being paged.

When I left Pittsburgh, Paul had decamped and Arlene was in the Buick wagon with me. I was surprised. She seemed to set great store on money; I had damn little at the time. The social positions of her two main beaux far exceeded mine. Life in either New York City or Bel-Air had to be far more attractive and comfortable than the nomadic existence that was my lot. Had she fallen in love with me? And I with her? I honestly don't know. I suppose we both thought we had found something we were looking for.

We traveled together for a few months, staying in hotels, making love; me performing in various eastern venues; she, by turns, bright-eyed with admiration, sulky, loving, bitchy. Arlene, I was soon to learn, was a born malcontent and an unreconstructed flirt. Sensational-looking as she was, every day we were together was trying, and more than once we vowed to break up and go our separate ways. At the eleventh hour, one or both of us would patch things up, and on we would go.

That's the way it was when we rolled into New York City in mid-July of 1956. I had to go to England; I invited her to come. She said she would meet me there. Why not come with me? She wanted to shop in Manhattan, look up some friends. I could just imagine what friends. I broke with her then, got on a plane, and flew to London (but not before seeing Steven and Melissa, who were now living in New York with Candy and Hal).

Having always been an Anglophile, you can imagine how knocked out I was to find that the English had discovered me through "Mountain Greenery." When I got there, the last week in July, the record was number two on their Top Ten list, and, within a week of my arrival, it hit number one. I had never had a genuine number-one record in the States, and I was beaming, inside and out. I immediately did the "Show Band Show," with Cyril Sta- pelton and his magnificent studio orchestra. He then wrote an article about me in one of the big Sunday newspapers. The headline read: MEL—HE WON A MILLION FANS IN ONE WEEK!"

My first British engagement was at a theater in Cardiff, Wales. My hit record stood me in good stead there, and business and the reviews were better than good. When I returned to my hotel in London, there was a message from Arlene: Please call me in Pitts- burgh. So—she had gone back to her mother's house. I delayed returning her call and went north to play the Empire Theatre in Glasgow.

I had been reading a fascinating book called *Ghosts in English Houses*. I checked into the Central Hotel in Glasgow, settled into my suite, and climbed into bed with that hair-raising volume. The only light in the bedroom was a single bulb, crowned by a green shade hanging by a long cord from the high ceiling. As I read about a particularly nasty apparition, I looked up at the light. It was swaying back and forth. Instant goose pimples! I looked around the room, dark except for the ray of light from the moving fixture throwing grotesque shadows on the walls. Slowly, the swaying stopped. I went back to my reading. In a few moments, the swaying began again. I got out of bed and checked the windows. Closed tight. No drafts of any kind in the room. I got back into bed, pulled the covers over myself, and almost reluctantly began, once again, to read about ghosts. For a good ten minutes, nothing happened. Then, slowly, the faded light fixture began to sway, this time more pronouncedly than before. I grabbed the phone and called the night manager. "Listen," I said, my teeth chattering slightly, "would you please come up here? I want to show you something."

Within minutes, there was a knock on my door. The manager was a poker-faced type, decidedly dour and Scots to the bone.

I pointed to the light. The fixture was perfectly stationary. "I want you to watch that light," I explained. He stood there, his hands clasped behind his back, watching the motionless fixture and eyeing the crazy American to his immediate right. We stood and stood. Nothing. He cleared his throat. I was about to give up the ghost (sorry) when the light began to sway again. Hard, from side to side.

"Look!" I yelled triumphantly, vindicated. "What the hell is that? I mean, why is that light swaying like that? There's not a breath of air in this room. For God's sake, what can that be?"

The man saw the title of the book on my bed, and he actually grinned. No—he smirked. "Well, sir," he said, in a fine, thick brogue, "it's easily explainable. This is a station hotel."

"What does that mean?"

"It means that underneath this structure is the main train station. Trains run through the hotel all night. And when they do, they set up a vibration that travels right up the walls and ceilings. You've no ghost in here, if that's what you're thinking—just a wee tremor from the choo-choos!"

He walked out laughing and, pretty soon, so was I, partly from relief. And, at that moment, I thought of Arlene. Whatever else I was feeling about her, I remembered her sense of humor. She

would appreciate this story, I thought. On impulse, I picked up
the phone and called her in Pittsburgh. Two days later, she joined
me in Scotland. Our first few days together were fine. The Scottish
audiences were rowdy and affectionate, and I was enjoying the
Empire. Toward the end of that week, my English agent, a dapper
little man named Harry Foster, called with some incredible news.

"Mel, my boy," he said enthusiastically, " 'Mountain Greenery'
is going such great guns that the Prince of Wales Theatre here in
London is willing to suspend their current stage production for
two weeks and put you in to top a bill of variety."

I could hardly believe it. The Prince of Wales was one of the
most prestigious theaters in Europe. The financial offer was more
than generous and, of course, I accepted at once. Arlene and I
celebrated. Suddenly, things began to go sour. Fighting broke out
between us again, and the press got wind of it. The British press
is famous for sniffing out sensational news, and the fact that Arlene
and I were unmarried and living in the same apartment made us
fair game.

The Prince of Wales fortnight went well, and, in one newspaper
interview, I let it be known that I was looking for a 1937 SS-100
Jaguar, a classic that resembled an overgrown M.G.-TC. A man
named Dennis King, who test-drove for the Jaguar Corporation,
called and offered to sell his SS-100 Jaguar to me. When he brought
it around, I was full of admiration. The car was in virtually mint
condition. His asking price was sensible, and I bought the beauty
on the spot. My British tour was nearly completed and I was
preparing to go home. I made arrangements with United States
Lines to crate the Jag and ship it to New York. Instead, they lashed
it to the deck, out in the open, and brought it to America uncrated.

When the car arrived in New York, it barely resembled the
automobile I had bought. The chrome had rusted, the paint was
streaked with sea water and peeling in places, and there were two
or three dents in the bodywork that hadn't been there when I had
handed over the car to the steamship company. I wanted to commit
murder. Instead, I left the car with old Mr. Zumbach, from whom
I had bought my early M.G.-TC. He promised to clean it up as
best he could, while I stayed in New York for a few days. When

I told him I had it in mind to drive the Jag out to the Coast, he laughed hard and long. Drive a twenty-year-old open sports car 3,000 miles? With no adequate heater? Drafty side curtains instead of proper windows? In October? *"Du bist verrückt,"* Zumbach told me. Perhaps I *was* crazy to think I could make that trip, but I was determined to try.

Arlene and I checked into the Meurice Hotel on West Fifty-ninth Street, and the more time we spent together, the more convinced I became that we were a mistake. I was going with the flow, in a sense, having adopted a wait-and-see kind of outlook where the two of us were concerned. Then something happened that tore the lid off the situation.

We went to a movie one evening and, afterward, stopped for a drink at Billy Reed's Little Club on Fifty-fifth Street. The cozy bistro was deserted at that time of night, an hour or so before the theater crowd piled in for late supper and after-show drinks. Being a nondrinking type, I nursed a mild vodka and tonic while Arlene ordered something a bit more potent. Into the bar came an acquaintance of Arlene's, one Jack Le Vien (né Levine), a producer of documentary films, I believe. Arlene turned to me, after introducing me to Le Vien, and said, "Mel, I want a few words with Jack in private. Would you mind going into the dining room and waiting for me?"

I excused myself and sat down at an empty table just past the bar area. A few words in private? What the hell for? Is this bloody dame with me or not? Blazing mad, I rose and walked into the bar. "Come on," I said to Arlene, grabbing her arm and pulling her off the stool.

"What? What are you—"

"We're leaving," I announced. I pushed the front door open and we were out into the night.

She pulled her arm away violently. "You may be leaving, buster. I'm not!" she informed me, her eyes flashing. "I'm going back inside and you can go to hell!" I could have strangled Arlene at that moment, but murder is against the law. Instead, I hailed a cab and went back to the Meurice. Arlene did not return that night.

In the morning, I packed my bags and took a plane to Toronto to play a well-known club there called the "Colonial." I realized resignedly that Arlene and I were not to be. Her volatility and her unpredictability were too unsettling; other men may have found those qualities exciting and provocative, but I found them enervating and unattractive. In spite of her great beauty, wit, and undeniable intelligence, I was glad it was finally over.

The phone calls from Arlene began during rehearsal at the Colonial. The owners weren't exactly rocket scientists, and their annoyance grew with each call. "Hey, Tormé," one of the bosses growled, "this friggin' broad's drivin' us nuts. F'chrissakes, pick up the phone and get her off our backs, will ya?"

Arlene wanted to get back together. I told her it wouldn't work. She cried. Maybe she would change if I made an honest woman of her. Maybe. . . .

You guessed it. Dummy (that's me) capitulated. I knew from the git-go that marriage between Arlene Miles and me was hardly made in heaven. But, by God, she was beautiful. And she did seem to love me in her own strange way.

I flew back to New York, picked up Arlene at the Meurice, collected my SS-100 at Zumbach's, and set out for California. We got as far as Philadelphia. By then, water and steam were gushing out of the radiator cap and the temperature-gauge needle was frozen to the top peg. I shipped the car to L.A. by truck. Arlene and I grabbed a plane to California. The date was October 29, 1956. My folks were set to pick us up at the airport. They hadn't met Arlene and weren't exactly jumping up and down over my impending marriage, so soon after the divorce from Candy. Still, they were resigned to the fact that their son was not the most sensible man in the world where women were concerned.

We landed. Everyone got off the airplane, except Arlene and Dummy.

DUMMY (to Arlene): What's wrong? Why—?

ARLENE: I can't. I just can't. I don't want to meet your parents right now.

DUMMY: But they're out there, waiting for us. What'll they think?

ARLENE: I don't care what they think. I'm not getting off this plane unless they go away.

DUMMY: But—

ARLENE: That's final!

I got off the plane, met my folks, apologized, told them Arlene was "nervous" about meeting them, and asked them to go home where I would call them after she had calmed down a bit. My mother grimaced, looked at my dad knowingly, and they left.

Arlene disembarked the empty TWA Constellation and we made for my Crescent Heights apartment, where we proceeded to have a *Guinness Book of World Records* fight. She wasn't so sure she wanted to get married, now that she was back in Los Angeles (near Bel-Air, I might add). She stormed out of my flat and, ostensibly, out of my life.

The next morning she called, assured me she had thought things over and was now certain we were made for each other. Please, Mel, let's go to Las Vegas and get married. Well, sports fans, you won't believe it but I agreed. We got to Vegas late in the afternoon on October 30, planning to get married that evening. Arlene panicked, got smashed, and passed out.

The next day was high-level-discussion day. Should we or shouldn't we? No boardroom decision at GM or AT&T was ever more thoroughly thrashed to a frazzle. Bells, sirens, and gongs were going off in my head: don't do it!

We got in a cab and shot over to the Chapel on the Strip or the Temple of Love or the Little Church of the West, I forget which. Inside, a "helper" greeted us. "Will you want music?" she asked.

I looked at Arlene. She nodded mutely. "Sure," I said. "What the hell?"

"Live or canned?"

"Come again?"

"Live organ music or recorded songs?"

"Oh, live. Live, absolutely," I said expansively.

"That'll cost thirty dollars," she warned.

"Uh, sure . . . sure. That's fine." We waited for the minister. We sat alone in the chapel. I felt that any minute one or both of us might bolt for the door and keep on going.

The minister appeared. He indicated that we take our places in front of his lectern. We complied. He cleared his throat. "Dearly beloved . . ." he began, in a mincing, lisping manner not far removed from the character espoused by the late Paul Lynde.

Getting through that ceremony without collapsing into spasms of uncontrolled hilarity was one of the toughest things I have ever had to do. Arlene shook visibly, a combination of nerves and suppressed giggles.

Then, blessedly, it was over, and the good reverend was instructing me to kiss the bride. Our teeth collided and again we did a masterful job of controlling the nearly uncontrollable.

We thanked the gentleman, turned, and walked back toward the entrance. Suddenly, as if by magic, there was organ music. *Live* organ music. "Because"? "I Love You Truly"? No way. The song being jauntily played was "I Can't Give You Anything But Love."

So help me God.

Arlene and I walked out into the cool autumn night. It was October 31. Halloween.

That should have told us something.

23.

CHAOS

I AM always surprised and amused at the strange turns our language takes. People sometimes say "After we got married, everything went downhill." Uh uh! Downhill is coasting—it's easy. "Uphill" is the struggle, the anguish, the problems. And so it was with Arlene and myself. Uphill all the way. The sexual relationship was great, and that was just about all the great there was. If we had fought before, that state of affairs only escalated after we married. And in addition to marital strife, my career was rocky as well.

While the records I was making for Bethlehem were going a long way toward freeing me from the "Velvet Fog" albatross, rock and roll had begun making deep inroads into the music scene. Middle-of-the-road artists were suffering in the process, and so were those whose bent was jazz. With the exception of the heyday of the Big Bands—that golden period between 1935 and 1945— jazz has almost always been tough stuff for the mass audience. In its simpler form, it was perceived as "happy" music, and I have always felt that Benny Goodman's initial success, beginning at the Palomar Ballroom in Los Angeles in 1935, was greatly attributable to the "danceability" of his music. After World War Two, progressive jazz tried to push its way into the public consciousness and, right away, jazz was in deep trouble.

"Bebop," as it was called, was cerebral, complex, and not suitable for dancing. Furthermore, its protagonists, perhaps in self-defense, took a hard line with listeners. With the exception of Dizzy Gillespie, there were few among the ranks of the beboppers who were willing to exhibit any kind of showmanship. Charlie Parker, Miles Davis, and many of their contemporaries were content to perform in an almost trancelike state toward the rear of the bandstand. "Back-of-the-wall cats" became a familiar catchphrase, and, while it was easy to understand the bebop musicians' frustration at being unable to communicate their brand of music to the larger audience, their apparent indifference to their listeners did little to help the overall jazz scene.

"Rock" music was simplistic by contrast, easy for the younger generation to digest, and it was being performed by the peers of the youthful. For the first time in memory, teen-agers looked to teen idols for their musical kicks. Older, better musicians were relegated to low visibility. It was tough to take, and I think that kind of rejection contributed to the downfall and, in some cases, the deaths, of some fine jazz players. I began to worry about *my* future in music. Perhaps it was time to look for other forms of employment.

One totally unrealistic alternative that occurred to me was a Walter Mittyish desire to become a commercial airline pilot. I had always loved airplanes and, with the onset of the rock era of music, I had an uncontrollable urge to hang up my singing gloves and enroll in a good aeronautical school. That urge lasted for about nine days. I was in my early thirties—too old realistically to opt for a career in aviation. Plus, my eyesight was limited and, physically, I would have had to go into training for at least a year to condition myself for the rigors of flying a large airplane. Enough Smilin' Jack fantasies. I had been a successful radio actor at one time; why not pursue that aspect of my talents?

My friendship with Edmond O'Brien was responsible for leading me back into acting. Eddie was an inveterate party-thrower. In his attractive house in Brentwood, he and his talented wife, Olga San Juan, made Saturday nights *de rigueur* for me and a wide variety of motion-picture people. On various evenings at the O'Brien home, I met Dean Jagger, Alan Ladd (a compulsive singer with a tin ear!), director Rudy Maté, and an almost endless cast of characters. Those were Eddie's two-fisted drinking days. He loved those evenings, and, in fact, they were great fun. Late in the

party, Eddie, in his cups, would get up and deliver Shakespeare
brilliantly. He was already having trouble with his eyes, and one
could sense the problem worsening with time. Just then, though,
he was riding high, and he was just about to do a 'Playhouse 90,"
that vaunted live-TV series that was the talk of television in the
mid-and late fifties.

Eddie had come to the Crescendo on the Sunset Strip to see
me perform, and now, on one of his famous Saturday nights, he
pulled me away from the din of the revelers and said, "Hey, pal,
I'm doing this thing at CBS with Rooney and Rod Serling. This
kid Frankenheimer's directing and, Jesus, there's a hell of a part
in it for you. Best part in the whole friggin' show, frankly."

I nodded absently, thinking it was the booze talking. It was
not.

On Monday, O'Brien called to say he had made an appointment
for me with Martin Manulis, the producer of the teleplay, which
was called "The Comedian." Surprised, I got over to CBS Television City and presented myself to Manulis's secretary. Presently,
Martin Manulis appeared and ushered me into his office. He was
a charming man with a warm manner, but his first words were
not encouraging.

"Mel," he said, "I promised Eddie O'Brien I'd let you read for
the part of 'Lester,' who is Rooney's brother in the play. I think
it's only fair to tell you that the part has been cast. Matter of fact,
it's a package deal. We hired a New York actor to play Lester and
his wife to play another role in the show. So . . ."

"Look," I said, "it's kind of you even to see me, and I understand
perfectly. Eddie is a great friend of mine, and I'm sure he didn't
realize—"

"Tell you what," Manulis interrupted. "Long as you're here,
why not read a scene from the show. We're doing a lot of other
plays, and perhaps we can find something for you later. Would
you mind reading for me?"

"Hell, no. I'd be happy to."

He tossed me a script and indicated page 24. He picked up a
second copy and began to read Rooney's lines. It was a highly
intense scene and it called for tears on my part. I sight-read the

scene, complete with tears. Sight-reading was my bag, dating back to my old radio days in Chicago. When we had finished reading, Marty gave me a long, hard look. He stood up. "Wait here," he said and went out of the offiice.

In a few minutes, a tall, lanky, dark-haired young man came in with Manulis. "Read it again with me, will you, Mel?" Martin asked.

We reread the scene with the same intensity and a fresh batch of tears on my part.

John Frankenheimer tapped his teeth thoughtfully with a pencil. Abruptly he rose, said, "Thanks, nice meeting you," and left. Marty Manulis thanked me politely for the reading and said I'd hear from them at some point. "Some point" was late that afternoon, when Marty called me to say they were paying off the New York actor and his wife and were prepared to offer me the part. I was bowled over. When they told me what the money would be, I called Eddie O'Brien in shock.

"Jesus, Eddie," I whined, "the money's lousy. I mean, two weeks' work for peanuts."

Eddie advised, *sotto voce,* "Pay them to let you do the part, kid."

He was absolutely right, of course. "The Comedian" turned out to be one of the greatest performing experiences of my life. Rooney and O'Brien were devastating. Kim Hunter, who played my wife, was faultless as was Connie Ford. They put me on my mettle.

During rehearsals at CBS, we came to a scene in which Rooney, as a kind of Milton Berle–Jackie Gleason composite, is berating, belittling, and humiliating his weak, dependent, parasitic younger brother, Lester. The Mick never heard of "saving some for the telecast." He is the complete actor, and every performance is imbued with the same intensity and realism. That, quite simply, is why he is great.

So, there we were, with the rest of the cast watching, as Mickey is reducing me to a squirming, sniveling mass of jelly. At that moment, I noticed out of the corner of my eye that Jack Benny had wandered into the hall and was standing near the door, his hand resting against his right cheek in that now-famous stance of his. When the electrically charged scene between the Mick and myself was over, Benny walked over to Marty Manulis and very quietly whispered in his ear, "My God, Marty! Rooney has really gone off the deep end, hasn't he? And poor Mel Tormé! I thought he was doing very well with his career. How can he sit still for that kind of abuse from Mickey?"

Martin Manulis laughed and explained that we had been doing a scene from "The Comedian." Jack Benny once again put his palm against his cheek, uttered his famous "Well!" and walked out.

"The Comedian" aired on February 14, 1957. The next evening I opened once again at the Crescendo, and the whole cast of the "Playhouse 90" drama turned out in force. It was an opening to remember. A few weeks later, Eddie threw another of his famous parties and, when I showed up, I was startled to find it was in my honor, to congratulate me on my performance in "The Comedian." Everyone was certain that Mickey, Eddie, and I would receive Emmys for our efforts. Mickey was nominated; Eddie wasn't, which was criminal, because his performance was nothing short of superb. I got a call from the Academy of Television Arts and Sciences. The man on the other end of the phone sounded embarrassed.

"Mr. Tormé," he began, "you have received enough votes to guarantee you a 'Best Supporting' nomination."

My heart leapt.

He cleared his throat. "The thing is ... we have decided this year not to have a 'Best Supporting' category. Sooo ..."

My heart sank.

"You still there?" the man asked.

"What? Oh. Yes ... yes. I'm still here."

There was a pause. "Well," he said at last, "I just thought you'd like to know that if we *had* had that category this year, you would have been one of the nominees." I thanked him and hung up.

An independent producer, Martin Lancer, called. He had seen the "Playhouse 90" and was doing a film called *The Fearmakers* at Goldwyn Studios. There was a supporting role in the movie for me. Not surprisingly, it was the same kind of weak-kneed character I had played in "The Comedian." I took the job. I needed the money.

One of the joys of being in that movie was working with Dana Andrews, who played the lead in this little mishmash about Washington and influence peddlers. I had always admired Dana's work and was delighted to find he was a friendly, gregarious guy who didn't take himself too seriously and who was professional to a fault. Those were his drinking days (he is now and has, for several years, been staunchly AA), but his fondness for the grape never interfered with his ability to perform, and he did so perfectly under the direction of Jacques Tourneur.

I went back to England for a second tour in the summer of 1957. It was not as successful as the first one had been, but things went well until one night at the Palace Theatre in Manchester. Just before my opening performance, I felt faint and the world began to spin. I collapsed and was carried into my dressing room.

The British press (no, that's not fair, a *certain segment* of the British press, famous for outrageous journalistic practices) reported that I had suffered a heart attack and had been unable to go on.

In America, the three major networks interrupted their scheduled programs and reported my "heart attack" as a "special bulletin." My mother saw one of those "bulletins" and nearly had a heart attack of her own.

I was furious. I had contracted, as had so many others, the Asian flu. The very next day, I had gone on the Palace stage, and performed as if nothing had happened.

When I got back to the States, my insurance broker called me.

"Er—Mel, what was all that 'heart attack' stuff about?"

I explained what had happened.

"Well, I'm afraid you're going to have to undergo a physical."

"What? Why?"

"Simple. All that stuff about a heart attack on TV and in the papers has caused your life insurance to be canceled. The insurer wants you examined before reinstating your policy."

There was nothing I could do but submit to an examination by an insurance doctor.

"Come on, come on, doc," I said, angry and impatient. "This is ridiculous. Let's get this over with."

After doing an EKG on me, he ushered me into his office.

"Mr. Tormé," he said, looking me straight in the eye. "I can understand why the insurance company wants to cancel your policy."

"W-what?" I exlaimed.

"Well, here it is, in black and white. There *is* an irregularity in your heartbeat."

I felt sick. "Oh, my God."

I then consulted a specialist, Dr. George Griffin, one of the leading heart specialists in the country. He put me through a far more rigorous examination than had the insurance doctor. The verdict?

"Your heart's as sound as a dollar—well, not today's dollar. Let's say a 1926 dollar, when a dollar was a dollar. Thing is, your sternum is slightly pressed against it. Nothing to worry about, but that's what caused the irregularity in the EKG."

I got my life insurance policy restored, but that was one incident that really shook me.

≡

At Red Clyde's insistence, I had participated in a huge Bethlehem project, a jazz-oriented version of Gershwin's *Porgy and Bess*. Other artists involved in the undertaking were Duke Ellington's orchestra, George Kirby, Sally Blair, Johnny Hartman, and Frances Faye, singing Bess to my Porgy. I hated the record. *Porgy and Bess* is very special to me, and I felt we belittled it with our polyglot styles and approaches. It became a cult favorite, however, so maybe I'm out of line.

I was under new personal management, Gabbe, Lutz, Heller and Loeb, with Bill Loeb as my special representative. Since I had, earlier on in my career, enjoyed a reputation as a "hard nose," I was bending over backward to be pliable and cooperative. It wasn't easy. I was still being booked into some places that were nothing short of odious. Still, my position in the business was not exactly at a high point, so I accepted dates I would have ordinarily turned my back on.

Arlene and I bought a house on Rising Glen Road in a new development above the Sunset Strip. I moved in with misgivings. In addition to my lagging work, how could I inhabit a permanent dwelling with my tempestuous wife?

Somehow, we stayed together. The fights, in concert with my career problems, made for an extremely unhappy existence. In April 1959, Arlene gave birth to a son, Tracy. He was a great-looking little skeeter and, for a while, a kind of ersatz calm prevailed on Rising Glen. Soon, though, Arlene seemed to grow more and more discontented. In truth, she should never have been married to me. She loved the good life—I mean the really good life, the kind you buy with lots of money. I simply did not rank financially with her former boyfriends.

The fighting started again and seemed to last right up to the end of the marriage, which was still four years in the future. The anomaly of a woman that beautiful being that difficult was hard to handle. I also have to take some of the blame. Things were not going well, and I was subject to some pretty radical mood swings. At those times, I would slink off to a little shack I had erected, and proceed to build model airplanes all day. There were days when, from sunup to sundown, I would spray, glue, and assemble airplane kits. It was good, necessary therapy. It also kept me away from Arlene and vice versa. I missed Steven and Melissa, living 3,000 miles away from me. Happily, I spent as much time as I could with Tracy and, on those occasions, there was peace between me and my wife.

Once again, I was booked into the Crescendo. Prior to that engagement, Gene Norman asked me if I would object to having Lenny Bruce on the bill. I adored Lenny, who was certainly one of the most brilliant comedic talents of the century. He had a reputation for being an *enfant terrible,* but had never shown that side of himself to me. I was thrilled to share the stage with him and told Gene Norman to sign him that day.

Lenny had done time for a drug bust. He had, if memory serves, gone through a plate-glass window at Schwab's Drug Store on Sunset Boulevard. He was being hounded by the police for his uncensored language in night clubs. Life, at that moment in time, was not exactly a ball for Lenny Bruce.

He played the Crescendo with me, sporting a bandage across the bridge of his nose, a souvenir of the Schwab's accident. Impishly, he spewed expletives right, left, and center. The Crescendo audiences loved every minute of it. He was "off the wall," breaking ground for a whole new generation of comics and for a totally fresh, censor-free approach to comedy itself.

At one point, he sought me out and shook my hand. "I have only two real friends—you and Buddy Rich," he said.

"Len, you're crazy. You have friends by the ton. Don't sell yourself short."

"Yeah, but what you did for me, you know, here at the Crescendo—"

"Hey, get one thing straight: I didn't do a damn thing for you—I did it for me. And for everyone in this town who wanted to see and hear you. Believe me, Lenny, you're helping business in the club. I'm not exactly at my hottest right now; I need all the help I can get. And you're it. Period."

In the ensuing months, before his death, Lenny called me many times and always alluded to that Crescendo date as having been one of the happiest of his career. You can imagine how that makes me feel.

During that engagement, I also experienced something bizarre and frightening. One rainy night, Arlene accompanied me down the hill to the club. As I walked into the foyer, an attractive young girl in a raincoat rose from a chair, smiled at me, and crooked a beckoning finger in my direction. Since I was on the verge of being late, I smiled back at her and asked Arlene to handle whatever the young lady wanted to see me about.

Ten minutes later, Arlene came down to the dressing room, her face ashen. "What's wrong?" I asked.

Shakily, she told me that the girl in the raincoat had gone into the ladies' room. When the attendant had politely asked her if she had come to see and hear Mel Tormé, the girl had replied, "No, I've come to kill him!" She then told the ladies' room attendant that she had heard me criticize Elvis Presley's singing during a radio interview. She showed the attendant a long, thin knife she was carrying in her coat pocket and informed her she planned to stab me with it at the first opportunity. The attendant slipped away and called the police, and the girl was taken away in handcuffs. Mark Chapman and John Hinckley are nothing new in the world of crazies whose adoration of entertainment figures can assume deadly intent. To be obsessed with anyone to such an extent seems sick in the extreme; singers and actors are flesh and blood, like everyone else.

Since the incident involving "the girl in the raincoat," I have stopped voicing my opinions with regard to other performers' talents and capabilities. I have come to believe that it is not for me to say who is "good" and who is not. What, really, is "good" music? I guess I would have to say that, for me personally, classical music tops the list. Jazz would certainly come next, and, while the list of "pop" music composers range from Kern to Stevie Wonder, the popular music scene is a little like Chinese food—you're hungry an hour later, no matter how good it tastes at the time. Still, a great deal of what is written in the pop, C&W, rock, and soul veins is delectable and satisying. Remember, however, that the foregoing is simply my opinion.

I am always in mind of the Noel Coward line from *Private Lives* that goes, "Amazing how potent cheap music can be!" As a singer, I'm grateful to the likes of Gershwin, Mercer, Arlen, Berlin, Kern, Janis Ian, Donald Fagen, Stevie Wonder, and Paul Williams for supplying me with material with which to earn a living.

Music, like they say, soothes the savage breast. In addition to singing it and playing it, I was—and am—an inveterate listener. More than once, music calmed me, moved me, saved my sanity, during my chaotic years with Arlene.

24.

PLATEAU

*L*IFE got weirder. Arlene came on a road trip with me. We were driving in the middle of Kansas when we began to quarrel. She insisted I stop the car. She got out in the middle of nowhere.

"I'll find an airport," she blithely informed me. "Good-bye."

I drove off. For a half-mile. I drove back. She was walking along the deserted highway. I coaxed her back into the car. It took ten minutes of concentrated threats and entreaties to accomplish this.

I had reached a kind of plateau, status-wise and money-wise. Happy-wise, things were lousy. Confidence-wise, I was beginning to be a basket case. Work-wise, the jobs were coming in drips and drabs. Wise-wise, I decided I wasn't being very wise. I took low-paying parts in a couple of Albert Zugsmith bleeders at MGM. *The Big Operator* was a loose remake of a Metro picture called *Joe Smith, American*. Mickey Rooney and Steve Cochran were the stars of this little "B" effort, with Mamie Van Doren supplying the curves. It wasn't very good and I wasn't very good.

Surprisingly, I was instantly cast in another Zugsmith gem called *Girls' Town* with the curvaceous Mamie once again, Paul Anka, and a cast that included Charlie Chaplin, Jr. First scene, first day of shooting features a gang rumble. Chaplin and I are fighting. He is supposed to "slug" me and knock me down. We rehearse. Chuck Haas, the director, calls for a take: "Action!" Chaplin slugs me. Right in the mouth. I feel my front teeth bend. Charlie says, "Sorry." The son of the Little Tramp. You'd have thought he would have learned how to fake a punch.

This landmark film was followed by yet another Zugsmith beaut at Universal, tantalizingly entitled *The Private Lives of Adam and Eve.* Mamie again, playing you-know-who to Martin Milner's Adam. Mickey Rooney played the devil, and I was a lingerie salesman. I avoided seeing the picture.

Then I got a call from James Clavell. I had met him when he was engaged by Martin Lancer, producer of *The Fearmakers,* to write a screenplay based on a book Lancer and I had optioned. It was called *Night Light,* and there was a great part in it for me. It was written by Douglass Wallop, who later gained fame by writing *The Year the Yankees Lost the Pennant,* which ultimately became *Damn Yankees.*

Clavell's knowledge and preoccupation with Orientals had once again manifested itself, this time in the form of an original screenplay called *Walk Like a Dragon.* It had to do with the Chinese experience in the Old West. Jimmy had sold it to Paramount and was going to try his hand at directing for the first time. There was a part in the picture he wanted me to play, the role of a psalm-singing, self-righteous character called "The Deacon," a man as conversant with gunslinging as he was with the church.

I accepted the part and it was an enjoyable experience on the whole, except for working with Jack Lord, the star of the piece. Lord tried "lording it over" everyone in the cast, giving all of us line readings, direction, and advice on how to act. That superb Mexican actor, Rodolfo Acosta, was ready to paste him one on several occasions, and I especially admired Clavell's temperance in the face of Lord's constant interference.

Jimmy told me he had wanted me for the Deacon role for several reasons. He had seen me in "The Comedian" on "Playhouse 90" and liked my work as an actor. He also knew I was very familiar with old Colt single-action army revolvers, the familiar six-shooter carried and used by cowboys since they were introduced in 1873.

There are scenes in the film in which I teach novice gunfighter James Shigeta to shoot. They involved some fairly deft gun handling, and I sensibly placed myself in the talented hands of Rod Redwing, revolver-expert extraordinaire. The routines he taught

me looked damn good on film; as a matter of fact, they were the
flashiest parts of the movie. It is my understanding that Jack Lord
had them cut to the bone. Guess I didn't take his acting lessons
as seriously as I should have.

I began bugging my manager, Bill Loeb, to book me out of
town. Anywhere, as long as it was away from the turmoil of the
daily fights with Arlene. At the same time, I was consumed with
guilt over leaving Tracy for long periods of time. I felt he needed
me while he was young, but the heated battles between his mother
and me were getting out of control. Strangely enough, I doggedly
clung to the idea that somehow, miraculously, the marriage could
be saved. That was foolish in the extreme, and, subconsciously, I
knew I was kidding myself. Yet, since I had not had the pleasure
of watching my two children by Candy grow through childhood
to adolescence, I was stubbornly determined to keep the marriage
to Arlene intact as long as I could.

I took to the road in a variety of cars: a 190 SL Mercedes
followed by a 300 SL followed by a new Corvette convertible I
had earned by writing all the station-promo songs and lyrics for
WCAU in Philadelphia. The "road" also included another trip to
Australia, this time to perform in concerts with Ella Fitzgerald,
as well as a solo engagement at a Melbourne nightclub called "the
Embers," owned by a man named Jim Noalls.

A word about Ella: just as Duke Ellington has always been my
idol as a composer/arranger/instrumentalist, so has Ella Fitzgerald
been my paramount influence as a singer in the jazz genre. Anyone
who attempts to sing extemporaneously—that is, scat—will tell
you that the hardest aspect of that kind of singing is to stay in
tune. You are wandering all over the scales, the notes coming out
of your mouth a millisecond after you think of them.

A horn player or a pianist presses the valves or the keys or
slides the slide and what he puts into his instrument usually comes
out very well in tune, since, with a piano, for instance, the notes
themselves are pretuned. A singer has to work doubly hard to emit
those random notes in scat singing with perfect intonation. Well,
I should say, all singers except Ella. Her notes float out in perfect
pitch, effortless and, most important of all, swinging. Her years

out in front of the great Chick Webb band of the thirties and forties infused her with the ability to sing rhythm tunes exhilaratingly and ballads in that sweet, curiously little-girl-like voice that was, and still is, simply irresistible. Talk about one of a kind.

Bethlehem Records had folded in the late 1950s and I had signed in 1958 with Verve, which was owned by Norman Granz. Ella herself was the prime artist on the Verve label. I had hopes of our recording something together, somewhere down the line.

Jim Noalls was a strange man. He met me at Sydney Airport in a lavender Oldsmobile convertible. I discovered that he was the black-sheep member of a wealthy coal-mining family Down Under. He dressed like a gangster and, in his gaudily furnished home, huge pictures of Bogart, Cagney, and Edward G. Robinson adorned the walls. Norman Granz, accompanied us on this tour since he was also Ella's manager. It was a conflict of interest all the way, and by the time the tour was over, I realized that Norman was not one of nature's noblemen.

When I returned to the States, I parted company with Verve Records. Almost immediately, I got a wire from Nesuhi and Ahmed Ertegun: "Would love to have you with us on the Atlantic Records label." I was overjoyed. I had read about the Ertegun brothers for years in *Down Beat* and *Metronome*. They were the sons of the former Turkish envoy to the United States and were famed as the owners of the biggest jazz record collection in the world. They were constantly reported as having attended virtually every jazz concert/jazz club/jazz event in the eastern United States and were generally acknowledged as being the number-one jazz fans of the day. I had never met the Erteguns, but their enthusiasm for the kind of music I was singing was good enough for me. I quickly signed with Atlantic through their West Coast representative. When I called Nesuhi to tell him how delighted I was to become a part of the Atlantic family, he was utterly charming, not to mention flattering. "After all, Mel," he said over the long-distance line, "there's you and Ella, right?"   .

Wrong. There were and are a lot of superb singers performing in the same category as Ella and myself. I did not, however, feel it was in my best interest to contradict the owner of the record company I was about to join. I thanked him profusely and hung up.

I went to New York to meet the Erteguns prior to playing one of my favorite places in America, the Red Hill Inn in Pennsauken, New Jersey, right across the river from Philadelphia. A large sign on the roof of the club proclaimed _Jazz in Jersey,_ and the owners, a warm, wonderful Italian family, were hosts to some of the greatest names in jazz. I was honored to be one of their roster of artists.

Nesuhi Ertegun was a slightly rotund, jolly little man with a pixie smile and a hearty handshake. Ahmed was bearded, saturnine, less outgoing but certainly affable. I was eager to proceed with my first Atlantic LP; I hardly noticed the posters on the office walls featuring Atlantic artists such as Led Zeppelin and sundry other rock and soul performers.

Nesuhi handed me a lead sheet. "Look this over, Mel," he insisted. "Herbie Mann just cut this for us as an instrumental. It's great! You could do a terrific vocal on this one. We would like to do a 'single' with you before we try an LP."

The song was "Comin' Home Baby." It was a minor-key blues tune with trite repetitious lyrics and an "answer" pattern, to be sung by the Cookies, a girl trio that had once worked for Ray Charles.

Can this be happening? I thought. I mean, come on. The Ertegun brothers? World's greatest jazz fans? What have I gotten myself into?

The rationale, of course, was that Herbie Mann, a jazz flautist of some repute, had recorded the tune. Why not a vocal by Mel Tormé? I pondered the problem. Record companies weren't exactly breaking down my door to sign me. Here, at least, was a large independent, interested in releasing a "Tormé" product. I looked in the mirror. Be flexible, Melvin, I warned myself. This is one single. _One._ Period. These guys didn't sign you to record garbage. They think there's you and Ella, remember?

I recorded "Comin' Home Baby." With pressure from Atlantic and who knows what form of perks and blandishments from the Erteguns, the record made the _Billboard_ charts. It was number nineteen for two or three weeks and then, bye-bye "Baby."

I was not surprised in the least. Why would kids spend their money to buy a Mel Tormé single when their own teen-age peers abounded on vinyl in the record stores? The Erteguns had tried their experiment with me and had made a little noise with it. Many DJs around the country had branded me a "sell-out" and chastised me for making a piece of junk like "Comin' Home Baby." It hurt.

Let's go on from here, I urged the Erteguns. Let's make some good records, ones we can all be proud of. Please. Nesuhi smiled his cheruby smile and informed me he was coming out to California soon and we would set my first Atlantic LP at that time. I breathed a sigh of relief.

I returned to Los Angeles only to discover that Arlene had gone out and bought a mink coat for herself. My finances at that time were shaky, but that was not the issue. When I bought a car or even an old Colt six-shooter for my collection, I would always consult my wife. It's called married life. Consequently, I was furious with Arlene, because of the sneaky way she had acquired that coat while I was back east. In the end, I paid for the mink and let her keep it for what I laughingly called an "early" birthday present. It was one more nail in the coffin of our marriage.

≡

One day, on her best behavior, Arlene told me she had been house hunting for us and had found a commodious, modern home in Beverly Hills on Shadow Hill Way, off Coldwater Canyon Drive. The asking price was not exorbitant, and, compulsive collector that I am, we were literally bursting out of the smallish Rising Glen residence. I liked the Shadow Hill property and, after a soul-searching session with my business manager, decided to buy it.

We moved in, Arlene, Tracy, and Arlene's thirteen-year-old daughter from a former marriage, Tami. Life will get better, Mel, I counseled myself. This house will make a difference, you'll see. Arlene will be happy here.

I looked upon what was happening in my professional life not as a "career" but as a series of jobs. I had no idea where I was going—I was simply happy to be making ends meet. And there was always the chance that my first LP for Atlantic might take off. I awaited Nesuhi's arrival in Los Angeles.

He finally appeared, as promised. He came to our new house, complimented us on the furnishings and decor, and produced, from an attaché case, a large stack of music and demo records. "Mel." He grinned. "I'm excited. So is Ahmed. We've found some great songs for you. This could be the best record you've ever made. Am I happy it's going to be on Atlantic!"

For the next hour or so, Nesuhi Ertegun, his eyes rolling, his chubby hips jiggling, proceeded to infest my Mackintosh-powered stereo player with the worst putrefaction I have ever had to endure. Each song sounded as if it had been written by someone suffering from arrested development. Not even *good* rock and roll. Arlene, who did have excellent musical taste, kept looking at me, shaking her head in disgust. Nesuhi was oblivious to our exchange, he was so caught up in the music, snapping his fingers, tapping his toes, shaking his body to the three-chord obscenities passing for songs. His eyes closed, a broad grin splitting his face, he would occasionally flutter his lids and look in my direction for approval. I smiled weakly. He was a guest in my house, after all.

When the nightmare was over, when the last record and the last lead sheet were placed on the coffee table, there was an embarrassing silence.

Sensing my concern, Nesuhi counseled me. "Mel," he advised sternly, "this is where it's at today. This is the real music, the only music. You gotta progress. There are some real hits in this group of tunes I played for you. Let me leave them with you. Go over them, absorb them. I'm going back to New York tonight. I'll call you in a few days and then we can pick and choose. Believe me, once you give these songs a chance, you're gonna love 'em."

He got into his rental car and pulled out of the driveway, waving a jolly good-bye. I stood there in shock. I went back into the house, closed the door, and sat down heavily in the den.

Arlene said, "I thought you told me these guys were great jazz lovers, good music fans."

"Yeah, well, so much for that," I replied. I gathered up the music and records and tapes he had left and filed them under *W*—

wastepaper. Then I went into the bedroom and located a few old *Down Beat* magazines I had found in a used book shop, with stories about the Erteguns and their love of jazz. I threw them in the trash can.

From that moment on, every record I made for Atlantic was a tooth-puller, even though I eventually got to record most of what I wanted. Even when Peter Nero chose me to sing his title song for the MGM movie *Sunday in New York* (1963), I had to plead, beg, and shout before the Erteguns and their minion, Jerry Wexler, would allow me to make a "New York" album by the same title. It became one of my most well-received efforts, and, as recently as 1984, it was rereleased by Atlantic and reviewed enthusiastically by *People* magazine.

It saddens me to say that some of the vilest people I have ever met are those who run and control the record industry. They hold the original patents on "creative bookkeeping" and if you think the foregoing is sour grapes, I wish you could be privy to the dozens of horror stories I have heard from musicians, singers, arrangers, and songwriters about the downright scurrilous activities of record executives.

Big and small, conglomerate or independent, they are all the same, with a few rare exceptions, like Carl Jefferson, owner of Concord Jazz Records. Someday, you are going to see many of the people in the music industry exposed and convicted and, believe me, it will be a scandal of the proportion of Watergate.

In 1962, I began riding motorcycles. Honda had "civilized" the normally noisy two-wheelers, and the open-air bug hit me hard. When I went to play the Carillon Hotel in Florida for two months (a happy respite from Arlene, a sad time away from Tracy), I borrowed a Honda down there and tooled around the causeway. I was a very unhappy man at the time and I am sure, subconsciously, that I was hosting a death wish. Keenan Wynn kept warning me that riding a cycle on the street was dangerous, crash helmet or no, and advised me to limit my activities to dirt roads. I didn't listen and, sometime later, I would regret not taking his advice.

I had done well at the Carillon in Miami Beach. They bought me again the following year, for an eight-week stint. This time, when I had been home, Arlene and I had had a shouting match that had brought police to our door on a complaint from our nearest neighbors. My mother and father had long since become disaffected with my wife and no longer came to our house. To say my domestic situation was impossible would be a miracle of understatement.

I sat in the Florida sun day after day, trying to figure a solution to my seemingly insoluble problems. I realized that being away almost constantly wasn't really helping things, merely delaying the inevitable. I felt cowardly in running away from Beverly Hills but rationalized my absences with the sure and certain knowledge that I was, after all, working, earning money, paying the mortgage, the food bills, and providing for my family.

One day the phone rang in my cabana. I picked it up and found myself talking to George Schlatter. He was about to go into production at CBS. Judy Garland had agreed to do a weekly show on Sunday nights starting in September of that year, 1963. He wanted me to write all the special musical material, to help Judy put medleys together, and to be a frequent performing guest on the show. He assured me we were going to "knock 'Bonanza' out of the box." My God! Judy was going to buck the behemoth known as "Bonanza"?

At first I turned Schlatter down flat. He persisted, calling me several times in Florida. Preproduction would start in mid-May. We would be shooting the first shows in late June and on into the summer. "Great opportunity, Mel. Judy wants you. You can stay home, off the road for a change, and put your writing as well as performing talents to work. Whaddaya say, Bunky?"

Suddenly, the solution to my problems seemed crystal clear. A new beginning, uninterrupted by my normally itinerant life-style. Might work. Might just save the marriage. I accepted George's offer.

Not the smartest move I ever made.

25.

BREAKUP

I HELPED write the Judy Garland show from May 1963 until late February 1964. It was a trying, tiring, frustrating, occasionally rewarding experience. The assignment was a mixed blessing, with the "down side" of the mix dominant. I had been as much a fan of Judy's as anyone in the world. But I knew she could create problems: tardiness, apathy toward coperformers as well as the creative staff, and I had heard she had become far too fond of Blue Nun Liebfraumilch as well as certain prescription drugs that affected her performances in general and her enunciation of lyrics in particular.

Much of what I had heard—and feared—was true. But God! It was fascinating working with her. During the eight and one-half months we worked together, my overriding feelings for the lady ranged from impatience and compassion, to disgust, admiration, and honest-to-God love.

I was always amazed over how she mentally rated guests on the show. If she liked and/or respected a given artist, or conversely, if she felt threatened by a performer's immense talent (the Barbra Streisand guest shot comes to mind), she would pull out all the stops and meet any challenge—real or imagined—head on. She invariably won the day, took the prize, beat the odds, raised her banner victoriously.

She also "walked through" several shows in which she felt the guest talent was inferior, uninspiring, unchallenging. She was pleasantly surprised a few times during the tenure of the series.

Case in point.

I had worked with a young Canadian named Rich Little a few times in Toronto. I thought he was, unequivocally, the finest impressionist I had ever encountered. I told Judy about him and suggested we use him on the show. She grinned evilly at me and said: "I hate impressionists. They make me f————." She purposely used the vulgarism for breaking wind that I find the most detestable word in the English language.

John Aylesworth and Frank Peppiatt, the head writers on the show at that time, as well as being Rich's fellow Canadians, joined me in trying to pressure Judy into relenting and giving Rich the exposure on American TV that he deserved. We finally wore her down.

"All right! All right, for God's sake!" she cried. "Book him. But no rehearsing with me, understand? Write a spot for him and I'll just introduce him."

"At dress rehearsal, right?" asked John Aylesworth.

"Hell, no," Judy corrected him. "On the air!"

"Jesus!" Peppiatt muttered under his breath.

We put together a "spot" in which Rich would do various impressions to the tune and lyrics of "The Man That Got Away." Sure enough, Judy was absent from dress rehearsal. Then it was "showtime." She came out on the stage in front of our 300-plus audience and, for the first time, read the TelePrompTer introduction:

"Here's a young man from Canada who is one of the finest impressionists to come along in years. [_How would she know?_] We're very happy tonight [_well, Peppiatt and Aylesworth and Tormé were, anyway_] to present, for the first time on television [_U.S. television, that is. He had made dozens of appearances on the top Canadian shows_], the very talented—Rich Little!"

Rich walked onto the stage and got his first glimpse of Judy Garland. She smiled graciously. He grinned. The band played the introduction. Rich launched into his impressions of Gregory Peck, Orson Welles, Jimmy Stewart. Judy's mouth dropped to half-mast in astonishment. Rich continued on with several more uncanny impersonations. He saved the best for last, however, beginning with the line: "The road gets rougher/ It's lonelier and tougher ..."

The voice, the manner, the indelible impression was James Mason, who had been Judy's costar in *A Star Is Born*, the film in which she had sung this song. I looked over at her. Her mouth was wide open in delight and astonishment. Afterward, she grudgingly admitted that John, Frank, and I were right: Rich Little was absolutely unique, the finest impressionist in the world. I gritted my teeth, unable to resist one minuscule barb.

"So tell me, Jude, did he make you f———?"

She raised her hand in a mock gesture of hostility, then slowly brought it down, with great gentleness, on my head.

≡

Christmas of 1963 almost turned into a disaster where the show was concerned. Late, late the night before our first major runthrough, I finally got caught "with Judy Garland on the Dawn Patrol" (the subtitle of my book about working with Garland).

She woke me out of a sound sleep and entreated me to come and get her at her house on Rockingham Drive in Brentwood. Since virtually every other colleague of mine had seen service on the Dawn Patrol, I figured my long-overdue number had come up.

I fetched a sleepless Judy and brought her back to my house where Arlene helped her bathe and get into bed. After Judy had fallen asleep, Arlene told me she had seen strange, lashlike marks on the lady's back. I shrugged that information off and rode my motorcycle over to CBS-TV City.

After informing producer Bill Colleran of the night's adventure, I tried reaching Glenn Ford, with whom Judy was having a romance. I called his home number, got his mother on the phone, and gave her my address in the hope that, should she locate him, he might go to my house, collect Judy, and bring her to rehearsal.

Hours later, the phone rang in my office. It was an agitated Arlene. Glenn had been to the house. He had been extremely excitable, according to my wife. "He acted like we had been keeping Judy prisoner and he had come to rescue her!"

Strange guy, Glenn Ford.

I survived the firings and hirings of a spate of producers, directors, choreographers, and writers. Three shows from the end, the manure hit the propellor. Thousands of dollars had been squandered in the process of what we had come to call "waiting for Judy." Her tardiness, her demands for changes—sometimes at the very hour of taping—had put the show into one hell of a financial hole. Judy and her production company decided to do the final three programs of the twenty-six as "concerts": no dancers, choir, or expensive sets. Just Judy—doing what she did brilliantly—entertaining an audience single-o.

There was nothing for me to do on those shows, so her company aced me out of the contract that still had three shows to run (as a writer), as well as four unrealized guest shots as a performer. It was understandable dirty pool and, while I was sympathetic to Judy's financial plight, I was also disturbed over the thousands of dollars out of which I was being bilked.

I sued, then abruptly dropped the suit. I wasn't being a "good guy"; I realized the money would probably be uncollectable, or at least, that it would be several years down the road before I saw any of it. I had taken the job to try to save my faltering marriage. That hadn't worked and the marriage, like a horse that had been poleaxed, fell down dead in the street.

All in all, I would not have missed the Judy Garland experience for the world, and when it was finally, irrevocably over and she had sung her last song, laughed her last laugh, bestowed her last kiss, and gone on, perhaps to greater heights than she had ever wished for or imagined, I came to realize there might be one hell of a book in the telling of her "last chance of many last chances," the 1963–64 Judy Garland television show.

I had switched managers again. Joe Shribman, of the famous New England family of band managers/backers, had taken over the reins of my career. In March 1964, having run the gamut with Arlene, I asked Joe to begin booking me back in clubs, hotels, and concert halls. I had occupied an office at CBS for almost nine months working on the Garland show. I wanted to get out, to breathe again.

One night, shortly after the Garland show was terminated, I was singing at the Hollywood Bowl. Arlene's masseuse called me backstage to tell me what I already knew: Arlene was running around with several men, one of whom was her hairdresser, a guy she had characterized to me as a "flaming faggot" but who, I later found out, was one of the prime studs in town, servicing not only my errant wife, but several other hapless cuckolds. The masseuse went on to say her reason for divulging this information was that Tracy had been almost completely given over to our household help, and, while they were both fine young Mexican girls, they were not Tracy's mother.

It was one hell of an anvil to drop on my head at that moment. I was about to go out in front of several thousand people and perform a medley of movie music I had only just learned. Singing that night was one of the toughest things I've ever had to do, but somehow I pulled it off. I moved out the next day and informed Arlene I was going to divorce her and seek custody of Tracy.

On the advice of my attorney, Dan Sklar, I hired private investigators to secure evidence with which to bulwark my case. The California divorce courts had not yet been legislated into the lunacy of "no-fault" divorce. If there was merit to a husband's case, if fault could be proved on the part of his wife, then a man had a chance of enjoying fair play and justice.

In June of that year, I flew to New York on the way to Denmark and an engagement at the Tivoli Gardens there. I stayed at the Wyndham on Fifty-eighth Street, where I had stayed many times before with Arlene.

The phone rang in my suite. I picked it up. It was Arlene. She was there, in the hotel. She wanted to see me, talk to me. I didn't think that was a good idea. She pressed the issue. Could she come up? I asked her what room she was in and told her I would call her back in a few minutes. The moment I hung up I called Dan Sklar on the Coast.

"Sweet Jesus," he exclaimed, "I was just about to call you!"

"No kidding? Why, Dan?"

"To warn you. Your wife is in your hotel, with a private detective. Her lawyer has advised her to get you in the sack."

"What? Are you kidding?"

"No, friend, I am not kidding. The idea is to get you to sleep with her. The detective comes in and finds you together. It's called 'condonation.' "

"What does that mean?"

"It means, Melvin, that by copulating with your wife, you acknowledge her infidelities and condone them. In other words, you forgive her. Your case and your custody plea go right out the window."

"Christ! What the hell do I do?"

"Get your ass out of that hotel pronto and, if you can, make for Denmark on the first available plane."

I took his advice. Arlene was furious. She found out where I was staying in Copenhagen, a small, quiet hotel called "The Park." She began bombarding me with calls, alternately sweet as sugar and haranguing. She threatened, then begged me to let her come and join me in Denmark. No way, José. I'd had enough.

When I left Denmark, I flew to England to do a few concert and theater dates. I ran into Stu Whitman at the Dorchester. He was in England making _Those Magnificent Men in Their Flying Machines_. On a free day, I went out to the aerodrome where they were shooting. I had become a private pilot the previous April and was all wrapped up in flying. The sight of the replica vintage airplanes they had built for the film gladdened my heart. Having been a founding father of the aforementioned Cross And Cockade Society, old airplanes (preferably ones with two wings), were my special cup of tea.

Later in the week, I made contact with an old friend, Cliff Robertson, who was in Britain making _633 Squadron_. He was also a student pilot and, on a lovely July Fourth evening, we drove out to Fair Oaks Aerodrome in Surrey, where a pair of RAF types as well as twin Tiger Moths were waiting for us. It was the first time I had ever flown in a helmet-and-goggles biplane. All those pleasures from my childhood came rushing up and patted me in the face: Smilin' Jack, Barney Baxter, G-8 and his Battle Aces; I was now one with them, tailchasing Cliff's Moth in the clear evening skies of England.

After we landed on the broad green field that was Fair Oaks, the RAF pilot who had been instructing Cliff gave him a nod and

Robertson beamed. He was about to solo in the Moth. He handed me his movie camera and asked me to take pictures of the blessed event. He took off into the waning sunlight, did a perfect circuit and landed the Moth in a "wheeler" landing: light forward pressure on the stick, no flare-out, front wheels touching down, then the tail skid falling gently into the grass and dragging the plane to a halt. It was beautiful.

The weeks in England had been pleasant. I hated to return to the States and the turmoil I knew awaited me there in the divorce courts. I didn't even want to look at my transatlantic phone bills to the folks and Tracy. I had to go home, no doubt about it. In the six weeks I had been abroad, I knew Tracy, who was now five, had changed, grown, and I longed to see him.

We had a loving reunion and I managed to avoid accepting any more engagements until the preliminary custody/support hearing at the end of August.

Arlene had been foolishly indiscreet, and when we went before Judge Alton Pffaf in the matter of temporary child custody, he listened to the facts carefully and granted custody to me. No one whooped or hollered or cheered a victory cheer. It was a no-win situation and, although I had at least gained the temporary right to take care of my little boy, the fight to keep him permanently was still to come. If I knew Arlene, it would be no-holds-barred.

I had an engagement to fulfill in Hawaii. I took my mother and Tracy along. It was a melancholy trip. I don't really think my son missed his mother that much; she had not been spending that much time with him at home. But, for the first time, I was in charge of Tracy, his welfare, his upbringing, his safety. Thank God for my mom, who took charge admirably. We had a long talk about Tracy's future. There was nothing in the way of a steady job looming in L.A. My greatest earning capacity was tied in with being on the road, and the money wasn't all that terrific. What if I *was* lucky enough to get permanent custody? How would I be able to raise my little boy?

When we returned to the mainland, I rented a small, cheery house on Club View Drive, just opposite the Los Angeles Country Club. It was a far cry from Shadow Hill Way, but it was comfortable and attractive. My parents moved in with me and together we gave the boy our attention. He seemed to thrive.

I had made a "trade-off" agreement with the Piper Aircraft Corporation. In return for an original song I had written and recorded for them that was to be used as a radio commercial, they let me have an airplane. Just after my birthday in September, my flight instructor, Duane Allen, and I picked up my new 235 Piper Cherokee and flew it from Niagara Falls, New York, to Santa Monica, California, with stops overnight in Peoria, Illinois; Lincoln, Nebraska; and Needles, California. For a budding pilot, it was great experience. At one point, we flew right through a towering cumulus cloud. "I want you to see how it feels," Duane explained. "Put it on autopilot. That thing'll fly this bird better than you or I ever will."

We bounced around inside that formation for four minutes, and it was frightening but enlightening. I made a night landing at Needles Airport, an uncontrolled field (no tower) with a huge mountain to your right as you make your downwind leg. Again, hairy stuff but valuable, if you intend to stay alive flying airplanes.

I met a woman named Cynthia Conroy—a real Irish beauty— and we began dating. Once again, I was booked into my old standby, the Crescendo. One night, Nat Cole came in to see me. He looked terrible. I was greatly distressed, unaware of his terminal lung-cancer illness. He was his usual gentlemanly, loving self, and I feel I sang well that evening because of his presence as well as Cynthia's.

The only thing that marred the evening was a table of outright hillbillies, who came close to wrecking the show with their needling, heckling, and insults. Several times, the maître d' cautioned them to be quiet, but to no avail. It was impossible to ignore them and, finally, foolishly, I gave in to my rising temper and threw some one-liners back at them.

After the show, Cynthia and Nat came down to the dressing room looking worried. "My God, Mel," Cynthia said, "I heard those ignoramuses talking just now. They're planning to wait for you and cut you up."

Nat echoed her concern. "Yeah, I don't like the look of it, Melvin. The creeps look mean. Let's call the cops."

Brave, dumb Melvin waved aside their advice. I picked up an empty bottle. So did Nat. "Let's go up and have a look." By the time we climbed the stairs and entered the showroom, it was deserted. We walked out into the night, Nat and I, empty bottles at the ready. The Strip was all but deserted, very little traffic.

Nat smiled at me. "This remind you of something?" he asked.

I smiled back. "Sure does."

We were remembering a similar incident that had taken place in Chicago, years earlier. I had been playing the Oriental Theatre. Nat, his wife Marie, Candy, and I had gone between shows to a fine little steak house nearby. As we ordered from the menu, a trio of rednecks parked themselves at the bar and proceeded to give us dirty looks and make offensive remarks about "nigger-loving white trash."

Nat and I had taken all we could from these walking pigs. We got up, over the protests of our wives, and walked over to the bar. I was too angry to think about how it would all turn out. The truth is, Nat would probably have held his own; I, in the tradition of feisty little guys whose assertions of bravado constantly get them into trouble, would have probably wound up in the hospital. It never came to that. Like the cavalry in a John Ford western, in walked Big John.

Now, Big John was *big*. An ex-fighter/bouncer, he worked for Nat in a majordomo capacity. One look at him and Joe Louis would have thought twice about tangling with him. He walked right up to the bar and said softly, "Some kind of problem here?"

"No, no problem, John," Nat answered him. "Just getting acquainted with these fine gentlemen."

"I see," said John, seeing.

We ate our dinners in peace.

Now, years later, at one-thirty in the morning in front of the Crescendo, we stood with empty bottles in our hands, looking around carefully. When we were satisfied the country types had departed, we said our good night and went our separate ways. I went back to Cynthia's place. She lived in a nicely furnished little cottage in back of her mother's main house off Melrose. As she pulled the drapes, I sat down on the couch, drank a Pepsi, and talked about the evening. She sat opposite me in an overstuffed chair and looked frightened. I tried to calm her down.

"Relax, Cynthy," I began. "Jerks like that love to shoot their mouths off. Hell, here they are in Hollywood, and they're gonna show us city folk they ain't impressed."

"I know," she replied. "But, God, Mel, if you could have heard them talk! One of them said, 'I'm gonna get that little bastard and kick his guts in.' Another one said, 'Yeah, let's take him apart.' Honest to God, they were serious. Be careful when you go home. Keep looking in the rear mirror. Please."

I grinned. "It's nice to have a beautiful girl care about you. You know, it's been a while since—"

The bay window behind the drawn curtain in back of me exploded in a roar of shattered glass. I dove to the floor and yelled to Cynthia to get down. We lay there, trembling, waiting for the next shotgun blast, because that is exactly what I thought it was. I was bleeding from several tiny cuts made by flying glass.

I crawled across the glass-strewn floor, picked up the phone, and called the sheriff's office. After waiting five or ten minutes for another onslaught (which never came), we cautiously opened the curtain. A huge, jagged hole disfigured the large window. I reached under the couch and retrieved a heavy object. Then I realized what had happened. Someone had come into the yard between Cynthia's cottage and the main house, taken a piece of clothing off the wash line in the yard, wrapped it around a brick, and thrown it through Cynthia's window. The sound of that window bursting was identical to a shotgun blast.

Deputy sheriffs arrived. It was after two in the morning. We told them about the incident at the Crescendo, and they took a lot of notes. After they had gone, I apologized to Cynthia. I was sure it had not been the rednecks; my best guess was Arlene. I was positive she was having me tailed with an eye toward having some ammunition in court, once the final divorce hearing began.

Cynthia seemed strangely distracted, like she wasn't listening.

"Cynthy," I assured her, "we were careful when we came here

tonight. I'm sure we weren't followed. At least not by those hicks. But possibly professionals are doing the job—you know, private investigators. Arlene has undoubtedly found out we're seeing each other. She's obviously discovered where you live. Hell, it could have even been her new boyfriend who did this."

Arlene's "new" boyfriend, supplanting the hairdresser, had been recruited right across the street from the Shadow Hill house. The nineteen-year-old son of one of our neighbors, he had dated Arlene's daughter Tami a few times. Now the mother took up where the daughter had left off, and this kid, whom I'll call Stan, had moved into my house and my bed.

Cynthia still wasn't listening. She seemed nervous and preoccupied. From information I later became privy to, it appears the Broken Window Incident was not attributable to either Arlene or the hillbilly hecklers, but to an infuriated boyfriend of Cynthia Conroy's.

I went flying during the early morning hours, getting to know my new airplane. I spent most of my nights with Tracy and the folks, watching TV or running movies or simply talking with the family and a few friends. I stayed mainly close to home, where I spent a quiet New Year's Eve.

It was 1965. I knew what lay ahead of me was not going to be pleasant—an extended court fight, the battle for my son, the expenditure of thousands of dollars for lawyers and court costs. I thought of Candy. That divorce had been civilized, even friendly. This one would be alley-fighting with no quarter. I forced myself to think about the immediate future, an upcoming two-week stand in early February at a private club in London called "The Cool Elephant." I loved England and the English. It would do me good to be there.

It would also change my life.

26.

JAN

THE Cool Elephant was a chic private club owned by the proprietors of the famed White Elephant Restaurant in Mayfair. A charming man named Leslie Linder ran the "Cool," and we instantly became friends. I was to be backed by a ten-piece band headed by saxophonist/arranger John Dankworth. His wife, an as-yet-undiscovered Cleo Laine, did the vocals with the band between shows. Opening night went extremely well and the resulting reviews were excellent. The club membership began showing up in droves. I was not surprised to learn they were mainly people connected with the entertainment business. Within a few nights of my opening, familiar movie names from English films began to appear.

I was determined to park my apprehension over the coming divorce in the farthest garage of my mind while I was in Great Britain. I became very social, thanks to an embarrassment of invitations. One Sunday afternoon was spent in the flat of Edmund Purdom. (Remember? He played the lead in *The Egyptian* for Twentieth Century-Fox.) Sean Connery and his then-wife, Diane Cilento, were also present, and it became a nice, relaxed day of food, jokes, talk, and opera, Purdom being a genuine authority on the latter.

I guested on a Dudley Moore–Peter Cook special, and was also preparing a BBC special of my own, which was to take place on the Friday prior to my Saturday closing at the Elephant. As I entered the club Thursday night, Leslie Linder greeted me with a twinkle in his eye.

"Well, dear boy, tonight's the night."

"Really? Why, Leslie?"

"Because right around that corner," he indicated the first booth past the entrance to the showroom, "sits Princess Margaret and her entourage. Plus, my friend, more film and show people than we have ever seen in this place."

He was right. It was one of those banner evenings performers dream about. Dudley Moore got up and played piano for me. Peter Sellers and his wife, Britt Eklund, were in attendance, as well as at least a dozen other English luminaries. One young woman I noticed turned my head a full 180 degrees. At the end of my performance, I quickly asked Leslie who she was.

"That's Janette Scott," he said. "One of our best-known film actresses."

Of course. I had seen many of her movies. Most were small films, although I recalled her in *The Devil's Disciple* with Kirk Douglas and Burt Lancaster. She was a genuine English beauty, and I told Leslie I wanted to meet her.

"Two problems, dear boy," cautioned Linder. "One, the princess has requested your presence at her table; you do understand that is tantamount to a royal command. Two, Miss Scott is with her live-in boyfriend, David Frost. They have been together for some time now, and I doubt if there is a remote chance of your even taking her to lunch, if that's what you have in mind."

I was disappointed but undaunted. I was shown to the royal booth and introduced to Princess Margaret, who bade me to sit. She was a totally delightful young woman who asked some interesting questions about life on the road, the quality of musicians in varying countries, and my opinion of the specialized audiences I found at the Cool Elephant. I was honored to be at her table, but I must confess my eyes kept darting along the wall, back to the booth where Janette Scott sat. I think the princess sensed my restlessness.

"If you would like to say hello to some other people, please feel free to do so."

"That's very understanding of you, ma'am." I smiled.

I rose, bowed, thanked her again, and made for Janette Scott. She was sitting with a friend, whose name, as I recall, was Diana.

Their escorts were nowhere in sight, table hopping presumably. Janette seemed especially happy to see me. I introduced myself. She laughed. "Oh, yes, we know who you are." We sat and chatted for several minutes. She was complimented when I told her that I had enjoyed her work since her appearance as Jimmy Stewart's twelve-year-old daughter in *No Highway in the Sky*, and she returned the compliment by informing me she had been a longtime fan of mine. I have always disdained predatory males and have tried all my life to avoid ever being categorized as one. Yet, I knew if I didn't at least explore the possibility of seeing her again, something important would slip away from me.

I took a deep breath and asked her to lunch at the BBC the next afternoon. I would have liked it to have been somewhere a bit more special, but I was trapped, rehearsing, and taping my special on Friday.

She took a pen and pad out of her purse and wrote down her phone number. "Call me, around noon, if that's convenient."

"It's convenient, it's convenient," I laughingly assured her.

Next day, I watched the clock. At noon, I asked for a ten-minute break from rehearsal and called her. Lunch, she informed me, was impossible, but perhaps—the line went dead. I looked at the phone in disbelief. What had happened? I quickly redialed her number. Busy signal. I called the operator, asked for verification. After a minute or so, the operator came back on the line. "I'm sorry, sir," she said, "that line is not in service."

"You're kidding. You mean—it's out of order?"

"I'm afraid so, sir. It might be off the receiver."

I was devastated. Why not just say no, thank you, I can't see you? For God's sake, why play games?

I rehearsed somewhat disconsolately for the next fifteen minutes. A BBC guard came up to me. "Phone call for you, Mr. Tormé."

It was Jan. "My phone fell off the bed and just came apart," she explained, laughing. "It's taken me fifteen minutes to put the damn thing together again."

Relief flooded through me. At least she wasn't a phony. She had called back.

"Mel, I've been out of the country, filming, for the last ten weeks, I only just returned yesterday afternoon, and, to be honest, David and I almost went somewhere else last night. The Cool Elephant was a last-minute decision. Of course," she added quickly, "we both wanted very much to see and hear you."

I waited, wondering where this was going.

"You, uh, you're there at the BBC rehearsing, aren't you, for your special tonight?"

"Yes, that's right."

"Yes, well, it's a bit sticky. You see, David does his show from there tonight. Almost at the same time as yours. And David and I, well, I'm sure you know—"

"You live together. Frankly, I know I'm out of line trying to see you, to perhaps take you to dinner—something. I'm going through a bad divorce, Jan. American guys have done to me what I feel I'm trying to do to David; who seems like a fine, bright fellow. Look, I'm sorry. Maybe—"

She cut me off. "Why don't I drop in tonight, to your dressing room at the BBC, and at least say hello. Would that be all right?"

My heart sank. I had so much wanted to get to know this girl. On the other hand, I knew what I was doing was wrong. She had a boyfriend. Where did I fit in? Nowhere.

I told her I would be delighted to see her again and would look forward to her visit that evening. I hung up and put her out of my mind. Or tried to. Ships that pass and all that jazz.

That evening, true to her word, she showed up in my dressing room before the taping, looking even better than she had on the previous evening. I wondered out loud whether she might be interested in coming back to the Elephant with me that evening and then literally bit my tongue. Tormé! She saw you last night. She's heard you sing. And there *is* David. What the hell are you doing? She was noncommittal but promised at least to say good-bye before she left—with David.

I taped the special, accompanied by a large orchestra under the baton of the inestimable arranger/conductor Wally Stott, with whom I had recorded on earlier visits to England. When I returned to my dressing room after the taping, Jan was there, waiting for me. "Where shall we have dinner?" she asked brightly.

We had dinner and talked. She came to the club and we talked some more. Later, she came with me back to the London Hilton where I was staying. We went upstairs to the International Club and had tea and sandwiches. And talked. We told each other our life stories. In depth. We found we liked the same kind of movies, music, books, and humor. At five in the morning, she looked at her watch. "Oh, my God," she said, "I'm flying to Cartagena, Colombia, tonight as a guest of the film festival there."

I stood up. She didn't. I sat down.

I had by now deduced that her relationship with David Frost had been long-standing, well-publicized, yet tenuous. I was certain she had no permanent plans where he was concerned. I took a deep breath.

"Listen, Jan," I said, not quite believing what I was about to say, "I know this sounds absolutely crazy, but—I'd like to marry you. I mean, I'd like you to marry me."

She looked at me for a moment, took a card and a pen out of her purse, and said matter-of-factly, "Right. Now, where and when do I come to you?"

We kissed. The decision was made to tidy up her affairs in England, once she returned from South America, and to come to California within two months. This can't be happening, I thought. She knows I won't be free to marry for a year. Yet, here is this English rose, willing to come and be with me in America, virtually forsaking her career in films. At that time, she was being seen on the movie screens of the world in a Paramount sci-fi flick called *Crack in the World*, opposite my old friend Dana Andrews. Jan was never a star of the magnitude of, say, Julie Andrews. Nor was she famous internationally in the manner of Julie Christie, Susannah York, or Samantha Eggar. She was, nonetheless, extremely well-known and respected in her home country, and she was, if not in heavy demand, being offered work.

"I was to go to Africa to make a film called *The Sands of the Kalahari*. I shall come to California instead." She said it with an air of finality.

We parted with great reluctance. I promised to call her in Cartagena the following week; I would be in New York, finishing up a record.

I returned to my suite, delirious with happiness. It was Saturday, almost six in the morning. Final night at the Elephant. Better get some sleep. If I could sleep. I settled in. Twenty minutes later, the phone rang. It was Jan.

"Darling," she said (Darling!), "I've forgotten my house key. No matter how hard I knock, I can't seem to wake David. Please, could you get me a room at the Hilton?"

"Jan, you already have a room here. Hurry back as quick as you can."

At two in the afternoon, she arose, kissed me good-bye again, and went back to her house in Chelsea to pack for Cartagena. Three hours later, there was a knock on my door. Dopily, I answered it. It was Jan, holding a large envelope in her hand. "If we're going to get married, you should know a bit more about me." In the envelope were stories, pictures, and a bio, dating back to the time when she was England's most famous child film star. I was half-asleep. I thanked her, kissed her, and fell back into bed.

Two days later, I was in New York in a recording studio, finishing an album for Columbia. I had had it up to here with the Erteguns and Atlantic and had signed with that company just before the new year. I had entered the ranks of Columbia artists halfheartedly. I could not believe Columbia record distributors, salesmen, publicity and promotion people were going to get very excited about having me on the label with the likes of Andy Williams and Tony Bennett to promote. In January of '65, just before going to England, I had gotten a call at the house from my manager, Joe Shribman.

"Melvin," his deep bass voice boomed, "Columbia is having a convention in Vegas at the Sahara. They want you to attend. It's next Saturday."

"Aw, Joseph, Joseph, I don't know. I'm going to England soon. I really don't want to leave Tracy, even for a night. Besides, I honestly don't feel I'm up to a big brawl like that. Not right now."

"In actuality, Mel," said Joe, using one of his favorite phrases, "I think it would do you good. Hell, take Tracy with you. Why not?"

In the end, I went. I took Tracy along, but it couldn't have been much fun for him, because it was mainly business. I was given a nice suite in the tower at the Sands, since the Sahara was overflowing. I agreed to meet some of the individual distributors, but I asked to be excused from the larger social functions. Joe, however, insisted that I attend the huge dinner being held that night for the entire Columbia family in the Convention Center of the Sahara. I felt lousy, with a cold coming on, and, again, I simply did not want to leave Tracy alone. Joe told me Columbia had arranged a baby-sitter with impeccable qualifications. Tracy himself finally tipped the scales, urging me to go and "have a good time, Dad. I'll be fine." I went, with misgivings.

The enormous Convention Center was jammed and noisy. Joe had arranged to have me sit with Bob Horton and his wife at a table way off to the side and back. That suited me just fine. Bob Horton was a charming, bright guy. In addition to being a good actor, he was a sometime-singer on Columbia as well as a first-rate pilot, having flown his own twin-engine airplane into Vegas. Joe had told him about my problems, and he did a wonderful job of diverting me by talking aviator talk. Being with Bob and his lovely wife that night was therapeutic. And the best was yet to come.

After Tony Bennett and Andy Williams had each sung a few tunes, Goddard Lieberson, high mucky-muck of Columbia Records, addressed the crowd. He read a list of names of Columbia artists in attendance. Each, in turn, stood up for a bow. Each was greeted with enthusiastic applause and whistles. I literally ducked my head. "I hope to God he doesn't introduce me, Bob." Horton smiled at me. When his turn came, he stood and waved to the friendly, hand-clapping throng. Lieberson looked at his list, then looked again, closer, as though he couldn't believe his eyes, as though there was a name on the list that didn't belong there—a misprint, a mistake.

"Oh," he said, offhandedly, "and, uh, a new addition to our artists' roster . . . um, Mel Tormé."

I stood up. So did the audience. Every single one of them. They began to cheer. Lieberson was flabbergasted. So was I. Dazedly, I waved my hand, smiled, and sat down. The crowd refused to stop. The cheering, whistling, and clapping increased. Now Lieberson looked angry. Horton nudged me, beaming. I stood again, slowly. The roar from the crowd was deafening. I was in shock. Lieberson actually had to hold up both his hands to quiet the audience. Gracelessly, he did not comment on the unexpected standing ovation. Others did. I got deluged at the table. People were slapping my back, shaking hands, congratulating me on joining the company and expressing good wishes and confidence that I was going to do great things at Columbia.

Shribman came over and put his hand on my shoulder. "What did I tell you, Melvin? Aren't you glad we came?" I nodded happily. When I got back to the Sands, Tracy was still awake, watching television with the sitter. When she had gone, I sat up with Trace a while longer and told him what had happened. I could see he was happy and proud of me.

Next morning, I went to a breakfast attended by some key Columbia distributors. After the overwhelming reception I had received on the previous evening, I was eager to make friends, to ingratiate myself with some of the people who could make or break me with the company.

I had hardly begun to drink my orange juice, when a good ol' boy from Texas walked over and threw an arm the size of a python around me. "Hah you this mornin'?" he inquired.

"Well, sir." I smiled. "I feel like I was born on Wednesday lookin' both ways for Sunday!"

"Hey, podner, I like that. That's a good un." He offered me his huge hand. "I'm Lester Levy [not his real name]. I'm from Houston and we are all mighty glad you're with the label."

"Believe me, so am I."

"Well, I should hope so! 'Specially after last night. How 'bout that welcome you got? Biggest goddamn hand of the evening."

"It sure was . . . exciting."

He leaned toward me. "Caused one hell of a fuss, too. Hear about it?"

"No. What happened?"

"Well, sir, ol' Ray Conniff's wife got her nose clear outta joint. She raised hell after with Goddard and anyone else she could collar."

"I don't understand. Why—"

"Aw, she was ticked off because the gang carried on the way they did over you and barely clapped when Ray was introduced. 'My husband sells millions of records for this company, and they give Mel Tormé a standin' goddamn ovation?' Man, you shoulda heard her."

"Well, in a way she's right. Conniff is a huge seller for this company. I can understand why she—"

"Oh, sure, sure. Ol' Ray's terrific. But hell, you deserved what you got last night. Lemme tell you somethin', Mel Tormé—you are long overdue."

"I am?"

"Hell, yes," he said, sitting down with me and assuming a more confidential tone. "Now, lookee. I been a fan of yours since way back. You've always had the ability to be a big record seller. But— if you don't mind my sayin' so—it's the product you been puttin' out all these years that's been the problem."

I nodded, waiting for advice. He patted my knee in a friendly gesture. "Know what I want to see happen?"

"No, Lester. Tell me."

"I want to see you start turnin' out the kind of records that Andy Williams makes."

I loved Andy's singing, always had. And I certainly envied his string of hits. "Well," I said, "you can't start a fight with me that way. Andy is one fine singer. Wouldn't have minded having first crack at some of his hits, if the chips had fallen that way."

"No, no, no, you don't get what I mean. It ain't the tunes I'm talkin' about. It's the kind of records you been makin'. See, I want to look forward to a Mel Tormé platter that don't get in the way, know what I mean? The kind you can play at, like, a cocktail party and it don't interfere with the laughin' or the talkin' and what-all. Get my meanin'?"

I got his "meanin'" full bore.

Now, here I was, a few months later, in a studio in New York, engaged in yet another exercise in musical futility, making an album for Columbia, the first of a few forgettable discs. At least now there was a bright side: my new love, Jan.

I called her in Cartagena.

"Darling!" she cried. "I don't really see the sense in my going all the way back to England. I'm halfway to you now, here in South America. Why don't I just come ahead to Los Angeles?"

One week later, accompanied by little more than a trunk full of ball gowns and a couple of bikinis, Jan got off the plane at Los Angeles Airport.

27.

CUSTODY

*J*ANETTE SCOTT was manna from heaven. She had given up *The Sands of the Kalahari* to come and be with me in America. She refused to let me pay her fare from South America to California. She found a small apartment in Westwood, moved in, and resisted all my attempts to pay her rent. She also ignored the combined efforts of her English agent ("My God! Are you giving up your career?"); her parents ("What have you become? A camp follower?"); and her erstwhile live-in boyfriend, David Frost ("When are you going to come to your senses and come back where you belong?") to induce her to return to Britain.

My parents were confused as well. They thought Jan charming and beautiful, but they couldn't figure out how I could have become so seriously involved with a potential new wife when I was facing a struggle in the courts with my current wife. Jan was understanding and, very quickly, she, my parents, and Tracy were doing a lot of smiling at each other.

I had several dates to play on the road. Jan insisted on coming with me. I wouldn't have had it any other way. The thought of her sitting alone in that little apartment on Wilshire Boulevard curdled me. It occurred to me that driving to these midwestern dates might be a nice idea. Jan had been to New York before but had not really seen anything of the United States outside of the Big Town. Now began a game of "musical cars" with Arlene.

I had earned, as full payment for some radio promos I had written for KSFO in San Francisco, a nicely kept, used Rolls. It had once been part of Red Skelton's fleet of cars, having been driven almost exclusively by Georgia Skelton, Red's wife. The idea of being a Rolls owner excited me and, when I had found the Skelton Silver Cloud II was available, I had made my deal with KSFO.

Now, having returned from England and New York, I discovered my car was missing. Arlene had sequestered it somewhere, and it looked as though I wouldn't see it again until we went to court for the divorce. I was ready to rent a car for the trip east with Jan when I got lucky. Arlene had exercised her weekend visitation with Tracy and had asked me to pick him up at a restaurant in Westwood, where she was having dinner with some guy. He turned out to be Manny Skar, a small-time "wise guy" from Chicago.

I entered the restaurant, checked out her dinner companion, came within an inch of giving her a tongue lashing for exposing my kid (all right, *our* kid) to such crummy company, thought better of it, took Tracy in tow, and made my way to the parking lot. Sitting there, looking beautiful, was my beloved Rolls. The parking attendant, who recognized me, came up and asked me for my ticket.

"Uh . . . I'm taking my son here out to a movie tonight, with some of, uh, his little friends . . ."

Tracy looked up at me quizzically. I squeezed his hand for silence. ". . . and so Mrs. Tormé will use my car [a Corvette] and I'll be taking the Rolls."

Without a word, the attendant handed me the keys to the Rolls and Tracy and I drove away. A petty victory, but, thanks, I needed that.

The strain of depositions began to gnaw at my insides, and I was grateful when the day to set out for Indianapolis and the first of my eastern dates arrived. I said a teary good-bye to Tracy, promising to call him daily and knowing he was in the best hands possible—my parents'. They worshiped him, and he seemed happy and adjusted to the notion that he would be raised jointly by his grandparents and me, should I be awarded final custody.

It was May, a beautiful time of year to be driving, and our trip was near idyllic. In the evenings, we stayed at the most attractive and comfortable places available. In the daytime, the weather was glorious, giving Jan a picture-postcard look at the Grand Canyon, the Rockies, broadening into the spring-dappled plains of Kansas, Oklahoma, and Missouri. We stopped where and when we wanted.

Jan seemed content to be on the road with me. I sang at the Governor's Ball in Indianapolis, just prior to the Indy 500. We sat among the privileged in the executive tower and watched the race with the owner of the track, Tony Hulman. From there, we went on to Detroit and a nightclub date at a charming little place called the "Act IV." We went to the movies, crossed over into Canada, did some sight-seeing . . . in general, life was better than okay. Why not? We were in love.

Jan had been married once before. Her ex-husband, Jackie Rae, was, coincidentally, an old friend of mine. A talented Canadian performer, he had also been one of Canada's leading Battle-of-Britain aces, flying a Spitfire and downing several German aircraft during that historic altercation. He had taken Jan up many times and had taught her some of the rudiments of flying. She seemed to have no fear at all of private planes, and she proved it during one particularly harrowing flying experience in my Piper 235.

After we returned from our eastern-midwestern tour in the car, I contracted to play two very lucrative one-nighters. An extremely wealthy Texan from Corpus Christi called my manager to say that his daughter's choice for the "entertainment" at her private high-school graduation party was me. I grinned when I heard that. "She must be living in a time warp," I cracked. "I thought my bobby-sox idol days were over long ago."

My manager laughed and said, "Listen, her father's got money he hasn't even seen yet. If he wants to buy you for his daughter's graduation party, who are we to argue?" He was absolutely right. The second date was a concert at Utah State University in Logan, Utah. I was trying to compile flying hours, and the triangulation aspect of the trip, Los Angeles to Corpus to Logan to Los Angeles, appealed to me almost as much as the money.

Jan readily agreed to come along. To backstop me, in case we ran into instrument weather, I hired a professional pilot named Jimmy London. He was overqualified and I felt secure in his company. The flight to Corpus was uneventful, made in clear weather and smooth air. Jan sat in the back seat of the Piper, reading, napping, and doing a little crocheting, relaxed and unperturbed. I did all the flying and London seemed to approve of the way I had been trained.

The Corpus Christi date turned out to be a sweet event. The young lady's father had spared no expense, and the evening turned into a festive, gala happening. From somewhere, a superb band had been culled, and, exhilarated by my work at the controls of the 235 that afternoon, not to mention Jan's company, I gave one of the best performances of my life.

The next day, however, was something else.

We headed for Albuquerque, planning to stay overnight and continue into Logan the next day. The weather got funny on us. Several layers of altocumulus blocked our way and we had to go skidding around them. That's no fun. My Cherokee was equipped with twin Omnis and an ADF (automatic direction finder), but no DME (distance measuring equipment) or transponder.

The latter instrument is vital if you are going to fly around in cloud conditions. Once you crank in a digital setting, determined by the closest air traffic control station, the transponder "squawks" your position to ATC in the form of a radar "blip." Once they "have" you on their screen, they can route you safely through weather and away from any threatening traffic in the sky. The very next addition I was going to make to my 235 was one of these mandatory accessories, but, at the moment, we were transponderless, and dodging around the towering cloud buildups was chancy and unnerving.

We made it safely into Albuquerque, tired and a little jumpy. After a good night's sleep, and a look at the clear sky the next morning, we were in much better spirits. That condition was to be short-lived. We headed for Logan and all went well until we neared the little college town. My navigation had been near impeccable (Well, actually, how brilliant do you have to be with a pair of Narco Omnis doing the work for you?), but suddenly Logan wasn't where it was supposed to be.

What is going on? I thought. Everything checks. We should be over Logan Airport right now. It's nowhere in sight! Now the thermals began kicking us all over the sky.

"False echo," said the laconic Jimmy London. "Signal's bouncing off the goddamn mountains. Don't know where the hell we are."

"Uh, Mel," came a voice from the rear seat, "please get us down as soon as possible. I have to—I need a rest room."

"Okay, honey. Take it easy. I'll do my best."

Jimmy's seat belt had been loose. Now we hit an unstable pocket of air and he was jolted half out of his seat, his head slamming against the airplane ceiling. Half-stunned, he sat back in his seat and groped for the seat belt–tightening strap.

"Oh, great," I muttered, starting to become slightly concerned. I looked at the fuel gauges. Gas wasn't critical at the moment, but I knew it could become a problem shortly. Jimmy was shaking his head, rubbing his neck. I looked out of the left-hand window. Mountains, rivers—but no Logan. Then, by sheer luck, there it was. I brought the Cherokee in for a bumpy landing and did a somewhat shaky show that night at the college.

Next morning we headed home. Over an appropriately named area called "Devil's Rocks," I lost my generator. That meant we were flying on the battery alone, with no radio or navigational aids functioning.

"We gotta go into Vegas and get it fixed," Jimmy yelled over the engine noise. I nodded okay and we pulled out our Jepp charts and trusted the airplane's compass. We found Sin City and, at McCarran Field, I had to fly directly over the runway so the tower would understand we were radioless. They gave me a green light-gun signal, indicating it was all right to land, and I did a 180, setting up my downwind leg. I looked down for the wind sock near the runway. It was stiff and straight.

On final, I was faced with a thirty-five-knot crosswind and had to "crab" the airplane onto runway one-niner. Hairy. After I landed, we found that a wire from the generator costing no more

than a couple of pennies had broken. It was quickly repaired
and we were once again ready to go. I had to take off using extreme right aileron and left rudder, hauling the 235 into the air
sideways.

At 800 feet the right door popped open. "Wonderful!" I growled,
as London examined the door latch. It was defective. He shrugged.

"I'll hold the door. You'll have to 'slow fly' this sucker."

"All the way to L.A.?"

" 'Fraid so. You'll have to order a new latch. They'll never have
one back there." He jerked his head backward to indicate a rapidly
disappearing Las Vegas.

Hot, tired, and discouraged, we slumped in our seats as I flew
back to Los Angeles at eighty-five miles an hour. At one point,
we could see cars passing us on the highway below.

≡

In a week or so, my divorce court date came up on the docket. I
was as ready as I would ever be. What I was not ready for was
the judge. His name was William Munnell. My understanding was
that he had been, until recently, a traffic-court judge and had
presided over few, if any, divorce proceedings. Compounding the
problem was my aforementioned attorney, Dan Sklar. He was one
of the finest entertainment lawyers in the business. I liked him
enormously and had chosen him to represent me purely on an
emotional basis.

It was a mistake. Even a layperson like myself could see that
Dan was in over his head. He knocked his brains out for me, but
what we had brought into court in the way of evidence was not
impressing Judge Munnell, particularly the way Dan was pre-
senting the case.

Munnell, at the outset, had said, "Well, you're going to have
to show me a great deal and prove a great deal before I'm going
to take custody away from the mother."

"Your Honor," Dan answered patiently, "Mr. Tormé has had
custody for over one year now. You would be taking custody away
from *him*, not her."

The judge shook his head stubbornly. "I don't care. The child's

place is with his mother, and unless . . ." This went on and on, to
my consternation, and growing anger.

In Sklar's office, later that afternoon, I warned, "You're too
tame in court, Dan. Forgive me, but this judge is making noises
like the trial is a formality, like he's going to automatically give
Tracy to Arlene."

"Problem is," Dan replied, "Munnell is an apple-pie, solid-
citizen individual who won't or can't accept the intricacies of our
evidence. In plain language, Mel, this case is above and beyond
him. He simply doesn't believe our witnesses or our evidence."

"Dan," I pleaded, "we need help."

"Help" arrived in the form of a New York lawyer named
Howard Redlich. Looking and talking like somebody out of a
Warner Bros. gangster movie, he breezed his no-nonsense way into
Sklar's office and took over. He told us he had been married to a
crazy lady who had brought his seven-year-old daughter, Heidi,
out west and settled in southern California. He followed, studied
California family law for a full six months, then went to court and
secured sole custody of his little girl. I liked that. A lawyer who
specialized in our kind of case and who had personally experienced
the same trauma I was now suffering.

We sat in that office interminably, indoctrinating Howard. As
I previously mentioned, California had not yet been so stupid as
to inaugurate a "no-fault" divorce law, so cookie-cutter justice was
not our main concern. Our problem was Munnell. How in hell
were we going to convince him that Tracy would be far better off
in my custody?

We resumed in court. Redlich was introduced as cocounsel. He
took the ball and ran with it. Against Munnell's obduracy, it was
like bucking the Forty-Niners' defensive line. I was really worried.
Howard said to relax.

The turning point came a few days later, in one of those totally
unpredictable moments that have to be a combination of timing,
luck, and God's will. I was on the witness stand, recalling the night
I had picked Tracy up at the restaurant in which Arlene was
having dinner with Manny Skar. I pointed out that Skar was a
hoodlum, certainly not fit company for my little boy, and that

Arlene showed poor judgment in exposing Tracy to him. I assured the court that I would never have socialized with a type like Skar and would certainly not place my kid in his company.

Objections spilled out of the mouths of Arlene's lawyers. "Your Honor, this is ludicrous! Manny Skar has never, at any time, been identified as a hoodlum. He has no known criminal associates, and this attempt to blacken his reputation, and Mrs. Tormé's, is rep-rehensible. Mr. Skar is a Chicago businessman. He was visiting Los Angeles for a few days and invited Mrs. Tormé and her son for a quiet dinner. We ask that any evidence with regard to Mrs. Tormé and her friendship with Mr. Skar be stricken as being prejudicial and irrelevant."

Munnell was about to rule, when my Uncle Art stood up. He had come to L.A. in an advisory capacity, concerned for me and Tracy and the eventual outcome of my case. Ever since he had lost his only child, Ira, in a tragic car accident, he had taken a particular interest in my kids. Now here he was, standing, ready to toss an evidentiary hand grenade.

"Your Honor," he said, "I am the plaintiff's uncle and a member of the Chicago bar. I beg the court's indulgence for a moment." He handed a newspaper to Howard Redlich, who glanced at it with widening eyes. Redlich shoved it in front of Dan Sklar, whose face also registered astonishment. "If it please the court," my uncle continued, "may my nephew's attorneys offer into evidence a copy of this morning's *Chicago Tribune*, with specific reference to the headline on the front page?"

Munnell beckoned Dan, who placed the paper in the judge's hands. For the first time, Judge William Munnell expressed emotion. He actually looked shocked.

The headline read: MANNY SKAR SLAIN MOB-STYLE.

The story went on to explain that Skar had been caught in an underground garage and pumped full of holes by persons un-known. Most importantly, the article went on to list Skar's noto-rious past and his known association with Chicago underworld figures.

Arlene's lawyers were visibly stunned. So was I. We had been waiting for a decent break, and here it was, gilt-edged. From that moment, I felt the judge turn around. He ordered psychiatric evaluations of both myself and Arlene, nodded affirmatively when we presented our evidence, and finally confirmed total and permanent custody of Tracy to me, with visitation to Arlene.

I was in a state of quiet euphoria. It had been a long and difficult trial. It had been draining, financially and emotionally. I went home, told the folks and Tracy the good news, picked Jan up, and brought her back to the little house on Club View Drive, where we all had a comfortable dinner together.

Now I would have to wait for a final decree from the court before I could marry Jan. We faced a year in limbo. We figured I would be free sometime around the middle of May 1966. In the meantime, Jan moved into the back bedroom of my house, and we played it very straight-laced for Tracy's and my parents' sake, as well as for the simple sake of propriety.

In those days, prior to VCRs, we ran a lot of movies at the house. Tracy and my folks loved that. They had grown fond of that little house and preferred staying in at night watching old films that I projected on a white-washed wall to going out to movie theaters. Jan and I selected many wonderful old classic pictures that we hadn't seen for years, movies we thought Tracy would enjoy seeing for the first time. Those were good evenings.

Jan bought me a chess set for my fortieth birthday and taught me how to play. She was very good; I was fair, but it was fun learning.

Tracy still loved going to the kiddie park at Beverly Boulevard and La Cienega. Saturdays, he rode the little Shetland ponies and the merry-go-round and even talked me into braving the big Ferris wheel. Funny, I was a pilot who loved to fly, but I did not like the Ferris wheel. Trace loved it.

The three of us loved to get into the car and head for Will Rogers Park near Pacific Palisades and the ocean. We would picnic and admire the animals and occasionally watch the polo players.

I had been awarded the house on Shadow Hill Way, but after what had transpired there, I did not ever want to occupy it again. Neither did Jan. I sold the house and bought the Club View home as a temporary stopgap. Tracy was in first grade, Jan and I hit the road, and, once again, life began to drift back to normal.

Six months after I obtained my divorce, Howard Redlich was killed in an automobile accident on his way to Palm Springs. He was taking his daughter, Heidi, for a weekend in the sun when he fell asleep at the wheel of his car. He woke in time to push Heidi out of the car, saving her life, but he was less fortunate. I stayed sad about Howard for a long time.

28.

DUKE

*A*LL was not roses for Jan and me. In trying to recoup some of the expenses of the trial, I was forced to work in some clubs I would not normally have played. It was embarrassing, shaming really, and, though Jan displayed real understanding, I behaved like a horses's ass on more than one occasion. I suppose I felt I had lured Jan to America to marry me under somewhat false pretenses. The Cool Elephant, where we had met, was elegant and "in." But many of the places in the States in which I performed at that time were considerably less than that. Back in England, perhaps I gave her the impression I was far more successful than I actually was at this stage of the game.

I got through the year fighting depression and my stalled career. I was writing more now. I contributed a couple of articles to the Arts and Leisure section of the *New York Times* and was gratified to see them accepted. More and more I was orchestrating my singing material. It was a hit-and-miss process for a while. Since I had never studied music formally, I asked tons of questions. Marty Paich, Shorty Rogers, and other arranging idols generously fed me information and advice. Wally Stott, from England, contributed a voluminous notebook full of string-writing examples.

I hadn't played Manhattan for a long time. Twice I had been offered three-week runs at Basin Street East. The money was fine but the billing wasn't. I would have had to be second-billed either to Fat Jack Leonard or Benny Goodman, who I worshiped musically. I chewed on both of these offers and eventually turned them down. New York was still the single most important city in

the world to me and, after the debacle of the Copa and subsequent
lackluster engagements in the Big Town, I had made my mind
up to either go back there importantly or not at all. Joe Shribman,
my manger, concurred.

Then one day, in September 1965, Shribman called me. "Melvin,
we've got an offer."

"Where, Joe?"

"Basin Street East. December. Three weeks."

"Uh-oh. Basin Street East, huh? Same old story. With who?"

"Duke Ellington and his orchestra."

"Well, I'd sure love that, Joseph, but you know what we decided
about playing New York. It would never work."

"No, no, Melvin. You would get top billing."

"What? You've got to be kidding."

"Never more serious in my life. Duke has agreed to take second billing. Or right hand to your left, whichever way it works
best."

"Joe, you must have gotten it wrong. There is no way Duke
is going to accept anything but one-hundred-percent top-headline
billing. No way. and frankly, even if by some crazy miracle he
agreed, I'd feel stupid and guilty about it. You know I idolize him.
You know how I value our friendship."

In point of fact, from the minute I had met my musical idol,
he had been extremely kind to me. Whenever I went to hear the
Ellington aggregation, he would announce that his "first-chair
percussionist" was in the audience and invite me up to play drums
on "Rockin' in Rhythm" with the band. What an honor that was!
To me, he was the prime genius of the music business, and to have
been befriended by him was the happiest circumstance of my
professional life. Here was my manager telling me my musical
hero was prepared to be billed under me. Unthinkable. I turned
the date down. Two days later, Joe pushed it again.

"Melvin, quit being silly. I'm telling you—Duke wants to play
this date with you. He says it's okay about the billing."

"Joe, who's telling you this?"

"Everyone. The owner of the club. Duke's agents. Everyone."

"Listen, I know I'm being stupid, but I don't think I can live with it. I'd feel strange every night, headlining a show with Duke in second position."

"I don't believe this. You have been screaming about going back and starring in New York. Now here's your chance and you're giving me a hard time."

Silence.

"Look, Joe, forgive me. There'll be other chances. I'd rather pass."

One week later.

"Melvin, they're back, nipping at my heels about Basin Street."

"You're joking? I thought we'd put that to bed."

"Me too, but they really want this date to work out."

I felt flattered as hell. I wasn't exactly in demand in the Apple. In the end I accepted. I wanted the job, wanted it badly. I also was concerned that if I continued to appear to be hard to get, I might never be offered the club again.

When the time came, Jan and I were lucky enough to borrow the empty Greenwich Village apartment of Bert Shevelove. He had been one of the creative minds behind *A Funny Thing Happened on the Way to the Forum* and was an old friend of Jan's. It was a beautiful little flat and we were happy there.

I had written five new arrangements in preparation for the Basin Street gig. I eagerly looked forward to rehearsing with my favorite band. That was my first mistake. Of the band's fifteen members, only eight showed up for rehearsal. We were opening that night! I panicked. No, no, no! I had waited a long time for this. I looked up in the general direction of God and prayed silently, Give me a break.

The rehearsal was a disaster. My charts were played with monstrous indifference and, had it not been for Louis Bellson on drums, John Lamb on bass, and my pianist, a fine musician named Jimmy Wisner, I would simply have had to walk away. At the end of rehearsal, I was nervous as a cat about the opening, which was only a few hours away.

I went back to the apartment and tried unsuccessfully to rest. That night, I headed with real trepidation for Basin Street East. I walked in through the stage door at 9:10 to prepare myself for

a 9:30 performance. A young comic named Joan Rivers was on
stage, trying to do her act. I say "trying" because there came, from
the manager's office, a commotion so raucous that customers' heads
were cranked around angrily.

What the hell is going on? I wondered. I walked into the office
and found myself in a hornet's nest. Joe Shribman was shouting
at the top of his voice at Arthur, the manager of Basin Street.
Duke Ellington's longtime mentor and agent, Joe Glaser, was also
in the middle of the fray.

"Goddamn it," yelled Shribman, "you told us—assured us—
that this billing situation was copacetic!"

"Well, shit," replied Glaser hotly, "no one told us! No one told
Duke. I'm warning you—"

"I was told that everything was fine with the billing!" Arthur
shouted, bristling. He held up a contract. "Look! Just look through
this friggin' thing. Duke doesn't even have a billing clause of *any*
kind on this piece of paper. Legally, we could omit billing him at
all."

"Okay, you try that," ranted Glaser, "and we'll take you to
court and—"

"Jesus," pleaded Joe, "can't we work this out? I mean—"

"I'm telling you for the last time," Duke's agent warned, "if
you don't give Duke top billing in all advertising, promotion, and
on the marquee outside, he's not walking on the stage for this
entire engagement. That's final, from Duke himself. The band'll
play for Tormé, but Duke will be the man who wasn't there!"

I stood in the doorway in shock. To have waited so long to
play this club, to have checked and checked again that Ellington
was satisfied with the billing, to face this on an opening night,
particularly in view of the fact that only half of the Ellington band
had rehearsed my music (and mauled it to boot), literally made
me sick to my stomach.

I walked into the office. "Look, you guys," I said, "I heard
everything. Duke and I are friends. Let me go talk to him, okay?
Let me explain. . . ."

"It's not going to do you one bit of good, Mel," warned Glaser.
"He's mad as hell."

"All right, all right. But at least let me try."

They agreed. I went to Duke's dressing room and knocked on the door. He opened up when I stage-whispered through the door that it was his "first-chair percussionist." He was dressed in a terrycloth bathrobe. A stocking covered his brilliantined hair. For the first time since I had met him in 1944, he seemed cool and unreceptive.

I sat down and told him everything, including my earlier refusals to play New York unless I could come back headlining. I informed him that I had not believed my manager when he had told me that Duke had been willing to accept second billing. Ellington would have none of it.

"Yeah, baby, well, I'm not mad at you, but, you know, I nearly just won the Pulitzer prize, and this is an insult and I can't help it if you're in the middle. If they don't fix the billing, I'm not moving."

Now the strain of the afternoon rehearsal, coupled with this new development, took its toll. I hated finding myself in a position of supplication, but I suddenly saw the whole engagement going down the tubes. Duke's attitude toward me, despite his disclaimer of not being mad at me personally, was also contributing to a sinking heart.

"Please, Duke," I begged him, "please don't do this. I'm sorry about the billing thing. Look, couldn't we compromise? Let them print half the ads with me on the left, and half with you on the left. Let me have top billing on one side of the marquee, you take top on the other side. And on the middle marquee, the big one facing the street, you take left and I'll take right. That gives you top billing on two-thirds of the marquee."

My idol was cold and adamant. No sale. I left his dressing room brokenhearted and disillusioned. I had heard that he could be obstinate and haughty. I had never before seen that side of him. It was shattering, to say the least.

A word about billing: There are probably equal amounts of ego and status involved in the matter of billing. There is also one other factor: businesss. If, say, a club owner comes to New York with the idea of buying Mel Tormé for his bistro in Cleveland, shows up at Basin Street and finds that Mel is not genuinely headlining in that prestigious music venue, he is liable to do one of two things: refrain from buying Mel at all, or alter his thinking on how much money he is willing to pay for Tormé. It's crazy, but I've seen it happen again and again. New York is the standard by which many promoters, entrepreneurs, and club owners do their selecting of talent, and, more than anywhere else, it is absolutely vital to appear there with as much stature as possible.

In fairness to Duke, he was fighting for the same thing that I fought for. My guess is that no one had even discussed the billing problem with him prior to that night, and his huffiness and anger were understandable.

Conversely, I had worked hard, sometimes against almost insuperable odds to make a name for myself. I commanded top billing everywhere else and had made my acceptance of this date conditional upon that clause in my contract. Duke had no clause— nothing of any kind. I guess when you're as big as Duke Ellington, you take it for granted that your position on the bill is automatically on top.

I went back to the office in a daze. To the questioning eyes of Glaser, Arthur, and Joe Shribman, I shook my head. Then it was time to change into my working clothes and go entertain the overflowing audience.

That performance was a debacle. Duke's band did not sport good music-reading musicians. It never had. Now these weak readers, half of whom had not even come to rehearsal, were about to *sight-read* my arrangements. The result was unforgivable. Rarely had my charts been so mangled, played with such astonishing disinterest. The lion-hearts were there, of course, knocking themselves out for me: Harry Carney on baritone sax, Jimmy Hamilton on clarinet, and Cat Anderson's fierce trumpet. Heroes without feet of clay. Total professionals. Total gentlemen. They cheered me on and played their hearts out for me, but they couldn't overcome the lethargy of the band as a whole.

Duke did not leave his dressing room all evening.

Jan and I returned to Shevelove's flat disgusted and despondent.

She had heard it all and had great sympathy for my untenable position.

"Jan, I think I'll just bug out. Quit. The hell with it. I don't think I can take another night of tension in that place, not to mention the totally shitty way the band played my charts."

"Don't do that, darling," she counseled. "Running away is liable to make people think you are in the wrong, and you're not. Stick it out and don't grumble. It'll work itself out."

I doubted her optimism but took her advice and continued.

Four days later, with Duke still *in absentia* on the stand, I guested on the "Tonight" show, where Johnny Carson asked me, in front of America, just what was going on at Basin Street East. The question took me by surprise, but I attempted to answer it evenhandedly. Carson told me afterward that I had handled myself correctly and well. Then he showed me a copy of the *New York Post*.

A columnist named Frank Farrell had written a column about the Ellington-Tormé billing squabble. I was characterized as a snot, a jerk, and an arrogant punk who had ranted and raved over the billing situation and had insulted Duke Ellington in his dressing room on opening night.

I read that column and my face flushed with rage. So help me God, for the first time in my life, a notion of violence swept over me. Perhaps my reviews at the Copa back in 1947 had been deserved, to some extent, but *this*—I fantasized about which of my Colt six-guns I would use to blow this son of a bitch Farrell away.

Then I calmed down and called him. In the quietest tone of voice I could muster, I told him the whole story. At the end, I did something I hated doing. I swore on the lives of my children that every single word I had spoken was the unvarnished, unhomogenized truth. I suppose what I was hoping for was a correction in the paper of what he had written—at the very least, an apology.

Farrell, a feelingless Irishman and a Duke Ellington idolator, said, "Well, what the hell. The story will probably generate a lot of business for Basin Street. You know, a feud between you and Duke. Makes good copy."

I hung up.

My felicitous relationship with Duke Ellington had been badly damaged. I had finally, unhappily, given in. Duke had his top billing. I had three weeks of hell at Basin Street, counting the days to the end of the engagement.

Postscript: Within six months, I returned there with top billing, costarring with Woody Herman. A smashing run.

One final comment: When Jan and I got married, months later in a foreign country, who should I run into in the lobby of the hotel in which we were staying but Duke and his entire band. He beamed, gave me a bear hug, kissed me on the cheek, and said: "Hey, baby. Love you madly."

29.

HONEYMOON

I TOOK a deep breath on January 1, 1966, determined to make it a good year, knowing it would be infinitely better with Jan as my wife. I was offered a series of concerts/club dates for that May in Tokyo, Taiwan, and Okinawa, the latter two for the military. Jan and I knew I would be free to marry right about then and thought it would be romantic to wed in Japan.

Living in the same house for several months had paid off where Jan, my parents, and, especially, Tracy were concerned. My folks adored my future wife and Tracy had warmed to her considerably. Arlene was in New York with her future husband, Larry Fisher, calling Tracy occasionally but not exercising her visitation prerogatives.

By the time Jan and I were ready to go to Japan, Tracy was actually eager to see us married and had even begun tentatively to refer to Jan as "Mom." And my parents felt that after two broken marriages I had finally lucked out. So did I.

I played four concerts in Tokyo. They were nicely received, if not world-shaking. I didn't care. I was about to marry the first lady with whom I had ever really been in love. The final divorce papers had been put aboard a plane in L.A. and flown to Tokyo. I went to the airport, saw them through customs, pocketed the envelope, and headed back to the Tokyo Hilton where we were staying. I ran into Tony Randall in the lobby. Sweet human being that he is, he volunteered to meet us at the British consulate later in the day, where we would undergo a second ceremony. First, however, Jan and I had to present ourselves to a Japanese ward

office (more like a post office, really), where we would be civilly
married according to Japanese law.

That ceremony was no ceremony. A Japanese civil servant sat
on a high stool scribbling in his native language with a long-handled
brush. After a few moments, we were handed a certificate, completely in Japanese. The clerk then smiled at us and said, in English,
"You married."

The affair at the consulate was considerably more festive, with
a proper wedding service, champagne, and congratulations from
both the British consul and his American counterpart, who also
graciously attended. Tony Randall laughingly informed us that one
member of the Japanese press, part of a substantial number of
media people who had shown up to cover the wedding ceremony,
asked him, "How it feel, Mr. Randall, to be getting married?" I
can only imagine Tony's reply.

Our honeymoon, in Taiwan and on Okinawa, was right out
of a 1930s screwball comedy/thriller. Instead of the big band I had
been promised by the Japanese promoter who had set up the tour,
I had five servicemen whose combined spirit was willing but whose
talents, to say the least, were weak. At least half of why a singer
delivers a successful performance is attributable to his or her backing. I have seen audiences respond poorly to performers without
their really knowing why the show failed. In many instances, it
was the inadequacy of the orchestra and/or individual players that
contributed to the unsuccessful presentation. Of course, sometimes
it's the performer who is at fault—I ought to know; like every
other performer, I have been guilty of that more than once! Generally, though, the quality of musicians supporting a singer or
dancer can make or break the evening.

The aforementioned servicemen were nice guys, but visibly
embarrassed by their inexpert playing. In the end, I had to sit at
the piano and play for myself—no mean feat, since my main
relationship with the piano is that of arranger/composer. George
Shearing I ain't.

I was supposed to do one concert only in Taipei. Suddenly I
found myself being asked to get on an old military C-46 and fly
to Tainan, some 200 miles away, to perform at a noncom service
club there. "Those men are stuck there for months at a time without

a grunt of entertainment or real recreation. Be a good guy, Mel, will ya, and go sing for them."

Jan and I boarded the airplane next morning. A C-46 is a stubbier, underpowered first cousin to the more stable C-47, or DC-3. The C-46 has a glide ratio comparable to a flying rhino stuffed with anvils. Lose an engine and you're history. I had avoided flying in one of those birds for years. Now, here we were, me and my brand-new bride, coming in for a landing at Tainan, the closest city to mainland China, in a dicey aircraft, whose every window was shuttered "for security purposes." Unpleasant to say the least.

Again, I had to accompany myself at the piano. The drummer played a set of drums that looked like they had seen service in the Spanish-American War, and he played like he was rooting the charge up San Juan Hill. The bass player had only a nodding acquaintance with written music and, most of the time, it sounded as though I was playing "Blue Moon" and he was playing "Mairzy Doats." Somehow, we got through the evening, and even ended together.

Jan and I opted for a late train back to Taipei. We had had enough of curtained vintage airplanes. I mean, after all, we _were_ on our honeymoon. We were told the train had compartments, which suggested some sort of comfort. We boarded at midnight and were directed to our cubicle. The sheets, pillowcases, bedding, and floors were filthy. We were dead tired but unwilling even to sit on the berths. Consequently, we stood up all night. Let me repeat that: we _stood up_ all night—nine hours coping with a rolling, clattering Chinese train.

The porter brought tea. We looked at it, looked at each other, and declined. In the morning, dead on our feet, we were scooped up by the military, taken to the airport, and flown to Okinawa. There is a good hotel on Okinawa. We were taken to the other one. I called the "good" one; no rooms to be had. We collapsed into a lumpy bed and slept for six hours.

"Jan," I said wearily, after eating something that vaguely re-sembled a meal, "we need a little R and R." I called our army contact and found there was a moviehouse downtown, playing the Burton and Taylor _Cleopatra_, which Jan had never seen.

"Let's go," she said enthusiastically.

I checked to make sure the theater was habitable. "Oh, it's fine, fine," chirped the army officer. "The best in town."

Halfway through the movie, Jan felt something brush her ankle. We looked down and saw a rat the size of a duffle bag scurry under the seat in front of us. Then another. And two more. We tiptoed out of the best theater on Okinawa, dreaming of the Chinese in Hollywood and the Bruin in Westwood.

When we were finally unceremoniously shunted onto a homeward-bound airplane at the end of this hellish honeymoon, I thought, what a way to begin a marriage. I must say, Jan laughed a lot through it all and I admired her attitude. I was humiliated. What could my new wife be thinking about me and my so-called career?

The folks and Tracy were glad to see us home safe and sound. I literally kissed the ground upon arriving at the Club View house.

For a few weeks, we puttered. I had found a new friend in Frank Tallman. The owner of several vintage as well as World War Two aircraft, he had come to California to take up where veteran pilot Paul Mantz had left off. Thing was, Mantz was still very much in evidence in the movie colony, actively plying his trade wherever stunt flying in the movies was required. Tallman wisely made friends with Mantz, and together they formed Tallmantz Aviation, the most formidable organization of its kind since the old days of Frank Clarke, Leo Nomis, Dick Grace, and the Squadron of Death movie-stunt flyers.

Tallman gifted me with a huge, brass-tipped wooden propellor. It was one of the ones he used on his old Standard J-1, which was seen extensively in *It's a Mad, Mad, Mad, Mad World*. That rickety biplane, ostensibly flown by a tipsy Ben Blue, was actually a beautifully restored example of what World War One trainers looked like back in 1917.

The prop reached from floor to ceiling. It needed restoration and Jan, Tracy, and I applied ourselves. We laid it down in the backyard and proceeded to sand, stain, and polish it. The results were worth all our efforts. It still stands in the corner of my den. On April 15, 1978, Frank Tallman was killed in a twin-engine airplane just outside Los Angeles. That day I sat for a long time, looking at the propellor, remembering him.

Marilyn Monroe with Mel, Sammy Davis, Jr., Milton H. Greene, and Jacques Sernas.

Mel substitutes for the great Gene Krupa with the Benny Goodman Trio on the "Spotlight Bands" TV show in 1952; Teddy Wilson is the famous pianist.

Peggy Lee and Mel during their summer replacement series, *T.V.'s Top Tunes*, for Chesterfield cigarettes. Perry Como hosted this show in the fall.

Mickey Rooney scolds his younger brother, Lester (Mel Tormé), as Lester's wife (Kim Hunter) looks on in a scene from *Playhouse 90's The Comedian*, 1957, Sonny Fox Productions.

Proud papa Mel with his second wife, Arlene, and their baby, Tracy, 1959.

Mel and Ella on the
Garry Moore Show, 1960.

J. PETER HAPPEL

GENE HOWARD

The Carlos Gastel "stable"—
(LEFT TO RIGHT) Carlos, Nat
King Cole, June Christie, Mel,
Peggy Lee, and Stan Kenton,
1959.

Mel with Judy Garland
during the 1963–64 run of the
Judy Garland television series.

Mel takes flight on the day his first airplane—
a *Piper Cherokee 235*—was delivered.

Mel in the title role of "The Handyman," the episode he wrote for *The Virginian* TV series. *Make my day.*

Mel, looking more like Tevye than Zack O'Brien, the animal trainer he plays in the 1974 film *Snowman*.

Besides hosting "One Night Stand," a TV jazz special, Mel
got to play drums alongside a pair of giants named Krupa
and Rich. Gerry Mulligan can be seen behind Buddy Rich.
Lionel Hampton was only one of the many name
musicians to participate. (1970)

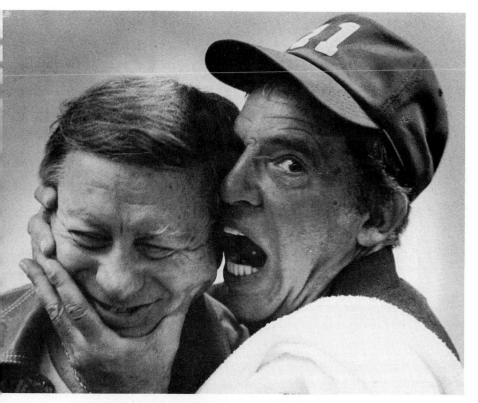

Buddy Rich yells into Mel's ear, "Hey, Tormé, you sing flat!"
during the making of their LP *Together Again for the First
Time*. Unfair, not true, unclean, Mel replies.

An historic gathering—an evening of tribute to
Willard Alexander, dean of band bookers, at
Buddy's Place. LEFT TO RIGHT: Buddy Rich,
Woody Herman, Alexander,
an unidentified gentleman,
Benny Goodman,
Count Basie, Stan
Kenton, and Mel.

Mel performing on the
Jerry Lewis Telethon in 1983.

Mel and his second father, Count Basie, who was once quoted as saying, "The way Mel sings, he should have been black."

Mel Tormé with his favorite judge, Harry Anderson of NBC's *Night Court*.

Mel's family (LEFT TO RIGHT): Daisy Ann, stepdaughter Carrie, Steve, Tracy, Melissa, and James.

Mel and Ali Tormé, 1988.

BILL EASTABROOK

A great pilot, he had lost a leg in a freak household accident years before. When I saw him right after the amputation, he had told me, in no uncertain terms, that he intended to requalify for every single one of his ratings just as soon as possible. He did just that in the most extraordinary act of determination I have ever seen. One of the most daring stunts he ever accomplished (even more tricky than flying the twin Beech through the billboard in _Mad, Mad World_) was shoehorning a WWI Jenny through the main street of a small Texas town, altitude three feet, during the filming of _The Great Waldo Pepper_.

My first-born children, Steve and Melissa, were now living in Beverly Hills with Candy and Hal. I reestablished a one-on-one relationship with both of them. It wasn't easy. They had grown up mainly in Scarsdale, where the Marches had lived while Hal hosted "The $64,000 Question." After the quiz-show scandals broke (in which Hal had absolutely no part), they moved to the Coast, a happy circumstance for me. In June 1967 I was offered a run at Talk of the Town in London. Europe's largest nightclub, it boasted a large chorus line in a variety show early in the evening and a headline performer—me—for the 11:00 P.M. offering. It was also the worst-paying job in Europe. Only the additional offer of my own "special" on the BBC made the trip financially feasible. Most important, I had not yet met Jan's parents, and this trip would allow me to do so.

The first time I laid eyes on Thora Hird, Jan's actress-mother, I knew I was in for it. I had seen her brilliant performance as Shirley Anne Field's "mum" in Olivier's _The Entertainer_. I now realized she had played herself in the film. Vastly opinionated, I perceived her as the dominant element in the Scott family. Her husband, James, was a quiet, likable man, from whom Jan got her good looks. He served as Thora's "manager." When we met, she was busy doing a series on TV as well as appearing annually in plays during the "season" in Blackpool.

For most of her professional life, Thora Hird had been a member of that vast army of supporting players so admirable in British films. Only recently, in the early and mid-sixties, had she come into her own as a TV series star. Every housewife in her age bracket identified with her. Her show was not unlike "All in the Family," and the character she played struck a responsive chord in thousands of English breasts. She was also a magnificent dramatic actress and an amusing storyteller. She basked in her success but sometimes exuded an irritating self-importance.

Privately, Jan would sigh and say, "My mother's stardom came very late in her life and she has trouble handling it." Thora and I circled each other warily throughout my marriage to her daughter and it was wearing, to say the least.

I opened at the Talk of the Town on June 6, 1967. Far away, another opening day was in progress—the first day of the Six-Day War between Israel and Egypt. The mini-war affected business throughout London and, specifically, at the Talk of the Town. I did my thing, performed on my TV special, with Jan as my only guest and the redoubtable Wally Stott conducting a largish orchestra. And then we scooted back to California.

In October 1967, I played a memorable two-week run at the Sands in Vegas.

I had just finished appearing at Harvey's in Tahoe when the call came from Joe Shribman.

"Listen," he said, "I just heard from Vegas. They got a little problem at the Sands. They'd like you and Don Adams ["Get Smart"] to come in and help them out."

"What's the problem?"

"Don't know, but the money's very good." He mentioned a figure. It *was* good. "So, could you take a plane outta Tahoe for Vegas as quickly as possible? They want you to open tonight."

"Can do."

Adams and I opened that night, and the packed house responded extremely well. Later that evening, Jack Entratter (now deceased), head man at the Sands, summoned me to his office. He had been the bouncer at the Copa in New York when I had appeared there in 1947. Now he was "Mr. Sands," a tall, slightly menacing character with the demeanor of an ex-boxer. I was not fond of him, particularly after an incident that had taken place during my Copa debut in 1947. One night I had asked permission to bring a young, talented performer named Sammy Davis, Jr., backstage, and he had snarled, "We don't let niggers in here!"

Now he scowled at me from behind his desk and said, "How the hell did you know?"

I stared at him. "Know? Know what?"

"About last night in here. About Sinatra."

"Sinatra? Was he here last night?"

"You kiddin'? Nobody told you?"

"Jack," I said patiently, "what are you talking about?"

"I'm talkin' about you. And the 'Run for Your Life' I watched in here tonight. You wrote it, right?"

"Right."

"What I'm tryin' to figure out is how you could get what happened here last night on the air so quickly."

"Hey, fill me in, will you? What happened here last night?"

"Come on. Somebody must have told you. Sinatra got mad as hell 'cause he was refused more credit in the casino. Now I look at this TV show you wrote tonight, and you're playin' the same scene Frank played in here last night. Same scene."

I was listening intently.

"The hassle at the crap table," Jack continued. "Then you insist on more credit and they refuse you, and you throw a fit and stamp out of the casino. I mean, I don't get it. How the hell—"

"Jack, I wrote that show months and months ago. We completed filming it well over *three* months ago. How could I possibly know what was going to happen here last night?"

"Yeah, but you taking Frank's place after what happened, and then playing the same scene on TV—one night after the commotion here...." He shook his head. "Fuckin' weird."

He was right.

Since no one had been offering me anything decent in the way of acting roles, I had written one for myself, an episode in the *Run for Your Life* series called "The Frozen Image." The story had to do with an aging singer, afraid of losing his youthful persona, who works hard at "freezing" that image by living in the fast lane of sports cars, heavy gambling, and generally outrageous, flamboyant behavior. In the process, he alienates his wife, friends, and business associates, until Paul Bryan (Ben Gazzara) intervenes and saves him from potential disaster.

Writing a teleplay wasn't too difficult. Producer Roy Huggins gave me an early "Run for Your Life" shooting script and told me to go home, study it for the proper form, and start writing.

I followed his instructions, read that script, and then commenced writing mine.

When I finally turned it in to Huggins, he looked at it and frowned. "Wait a minute. This script is double the length we need. How come?"

"I don't know, Roy. I read the sample script you gave me, counted the pages, and tried to duplicate the length."

"Ohmigod!" He laughed." I gave you one of our two-hour special shows to study. I'm so sorry, Mel."

Cutting that one down to one hour was a job and a half in itself. But it was fun, and having watched more movies than I could possibly count, it was interesting to be involved in the creation of a film rather than merely being a viewer.

The reviews sparkled. Dave Kaufman, a tough critic for *Variety*, called it "... one of the superior segments in the 'Run for Your Life' series ..."

In addition to "Run for Your Life," I appeared on several TV variety shows, Garry Moore's among them. Carol Burnett had come into her own on Garry's show and was heading for big things in television. I felt confident I would make several appearances on her new CBS program.

I tried my hand at executive producing. I had come up with a sort of alter-ego notion to "Laugh-In." I called it "The Singers." All the humor would spring from music and musical guests. My agents liked it. So did CBS, who saw series possibilities and proceeded to fund a special toward that end. I wrote all the musical material and, together with a team of talented writers and line producer Bill Foster, we got "The Singers" off the ground. The cohosts were Michele Lee and Jack Jones. The "regulars" included John Byner, Bobby Van, Gerry Grainger, Charles Nelson Reilly, Marilyn Michaels, and Harve Presnell.

The special guests were Frankie Laine, James Farentino, Ricardo Montalban, and Edward G. Robinson. Cliff Robertson flew all the way in from Australia to perform aerobatics in Bud Gurney's old Gypsy Moth, simultaneously singing a medley I had put together of predictable tunes relating to his flying maneuvers ("I'm flying high, but I've got a feeling I'm falling," and so on). It worked beautifully, and having Academy Award winner Cliff on the show did not hurt our ratings one single bit.

Again, the show was praised by critics, with more than respectable numbers. Again, I came close to being the executive producer and co-owner of a series in partnership with CBS, although they failed to sell it.

I continued writing, cranking out a story for *Guns* magazine.

I went to Cross and Cockade meetings with my mutual-interest-in-aviation buddies.

I pursued my gun-collecting hobby.

I flew my airplane.

I sang.

And waited.

30.

SAMMY

*A*ND waited.

There comes a time when, with your hopes unfulfilled and your expectations diminished, you begin to think, "Is this all there is?" If you're a realist (and, to a great extent, I am), then a kind of resignation sets in. All right, okay, you win, God (or fate or The Force or whatever), I accept the hand you've dealt me. So I'm not going to be the superstar I always believed I'd be. So I won't be a huge megabuck earner. So I'll never have a million seller. I can handle it, live with it, make the best of it.

Trouble is, giving in means giving up, at least to me it does. I always believed there were better times a-comin' for what I still doggedly called "my career."

The year 1968 slipped away from Jan and me. I played a lot of dates, made good money, but without really making it to the "main event." I was like a boxer in the ring, jabbing, jabbing with my left, waiting for that all-important opening into which I could slip a good, hard right cross. About the most significant thing that happened was the purchase of a new house in Beverly Hills.

My mother, who had become a real-estate broker, had been scouring west L.A. and Beverly Hills for a bigger house for Jan and Tracy and me. She met us at the airport one day, as I was returning home from a concert date, and drove us directly to a large, beautiful house on Coldwater Canyon Drive. The woman occupying it was a widow whose children were grown and gone. She rattled around that house, she said, all alone and lonely. She longed for a nice apartment or condo. She liked us. We loved the house. Sold.

Happily, we found ourselves "rattling around" our new living space. A big house on a large piece of land, our new home boasted a tennis court, a swimming pool, a guest cottage, a projection room (Whoopee!), and two separate gardens, not to mention a cluster of roomy bedrooms and baths upstairs as well as a commodious living room, den, billiard room, and formal dining room. The house had been built in 1936 by an old friend, Ray Heindorf, the musical director for many years at Warner Bros. Studios. He had been very kind to me when I had been under contract there, and it was nice to think I was now living in what must have once been his pride and joy.

Jan and I decided we wanted to have a baby. Strangely enough, it wasn't simple. I had made three children with two other wives as easily as rolling off the proverbial log. This time, we couldn't find the right formula. We went to a famous clinic in Los Angeles and boned up on temperature readings, fertile times of the month, and other ploys for getting good and pregnant.

We had a lot of fun trying, but still no luck. "God," I said to Jan, one exhausted night, "if you ever are 'with child,' I hope the little bugger knows how badly he or she was wanted."

One day in April 1969, Jan beamed with the good news: Contact! The blessed event was due in December. We celebrated and I gasped a sigh of relief.

I did several guest shots on "The Carol Burnett Show." After the madness of the ill-fated Judy Garland series, working with Carol, Harvey Korman, Vicki Lawrence, and Lyle Waggoner was pure pleasure. Rarely, if ever, was a more professional, talented company assembled under the roof of CBS Television City.

I was still foolishly riding a motorcycle. You'd think I would have learned my lesson, but dumbness dies hard. One day, in 1969, I rode the Yamaha up into my driveway, turned off the engine, and said, to no one in particular, "That's it!" Don't ask me why. I have never ridden a bike since.

My flying was suffering. I felt guilty when I thought about my beautiful *new* airplane, one of the first Cherokee Arrows off the Vero Beach Piper line, sitting and rusticating, waiting for me at Santa Monica Airport. There didn't seem to be enough time to fly the damn thing and stay current. When home base is a high density area like L.A., you'd better be sure to spread your wings a lot and stay proficient. I couldn't, and I finally gave up trying; 3728 Tango went back to Piper.

The reviews and subsequent favorable comments on my performance both as actor and writer in the "Run for Your Life" segment inspired me to write an episode for "The Virginian," another Universal series, starring James Drury, Doug McClure, and a slew of superb supporting players.

I adapted my first book, *Dollarhide*, written in 1955 but never published, to fit the "Shiloh" locale and family and presented the adaptation in treatment form to executive producer Norman MacDonnell and Joel Rogosin, the line producer. They bought the story and agreed to let me write the teleplay and to play "The Handy Man," my retitled effort.

"The Handy Man" was beset with problems, one minor, several major. The minor problem was Norman MacDonnell. He simply refused to believe I was writing the script. He was sure Joel Rogosin was the real author. Joel agonized over this. We had become friends and he liked what I had turned in as a final script. So did MacDonnell. He just didn't believe the work was mine.

Then came the matter of "okay." In a few scenes, I had used that well-worn term of assent. "No, no, Mel," warned Joel, "that's a house rule around here. No one ever says 'okay' on this show. They always say 'all right.' Never 'okay.'"

"Why?" I asked him.

"Well, because Norman says no one used 'okay' back in those days in the West."

"Norman is wrong," I said, having had my fill of Norman and his obstinate doubts about what was what. "In the 1880s, in New Mexico, there was a well-known rancher named O. K. Wright. His cowhands, the townspeople, and everyone who came in contact with him called him, of course, O.K. Because his last name was Wright—get it, Joel?—sounds like 'r-i-g-h-t'—his initials became synonymous with 'all right.'"

I knew I sounded like a smart-ass, but other than WWI aviation, my unabiding passion was the Old West and the characters who inhabited it. I had amassed a huge library on the subject and was a devout student of the genre. I longed to tell MacDonnell that, just before the quiz show scandals broke, Mert Koplin, the executive producer of "The $64,000 Challenge" had signed me as a contestant to compete against Virgil Earp, Wyatt's descendant. Subject: the history of the Wild West. Koplin had grilled me for four hours one day in New York and thought I would beat Earp, who had already won $32,000 on "The $64,000 Question."

Still, my story about old O. K. Wright fell on deaf ears. The "okay" rule stubbornly stood and I had to substitute "all right" every time the dreaded pair of letters appeared in my script.

The major problems were manifold.

"The Handy Man" went before the cameras nine days before Christmas. There was a definite feeling on the set of "Come on, let's get this thing done. I gotta go do my Christmas shopping." It was unsettling, particularly if you are not only the guest star but the writer.

Abner Biberman was assigned the director's chore. He was a nice little guy and I had enjoyed his work as an actor in films for years. I was concerned about his directing, however. He seemed more interested in getting long shots of horses and riders, silhouetted against the morning sky, than pulling performances out of the actors. To save money, "The Virginian" company habitually let stunt men and wranglers deliver lines, sometimes "key" lines. Well and good, if those individuals have any acting ability.

On this show, however, some important lines were mumbled unintelligibly by nonactors and the other guest star in the piece, an up-and-coming young mummer with the right drawl, who was hopelessly in over his head. He spoke the lines as though he were in a high-school play, with no understanding of them at all, and, boy, that bothered me.

To make matters worse, I suffered an injury during the third day of shooting. I had written a scene in which Paul Mantee is supposed to rough me up and slam me into a wall.

"Make it look good, Paul," I whispered just before Abner yelled "Action." Paul did, and I ended up with three badly bruised ribs. I had to be taped in order to continue. Paul felt lousy and apologized over and over again. I had brought the injury on myself, and I kept assuring him it had been my fault, not his.

On the fifth day of shooting, a Monday, I was assigned a horse named Buster. "Gentle as a lamb," the wrangler assured me. "No sweat."

I have ridden a lot of horses, but there is no way I can be characterized as a good rider. Buster and I made our way up a fairly steep incline. I neck-reined him into a 180 and waited for Abner to yell "Action," so that we could make our way *slowly* down to where the camera was. Buster had been in the barn all weekend; he wanted to run. When Biberman waved his arms at us, Buster took flight and I hung on for dear life.

No amount of "Whoa, Buster" or "Easy, boy" or "Pull up, you mangy son of a bitch" would deter Buster. Even though I was taped as tight as a mummy, the pain from my injured ribs was indescribable. I still can't believe I made it all the way down that hilly slope without falling off and breaking my head.

All things considered, "The Handy Man" fared well with the critics when it aired weeks later. I felt I had gained a foothold at Universal. I was encouraged to write more scripts, series ideas— whatever I wanted. The best thing that happened to me at Universal was meeting a man named Dale Sheets. He was a vice-president in charge of special television projects and a protégé of MCA's boss, Lew Wasserman.

Dale and I became friends. He was an old acquaintance of Shribman's, and we hit it off instantly. Sandy-haired, good-looking, and possessed of a winning personality, Dale was simply an admirable guy. In the near future, he would become more than just a good friend; he would take over as my personal manager. But I'm getting ahead of myself.

Out of the blue came a call from Sammy Davis. "I'm going into Harrah's in Reno for two weeks in November and then into the Sands in Vegas for a month. I've got one hell of an idea. You and me. Just the two of us. Sort of *mano a mano*, know what I mean? You write the special material, like you did for Garland. We'll rehearse like mad. I mean, total perfection. Everything down pat, dig? Nothing like the Rat Pack bashes. We'll show them two performers who sing, dance, play drums—do it all. But completely rehearsed, really structured. What do you think?"

I was blown away by the idea: Sammy, indisputably one of the great multitalents of the age; myself, given an opportunity to write the kind of special material I enjoyed creating and performing. "I think, Samuel, it is one bitch of a thought."

"Great. Start writing."

He then made me an offer I should have refused. The money was low. The special material? I was to "throw that in." With slight misgivings, I accepted.

I began writing. When I was finished, I had turned out some of the best lyrics and music of my songwriting career. Were I to have charged for the material, I would have asked five figures. In the spirit of cooperative participation, I sat down and wrote a big band arrangement for our opening song, a ditty about our divergent life-styles called "Funny Clothes." As I have mentioned, I am not a schooled arranger; writing the chart ate up a lot of time.

The night prior to leaving for Reno, I let myself be inveigled into going head to head with Sammy on "The Movie Game" show on channel five. Hosted jointly by Army Archerd and Larry Blyden, the show was an enjoyable exercise in movie trivia. I had appeared many times and had never lost. Neither had Sammy. Now, the two "champs" were each captaining a team for the ultimate championship.

We were so closely matched that winning was a matter of answering the final question: Who had won three Academy Awards? Sammy jumped the gun, before Blyden finished the question, and proudly answered, "Walter Brennan." The subsequent clues would have revealed his mistake. Brennan had indeed been awarded three Oscars. But so had Katharine Hepburn. I waited for the question to be put in its entirety and then answered it correctly. My team had won.

Sammy was disconsolate. He said, "I let my people down." He actually said that, shaking his head slowly from side to side. He gathered up his troops and faded into the night, without even saying good-bye. Great, I thought, tomorrow we open at Harrah's. This is going to be interesting.

When I arrived in Reno, the first thing that caught my eye was Harrah's marquee: "Sammy Davis." Period. When I protested the lack of billing to Sammy, he said, "Hey, baby, I've got nothing to do with that. Go see Doug and Pat."

"Doug and Pat" turned out to be Doug Buschhausen and Pat

Franz, a pair of Tormé-haters, who were the booking agents for Harrah's. They had never booked me before, never *would* have booked me if it hadn't been for Sammy's insistence. When I opened my mouth to discuss the billing problem, they fired converging barrages of verbal assault at me. How dare I ask for billing? Who the hell did I think I was? They didn't want me in the first place. And so on.

I have never walked away from any engagement; that day was the closest I ever came. Jan and Dale Sheets talked me out of it. Sammy, reveling in his element, finally conceded that I ought to have some billing on the marquee. The result was humiliating: MEL TORMÉ in letters one-quarter the size of Sammy's. So much for "*mano a mano.*"

That night we opened. Far from the weeks and weeks of preparation and rehearsal we had agreed on, Sammy and I had had two talkovers prior to opening. We did exactly one song together, the one for which I had written an orchestration. During the entire two-week run at Harrah's, two of his "aides" stood in the wings of the stage with cue cards, and Sam would turn right and left, singing the printed lines.

Discouraging? Hell, yes. I had invested in new "mod" outfits so that Sammy and I would be dressed alike in those few short moments we spent together on stage. Puffy-sleeved silk shirts, tux-type pants with matching vests, clothing that Sammy espoused but that I would never wear again. What can I tell you?

Watching Sam perform every night was a revelation. First of all, he is the best tap dancer I have ever seen, virtually the Buddy Rich of tap dancers. The clarity and syncopation of his taps are nothing short of astonishing. His vocal impressions were matchless, and his singing was in tune and swinging, as well as plaintive during his balladeer moments.

There were nights when the audience was too unresponsive. On those occasions, Sammy would pull out all the stops. He would inveigh every trick, every nuance, every ounce of showmanship he had learned in a lifetime of performing in front of audiences. Damned if he didn't pull it off every time. He would stubbornly persevere, as if to say: All right, you bastards, I'm going to get you. I don't care if I have to stay out here for two hours; you're going to jump to your feet when I'm finished. Sometimes it took nearly two hours, but when he had sung his last note and tapped his last tap, every single person in the audience was standing, clapping, whistling, and cheering.

I have often wished I had that same, dogged intestinal fortitude that Sammy Davis exhibits. I have rarely dug my feet into the stage, lowered my head, pawed the ground, and snorted: "All right, I'm gonna get you." I wish I could. I don't know, maybe I'm too foolishly proud. Maybe I don't have that superstar mentality. I figure, given an even chance, I can pretty well hold my own with any given audience. If I sense resistance, apathy, or hostility in the crowd, I simply do my best and hope for a better shake from the next group of nightclubbers who come to see me. Sammy, though, won't take "no" for an answer from any audience. He's an awesome talent, and, I'm happy to say, we are still friendly.

Through Carol Burnett, I had made friends with one of my acting idols, Edward G. Robinson. He was a warm, loving little man, and being a guest in his home on several occasions, savoring his famous art collection, was one of life's highlights, as was his wife, Jane, a no-nonsense, outspoken, and witty woman.

Eddie, discovering that I was Jewish, used to delight in calling me *boychik*; his attitude toward me was positively fatherly. "So, boychik," he would say, patting my hand, "where have you been? How's life going?"

Eddie had kindly come to a party in the fall of 1969 held jointly for me and Dolly Martin, Dick's wife, with whom I shared a September 13 birthday. Dick and I had become friends due to our mutual passion for movies, and he had elected to throw a birthday bash for us. The World Series was looming, and that night a pair of baseball fans named Tracy Tormé and Edward G. Robinson got together and huddled over the vagaries of the season.

Later in the year, Eddie became seriously ill. Everyone who loved him agonized over his misfortune. Then I heard from Jane that he had gotten much better, and that they were having a huge, celebratory evening at their house in conjunction with Eddie's recovery and his seventy-sixth birthday on the twelfth of December. Would we please come?

Jan was thick with child, due momentarily, but we couldn't

pass seeing the Robinsons. It was a wonderful night, with loving testimonials to the man of the hour and a touching, literate speech by Eddie himself that had most of us dewy-eyed. When he hugged me good night and kissed Jan on the cheek, we had no way of knowing his illness was terminal.

I'll never forget that night or the next one either. Our first child was born that evening, December 13. I grinned when she came into this world on that date. December *13*! A "thirteen" baby, like her old man. How 'bout that! She was gorgeous.

Perfectly formed, with a hint of strawberry-blond hair, courtesy of my reddish-blond beard and her mother's slightly burnished locks, we decided to call her Daisy. "Oh, my God," my mother moaned. "That child will grow up to hate you for giving her that name." But in a world full of Shirleys and Shellys and Cyndis and Cybils and Jonis and Janelles, Daisy sounded wonderfully old-fashioned and feminine to us.

We modulated into the seventies full of joy and hope and a lot of love. The only sad note was bringing my relationship with Joe Shribman to an end. I have never had a finer man represent me. But I wanted to try going in a different direction, and I sought a personal manager with a fresh perspective on what might be done to advance my career. Joe and I parted on the very best of terms. He passed away in 1986.

Dale Sheets was still a few months away from coming into my life as manager, friend, brother, and partner. As an interim representative, I got together with an old acquaintance named Jess Rand. Jess had been the supereffective publicty man for Sammy Davis, Jr., for many years. Then he took over management of The Lettermen, the highly popular group of singers who had made many hits for my old alma mater, Capitol. Mainly, I was looking for a new recording situation, and, with his clout at Capitol, Jess practically assured me he could get that company to take me on.

True to his word, Jess convinced Capitol to sign me. A ray of hope at that now firmly committed rock-pop label was Dave Cavanaugh, a holdover from the old days. I knew he liked my work, and it could be—it *just* could be—we might put out something decent together. My hopes were dashed at our first meeting. Dave,

looking tired and disillusioned, informed me that the word from
"on high" was for me to make an LP "covering" some current
hits. It was Columbia Records all over again.

I did two LPs for Capitol that year, both of them wonderfully
forgettable.

On the bright side, my social life, for the first time in a long
time, was positively thriving. Sundays became, for a lot of nice
people, a habit at my house. Ricardo Montalban, a longtime friend,
was also one of the town's better tennis players. He and his beautiful
wife, Georgiana, began coming by virtually every Sunday for tennis,
dinner, and a movie in our projection room. The guest list soon
expanded to include Dick Martin and his Dolly, Jonathan and
Eileen Winters, and George and Revel Kennedy.

Within a month or so, the Sunday group burgeoned. It was
not unusual to find thirty or more tennis-playing movie lovers
attending these evenings. There was a lot of good feeling in the
house right about then. And good conversation over the buffet
dinners that Jan insisted on preparing herself.

There was one particular night I will always remember. Jan
and I had a special evening for actor Ben Lyon and bride-to-be,
Marion Nixon. The house was packed and the mood festive. Tom
Mankewicz called to ask if he could bring a couple of friends who
were visiting from New York.

"Hell, yes," I assured him. "The more the merrier."

His friends turned out to be Paddy Chayevsky and George
Plimpton.

I had been lent a print of *Hell's Angels* by Astor Pictures president Bob Savini. No one had seen the film in years, since it had
been withdrawn by Howard Hughes. We ran it that night, in
honor of Ben Lyon, the star of the film. Everyone was wiped out
by the aerial scenes as well as the torrid stuff between Ben and
Jean Harlow. When the party broke up at two in the morning,
Plimpton shook hands with me and grinned, "This is the best
evening I have ever spent in Hollywood." Paddy Chayevsky echoed
his sentiments, and we were friends from that moment until his
untimely death on August 1, 1981.

Ben Lyon was especially touched by Jan's thoughtfulness. He

had been the chief talent scout in England for Twentieth Century Fox in 1951 when that company bought Nevil Shute's *No Highway* and was preparing to film the book. A key role in the film was that of a twelve-year-old girl, the daughter of the movie's protagonist, an aeronautical engineer played brilliantly by James Stewart. Lyon chose Jan, then the most popular child film actress in England, to play the part. The party that night was by way of thanking him for his kindness to her many years before.

I was singing, writing arrangements, and working on a book. That book would create quite a stir of controversy when it was published in 1970. It was a chronicle of the day-to-day events that took place during the troubled, chaotic, albeit sometimes inspriring, run of the Judy Garland TV show. I had been making notes for the better part of two years, ever since I had heard that John Bradford, a head writer on the Garland show (and, coincidentally, the brother of my old songwriting partner, Bob Wells), had annouced that he intended to write a book about his experiences on the show (he never did).

Shortly before Judy died in April 1969, I felt it was time the story was told. I dove into work on my book.

31.

RAINBOW

*T*HE critics were very kind to *The Other Side of the Rainbow*. James Bacon, writing in the *Los Angeles Herald-Examiner*, called the book "honest, interesting, compassionate." The *Hollywood Reporter* proclaimed it ". . . a great achievement." Andrew Sarris of the *New York Times* praised: "Tormé's book is a knowledgeable and lucid tribute to its subject," and the usually staid *London Times* pronounced *Rainbow* to be ". . . a stunning tour de force."

In interview after interview following the publication of *Rainbow*, the most-often asked question was, "Why did you write this book?"

My standard answer was straightforward and truthful. I had read newspaper accounts about a pair of personal appearances of Judy's; one, relating an embarrassing mob scene in Australia when, after she had kept the stadium crowd waiting over an hour before finally appearing, the assembled throng of Garland-lovers booed her off the stage, and, even worse, the second involved a subsequent disaster in London (at the Talk of the Town, I believe) when once again her tardiness so enraged the audience that they threw food at her.

I was mortified to read of these humiliations. I was also unsurprised by Judy's lack of punctuality. She had kept the entire work force of "The Judy Garland Show" waiting for hours, time and again, back in 1963–64 during the tenure of her ill-fated CBS TV series. The studio audiences were sometimes left sitting in their not-so-comfortable seats for hours on end before being treated to Garland's presence.

Since I was well aware of her trauma during childhood (allegedly, her mother was the quintessential stage mother), as well as her self-described internment at MGM in the '30s and '40s. I began work on the book about my experiences with her at CBS.

I didn't want to write a full-blown biography of Judy. Frankly, that was a project that held no interest for me. If, however, I could put down a personal account of our daily association while we worked together on her show, perhaps the potential readers might better understand her insecurities, her fear of failure and/or rejection, as well as her intermittent bursts of temperament and her occasional tyrannical use of superstar power.

Having been her musical adviser and occasional confidant on the show, and having written most of the special musical material for her and her parade of guest stars, I felt eminently qualified to recollect the events, conversations, little dramas, the funny and unfunny incidents that went to make up "The Judy Garland Show."

I had completed two and a half chapters when, on April 22, 1969, Judy died suddenly in London. I stopped writing for a few months, then decided to resume.

When my book was finished, my literary agent, Sterling Lord, happily sold it first crack out of the box to William Morrow and Company. I couldn't dream, at the time, what a storm the book would create.

After the excellent reviews came the hate mail. "You are beneath contempt!" wrote one Garland cultist.

"How could you do that to our Lost Princess?" shrieked another sycophant.

There were fewer than thirty letters like that, yet each one stung. I reexamined the book. I reread the reviews. One particular word seemed common to most of them: "compassionate."

I decided that most of the letter writers were the kind of fans who would read *anything* about Judy with a jaundiced eye. These were people who, in their obsessiveness with the Garland legend, refused to believe she ever went to the bathroom or scratched her behind or uttered a single vulgarism or expletive. "Lost Princess," indeed.

I always felt what made her marvelous and unique were her

bawdy sense of humor and her amazing command of truck driver language, earthy enough at times to shrivel the skin off a grape.

I took a lot of flak over that book. No complaints. I wrote it and I had no intention of avoiding the heat by "staying out of the kitchen."

One night, while I was appearing in Vegas, the radio blared forth the news that Sid Luft, Judy's ex-husband, was suing me and William Morrow for $100,000 each. He took exception to a quote I had used in the book. The words were Judy's. On the phone with me one evening, she had offhandedly used a phrase to describe Sid that, in Victorian times, was construed to impugn one's parentage. By 1970, the two-syllable word was in common conversational usage, a simple synonym for "jerk" or "rascal" or "creep."

Sid Luft preferred to live in the past, however, and commenced litigation. I went back to my book. On page 62, I had written: "I had met Sid Luft, Judy's husband, on a few occasions and had found him to be charming and likable." I had said nothing but nice things about Sid in _Rainbow_. Why the hell was he suing me over something _Judy_ had said?

In the end, the judge threw his suit out of court. Tenacious to the end, he appealed and lost again. My legal costs? Exactly $10,000. Thanks, Sid.

The Garland kids, particularly Lorna and Liza, were especially vocal in denouncing me. When someone told me that Lorna had been a guest on the Virginia Graham TV show and had branded my book "a pack of lies," smoke poured out of my ears. To dislike a book about one's famous mother is one thing; to call my book "a fake" and "a fraud" is waving a very red flag in front of my bullish eyes.

Virginia had pursued me to do her show for some time. Now I called her and asked to go on. "Yes, Virginia, I'll sing, but I am basically showing up to refute Lorna Luft's reckless, untrue allegations about my book." I armed myself with a few annotated reviews, which complimented the book for its honesty and compassion, and went to the TV studio. I dutifully sang the two obligatory songs, then moved to the interview area alongside Virginia.

"Virginia," I began, "I heard about Lorna Luft's visit to your show and some of the things she said regarding the book I wrote about her mother, Judy Garland. I can certainly understand her sensitivity where her mother is concerned, but I can't allow her remarks to go unchallenged." I took the underlined reviews out of a manila envelope. "I would like you to see—" That's as far as I got.

Virginia looked at me accusingly. "Mel, you're such a nice guy. Why would you want to write a book like this?"

I blinked. "Whoa, now, Virginia. When you read some of these—"

"No, but, I mean, really, why did you write this kind of book?"

My work was cut out for me. Patiently, I asked, "Have you read my book?"

She plowed onward. "With your wonderful talents, and knowing what a great talent Judy Garland was, what prompted you to sit down and write this sort of thing?"

A tad louder now, I repeated my question. "Virginia, have you read my book?"

"Mel, you know, I *adore* the songs you write, and the way you sing. I'm a big fan. But don't you think it was unnecessary to sit down and—"

At the top of my lungs, I shouted, "VIRGINIA, HAVE YOU READ MY BOOK?"

The audience gasped audibly. Virginia blanched, the color actually leaving her cheeks. "Well," she finally answered, "n-n-o, no I haven't. But—"

"Then shut your mouth, dear! You haven't the faintest idea about its contents! I would have hoped you would have done your homework so you might discuss this with me knowledgeably. But you didn't, and you obviously don't know squat about *The Other Side of the Rainbow*." I turned a switch inside my seething head, smiled sweetly, and said in a perfectly charming tone of voice, "Now, then, shall we talk about something you *are* qualified to discuss?"

You can imagine how the rest of the interview progressed. (Years later, Virginia came over to my table at a New York restaurant, apologized for casting aspersions on a book she had not even read, and actually thanked me for calling her to task with my outburst. That's class.)

I kept hearing about Liza and Lorna and their vilification of "Eggs Benedict Eyes," their favorite nickname for me. Then, one evening, I caught them on "60 Minutes." The sequence was mainly about their illustrious mother and her hilarious peccadilloes. They burst into gales of girlish laughter as they recalled how they had stayed with "Momma" at the Plaza in New York, running up a large bill for several days and then, short of funds, sneaking out of the hotel in the dead of night, the bills unpaid.

"Was that bill ever paid?" asked the interviewer.

Liza and Lorna looked at each other, smiled, and said, "No."

I found it fascinating that the girls would tell a far bigger audience than my book ever reached about Judy skipping out on a hotel bill. It seemed hypocritical to me to hear about Lorna Luft's constant sniping at my book vis à vis her lack of taste in recalling the Plaza incident. Were they, in effect, saying, Momma is our private province? Only *we* are permitted to tell the world that she was funny, flighty, feisty, foolish, feckless, fabulous?

If that was the case, they were in for even greater surprises. Shortly after my book came out, several others were in the works. Gerold Frank, well-known author of *The Boston Strangler*, began calling me. "I'm writing a biography of Judy Garland, Mel. Could you talk with me about her?" I asked him why he wanted to talk to me. "I read your book and not only admired it, I envied you enormously."

"I don't understand. Why?"

"Because I never met Judy Garland. Everything I write in this book of mine is being accomplished through research and interviews. You had the good fortune to have worked with her, to have written your book from the perspective of personal contact. That's what makes what you wrote terribly special."

I thanked him for his kind words and tried to be helpful.

Soon other books began to appear. If the Garland brood and other of Judy's friends and admirers thought my book was "muckraking," I wonder what they thought of the subsequent efforts, some of which were downright scurrilous and cruel.

One of Judy's acquaintances who has been constantly insulting

about *Rainbow* is Glenn Ford. In rereading the Garland book, I
don't feel there is anything in it with reference to Glenn Ford that
is damaging or inaccurate. I have always regarded him as an
extremely talented actor. He persists in villifying me publicly and
privately for having written the book. I guess I am fair game. As
I said earlier, if you don't like the heat . . .

On the positive side, Liza and I kissed and made up at a party
during the Christmas season of 1976. That mutual affection holds
to this day, I'm happy to report.

One final note: When the spate of Garland books appeared,
Walter Clemmons, the respected literary critic for *Newsweek*, reviewed them on a full page titled JUDY, JUDY, JUDY. His final
comment commended the reader to skip most of them, since "Mel
Tormé's book on Judy Garland is still the best of the batch."

32.

SNOWMAN

*A*T approximately 6:17 A.M. on February 9, 1971, the world began to shake. The attendant rumble sounded like an old Big Boy steam locomotive rushing past our windows, tearing the shutters to pieces, dislodging the masonry, and converting us into the inhabitants of a giant blender, made all the more terrifying by occurring in pitch blackness, thanks to an electrical failure and how dark the mornings were that time of year.

I'll never know how I did it, but I leapt over the half-sleeping form of Jan and raced out into the hallway, turned right, and ran into Daisy's little nursery. At the same time, I yelled into Tracy's adjoining bedroom, "Get up, Tracy, and come stand in the doorway!" Trace was there before I had finished barking those orders. The house was shaking as though a giant hand had closed over it and was intent on breaking it apart. I felt for Daisy in the blackness of her room, grabbed her, and stood in her doorway, holding her in my right arm and steadying Tracy with my left hand.

After what seemed like an hour (the actual quake lasted only seconds), the shaking, rumbling, and roaring stopped. Jan rushed out to us. We could not see each other, but at least we could cling together. Now we realized the burglar alarm was ringing like a bell from hell.

I felt my way along the landing bannister to the stairs. I ran blindly down to the bar where the turn-off switch was, groped for the key, found it, and switched off the alarm.

Now came the aftershocks, not as intense as the original quake but scary nonetheless. We began tensing for them, and they seemed to occur at regular intervals. As it grew light, I walked back into the bar area. My heart nearly stopped. The floor of the bar was totally covered with broken glass. All the tumblers and wine goblets had fallen from their shelves in the initial shock, and there did not seem to be a single square foot of floor that wasn't sporting upturned, ugly shards of broken glassware. How I had avoided being seriously gashed in my barefooted attempt to turn off the alarm is something I will never know.

In the uneasy weeks that followed, the aftershocks continued. No matter where Jan and I were—out to dinner, at a party, shopping—whenever the slightest trembler occurred, we raced for the car and sped home. The earthquake had really spooked us. What we were most grateful for was the age of our house. Built in the mid-thirties, it had withstood the disaster with virtually no structural damage.

In the wake of the Garland book controversy came an offer from Alan Landsburg, a documentarian formerly employed by David Wolper. With nostalgia all the rage at that time, Landsburg had an idea for a show to be called "It Was a Very Good Year." I would be the host and line producer. The show would examine the news events, music, politics, movies, car models, advertisements, *et al.* of a given year each week. I loved the idea and hated the title. "Alan, for God's sake," I argued, "how do we call 1942 a 'very good year'?" Landsburg stubbornly insisted on his title. I wanted to call the show "Sentimental Journey," although even that title didn't really suit the subject matter perfectly either.

When the first segment finally aired, beginning in April 1971, it was well-received by critics and public alike. It easily outrated the show that had occupied that time slot previously. Thanks to Landsburg's talent in the editing room, each show became an eye- and ear-catching collage of memories. My proudest moment in connection with "Year" came one night at a party out at Jack Lemmon's beach house. Three of my heroes were present: Gregory Peck, Richard Widmark, and Alan Arkin. Each made a special point of telling me I had captured his Tuesday nights with our program.

Sadly, in spite of good ratings, it was a bartered show, stuck in a 7:30 position on ABC. Since ABC was not a partial owner, they dumped us after seventeen segments had aired and replaced "It Was a Very Good Year" with one of their own programs. I was sorry to see the project end, but we had had a good run.

Off I went, on the road once more. Sometimes Jan would pick up baby Daisy and accompany me. Mostly she stayed home, which was healthier for our daughter, but ultimately injurious to our marriage. The dilemma of any traveling man, be he lingerie salesman, airline pilot, or entertainer, with regard to having children, is very nearly insoluble. Still, I wouldn't trade a single child of mine for anything imaginable. They are the delights of my life. It isn't easy to be a parent, especially in these permissive times, but, having been one since the early 1950s, I can just imagine how empty and pointless my life would have been without my five kids.

I am, admittedly, part dreamer, part realist. The latter side of my nature knows what it means to tie a wife to the family home once a baby comes into her life; add being apart for weeks at a time and you put one hell of a strain on any marriage. Absence *may* make the heart grow fonder, but you can't prove it by me.

In December 1972, Jan walked into my den/office in our house and quietly informed me she was going to have a baby the following August. I was delighted. We had been trying to create a brother or sister for Daisy who would be reasonably close to her own age. Tracy was crazy about his new little sister, but he was now thirteen years old and going to junior high, with a truckful of friends his own age. So, a new little one on the way. Great.

I was a bit nonplussed by Jan's low-key announcement of the future blessed event. She gave me the news with a slight shake of her head. Was it disbelief? Disappointment? I couldn't tell. Her subdued attitude surprised and disturbed me. Hadn't we been trying like crazy to get her with child again? The tests, the body-temperature readings, the works? What was wrong? Little did I know.

1973.

Out on the road. I call Jan.

"How are you feeling?"

"Fine." (A trifle too cheery? Am I detecting things that aren't there?)

"How's my Daisy?"

"Growing. Lord, she's beautiful."

"Well, hell, look in the mirror and you'll see why."

Silence.

"Sure you're all right?"

"Hmm? Oh, yes. Of course. Certainly."

What the hell *is* going on? I wonder.

The year progressed inconsequentially for me with the exception of the arrival of my fifth child, James Scott Tormé, on August 13. He was some beautiful baby, with Jan's well-chiseled English nose, which she, in turn, had inherited from her dad, "Scotty." I have never been hooked on numerology or any of the other attendant craziness with regard to astrology or tarot cards or crystal balls. I do, however, think it interesting that Daisy was born December 13, James on August 13, and I first saw the light of day on September 13. There's a message there somewhere.

I played several dates on the road and earned enough money to buy the groceries, pay the bills, and put something aside as well. All in all, neither a bad nor a particularly good year. Average. Adequate.

≡

The new year started out downright promisingly. I was offered the lead in a movie, to be shot in Utah in February. I was fascinated by the prospect of playing the character described to me by producer-director Kent Bateman. First, though, I had to extricate myself from a commitment to appear as a guest on a Monsanto TV special that featured Benny Goodman. I hated to do that, because, despite Benny's erratic behavior at times, I idolized him. On the few occasions in the past when I had worked with him, mainly on TV specials, performing with the undisputed King of Swing always got my heart pumping a little faster.

Working with Benny was always a treat and trial. Artie Shaw was an entirely different ball of wax. Highly intelligent, able to discuss a wide variety of engrossing subjects with insight and authority, Artie is someone with whom working was always a treat and often instructive. I always regretted his having forsaken the clarinet at a far-too-early retirement from the music business. When he began occasionally to front the newly organized Artie Shaw Orchestra, it was a pleasure just to see him standing in front of sixteen musicians, even though nary a reed touched his lips. I was thrilled to share the stage with him at the Hollywood Bowl a few years ago. When Darlene Chan, producer of Jazz at the Bowl, approached me in the parking lot of the Bowl looking distraught and informed me that Artie had commandeered my usual dressing room, I smiled, patted her hand, and said: "Hey, Darlene. He's Artie Shaw. He gave me my first break as a solo singer. He's entitled."

Now then. Benny.

Of course, stories abound about Benny. Funny stuff.

Like the time one of his "girl" singers went to his house to rehearse and complained of how cold it was in the rehearsal room. Benny nodded, walked out of the room and came back wearing a sweater.

Or the one Leonard Vannerson, his onetime road manager, told me. After a one-nighter, Leonard, driving Benny's car with the King alongside him, informed the maestro that Chris Griffin, Goodman's lead trumpet player, was leaving the band in two weeks. At that very moment, a tractor-trailer truck swerved into their path, and to avoid hitting it, Leonard cramped the wheel of the Cadillac to the right and crashed into a ditch, crumpling the right fender against the tire.

Benny, his overcoat thrown over his shoulders, sat on a rock in silence as Vannerson took the truck driver's license number, filled out a form for the police, who arrived shortly after the accident, and helped a tow-truck driver free up the right tire so he and Benny could continue on their way. This all took about an hour.

Finally, Benny and Leonard set out again, Benny not having uttered a word in all that time. They drove for another forty minutes before Benny broke the silence.

"Gee, Leonard," he said. "Why does Chris want to leave the band?"

I was secretly delighted when Monsanto refused to release me from the obligation. Bateman pulled out a few stops and moved the shooting schedule so that I could begin the picture the day after taping the Goodman show.

When B.G. asked me what I'd like to do on the show, I suggested, among other tunes, "How Long Has This Been Going On," a fine Gershwin ballad he had recorded years ago with Peggy Lee. Benny put his forefinger in his mouth, like a little kid pondering which flavor of ice cream to select. "Gee," he said, "I don't know. We haven't got any parts on that one."

"No problem, Benny," I answered. "I'll sit down right now and knock out some rhythm parts."

"Great. Just great."

I sat at the piano for a full twenty minutes, writing piano, bass, drum, and clarinet chord sheets, while Benny sat in a chair ten feet away, reading the paper.

When I finished, I called to him: "Okay, Benny. I've finished with these parts on 'How Long Has This Been Going On.' "

He looked at me. "Aw, Mel," he said. "Let's not do that tune."

Figures.

Ah, well. He was a one-of-a-kind virtuoso and ten years later, in 1983, he came to see me at a New York nightclub and sat with me for an hour between shows talking about the old days.

When I asked him about his various drummers (he was reputed to hate drummers in general), he waved them aside and said: "There was only one drummer. Gene."

I tried to extricate some praise from him for Ralph Collier, who had played so cleanly and crisply on his single of "Clarinet à la King."

"Too rigid," he pronounced.

"How about Sid Catlett?"

"Okay, but he wasn't Gene."

"And Davey Tough?"

"He kept damn good time, but Gene was the best."

It warmed my heart to hear him extol the virtues of Krupa. They had not always seen eye to eye, but Benny was nothing if not honest and honorable where his evaluation of musicians was concerned.

He talked a lot about Fletcher Henderson, his favorite of all the arrangers who had worked for him. I mentioned how much I also loved the early 1940s band with Lou McGarity on trombone and Mel Powell on piano and how I especially admired the futuristic charts by Eddie Sauter.

He wrinkled his nose and looked at me as if I were crazy.

"Naw. I never really liked that band. Fletcher. He was *the* arranger. And my first band back in the thirties was the best I ever had."

Was Benny having an attack of nostalgia that night in 1983? Who knows? Who cares? It was just very enjoyable sitting there, listening to the King of Swing expounding, reminiscing, and being warm and extroverted in the bargain.

We shot the Monsanto special at the Rainbow Room, high atop Rockefeller Center. Benny was in good form, courteous and seemingly happy to have me as a guest on the show. We did "Lady Be Good" together, with me supplying the "scatting" and Benny playing the answers to my vocal riffs. What I really wanted was to join him the next evening in Carnegie Hall and play drums on "Sing, Sing, Sing," which I know as well as the national anthem. Whether or not I could have aced myself into that drum spot was academic in any case. Kent Bateman and the movie crew awaited me in Salt Lake City the very next day.

"Snowman" was the working title of the film. I played Zak O'Brien, trainer of a pair of famous TV stars: Romulus the Wolf and Caesar the Golden Eagle. "Caesar and Romulus" is a highly rated TV series, and, as the movie begins, I am about to fly my two talented friends, via my private plane, from Denver to Burbank to pick up their "Patsy Awards" on a TV special created for just such an occasion. I load the wolf and the eagle into the aircraft (a twin sister of my own Cherokee Arrow) and take off. Somewhere over the wild, snow-enshrouded Utah wasteland, I encounter an uncharted blizzard. My radio goes out and soon I develop engine trouble. I am forced to try to get the plane down safely. It is night and I become disoriented. The plane crashes. I and my two companions survive the crash and escape the fire that consumes the Cherokee. Romulus runs free and disappears. Caesar stays with me.

The rest of the picture is a survival story. Zak improvises a
pair of snowshoes from the wreckage and fashions an ersatz sled
with a rail for Caesar. He also has found a walkie-talkie, undam-
aged but minimally functional, as well as a suitcase containing
outlandishly colorful golf clothing he had been bringing to his
partner in Burbank, played by William Shatner.

Zak trudges through the bleak landscape that goes to make up
the snowy Utah wilderness. His leather flying jacket is hardly warm
enough for the icy winter cold. He opens his partner's suitcase and
proceeds to put on a garish golf sweater and an equally colorful
sport jacket. Later on, he repeats the process, until he looks like
an outrageous circus clown trekking through some kind of white
hell on the way to oblivion. Are he and Caesar ever found? And
what of Romulus? Does he survive or perish? Watch it on TV
and find out for yourself. Channel thirteen in L.A. has run the
movie several times in the last few years. It was also released
theatrically as *Challenge to Survive*.

I played Zak with a beard and moustache that were applied
every morning by a marvelous guy named Norm Pringle. He had
retired to Salt Lake City after having been, for many years, one
of the top makeup men at Warner Bros. in Burbank. I had met
Norm back in the days when I had been a Warner Bros. contract
player. I was grateful that Bateman had found him and lured him
out of retirement to do our movie. Having a beard and moustache
applied to your face with spirit gum at 5:30 A.M. on successive
wintry mornings in a cold trailer out in the boonies is no laughing
matter. Norm's humor and understanding helped ease the pain.

Brian Renfro, of the famous Renfro animal-training family,
supplied the eagle, whose real name was Baby and who, in fact,
was a lady eagle. Golden eagles are naturally quite fierce; Baby
was the only trained specimen in the world. That bird and I became
friends, and I actually got to love her. There are scenes in the film
where, after Caesar is flying around, hunting for game at Zak's
command, she flies back to where Zak is waiting and comes to
rest on the gauntlet he wears on his right arm.

Having a large eagle flying right at you at forty miles an hour
can be somewhat unnerving. After several runs, though, it seemed

perfectly natural to stand there, with my gauntlet-covered arm raised just in front of my face to receive that onrushing bird. Baby was a joy.

There were a couple of hairy moments. One of them involved a large bear that Zak encounters on his journey. The bear was supposed to have been a docile, trained animal. He was something less than that. When he started to come at me, the trainers jumped between us and calmed him down. "Maybe he's heard me sing?" I wondered out loud to general laughter.

Another unsettling incident took place in a large field at the foot of a low mountain range. The snow was kneecap high. On "Action," I was to run as hard as I could, camera right to camera left, believing that I had spotted Romulus in the lower range of one of those mountains. I was wearing two of the wild-and-crazy golf sweaters and two sports coats over my leather flying jacket. I could barely move in that regalia. Now I was being asked to run through knee-high snow. Jan and Daisy had come to the location to visit. As they watched, I dutifully performed the director's bidding for the cameras.

"Faster, Mel," yelled Bateman. I tried to comply. Running through that snow meant lifting my legs as high as I could and trying to mush through. It was brutally tiring. Kent kept egging me on.

"Keep running. All the way to the foot of that hill. Don't stop. Keep going." I made it, barely. I fell into the snow, my heart banging against my rib cage. I fought to catch my breath. I began to gray out, that same dimly remembered feeling I had once had during a very tight turn I was making in my airplane, with the "G" forces pulling the blood out of my brain.

I'm having a heart attack, I thought vaguely, slipping toward unconsciousness. I briefly flashed on the false alarm I had years before in Manchester, England. Then there were anxious faces above me, including Jan's and Daisy's, and slowly, slowly, my vision began to return and my breathing became deeper and easier. That scared the hell out of me. Later in the day, a doctor examined me very carefully and concluuded that I had merely hyperventilated and that my heart was still as sound as a 1926 dollar.

Hairy incident number three: At one point, Caesar and Zak take refuge in a mountain cave. There, they accidentally come across a small mountain lion cub. "He's a cute little thing, Mel. No sweat. Pick him up. We'll get some good stuff with the little guy."

I picked him up. And let him go. The minute he was in my arms, the little cub turned into a squirming, clawing, biting bundle of dynamite. Nothing I did pacified him. It was the one bit of direction that made me balk. Later, Brian Renfro, who was not the cub's trainer, said, "Good move, Mel. That damn little cub is wild and dangerous. You could have really gotten hurt."

In May 1974, I acceded to Jan's wish to take a family vacation in England. While I had spent a goodly chunk of money converting our pool house into a pleasant guest cottage for her parents during their frequent visits, I realized Jan was patently British to the bone and missed her native soil.

We stayed with her mother and father in their tiny house off the Bayswater Road in Leinster Mews. It was crowded and uncomfortable and, worst of all, lacked any kind of real privacy. Jan's mother and I were not exactly compatible, and I was not sorry to leave when work called. Jan opted to stay on for a couple of extra weeks. Why not? She was in the bosom of her family; she was seeing old friends and, as I later discovered, new ones.

I went to play Harrah's in Reno with Jerry Lewis. One evening, after having called Jan in London, I walked somewhat dazedly into Jerry's dressing room between shows and told him I was having a problem. Jan was being evasive about when she was coming home with the children. The problem resolved itself when she called unexpectedly the same evening and announced she would take the next plane. Further, she would bring the kids to see me in Reno and we could drive back to L.A. together. I was relieved and delighted.

≡

I had appeared on the Jerry Lewis muscular dystrophy telethon many times before, but that year, 1974, was a particular kick for me. I began the telethon in Las Vegas with Jerry. At midnight, I boarded a plane for New York City. I landed at Kennedy and sped by limousine to the New York TV studio, where I proceeded to host the Manhattan portion of the telethon until it ended. The New York "take" was the greatest it had ever been. Jerry showed up a few days later for my annual post–Labor Day opening of the new season at the St. Regis.

Opening night, I debuted a seventeen-minute medley of Gershwin music it had taken me two and a half months to arrange. I remember Jonathan Schwartz, one of the Big Town's radio lights and a longtime friend, coming backstage after the show and saying, with a broad smile, "The Gershwin medley's too short." And meaning it. That was an evening full of love and excitement. Jan was not there, unfortunately. She was home with year-old James. Her presence would have made the evening complete.

Midway through the St. Regis run, Jerry Lewis picked me up at the hotel in a limo, carted me over to a camera store, and presented me with a fine Konica 35mm camera and an even better Macro zoom lens. Back in the car, he handed over a gift-wrapped box. I opened it to find he had special-ordered a quantity of memo cards with my name embossed at the bottom. I had once admired some of his, in his dressing room at the Sahara in Vegas. That is a mistake. You can never admire anything of Jerry's out loud. He'll either buy you a duplicate of what you mention or give the coveted item to you on the spot. In the case of the memo cards, he had waited until that day and presented them to me—10,000 of them. It was September 13.

Forgetting his genius for comedy for a moment, Jerry is one of the most informed, intelligent persons I have ever met. He has been parodied, in some instances mercilessly and unfairly, for his devotion to the cause of muscular dystrophy. I know, firsthand, how genuine that dedication is. Jerry works tirelessly on behalf of M.D. 365 days of the year. He does "good stuff" endlessly. I am proud to call him and his wife, Sandy, friends.

Late in the year, I hired a young drummer. His name was Don Osborne, Jr. He was the son of Don, Sr., who was the president of Slingerland Drums, a product I had endorsed for many years. He was also a Buddy Rich protégé. He played drums in the style

I admired but he was timid as hell. Consequently, when he joined me on New Year's Eve at the Hyatt in Houston, he played with so little gusto that I was sure I had made a mistake in hiring him. Donny was quite young, in his early twenties. A tall, slim, blond lad who would not have been seen dead in an unpressed pair of pants or unshined shoes, his taste in clothing—with a preference for Brooks Brothers suits and jackets—was impeccable. He made it clear to me that he was determined to keep his newfound job, and that he was diametrically opposed to the kind of attention-grabbing antics practiced by certain other drummers.

"Well and good, Donny," I informed him that New Year's Eve at the tail end of 1974. "But bring the pendulum back toward center. You're way over to one side. I appreciate your outlook on what a drummer is supposed to do in backing a singer, but don't confuse strength with showing off. I want you to kick the band when the arrangement I write calls for it." Donny, who kept calling me "Mr. Tormé" for the better part of the first few months he played for me, shifted gears and turned into a magnificent drum accompanist.

He has been playing for me ever since.

33.

FRIENDSHIP

*D*URING the 1974 engagement at the St. Regis, I had been backed by a fifteen-piece band, led by one of the greatest lead trumpet players of all time, Al Porcino. He had played on a number of my records as well as Sinatra's, Peggy Lee's, and more Big Band LPs than I could possibly enumerate. He had finally taken the quantum leap from sideman to leader, and a friend of his had prevailed upon me to persuade the St. Regis management to hire Al's new band to back me. The hotel was amenable and the band, a crisp, roaring brood, came on like Buster's proverbial gang.

Al's friend came to me and announced he was bankrolling an Al Porcino album, to be made "live" in the Maisonette Room where we were working. Would I do Al a favor and sing one song on the album? I said yes. That "yes" wound up being a Mel Tormé LP with backing by Al Porcino's band. I was to receive a $5,000 advance against a percentage of the ultimate royalties.

Al's pal took the tapes to the one company I detested, Atlantic Records, sold the album to them for $19,000, and took off. The musicians never got paid, Al never saw a penny, nor did I. The record, called *Mel Tormé: Live at the "Maisonette,"* has been re-released again and again. I have yet to see one penny from Al's pal for my participation. Ironically, that LP earned me a Grammy nomination for "Best Arranger."

In 1973, Buddy Rich had "fronted" a little club called "Buddy's Place" on Second Avenue and Sixty-second Street. One night he cooked up a prank that was really funny. I had been playing the

Maisonette. I called to tell him that I and a good friend, Rudy Behlmer, were going to come and hear his last show on Saturday night. Buddy seemed delighted.

When we arrived, the place was jammed. Rich, heading a sextet in those days, played a knockdown, drag-out set that left everyone breathless. When the cheering subsided, he made his way to the microphone, a towel wrapped around his neck.

"Thank you," he puffed, holding up his hand for silence. A few people continued to stamp and whistle. He glared at them, then smiled. "I don't blame you. I know I was great."

More cheers. "I just want to take a minute to introduce one of my best friends. I'm really flattered that he came over tonight, after doing two shows of his own over at the St. Regis. What else can I say, except—Ladies and gentlemen, the absolute greatest— Mr. Mel Tormé!"

I smiled and stood up.

Not one person applauded.

Not a single soul.

Total dead silence.

My jaw dropped and my eyes popped. Ten seconds went by. I looked at the audience, dumbfounded. They looked at me. Then came a burst of laughter from every single person in the room and wild applause.

In that split second, I "got it." Rich had preprogrammed the entire audience. ("Listen, everyone. Tormé's coming over. Now, when I introduce him and he stands up, I don't want to hear one single whistle, hand clap, or cheer. Dead silence, understand? He'll flip.")

It was a great gag, and no one laughed harder than I.

In 1975, Buddy Rich expanded his Buddy's Place operation and moved to a spacious downstairs facility near Madison Square Garden, directly across the street from the old Hotel Pennsylvania, where he had made musical history in 1939 with the Artie Shaw band.

Stanley Kay, Buddy's manager, idolator, and friend, prevailed upon me to play the club for a pair of weeks. He didn't have to do much prevailing. My old hangout, the St. Regis, had closed the

Maisonette Room in the spring of 1975. There really wasn't much
to choose from in the way of a Manhattan venue. Buddy's new
place seemed tailor-made for me. His band would accompany me.
It sounded like it would be fun.

Buddy barked orders in the club as if he really owned it. In
fact, he was merely paid for the use of his name on the masthead.
Marty Ross, a shrewd young restaurateur, was the actual owner.
The food at Buddy's Place was magnificent, and no wonder. Marty
had previously owned a superb little eatery called "Marty's Bum
Steer" in the East Seventies. The quality of his food drew the
cream of New York society and celebrities as well as raves from
the food critics.

Opening night, Rich was already knee deep in "shtick." I came
to work to find all my clothes gone. Buddy, highly agitated, informed me there had been a robbery. The police had been notified;
they were working on it. Meanwhile, I would have to go on, in
front of a packed house, in my street clothes. Knowing Victor
Venom's penchant for practical jokes, I shrugged and said, "Let's
go." When his gag bombed, he immediately produced the missing
garments and we got down to business. The rest of the engagement
went like wildfire. I signed to return in the fall.

I was doing my level best to maintain a decent balance between
home and the road. With one new baby, one toddler, and a teen-
ager in our house, I planned my dates away from home very
carefully so I could spend some meaningful time with the children
before they began calling me "Uncle Daddy."

≡

I had no idea how the value of my gun collection had escalated
until a good friend, writer, and gun expert, Larry Wilson, informed
me that a certain old Colt I owned was worth a fortune! Furthermore, he tempted me with the information that an outrageously
wealthy Connecticut gentleman named John Solley, heir to the
Lilly & Co. pharmaceuticals fortune, was very interested in pur-
chasing that gun. The staggering price Larry mentioned knocked
my socks off.

Back in 1954, while playing the Chicago Theatre, I had been

told about a fabulous Colt Single Action Army Revolver, currently in the hands of one Ted Busse, a salesman for Klein's Sporting Goods Store on the near North Side. I had to have a look at it. That gun was the finest, the most beautiful Single Action ever produced. A rich charcoal blue, it was profusely and delicately engraved. Bands of gold encircled the fore and aft ends of the five-and-a-half-inch barrel. The frame of the gun, as well as the cylinder, was gold inlaid. The top of the backstrap or grips sported a finely outlined fleur-de-lis. The handles were pearl, with a sensitively chiseled example of Columbia, the Goddess of Liberty, gracing the right grip. The gun lay in a bed of purple satin, within a suede-covered box. My God, I thought at the time, even antigun fanatics could appreciate this work of art.

Ted Busse was adamant: $750 would buy the gun—not one cent less. In 1954, that was a lot of money for a firearm, even a beauty like the one in question. Two good friends, Bob Courtney and Ron Wagner at the Colt factory in Hartford, came up with provenance on the piece.

It had been fabricated by Colt on special order from Sears, Roebuck in Chicago and shipped to them in October 1897. Sears displayed the "one-off" showpiece in their sporting goods department for a long time. In an early 1900s Sears catalogue, they advertised this "one-of-a-kind cowboy revolver," and offered it for sale to the first taker at $50.

The weapon remained in Chicago, passing from one owner to another, until it fell into the hands of Ted Busse.

I spent several sleepless nights wondering whether or not to spend such a sum for a gun. I was not making great money in 1954. Was I crazy, contemplating ownership of an expensive piece like the Sears Colt?

In the end, I bought it, with trepidation.

In 1975, Larry Wilson informed me that John Solley had agreed to buy it for $100,000. You needn't count the zeros. You read it right. One hundred thousand dollars. It was past believing.

The James Scotts were once again in America, visiting Jan. Two friends of ours, the Larry Rosenblooms, hosted a lovely dinner party in honor of Thora and Scotty's visit. As we enjoyed the meal, I mentioned in passing the offer on the gun.

"Sell it," said Stephanie Rosenbloom. "Pay off your house with the money. Jan and the kids will never have to worry about a roof over their heads again. In case anything happens to you."

At that moment, I glared at Stephie. How insensitive! Sell the crown jewel of my collection? Unthinkable!

The more I thought about it in the ensuing weeks, the more I realized Stephanie was absolutely right. While I had long since given up my own light plane, I still flew an enormous amount of miles each year on commercial aircraft.

I was approaching middle age, when ailments and even serious health problems become more and more possible. What if something *should* happen to me? A heart attack? An incurable disease? Wouldn't it be wonderful to know the house was free and clear? What peace of mind that would instill.

I bit the bullet, and summoned John Solley and Larry Wilson from their homes in Connecticut. I nearly *did* have a heart attack when John, a gruff but gentle individual in his upper sixties, examined the gun.

"It's not mint," he grumbled. "Not mint."

He had every right to make that comment. For one hundred big ones, the gun had better be pristine. The Sears Colt was very close to perfect but not quite. It had a few abrasions in the blueing, minuscule to be sure, but detracting nonetheless.

We haggled. We had dinner. We haggled some more. Jan maintained a strangely detached attitude throughout. At one point, I asked her, "Is anything wrong? Aren't you glad about this? We'll pay off the house—"

"Suit yourself," she replied. "Sell it or don't sell it. Makes no difference." I was a bit angry with her response. Like all show folk, I am given to a little selfishness. Here I was, being unselfish for a change, selling my treasured Colt to pay off our house, and my wife was shrugging off the gesture.

John Solley insisted on my including two other guns in the bargain. By now, I was so infused with the idea of owning my house free and clear that I agreed and the deal was made.

That night, in bed, just after turning out the light, I chuckled and said, "A hundred thousand dollars! For one gun! I don't believe it!" Jan treated me to a chuckle of her own. I omitted telling her that it had become a three-gun deal. Her apathy over the transaction earlier on had bewildered me. No sense in compounding whatever problem she was having with this situation by involving her any further.

≡

I opened the 1975 fall season at Buddy's Place, this time commencing September 8 and ending on the 20th of that month. Rich's juvenile sense of humor was working overtime. He had planned an elaborate practical joke that might have had serious repercussions.

Stanley Kay and Marty Ross let me in on what Buddy had cooked up for me. He had arranged with a couple of his buddies, a pair of plainclothesmen from a precinct house, to come into the club just before the first show, pretend to be hoodlums, abduct me, drag me out of the place, up the stairs, throw me into the trunk of a car, and drive around town for an hour or so before returning to the club and letting me in on the merry "gag."

Only the angry, forceful intervention of Stanley, Marty, and Buddy's wife, Marie, prevented this stupid stunt from actually taking place. Had it come off, I would have either have had a heart attack or I would have run amok.

Rich sulked about his aborted practical joke. He figured out another one for closing night. The place was jammed. Rita Moreno, then starring in *The Ritz*, had purposely rushed her show that night so she could come to my closing performance. Gary Berghof, of M*A*S*H fame and an amateur drummer, was in the audience. The band played its final set. Now it was my turn.

I stepped out in front of the orchestra and began to sing. Twelve minutes into my act, Buddy walked onto the stage and stopped the proceedings cold. Hands behind his back, he announced, "Ladies and gentlemen, I want to thank Mel for a marvelous engagement. [Applause] I'm particularly proud of him because he's been dieting all the time he's been here. Tonight, closing night, I think he deserves a little dessert." Before anyone could stop him, he slammed me in the face with a lemon meringue pie. Not, mind you, one of those show-biz shaving-cream prop pies, but a genuine lemon meringue job that went way beyond my face. Women shrieked out in surprise and disgust as their dresses were splotched with whipped cream and meringue. Men were furious to find their pants and jackets suddenly fouled by flying goop.

Buddy laughed.

I stood there covered in dripping lemon pie. My suit was ruined and so was the show. Twelve minutes into my performance, it was all over. (Why, in God's name, hadn't he waited, at least, until the end of the show?)

I went backstage, having apologized to the audience for the shortened performance, and tried to clean up. The sink in that makeshift dressing room was one of those tiny affairs, and I simply could not wash away the gunk. My hair felt like I had doused it with a full tube of Brylcreem and, of course, my suit was a complete disaster. Buddy walked into the dressing room, patted me on the back, and said, offhandedly, "You're a good sport." That was it.

I walked out into the club. It was empty, except for Marty, Stanley, and a young couple. The girl, who was celebrating her sixteenth birthday, was weeping copious tears.

Seems her mother was a fan of mine, had raised her on my records, and, as a birthday treat, had made her a birthday present of my final show at Buddy's Place. All twelve minutes of it. I felt itchy and sticky and thoroughly disgusted. I walked up to the piano, sat down, and sang two songs for her. I never felt less like singing, but she really seemed brokenhearted, and I felt I owed her a few tunes.

After she left, we held a post-morten on Buddy's untimely act. Stanley Kay, shaking his head in anger, said, "Jesus! Do you know how he [Buddy] reacted when Marty and I raised hell with him about it? He pouted like a little kid and said, 'Okay, so we won't have fun anymore.' I can't believe it! Seriously, what the hell is wrong with him?"

Marty added, "It's incredible! He's a genuine genius who sometimes acts like a ten-year-old juvenile delinquent. I'll never understand him."

There wasn't much I could say. What a putrid ending to an otherwise superb engagement. I went back to the hotel and thought about what Rich had done. A faint glimmer of suspicion about our relationship nudged its way through the solid door of my affection and admiration for him. I was beginning to get the feeling that Buddy Rich didn't like me. He had thrown that pie with such relish, such wide-eyed glee. Was I being paranoid?

Perhaps.

Perhaps not.

≡

On those occasions when I was at home, Jan and I tried to maintain some sort of social life. Dick and Dolly Martin were the people we saw most frequently at that point. Dolly, being English, was very comfortable with Jan. Dick's love of old movies matched mine easily. He had bought a new house off Benedict Canyon Road. Thanks to a friend he had at MGM, he was able to borrow prints of some of the great MGM classics. At least twice a week we would dine at each other's home and run old movies. It was good fun and particularly relaxing for me.

The road was taking its toll. I had begun to feel disenfranchised. Where did I really belong? Where the hell was I going? The treadmill seemed more inexorable and pointless than ever. The evenings in Beverly Hills with Dick and Dolly and my wife came to mean far more to me than they would have had I been living a normal existence.

Dolly Martin was a delightful, caring young woman. At the dinner table, she would feign mock exasperation and pretend to scowl at her husband. "When are you going to have Mel guest on 'Laugh-In'?" she would scold him.

"Dolly," I would admonish her.

"Dolly," Jan would echo.

"Dolly," Dick would say for the hundredth time, "nothing would make me happier. You know that and—"

"Dick," I would remind him, "puh-leeze! Let's not mix business with our personal relationship. I don't—"

"No, the thing is, Melvin, Dolly's right this time! I realize that while Schlatter* was co-owner and producer, it was probably too uncomfortable to contemplate. But now," Dick said, "now Dan [Rowan] and I have bought Schlatter out. We're the owners of the show! And we've got Paul Keyes back. You're right, Dolly; now's the time to get Mel on the show. Matter of fact, I'd like to build a whole show around music with Mel as the guest star."

I went the route of protestation. Friendship was one thing, business another. I did not ever want to take advantage. Dick suddenly became adamant; he would hear of nothing less than a solid Mel Tormé guest shot on "Laugh-In." And so the evening ended.

On the way home, Jan said, "What do you think, Mel? It would be wonderful if they built a show around you, wouldn't it? You could certainly use the TV exposure."

She was right. If it came to pass, being the prime guest on "Laugh-In" would not only be beneficial to my career, but it would certainly boost my sagging road-bound spirits.

A few nights later, we were once again invited to dinner and a movie at the Martins'. Dick had gotten a really old MGM goodie, _The Wet Parade_, one of the few I had missed during my lifetime of manic moviegoing. I was excited at the prospect and delighted that the other guests for dinner were the Carroll O'Connors.

Dinner was fun, anecdotes and one-liners flying back and forth. At one point, Dick cleared his throat and said to me, "Mel, about 'Laugh-In': I talked it over with Paul Keyes. Hey, he's a big fan of yours, by the way. I told him there were only three musical people I wanted to have as guests on the show: Bobby Goulet, Steve Lawrence, and you. Well, he passed on Steve and you. He only okayed Goulet. I'm sorry."

*George Schlatter, my old mentor on the ill-fated "Judy Garland Show," had once told me, on the eve of his firing, that I was a "true friend," a real "stand-up guy," and that he would never forget how I had defied officialdom at CBS and told the big guns what I thought about their dumping him and how it would destroy Judy's confidence, in particular, and the quality of the show, in general. Stupid me! How could I know at the time that Judy, seeming to gnash her teeth and wail over Schlatter's dismissal, had actually ordered the firing herself? George, grossly humiliated, had never, to my knowledge, hired anyone in any capacity who had been associated with the Garland show.

Dolly was suddenly genuinely angry. "Dick, that's ridiculous. You're the producer now. You own the show. Why should Paul Keyes have the final word on who guests and who doesn't?"

"Honey, you don't understand. We've been trying to get Keyes back on the show for a long time. Now that he's rejoined us, we don't want to make waves. We're happy to defer to his taste and his judgment. I mean, I would love to have Mel do a guest shot, but—"

"Whoa, hold it," I interrupted. "Please, let's not ruin this evening. I would have loved to have done the show, but, what the hell, if it's not to be, well, kismet, right? And, Richard, if Paul Keyes has turned Stevie Lawrence down, well, I'm in good company. I think he would have also made a great 'Laugh-In' guest, because, in addition to being one hell of a singer, he's a very funny guy. So . . . maybe next year Paul will okay Steve and me. Either/or, right?"

We dropped the subject then, and I was strangely relieved. We had gotten very close to the Martins, and I did not want anything to sully our friendship. Jan was not particularly thrilled with Dick but she was superfond of Dolly, and, generally, our evenings together were happy ones.

On the way home that night, I told Jan I had been in dead earnest about the blown chance at a guest shot on Dick's show. "It gets in the way, Jan. Honestly, I'm actually glad it didn't come off."

"Gee," she mused, "I wonder if Steve Lawrence knows he was turned down as well."

"Hmmm. Don't know."

That was a Saturday night in December. On the following Monday night, I had a slight cold. I stayed in bed and turned on my pal's show.

"Tonight, on 'Laugh-In,'" intoned Gary Owens, his hand covering one ear, "our special guest is Steve Lawrence."

I got out of bed, walked into my adjoining sitting room, closed the door, sat down in a rocker, and shook my head in disappointment.

How could a friend do that? Why would Dick tell such a stupid lie? Obviously, the show had already been taped and was "in the can" when, just a few nights previously, he had told me Steve had been nixed by Keyes. To look me in the eye and tell me what he had told me was the height of duplicity and insensitivity.

Daisy opened the door. "What's wrong, Daddy? Why are you sitting here in the dark?"

"It's nothing, darling. I've got a headache from this cold, that's all."

Jan came in. "Look, I know you're terribly hurt by this. How rotten of Dick! But Daisy's worried about you."

"Look, Jan, at this moment I am feeling putridly sorry for myself, so kindly allow me to wallow in it, will you? Just take Daisy, close the door, and leave me alone for a few minutes. I don't think that's asking too much, in view of the fact that my friendship with Dick Martin just came to an abrupt end, do you?"

Jan shook her head, took our little girl by the hand, and left the room. I was having trouble with my wife's attitude. She seemed phlegmatic and insensitive to my feelings. That wasn't like Jan.

Business, in the form of a post-Christmas engagement at the Fairmont Hotel in San Francisco, carried me blessedly out of Beverly Hills. I took the whole family with me so that we could have New Year's together.

Jan and I were slightly estranged. Perhaps she disdained me for reacting as I had to the Dick Martin disappointment. Perhaps, when you have been through the Battle of Britain and been deprived, early on in life, of the simple pleasures and necessities, as had Jan, a brokenhearted display like mine seems unacceptable in the stiff-upper-lip tradition of British stoicism. She apparently missed the point entirely. I didn't gave a damn about the guest shot. The loss of a friend, however—the disillusionment—that was heavy. Why couldn't my wife understand that?

One happy note: on New Year's Eve day, we were all invited to lunch at Bing Crosby's beautiful home in Burlingame, just outside of San Francisco. Months earlier, a disc jockey had called me long distance from Boston in order to play a tape for me over the phone. To my complete amazement, the tape contained an interview between said disc jockey and Bing.

D.J.: "Bing, if you got stuck on a desert island with nothing more than a phonograph and a few records, whose records would you most want to have?"

BING: "Well, of course, some of the great jazz players—Teagarden and, oh, you know, guys like that. Oh, and Mel Tormé's records. . . . I tell you, any singer that goes in to hear this guy sing has got to go out and cut his throat. He's the most fantastic musical performer I think we've ever had . . . the best musical entertainer I've ever seen."

Bing's remarks were thrilling. I wrote him a letter of thanks and asked if he would mind if I used some of what he had said in my publicity releases. He responded immediately by mail and not only agreed to allow me to quote him, but added even more plaudits in his letter, which he suggested I use freely. He had come to see me at the Fairmont the previous year. I had been told he enjoyed my performance, but I had no idea to what extent. Now, the greatest popular singer of our century (along with Sinatra) was praising my work with kudos that were positively mind-blowing.

Luncheon, New Year's Eve day, 1975. Jan, the kids, Harry Crosby, Mary Frances, Kathryn, Bing and myself. A funny, loving, gabby meal in Bing's formal dining room. Then the Groaner leads us into the Music Room. Sans toupé, comfortable, and totally without pretense or inhibition, he calls to Harry, "Go get your guitar." Harry complies. Bing asks Harry about "that James Taylor tune I like." Harry begins to strum; Bing slips into the song. Just like that. Bing Crosby, in his music room, singing for us. Incredible! Bing then asks me to sing. I go to the piano and let him hear a new Christmas song I have written called "Christmas Was Made for Children." He likes it. Says he wants a copy and would like to record it in the near future. My egg nog runneth over.

It is time to go. He summons his chauffeur, and the Rolls is brought up in front of the house. As I am getting into the car, Bing says, offhandedly, "We'll see you tonight at the hotel."

I step back out of the car. "Bing," I say, "you're kidding. New Year's Eve? At the Fairmont? My God, it'll be packed! People might hassle you. I mean—"

Bing grins. "We'll see you tonight. First show."

Sure enough, the Crosby crew showed up en masse and were among the most vociferous clappers and whistlers that evening. I watched them from the stage of the Venetian Room and then looked over and saw Jan, looking beautiful in a brand-new dress, I thought: I have a loving wife, gorgeous children, and Bing Crosby thinks I'm the best singing entertainer he's ever heard.

I was nothing less than euphoric. Unfortunately, the new year I had just glided into would wind up being the most painful, traumatic, and devastating year of my life.

34.

RUMBLINGS

THE success of *The Other Side of the Rainbow* had prompted me to begin work on a new book. It was a novel, tentatively called "The Thompson Man." Not surprisingly, the central character became, as the book progressed, a world-famous singer; but that was only incidental to what the book was really about. At the core of the novel was a broken family: a willful beauty of an Irish girl from the coal-mining hills of Pennsylvania; an illegal Polish immigrant, sought in Russia for the murder of the Russian officer who had killed his mother; and their son, Martin Wynocki, who eventually becomes "Marty Wynner," the protagonist of the story.

By the beginning of 1976, I had worked long and hard to complete it. I had researched the book to death, talking at length with several Polish people who were kind enough to supply me with Polish phrases peculiar to the World War One era. The syntax, the colloquialisms of each decade, from 1916 until the mid-1970s, were very carefully implemented, since one of my pet peeves in reading other people's work is a lack of attention to detail. I've noticed this especially in crime novels where even superior writers, not having done their homework, insist upon having their heroes snick off the safety on Colt or Smith & Wesson .38 snub-nose revolvers. (Ain't no such animal as a safety on those guns.)

Happily, that was the one problem I did not have, having owned hundreds of guns by the time I began writing "The Thompson Man." The title itself referred to a nickname Marty is tagged with during his participation in World War Two as a sergeant with the 101st Airborne during the Battle of the Bulge. He has become superproficient with the Thompson submachine gun. He resists all efforts by his superiors to get him to discard the obsolete, unwieldy weapon for more current firepower. His squad, amused by his stubborn loyalty to the gun the gangsters and G-men used during the Roaring Twenties, begin calling him "the Thompson Man." In June, I placed the manuscript in the hands of my literary agent, Sterling Lord.

On January 20, 1976, I went to Holland to receive the Edison Award for Best Male Vocalist. It was a signal honor. The Dutch have a singular award for the arts: the Edison. It was akin to winning a Grammy, and it made for an encouraging beginning to the new year.

Then, on February 29, as I've mentioned, I was nominated as Best Arranger for my "Gershwin Medley." That nomination as an arranger made me prouder than any other. I appeared on the Grammy Awards program with Ella Fitzgerald. We sang a knocked-out, scat version of "Lady Be Good." It received, according to a subsequent letter I got from the president of NARAS, the National Academy of Recording Arts and Sciences, "the longest single standing ovation in the history of the Grammy Awards."

Great. So where were the record offers? I had been without a recording contract for a few years at that time, and, standing ovation to the contrary, there were no record company execs rushing up to me with pen and contract in hand. Well, no, that's not quite true. There was one.

His name was Norman Schwartz. His reputation preceded him. He was a fierce promulgator of good music, particularly jazz. He owned a small record company called Gryphon Records. He had recorded, in recent months, Lena Horne, Woody Herman, and Michel Legrand. I had heard the Lena and Woody sides. They were among the best things those two artists had ever done.

Schwartz was a beetle-browed, swarthy man in his late forties or early fifties. He was certainly making some of the finest records in the business at that point. He was knowledgeable about music, and his taste in musicians, arrangers, and the like was impeccable.

"What the hell is going on?" he demanded, that night at the Grammy Awards. "You're the best goddamn singer in the world today. . . ."

"Norman, let's not go crazy. It's very nice of you to—"

"Hey, I don't say what I don't mean! For my dough, you are the best. You should be recording. Constantly." He looked around and waved his arm in the general direction of the milling crowd. "None of these assholes—not one of them—has the brains to grab you for their dim-witted companies. Well, damn it, I do. I want to make records with you. And I can tell you right now, they'll be the best frigging records you ever made." I signed with him.

The first two weeks in May found me paired with the Buddy Rich band at the Waldorf Astoria in New York. As usual, the incident at the now-defunct Buddy's Place was glossed over. Rich and I were sensible musical partners, and the good, if not spectacular business, as well as the superb reviews (especially from Rex Reed) reflected the success of our combined efforts.

On June 1, we repeated our collaboration at the Hartman Theatre in Stamford, Connecticut, for a one-week stand. Perhaps I should have spelled that "one weak." It turned out to be the most hilarious engagement of my (and Buddy's) entire career. Opening night, in the 2,000-plus seat house, we drew 107 people. We were stunned. It's a fluke, we decided. Monday night. Connecticut. Smallish town. No sweat. It'll pick up and be great by the weekend. It was worse Tuesday. Disastrous Wednesday. Humiliating Thursday. Horrific Friday. Not-to-be-believed. Saturday night, we drew our biggest crowd: 231 patrons.

Rich and I nearly collapsed with laughter. I was sorry business had been so inexplicably bad at the Hartman, but I simply could not brood over it. Jan and the kids were waiting for me in New York, so we could board the *QE 2* and head for England.

In early springtime, I had received an offer once again to play the Talk of the Town. The fee, as usual, was ludicrous, but Jan so very badly wanted to go that, against my better judgment, I agreed to accept the offer.

Thora and Scotty met us at Southampton, and we made our way via the boat-train to London and the flat the Scotts had arranged for us. It was contiguous to their mews flat, just off Bayswater Road. We had brought with us Pauline Lilley, our housekeeper/nanny. Jan and I shared one of the two bedrooms in the old-fashioned walk-up; Pauline bunked with the children.

England, in general, and London, in particular, sweltered in the worst heat wave to hit the British Isles in a decade or more. The aging dinosaur of a flat Thora had found for us was not air-conditioned and uncomfortable in the extreme for me. Not, perhaps, for a Briton, whose running gag was usually, "Oh, yes, we had a lovely summer here one Thursday last July." My idea of a great summer is refrigerated rooms to work in, play in, eat in, and sleep in. I go to bed in the buff and sleep well only when I can draw the covers up over my shoulders and relax in the cool.

The heat in London that summer was oppressive. The grass in Hyde Park had turned a sickly yellowish-brown. Walk four blocks and your clothes stuck to your body in clammy wet patches. The humidity sucked energy out of you until the simplest moves, the lightest chores, became burdensome.

Consequently, I was surprised to find an overflowing house waiting for me at the Talk of the Town on opening night. The "Talk" was comfortably frigid and the audience was "hot," a rewarding combination for me. The result was a genuine smash, and there was a huge crush of people squeezing into my dressing room after the performance. One of them was Roy Moseley, a publicity man and an old friend of Jan's. Another was Kevin Francis, son of Freddie Francis, a well-known British cinematographer, and a new friend of Jan's.

He was a slightly corpulent young man in his late twenties. Along with his weight, he carried a self-satisfied Cheshire Cat smile and wavy dark hair, combed and cut the way they did it in 1944. He worked hard disguising what Jan used to call a "common Cockney accent." At this, he failed.

Now Kevin stood, in the front of my dressing room, directing traffic. Roy Moseley made his way over to me. "For God's sake, Mel," Roy said, indicating Kevin, "who in hell let that twit in here? I was just now standing next to him. He's acting like this is _his_ dressing room. He's already insulted..." Roy named a celebrated guest who had taken umbrage at Francis's rudeness and had left in a snit. "Why don't you just tell him to get out?" asked Roy.

"Well," I answered, flush with the success of the evening, "he's

Jan's friend. You know, she made a movie with his father a few years back, and in the past couple of years Kevin has been coming to America, trying to peddle these movies he's been producing—"

"Movies? Bloody crap! 'Z'-grade facsimiles of the Hammer horror films. Just because Kevin fancies himself a producer does not, in point of fact, automatically make him one. He's a shit, Mel. You oughtn't to have him around."

"Can't do much about that, Roy, without offending Jan and, ultimately, Freddie."

We left it at that, but I knew what Roy meant. Kevin's attitude was nothing short of supercilious. But Jan seemed to find him entertaining, and, since he was English, the son of a onetime colleague of Jan's and amusingly nerdlike, I put up with him.

Anyway, Kevin wasn't the problem. The problem was the heat. I simply could not sleep, and I must sleep in order to sing with any credibility. I was struggling each night to be worthy of even the pittance the Talk was paying me. I was out of sorts, tired, cranky, and occasionally inhospitable. I thought Jan understood my cantankerousness.

In addition, we were cottage hunting, against my better judgment. Jan had talked to me months before about the possibility of buying a small, inexpensive country cottage somewhere in England. At first I was surprised and disturbed. I had just sold three of my best Colt revolvers to pay off our Beverly Hills house. Now she wanted me to buy a second house? In England? What had happened to my sensible, practical, understanding wife? Buy a house we would live in for, at best, a couple of months during the summer each year? Or, possibly, every other year, if we were lucky?

"Oh no, darling," she had said brightly, "my idea is for us to live there six months a year and here in America six months a year."

"Jan," I had begun patiently, "what are you saying? Live there six months a year? What do we do for money? What do I do about my work?"

"Your work, dear heart," she countered, "is also writing music, arrangements, and books. You could sit in England and write other people's acts. God knows, lots of singers practically hound you to do so. You could sit in the garden of a lovely country cottage and turn out novels and articles for the newspapers and—"

"Darling, for heaven's sake, you're dreaming. I'm basically a singer. That's my identity with the public. I have no pretensions about being a great writer. I write articles for periodicals and newspapers and books because I enjoy doing it, not because I expect to make a real living at it. I arrange music only for myself; you know I'm totally unschooled in that department. Arranging my own music is a tedious chore. I'd go crazy, sitting at a piano, writing charts for someone else. As far as doing someone else's act—writing the special material, putting together medleys, and the like—Christ, I had enough of that during the Judy Garland mess."

"Yes, but just think how wonderful it would be if—"

"Jan, love, I'm a singer. For better, for worse. In my sickness and in my health, I'm a singer. That's what I do."

"All right, then," she continued stubbornly, "then sing. Six months a year. The other six months we can live in a lovely little cottage in Hertfordshire or—"

"Come on, love, you're not thinking. There is no continuity to any career on the basis of performing half a year and then taking the other half off. In six months of being away from the music scene and not actively performing, I'd be dog meat."

Now in the blasting heat of the summer of '76, we went traipsing around England, house hunting. My heart was not in it, but, if it made Jan happy and if we could find something affordable, a genuine bargain, why then . . .

Kevin Francis had become ever-present. ("Doesn't he have an office at Pinewood, Jan? The guy never seems to do anything. It's like his life's work is driving the kids and us around.")

No comment from Jan.

The weeks dragged on. Five of them. Even the cinemas were musty and close. As wonderfully as the engagement was going and as kind as the critics had been, I couldn't wait to get the hell out of England and back to the land of Fedders, Carrier, and Hotpoint; to freezing hotel rooms and icy movie houses and restaurants.

I confided this to Kevin one day. He had chauffeured us around so much that I felt it would be impolite not to accept his invitation to a men-only luncheon. "I have yet another problem, Kevin." I told him about Jan's manic desire to buy a cottage in England and live there for twenty-six weeks of the year.

"It simply isn't sensible," I concluded. He agreed.

Cottage hunting continued, but time was running out before we were due to return to the States.

The nightclub engagement came to a halt, finally, during the second, smothering week in July. I was asked by the management to extend the run for an extra two weeks. I could not, since I had commitments back in the United States. It was the year of the Bicentennial. I had been asked to sing in Philadelphia on the self-same steps of the art museum where "Rocky" had flexed his muscles and captured the American fancy.

The plan was as follows: I would go back to the States and fulfill the Philadelphia commitment and other dates while Jan remained with the children in Britain, visiting with her parents until mid-August. Then she and the kids would meet me in Fort Lauderdale, Florida. We would board the Sitmar liner, *Fairseas*, and would end the summer with a beautiful Caribbean cruise, before Daisy and James returned home for school in the fall.

The night before I left, Jan suggested we make love.

It was to be the last time, ever.

35.

HEARTBREAK

ON July 16 I went back to the United States. There were tears and good-bye waves from my kids, a seemingly reluctant-to-see-me-go embrace from my wife, and a polite, if not particularly warm, farewell from my in-laws. Jan promised to pick up the prepaid airline tickets awaiting her at National Airlines' office in London within the next few days. We would all rendez-vous in Florida on August 23 and board the *Fairseas*. Two days later, I did indeed sing for 18,000 people in Philadelphia. It was one hell of an experience, and (don't laugh, here it comes) it made me proud to be an American.

I then fulfilled a week-long stand at the Melody Tent in Hyannis, Massachusetts. I had put too much weight on in recent weeks, so I placed myself in the hands of a health club while I was there. During that week, pounds and inches began to disappear, and I was determined to continue the good eating and exercising habits being taught to me.

I went home from Hyannis. I puttered around the house, went to movies, did my calisthenics, adhered to my newfound diet, missed my wife and kids, and called them frequently.

"Oh, darling," chirped Jan over the transatlantic wire, "the weather's beautiful here today. It's cooled off a bit and I took the children for a long walk in Hyde Park. Then Kevin came over for lunch and . . ."

Two days later: "Darling, we all had a lovely day in the country. Kevin came round with the car and I prepared a picnic basket and we all—"

"Jan, have you picked up the tickets yet? Time's getting a bit short and—"

"Oh, not to worry. Loads of time."

"Well, I'd feel a lot better if you picked up the—"

"I will, I will. Next few days."

"Good, good. Well, my love, I'll call you Tuesday morning, eight o'clock, my time."

"I'll be waiting. I love you."

Monday, August 9, I had quite a few errands to do. I found myself in west L.A. near a storage facility where I kept several cartons of old records, many cans of film, and even some clothing with which I was reluctant to part. As I pulled up across from it, my heart sank. The large drive-in door was blackened with smoke damage, as was the rest of the building.

I was driving my Silver Cloud Mark III Rolls. I tore out of the car, leaving it standing with the engine running in the middle of the street, abreast of a drug rehab center. I ran into the Van & Storage to find poor Mr. Johnson, the owner, sitting in his fire-damaged office, virtually in tears.

"Couple of kids did it," he explained. "Set fire to one of the outdoor storage pallets just for fun. Fire caught on to the building. Ruined. Ruined. I've owned this place for twenty-seven years. Now, in one night, it's gone. I can't believe it."

I ran into the warehouse to where my things had been stored. Water damage everywhere, Everything ruined. I walked slowly back to my Rolls. Amazingly, it still stood there, purring.

I was forlorn about the loss all day. Even though most of the stored items had been mine, I still hated the thought of calling Jan and telling her the news.

Next morning, at 8:00 A.M., I dialed the number of the flat in London. "Good morning, love."

" 'Morning, Mel."

"Well, sweetheart, I'm afraid I have some rather bad news."

"Mel, are you alone?"

"Bellaire Van & Storage caught fire day before yesterday. All my stuff there is wiped out. Ruined. You should have seen the—"

"Mel, are you alone?"

"Yes, of course. Why?"

There was a pause, then, "Mel, I'm not coming back. Ever. I don't love you anymore. I hate Beverly Hills. All of our friends are too old for me. I'm staying here, with the children. If you want to see them, you'll have to come here."

Time seemed to stop. I shook my head. This had to be a dream. I would wake up momentarily, pick up the phone, and call Jan at eight o'clock as we'd arranged.

Sadly, it was no dream. I spent the next four hours on the phone, trying desperately to talk Jan out of her decision. Coldly, she urged me, "Get it all out, talk as much as you wish, but it will do no good. My mind's made up, Mel."

Finally, emotionally and physically exhausted, I hung up the phone. My mother and dad had arrived at the house midway through the conversation. They stood in the doorway, hollow-eyed. Tracy had awakened and had heard at least half the phone call. His mouth was set grimly. He had called Jan "Mom" since almost the very beginning of our relationship. Now, "Mom" was summarily dismissing him from her life. She hadn't been "Mom" at all, merely a woman who had shared his father's life for as long as she cared to.

Ten years. We had been married ten years. I had been certain this was to be my final marriage, a marriage to the grave. I had never loved any woman the way I loved Jan. Why? What had I done? The answer was too complex to comprehend on that Black Tuesday when my marriage came to an end.

Melissa and Steven, young adults now, came over to the house. Everyone did their best to console me. I walked through the house like a madman, again and again, shaking my head and mumbling to myself. I kept remembering a quote out of Judy Garland's mouth during the run of her 1963 series: "Mel," she had said earnestly, "I know I have my faults, but, you know, one positive thing about me is—I'm decent. I'm a decent human being."

Now I paused in front of a mirror. I'm decent too, Judy, I thought at that moment. I have been a decent father and husband. I have loved my wife and kids unrestrictively. Decently. How could Jan do something this *indecent*? The Jan who had spoken so impersonally that morning, so unfeelingly, was a Jan I did not know, had never met in an eleven-year relationship. My God, does anyone ever know anyone? How could I have been so blind?

Easily. There had been warning signs. I had ignored them. I thought we had a superb, loving marriage. Certainly there were obstacles, but who the hell doesn't encounter problems in ten years of marriage, a condition I had once heard called "the greatest invasion of privacy known to mankind"?

Then it was evening, the evening of the tenth. I sat on the front steps of my house, my head in my hands. Daisy. James. When would I see them again? And my wife? When would I lay eyes on her? What would it be like? I had engagements to fulfill, starting with a trip the very next morning to Great Gorge, New Jersey, to play the Playboy Resort Hotel, and then on to the Lake Geneva, Wisconsin, Playboy Hotel.

Tracy wanted me to ignore my obligations, fly over to England immediately, and "beat the hell out of that lying bitch. Do you realize she's strung you along, phone call after phone call, right up to today, when she knew you had to leave for Great Gorge tomorrow? She planned all this, Dad. Every goddamn bit of it. She tricked you into going to England with the kids; she tricked you into leaving her there when you came back; she tricked you into believing everything was okay. Damn her to hell!" He let loose some language I had never heard out of his mouth before.

I couldn't blame him. I felt as abandoned as he did.

Nighttime. My folks begged me to go to sleep. I sank, exhausted, into the bed Jan and I had slept in together for over a decade. In the morning, I discovered my dad had sat up in a chair all night, watching me. He was afraid I might do something stupid to myself.

Before I left for New Jersey, I called Max Fink. He was the lawyer who had negotiated for Bob Wells and myself when we sought the publishing rights, as well as the writers' share, of "The Christmas Song" once the twenty-eight-year copyright had expired. Fink had gotten the case settled out of court, and Wells and I gained the lion's share of the rights to "The Christmas Song." Naturally, I had great confidence in him.

I explained to Max what had happened. He was in his mid-seventies, pleasant but a low reactor. He had just married a woman decades younger than he and was in the early throes of marital bliss. The breakup of a marriage was anathema to him at that moment in time. Plus, he was not, by the furthest stretch of the imagination, a divorce lawyer.

I told him I had to leave for Great Gorge. What was I to do? Calmly, maddeningly phlegmatic, he told me he would appeal to the court to have my children returned to their father and their native country. He was the only lawyer I had had any dealings with for a long time. Poor Howard Redlich was in his grave. I told Max to go ahead.

I landed at Newark Airport. Happily, Tracy decided he should go with me. I did not object. I was grateful for his company. My drummer, Donny, did not recognize me at the airport. He had brought along his about-to-be bride, Gail. She looked right past me until Donny finally pointed me out, an astonished look on his face. I really looked like hell. I muttered the news to him. The poor guy was shocked. He had just come back from England with me. There had been no sign, no intimation of a breakup in my marriage. He was as stunned as I had been the previous day.

I performed that night before a large crowd. Don't ask me how; I honestly don't know. I stood there. I sang. I walked off the stage. Tracy practically led me to my suite. Ironically, the only major ballad in my books at that time was "Breaking Up Is Hard To Do." Against everyone's advice, I sang it, a tiny bit of home-grown masochism in the night.

Four days later, a walking ghost named Mel Tormé opened in Lake Geneva. I was in anguish. For once, I was aware of the disadvantages of not being a drinker or a drugee. Malted milkshakes were hardly comforting at that point, on top of which, I couldn't keep anything down.

Saturday afternoon, August 21, Donny got married. In my suite. The Playboy management refused to provide Donny and his bride with a suite in which to have the nuptials performed. Mine was the only one available commodious enough to accommodate the wedding party and guests.

I stood up for Donny, one of the toughest things I have ever had to do, under the circumstances.

At the end of the ceremony, I walked into the bathroom, locked the door, pressed a bath towel to my face, and cried steadily for over two hours. Poor Donny and Gail. They—not to mention Tracy—felt helpless. Everyone wisely left me alone. I sat there, on the closed toilet seat, and cried uncontrollably. At one point, I said to myself: Come on, this is insane. You've got to sing tonight. Stop crying; force yourself. Use some self-control. To no avail. Finally, my tear ducts simply dried up and I was out of tears.

Now we all flew to Florida to board the *Fairseas*. I had contracted to perform on the cruise. There was no way out of it. I walked around in a stupor. Tracy, God bless him, stayed by my side, pointing me in the right direction. I count it fortunate that he had no access to Jan at that moment; I think he would have beaten her to a pulp.

Dale and Joan Sheets had joined us on board. Their friendship and support meant the world to me. Coincidentally, John Solley, the man who had bought my Colt revolvers the previous September, had booked passage on the ship with his delightful wife, Fern. He had been having health problems. When he saw me and was told what had happened, he became physically ill and was eventually taken off the ship in a wheelchair.

Evening. Dale, Joan, Tracy, Donny, and Gail gather in the main dining room for dinner. I walk in, sit down, and stare mindlessly at the food in front of me. Tracy begs me to eat. I shake my head and walk out onto the deck. I look at the calm, unruffled Caribbean. I pretend it is the Atlantic. A long way across are my wife and kids. What are they doing at that moment? Is there another man in Jan's life? Is that why all this has happened? I stand at the rail and grip it tightly. I resist a frighteningly powerful urge to throw myself overboard. I turn and look toward the dining room. Tracy and Dale stand in the archway, ready to stop me from being impetuous and asinine. I smile a dumb, weak smile and rejoin the table.

The next morning, there is a faint, cold ray of sunshine: a wire arrives from Max Fink. Judge Nancy Watson of the Superior Court of the County of Los Angeles has granted me full custody of my two detained children.

Now, how do I get them back home?

36.

TRAUMA

O N September 1, I flew back to Los Angeles to my anxious
parents and my empty house. Before me was the task of
telling friends about the breakup. I wondered how they would
take the news. Because of Jan's beauty and English charm, I had
always felt that most people we socialized with favored her over
me. In a funny way, I had always liked that idea. To have a wife
so admired was a kind of tribute to my luck and taste.

I took a deep breath, picked up the phone and called Anna
Lee Nathan. She had been a British beauty in the thirties and
forties (and still is), more famous as an actress in America (as Anna
Lee) than in her native England for her roles in John Ford's *How
Green Was My Valley* and *Fort Apache*. Her husband was Robert
Nathan, one of America's true poet laureates, with a devoted cult
following, thanks to his superb novels in the thirties and forties,
not the least of which was *Portrait of Jennie*.

Anna was flabbergasted. "My God," she said, "how could Jan
have done this? To have gotten you over there, to have pretended
all was loving and well until you returned to America? It's so . . . so
un-British. So totally without honor."

That was Anna. Fiercely English and doggedly honorable in
her outlook and actions. Robert got on the phone. Although still
vital, and possessed of a clear, keen intellect, he was pushing eighty
and growing feeble. "You know, Mel," his slightly cracked voice
came through, "it's you Anna and I love, not Jan. You have been
the basic reason for our friendship." I could have wept, but I was
temporarily out of tears.

I thanked them both for their understanding and loving words.

I called Ricardo and Georgiana Montalban. They had been frequent guests in our house for the past several years. They took the news badly, particularly Ric. At 2:00 A.M. the next morning, he woke me out of a restless sleep.

"Melito," he said, in that now-famous "crushed velour/Corinthian leather" voice of his, "I can't sleep. It's unbelievable. How could this have happened? She always seemed so happy, so in love with you. It's—it's as crazy as if Georgie and I were breaking up. It's—it's insane! We simply cannot believe this has happened." We talked for almost an hour. As I recall, he had an early studio call that morning, yet here he was, agonizing over my broken marriage. So was Georgiana.

Reluctantly, I dialed the Richard Baseharts. They lived just above us, off Coldwater Canyon. Diana Basehart, a brilliant sculptress, greeted me cheerily.

"How was England, Mel? How is Daisy? Does she want to come up and spend the day with Gala?" Gala, the younger of the Basehart daughters, had become great friends with my little redhead. The vivacious Diana, obviously happy to hear "we" were back, instantly invited all of us to dinner. Before I could speak, she said, "Oh, here's Richard. He's dying to say hello."

That magnificent voice purred through the receiver. "Mel! Glad to have you back. Diana says you and Jan and the kids are coming to dinner. That's great! I—"

I interrupted and laid the news on him. Stunned silence followed. Diana picked up the extension phone and heard it all. God bless her, no-nonsense woman that she is, and English to boot, she said quietly and firmly, "Don't move. We're on our way down to you right now."

They stayed for over three hours, listening to the saga of the end of my life with Jan. They also surprised me by saying forthrightly that they were with me all the way.

The Nathans, the Montalbans, the Baseharts. Funny, I thought, after Richard and Diana had gone, how it sometimes takes a catastrophe in one's life to find out where you really stand with people. The total supportiveness I had received in the past several hours from six sensational friends had bolstered my spirits considerably.

Rich Little and his English wife, Jeannie, were next on my list. Not surprisingly, Rich was angry and hurt for me and Jeannie expressed sympathy and support in strong, loving terms. I followed that call with two others: Bert and Muriel Slatkin, she the daughter of the owner of the Beverly Hills Hotel, he the manager of same; and the Larry Rosenblooms, he a sweet-natured insurance broker, she the same Stephanie who had, a year earlier, urged me to sell my Sears Colt and pay the house off, so Jan and the kids would always have a home.

Stephanie, who really loved Jan, collapsed in tears. Larry was predictably pragmatic and thoroughly sympathetic. Bert, a teddy bear of a man, sincerely offered to do anything he could for me. Muriel alone was the dissenter, siding with Jan.

"Are you kidding, Muriel?" asked her best friend, Stephanie Rosenbloom. "Why, for Christ's sake?"

"Well," Muriel replied defiantly, "I automatically side with Jan because she's a woman and so am I. I just naturally side with the woman."

Muriel was having enormous trouble with her own marriage at the time, and, as silly a statement as was the one she had made to Stephanie, to some degree I understood it. Stephanie did not. Muriel's obstinate stand, based on gender and nothing more, broke up the long-standing friendship between the Slatkins and the Rosenblooms. That hurt me deeply; to realize that my problems had caused pain and chaos for other people was terrible.

Finally, I called Rudy Behlmer.

Rudy and I had met several years before, when Jan and I had been prowling the aisles at a Hollywoood Boulevard reading emporium called "Cherokee Books." He was a tall, slim, dark-haired individual, a good-looking man, then in his late thirties like myself, with an infectious smile and a compulsion for collecting books and films that equaled my own. We had begun talking that day because we were both searching for old Big Little Books, movie memorabilia, and the like and were delighted to find we had so many interests in common.

At that time, he was married to an attractive woman named Sandy. They had a young son, Curt. Rudy worked for the Leo Burnett Agency in Hollywood, producing some of the cleverest, classiest TV commercials ever seen on the tube.

Knowledgeable beyond belief about movies, he began teaching a film course at Art Center College of Design. In addition, having written (with Tony Thomas and Clifford McCarty) the definitive book, *The Films of Errol Flynn,* he had embarked on the gargantuan task of assimilating, editing, and commenting on the mass of documents, wires, and interoffice communiqués known as the David O. Selznick papers.

Memo from David O. Selznick became a huge seller, almost from the day of its publication. Other superb Behlmer books, such as *Inside Warner Bros.,* followed. Film historians, students, teachers, aficionados, and just plain movie buffs have been enriched by the expertise of Rudy Behlmer. We had become good friends.

Now, I picked up the phone and called him. The tone of my voice told him something was wrong.

"How about meeting me for dinner, Rude? Hamburger Hamlet on Beverly Drive okay?"

"Yeah, sure, fine. But can't you tell me what—"

"See you at seven."

The look on Rudy's face that night upon hearing about Jan and me is indescribable. Let me just say that his face actually fell. "But you two were always hugging and kissing. I mean, it was revolting and all that, but anyone could see she loved you. This is ridiculous!"

"Well, good pal of mine, I've been living with it since August tenth and I still can't believe it."

He chewed his hamburger thoughtfully. "So? What's next? You've got custody. When and how do you get your kids back?"

"I honestly don't know. Max Fink is an old man. I was desperate when Jan lowered the boom that morning. And I was on my way to New Jersey. So I hired him, but he doesn't understand what I'm going through. Well, hell, why should he? He's basically an entertainment lawyer. He's content to sit and wait and see what develops. I've got to replace him, find someone who will go into action for me instantly."

"Anyone in mind?"

"Yeah. I spoke with Edana Romney this afternoon. You met her at my house once, remember? She's recommended a lawyer who specializes in divorce and particularly kids who are kidnapped by one parent or the other."

"Hmmm. So what's the deal?"

"The deal, Rudolph, is this: I have to go up to Concord, near San Francisco—"

"Melvin, I know where Concord is. I was born and raised in San Francisco, remember?"

"Oh yeah, right. Well, anyway, I have to go and sing at the Concord Jazz Festival day after tomorrow. Then I'm going to fly back, look up this lawyer Edana has told me about, and, if I like what the guy has to say, I'm going to hire him. Then I am going over to England as fast as I can, with Judge Watson's custody order in my hand, and appeal to the English court to honor the order and surrender custody of Daisy and James to me. After all, they're American kids, not British subjects."

"Sounds good to me. By the way, who's this lawyer Edana is recommending?"

"His name is Marvin Mitchelson."

37.

MARVIN

I JUST got a chilling mental picture of you, kind reader, stifling a yawn, thinking, Why, in God's name, is Tormé making me privy to all this personal stuff? Divorces, marital trauma, failed love affairs . . . who cares? Why must I wade through this uninteresting trivia?

Frankly, it's no fun to bare one's soul, particularly in the painful areas of broken marriages and child custody. There is, however, a reason for all of the foregoing information.

During the normal course of his working hours, a butcher would probably say, "Shall I trim off the fat, Mrs. Jones?"

During the normal course of his working hours, you might expect a lawyer to remark, "I think we can settle this out of court, Mr. Jones."

During the normal course of his working hours, it would be natural for a dentist to warn his patient, "You're going to lose that bicuspid if you don't brush harder, Mr. Jones."

During the normal course of a singer's working hours, he/she will be dealing vocally with subject matter pertaining to a) I love you, b) I loved you and lost you, c) I love you but you don't love me, d) I loved you and lost you and want you back but I know that's hopeless because you love another . . . and so on.

You get the picture.

Which is not to say that a butcher or a lawyer or a dentist suffers the hurt of a broken marriage one whit less than a singer. It is simply that most people are not immersed in the pain of a breakup as *part* of their routine workday. A singer is.

Even an actor or actress can escape by becoming someone else through his or her art—a schoolteacher, a politician, a gangster, cop, or 1,001 other disguises. A singer is trapped within the narrow confines of the popular song, and the popular song, nine times out of ten, usually has to do with the subject of love.

Certainly there are singers who perform, by rote, those songs of flourishing, lost, or unrequited love. I am acquainted with one who sheepishly admits to warbling love songs and torch songs in front of an audience with his mouth only, while his brain is searching for an answer to his missed birdie on the ninth hole earlier in the day.

I frankly envy that facility. To be able to perform creditably and convincingly and separate the hurt from the work would have been just what the doctor ordered. Unfortunately, I have never been able to accomplish that feat. And so every time I sang a love lyric during those unhappy periods of my life when I was going through the turmoil of separation and the trauma of court appearances, the mental injury and the damage to my broken heart (forgive the timeworn phrase) was almost irreparable.

It absolutely affected my work and in some ways strengthened it in the long run.

≣

I still don't know how I made it through my concert at Concord Pavillion on the night of September 6. Mercifully, it came to an end. Next morning, I boarded a plane for L.A. and went directly to Marvin Mitchelson's office in Century City. His official digs were attractive and warm, a far cry from Max Fink's sterile environs.

I took to Marvin at once. Tall, gray-haired, with a boyish face and an affable manner, he seemed instantly in touch with my pain. As I sat in his private domain, drinking tea and telling him what had happened, he kept making the same markings again and again on a large legal pad. When I finished, he showed me the pad, upon which were scribbled two words: CONSPIRACY/FRAUD.

"You've been had, Mel," he said as gently as possible. "Your wife planned this, unquestionably. She got you to go to England so she could be with her friends and relatives in safe, familiar surroundings when she lowered the boom on you."

"What do I do, Marvin?"

"What do *we* do, Mel. We. You and me. It's simple. You have custody, given to you by the superior court. I'm going to call England and hire the finest barrister and the best solicitor I know there. Then you and I are going to get on a jet, go there, and apply to the English court for comity."

"What's 'comity'?"

"It's a reciprocal arrangement between our two countries. It means that if, for example, someone from England kidnaps his or her own children and brings those English kids to the States without the other parent's consent, our courts should, and usually do, order the abducting parent and the kids back to where those children belong, to their country of birth. That's where the matter of custody and divorce is supposed to take place."

"You mean the English court will absolutely—"

"Ah, ah. I didn't say 'absolutely.' I said we'd go over and apply to the high court. Comity is a tacit arrangement between our two countries. It isn't absolute. It's the justice's—that's what they call their judges—it's at the justice's discretion."

My heart sank. "What if we fail in the English court?"

"Why, then"—Marvin smiled more broadly—"we move on to Phase Two."

"Which is?"

He filled me in on Phase Two, a plan right out of an Ian Fleming novel.

≡

Two weeks later, we arrived in London. The press was there to meet me at the plane. I looked haggard, pale, lousy. I told them as much as I felt I could without compromising what our position was going to be in court. Marvin's English detectives had finally found out where Jan and the kids were. She had rented a house near Pinewood Studios. That was all Marvin would tell me. She had been served with our papers by my English attorney. Her solicitor had replied. They would see us in court.

Marvin had hired, in my behalf, Sir Peter Rawlinson, former attorney general of England. A tall, handsome man, he made me smile ruefully as I thought about the number of English courtroom films I had seen throughout my lifetime, with Sir Peter's virtual doubles playing the roles in make-believe that he would soon enact for me in real life. We talked. Notes were taken. Heads were shaken. There were grunts, coughs, grimaces, and some sympathetic nods.

Dinner at Trader Vic's in the London Hilton. (God, it was tough, walking into the hotel where Jan and I had made love on our first date, back, back in another century.) The dinner was to effect a meeting between myself, Marvin, and a wiry, tough-looking little guy who was introduced by his first name only: Barry. He outlined his plan for Phase Two, should that exigency become necessary. I sat and listened, wide-eyed. Yet I knew I would approve the plan, should we fail in the English court.

Came the day.

I walked into court with Marvin and Sir Peter. I looked around. A woman I had never seen sat at the far right of the room, talking in hushed tones with some men. I looked closer. It was my wife, whom I had not laid eyes on in over a month and a half.

I attempted civility. "Hello, Jan," I said quietly.

She glared at me with a fierceness that would have pulverized Mister "T."

Hurt and rage comingled within me. How dare she, I thought. She broke the marriage up, she absconded with our kids....

That was for openers.

Marvin and Sir Peter were reading her attorney's answer to our plea to the court. I heard Marvin suck in his breath. He and Sir Peter looked at me with genuinely sorry-for-Mel eyes. Marvin snorted softly and handed me Jan's answer to our complaint. He pointed to a particular paragraph. In it, Jan stated that she was having a love affair with Kevin Francis and that she wanted to marry him. My face went from gray to dead-white.

It was all over soon. Justice Hollings was what I expected an English judge to be: utterly fair and impartial. He heard the evidence and promptly ordered Jan and the children back to America,

which, he intoned, was the proper place for the hearing of testimony
in the matter. I walked out of the court stunned. I was relieved
to know we had won the first round. I simply could not believe
that a short ten years after the madness in a Los Angeles courtroom with Arlene, I had been hurled into an almost identical situation: a custody battle and my wife having an affair with another
man.

It was raining. We got into the hired car. Marvin put his hand
on my shoulder. "Want to see your kids?" he asked.

I nodded mutely.

He gave the driver the address. We drove for a half-hour, finally
pulling up in front of an attractive house in the suburbs near
Pinewood Studios, where Kevin Francis had his office. It was
raining harder now as we were met at the door by a nanny. She
let us in. There were Daisy and James. They acted as though they
had never seen me before, there in the house their mother shared
with them and her lover. It was a stiff, unsatisfying meeting. I told
them they were coming home, to America, within a week. They
nodded absently, almost vacant-eyed. My chest (what there was of
it—I had lost over thirty pounds since August 10) felt constricted.
As I held my unresponsive children in my arms and looked around
at this furnished house my wife had rented with Kevin Francis, I
found I was having trouble breathing. My eyes felt as though they
had sunk three inches into my face. Standing there at that moment,
clutching James and Daisy, I suddenly felt like an intruder in a
settled, foreign household. For one overwhelming moment, it was
as though our house on Coldwater had never existed. I'm really
in the Twilight Zone, I thought.

I broke the awkward moment, clumsily kissed the kids good-
bye, and walked back to the car in the pouring rain. We began
the bleak drive back to London in silence. Marvin put his arm
around my shoulders and patted me, understanding.

≡

I arrived back home in time for my fifty-first birthday on September
13. It was a somber affair with my friends, the Montalbans, the
Nathans, the Rosenblooms, and the Slatkins, hosting a quiet dinner

for me at the Beverly Hills Hotel. At least I was able to say the kids would be back within a week. Oh, yes: Jan would return to fight things out in court.

Ten days later, Jan and the children arrived back in California. They had had a long, tiring flight. Jan was naturally edgy. Tracy, who was seventeen at the time, had seen me move, a few days earlier, into the pool cottage I had originally modified into a guest-house for Jan's parents. I had agreed back in the English court to occupy the cottage and let Jan and the kids stay in the main house. I simply could not stand the idea of moving to a hotel and visiting Daisy and James on weekends. I had had enough of that during my divorce with Arlene. Living in the cottage would at least afford me the opportunity to see the kids in the morning before they went off to school (James was in preschool, Daisy in first grade) and maintain daily contact with them.

Tracy, upon their arrival, asked Jan if he could take the kids out to the cottage to see me for a few minutes. Jan, tired, frustrated at having been forced to return to the States, refused Tracy's request. He insisted heatedly: Dad hadn't seen the children for more than one hour in almost two months. Surely it wasn't too much to ask—

Jan slapped Tracy soundly.

I don't think she knows, to this day, how close she came at that moment to having her face smashed in. Tracy is a big, strong young man, and a jock who excels at sports. He had already been through enough trauma in his young life during the messy divorce between his real mother and me. Now his sense of family, of belonging, had once again been shattered. When Jan slapped him, he roughly shoved her away from him, and had to fight for control. His hatred for her is only exceeded by his overwhelming love for James and Daisy. Seldom, if ever, have siblings been as crazy about each other as these three of my offspring are, and the love seems to increase with the passing years.

That first night in the cottage was tough. I stood at the sliding glass doors overlooking the pool and gazed at the house. Inside were my children and the wife I had loved and worked for for the past ten years. It had never occurred to me that my personal life, so settled and in control, would suddenly fracture into unmendable pieces. I felt a terrible sense of isolation.

I told myself that all this would pass, that one day my life would once again be in order. I looked back into the cottage and thought: How bad could this be? Jan's folks stayed in here for as much as three, four weeks at a time. In a month or two, this will all be behind me.

As it turned out, I lived in that little guesthouse for a year and a half.

38.

ALI

I WENT on a binge of mindless dating. Mitchelson had assured me that I was free to be seen with whomever I pleased. Almost daily, I would show up at the Polo Lounge of the Beverly Hills Hotel with a good-looking lady in tow. In the evenings I would appear at the Saloon or Le Bistro or Gatsby's or at a party, squiring Jane Seymour or Donna Mills or Stella Stevens. See, world, I was trying to say, my wife threw me aside for a younger man, but look! Look at me! I'm still attractive to women. Beautiful women. They like me. I can't be as worthless as I feel right now.

All those nights out served two purposes: I had to eat somewhere and being in the company of those young beauties was helping to counteract the loss of self-worth I was experiencing. Bloody hell, those dates were a bore! Not from my standpoint, understand; the ladies were uniformly lovely, interesting, and sympathetic. Me! I was the bore! I simply could not resist discussing what had happened to me. It's called "ventilating." I went on and on. The funny thing was that every time I took someone out, I had the strange feeling I was cheating on Jan. I suppose I am a classic creature of habit.

We were getting ready for a round of depositions in the forthcoming divorce. I got wind of the fact that Kevin Francis was planning a trip to California. I called Marvin and told him I wanted to apply to the court for a restraining order that would keep Francis from seeing my kids.

Serving Jan and her boyfriend became a problem. Sensing that something like a court confrontation might take place over Kevin, she proceeded, once he arrived in mid-October, to play secret agent. She would get into her car, drive circuitously, make unexpected U-turns—anything to shake off the real or imagined "tail" she was certain I had "sicced" on her. She was absolutely right. Marvin had hired, on my behalf, a private detective agency to serve the papers on both her and Francis. It wasn't easy, but it was finally accomplished. A hearing was set before Judge Saeta in Los Angeles Superior Court for the twenty-ninth of October.

I sat in the courtroom that day and watched a smirking Kevin Francis play word games with my attorney.

MARVIN: Are you in love with Mrs. Tormé?

KEVIN: Everyone in England is in love with Janette Scott.

MARVIN: (Patiently) Please answer my question, Mr. Francis. Are you in love with Mrs. Tormé?

KEVIN: I told you. Everyone is—

JUDGE: Answer the question, Mr. Francis.

That sort of cute stuff went on until the lunch break.

Waiting to go back into the courtroom after lunch, I was standing in the corridor, discussing the morning's testimony, when an extremely good-looking redhead walked by, looked at me, and smiled. I smiled back. That smile I got must have been a good omen. Wonder of wonders, back in the courtroom, Judge Saeta issued an ironclad order forbidding Kevin Francis to see, contact, or give knowledge of his presence in California to my children. I was grateful to the judge beyond measure and told Marvin I wanted to thank him. Marvin grinned and told me that just wasn't done. I must say, I'm sorry I did not have the opportunity to offer my thanks to Judge Saeta, since, as things turned out, that day in his courtroom was the first and last time I got anything resembling justice from the Los Angeles Superior Court in the matter of *Tormé* v. *Tormé*.

When Marvin and I walked out into the corridor again, I felt better than I had in over two months. Coming toward us from the opposite direction was the redhead. As she passed, she handed me a folded piece of paper and walked away without a word. Marvin and I looked at each other in complete surprise. Written on the paper was the name "Ali" and a Beverly Hills phone number.

I smiled sadly at Marvin. "Funny, isn't it," I said. "A few yards away from us sits my wife of ten years, chatting with her lover. It's killing me inside. All of a sudden, a pretty lady walks over and hands me her name and number. And I'm damned if I'm not flattered and, Marvin, I'm embarrassed to say, interested. There must be something very wrong with me."

Mitchelson laughed. "There's not a damn thing wrong with you, friend. You've felt like crawling into a hole somewhere and dying. A beautiful gal walks up and hands you an invitation to call her, and that's just what the doctor ordered." He put his hand on my shoulder. "Mel, Mel, Mel," he said in that curiously excitable manner of his, "I know what you're going through right now, but all this will pass, believe me. In the meantime, know what I'd do if I were you?"

"No. What?"

"I'd call that beautiful redhead."

A few days later, I called Ali. When she answered the phone, I thought, for one fleeting moment, Good God, what if this handsome lady has one of those high, nasal voices. Or a hillbilly twang? Or a Brooklyn accent?

My fears were groundless. I asked her why she had plunked that note into my hand.

"I saw you seven years ago, at the Sands in Vegas. I thought the show was wonderful, particularly because you seemed so completely happy to be up there on the stage, singing. The other day, in the courtroom corridor, I looked at you and I've never seen a sadder man. I gave you my name and number because I thought you might need someone to talk to. I read the papers. I know what you're going through. If it would help to talk with a sympathetic admirer, I'd be glad to see you some evening."

We went to dinner that night at La Cantina, a small, charming restaurant on Santa Monica Boulevard. Her full name was Ali Severson. She was in her early thirties, with luxuriant chestnut-red hair, wide-set green eyes, and the kind of natural beauty you would expect to find in a girl of Swedish descent who hails from a tiny Minnesota town called Brewster, population 500.

"What were you doing in court the other day?" I asked. "Are you also getting a divorce?"

She shook her head. "I was divorced seven years ago. I have two kids, a boy and a girl. And I intend to raise and support them with as little help from my ex-husband as possible. I was in court doing some legal-aid work. I'm a law student at USC."

"Uh huh. So. I assume you walked into my courtroom that day and—"

"No, I didn't. I didn't want to. I knew you were in there and, from everything I've read so far, I honestly felt watching you in court would be too painful, particularly after having seen the other side of Mel Tormé in Vegas a few years ago."

She then asked me to tell her what had happened to my marriage. She asked me! By that time, I had begun to realize what a crashing bore I had become to friends and strangers alike, blabbing my tale of woe. I told her as much. She waved that aside and said she wanted to hear if I wanted to tell her. I kept it as short as possible. I sensed that here was one magnificent woman—quiet, intelligent, and beautiful. I had no idea at that moment where we were going, but I was strongly attracted to her, and the last thing I wanted to do was ruin a possible relationship before it had the opportunity to spread its wings and fly.

Ali listened. Really listened. Along the way, she asked pertinent questions. She seemed genuinely concerned; she didn't patronize me. She made no value judgments on either me or Jan. I thought: This lady's going to be a good lawyer. She seems pragmatic, cool, and super bright.

And beautiful. Beautiful in a way I had never gravitated to before. My three wives, Candy, Arlene, and Jan, had all possessed that kind of glossy, model/actress/movie starlet prettiness that makes other men covet your conquest and envy the hell out of you. Ali was every bit the head-turner my wives had been, but in a far subtler way.

From that evening on, I began to see Ali exclusively. Her time was taken up studying law at the University of Southern California and with the practical experience of handling legal-aid cases, to say nothing of being a mother. I came and went, doing a concert here and a nightclub engagement there. I felt like singing about as much as I felt like putting my hand in a blazing fire. I had no choice, however, since it was absolutely imperative to earn enough money to defray the smashing costs already incurred by the ongoing divorce action.

There were nights out with Ali when my mind simply could not turn off the mental pictures of what had happened to my life. I was probably a dangerous driver at those times. I would experience a sudden rush of rage and grip the wheel so tightly it threatened to break in my hands. Ali would call it to my attention and I would force myself to release my grip. Otherwise, she never complained. She listened to my problems with patience and empathy and administered tender, loving care in equal amounts of sensitivity and good humor.

It was months before the dissolution proceedings came up on the docket, months of depositions, including a trip to England to depose Roy Moseley. Norman Schwartz had arranged for me to record an album there with a young, brilliant arranger named Chris Gunning. I got off the plane at Heathrow at 7:00 in the morning with almost no sleep. I was singing with a thirty-eight-piece orchestra at Olympia Studios at 9:00 A.M.

It was the first time I had been in England since my court appearance there in front of Justice Hollings. The fatigue I felt that morning coupled with the emotionalism of being in a country I loved, the city in which I had wooed and won Janette Scott, combined to fashion *Tormé: A New Album*, the record many people believe is the very best album I ever made.

I needed a lifting of spirit, and when news came that I had just won a second Edison Award in Holland, my sagging heart soared a few inches off the ground. The timing was perfect. If I had ever needed a morale boost, it was at that precise moment.

39.

DIVORCE

*T*HE case began.

I have no idea how good an attorney Marvin Mitchelson is. Given what I saw in court over the period of the next six weeks, I doubt any lawyer could have functioned more successfully than Marvin did.

He had become a great friend, an evening companion, and a frequent phoner; in short, he was exactly what I had needed to get me through the trying period of time spent living ignominiously in the guest cottage. We had won the battle to stop Kevin Francis from seeing my kids. Now, however, we were about to fight the war, a war that is repugnant to countless thousands of California fathers and husbands who find themselves in a no-win situation the moment they enter Los Angeles Superior Court.

Since 1970, a no-fault divorce law had been entered on the books of California jurisprudence to alleviate the burdens of the overworked judges and the crowded courtrooms. Many lawyers with whom I have spoken despise no-fault, since it stacks the cards time and again against the injured party in a divorce action. And, of course, since the still-current terminology regarding the wife in such an action is "innocent spouse," the chances for a father to obtain custody of his children are laughable. I had been awarded custody of Tracy ten years earlier when "fault" was still part of the legal process. Now, in 1977, I realized that securing custody of James and Daisy was next to hopeless.

Early on in the trial, Jan had agreed to joint custody, and I was grateful for that. It was to be one of two positive things to come out of the case. Marvin negotiated with Jan's lawyer and got an agreement about the value of our house. That house meant a lot to me. James and Daisy had known it as their home since their respective births. Naturally, it held a lot of memories for me, some of which had turned sour, yet it had been home to me for almost ten years. My life was in such a disarray that I think having to pack and move, when the whole pattern of my professional existence was pack-and-move, might have finally and irrevocably done me in. I had to come up with a large amount of cash to buy out my wife's share of our community-property house. The only way to accomplish that was to sell my prized gun collection, which I did. That killed me a little more inside, but it had to be done.

The rest of the case?

Jan had hired as an attorney the single cruelest man I have ever laid eyes on. He obviously relished raking me over the coals. The judge? Marvin had warned me at the outset that the luck-of-the-draw judge we got was far too inexperienced to understand the complexities of our pleadings. Mitchelson was absolutely right. Jan's lawyer postured and smirked his way around that courtroom, and, shortly, the victim (that's me, in case you have forgotten) became the villain.

Johnny Carson once said, "All we Americans are suckers for an English accent." That certainly applied to my divorce case: the judge blatantly disregarded me and my testimony and positively beamed at Jan every time she opened her mouth. I suffered through this madness in court for almost six weeks.

Finally, I listened in disgust while the judge read his findings. Early on, he had stated that he did not write his findings. "I make pro*nounce*ments," he had bellowed. ("Holy shit!" Marvin had muttered, shaking his head.) Perversely, that judge wound up reading a multipage *written* decision that was the rottenest single "review" I ever got, while Jan's attorney shot me sneer after sneer from their side of the courtroom.

Then the courtroom was empty. I sat there, feeling one hundred years old. Everything I had ever felt or thought or believed about fair play and justice, all the naïve values of good and evil I had been infused with during my growing-up years—right and wrong as portrayed in Depression-era movies, on the radio, and in the Sunday funnies—died that afternoon in L.A. Family Court.

Marvin led me wordlessly to the parking lot. We got into his car and headed for Beverly Hills. I sat and looked out the window, still unbelieving. Finally, in the gentlest tone of voice I had ever heard him use, Marvin said, "Mel, Mel, Mel, what can I say? You got screwed. Badly. It was horrible. If I ever wanted to win a case in my life, it was this one, because my client was in the right. You were wronged. Wronged by your wife, by that son of a bitch, Kevin, by her attorney, and, worst of all, by the judge."

I continued to stare silently out the car window. Marvin held his thoughts for a while. As we neared his office, he said, "It's not all bad, though. You got your house."

"Yes, Marvin," I agreed quietly. "All I have to do is sell my gun collection to keep my house. I started that collection when I was a kid. It always was my proudest possession, next to my wonderful wife and my kids. Now I have no wife, no gun collection, and a pair of little kids who will have a visiting daddy from time to time."

Marvin shut up.

I went back to the cottage and called Ali. "Well, Ali, I lost."

She laughed. "Come on, Melvie, this is no time to be cute. What happened?"

"It's simple. I lost."

There was a pause. "Mel," she said, in an entirely different tone of voice, "are you kidding?"

I told her what had happened. She seemed more demoralized than I. Ali's faith in the system was fashioned from the same kind of bedrock as mine had been. Her values were solidly midwestern, her belief in right triumphing over wrong unshakable.

"Mel," she finally said, "knowing what I know, not only from you but from all the people around you who are aware of what you've been through, what you've just told me completely kills any thoughts I might have had about practicing family law. This is the craziest thing I've ever heard." True to her word, Ali became a tax lawyer.

Later that day, Marvin called me to see if I was all right. I was very grateful for his solicitude, but, of course, I wasn't all right and told him so. The children had called me to ask where their mother was, since dinnertime was approaching. I mentioned that to Marvin, who hemmed and hawed and then admitted she was celebrating at her lawyer's office with champagne and hors d'oeuvres.

My stomach turned. I hung up on Marvin, went to the bathroom, and vomited. The saddest day of my life was being laughed about in a lawyer's paneled quarters.

It was like hearing about someone at a cemetery opening a freshly dug grave and dancing gleefully around it.

40.

RECOVERY

I HAVE always firmly believed in a balance in the universe. For every negative, there is a positive; for every downer, an upper. All through my life, time and again, that philosophy has held true.

Certainly, I had lost my wife, the opportunity to raise our kids, and a great deal of money. The legal costs alone came to a staggering $168,000. The weeks in court were enough to smash me to my knees.

Yet, I forced myself to look at the brighter side. I had my home. It would be months before I could actually move back in; Jan had to find a suitable house for herself and our children. But one day, in the not-too-distant future, I would be back in the house. The kids would sleep in their own bedrooms when they came over on weekends and holidays.

I had my health. Amazingly, it had not broken down during the long, unhappy months leading up to my court appearance. I was able to work, to try to rebuild my shattered bank account.

I had real friends, from Dale and Joan Sheets to my business manager, Bob Ginter, as well as all those people who had stood by me and, in some cases, even testified for me.

My novel, *Wynner* (formerly called "The Thompson Man"), was scheduled to be published by Stein & Day, and I had received a substantial advance against royalties.

Most importantly, I had Ali.

If I had never given any credence to predestination before, I became an instant believer when I found out, weeks after our first date, that Ali and I were as star-crossed as it is possible to be. Our second encounter, that day back in October 1976, had occurred because the case she was handling in the adjacent courtroom had been dismissed unexpectedly. She had fully expected to be tied up in that courtroom for many more hours. So had I, in Judge Saeta's bailiwick. Had Ali's case been dismissed five minutes earlier or later, or had mine dragged on into the late afternoon, I wouldn't be writing about her at this moment.

The multiple *Down Beat* and Edison awards I had won as "Best Male Jazz Singer" seemed to have started something. George Wein, the longtime entrepreneur of the famed Newport Jazz Festival, paged me for a concert in June 1977, at Carnegie Hall. Costars: two musical giants named George Shearing and Gerry Mulligan. The chemistry between us worked perfectly. The reviews were thrilling. More concerts followed. It was a fortunate triumvirate. Mulligan and Shearing shared my musical tastes exactly. They seemed to admire my approach to singing as well as my drumming and arranging. My respect for their talents was boundless. George's pianistic touch with his extraordinary mental storehouse of an exceptionally broad spectrum of music, and his ability to transform the most mundane pop tune into a thing of musical beauty was something to be envied, admired, and appreciated.

Mulligan had long been one of my favorite arranger/composers. His historic charts for the groundbreaking Miles Davis nonet back in 1949 were the inspiration I had needed to become an arranger. He had brought to the baritone saxophone a tone unlike any I had ever heard before. Most baritone players capitalized on the harsh, gutty sound seemingly indigenous to that horn. Mulligan played it like an overgrown tenor sax, a latter-day Ben Webster, whose tenor had graced and embellished the great compositions of Duke Ellington for so many years. Mulligan's wide grasp of musical styles, from Dixieland to bop and beyond, plus his knowledge of old tunes, almost matched George's. Every concert with them was joyful beyond description.

Timing is everything, particularly in the music business. A real renaissance was taking place. Young people were coming to our concerts—not teenyboppers, but seventeen- and eighteen-year-olds and upward. They were showing up in substantial numbers to find out what this "jazz" thing was all about. We theorized that these kids were looking for something more complex, more sophisticated than what they had grown up listening to—an alternative, not a substitute, to that simpler form called "rock and roll."

I think they came away from our shows realizing that rock owes its parentage to jazz, that there is an immutable link between the two, and that all that is needed on the part of the young to appreciate jazz is exposure to it.

≡

Buddy Rich's nightclub had gone under. The real owner of that club, Marty Ross, had opened a restaurant on Third Avenue and Seventy-second Street called "Marty's." It had become one of Manhattan's finest. Now Marty, always a jazz fan and all-around music lover, wanted to expand his operation into a small nightclub featuring singers only.

Would I come in for two weeks and try the club on for size? My manager, Dale, got into it with Marty. Thank God, (and Dale!) we were faring well, seeing a steady rise in my weekly fee as well as my one-night concert price. Marty's room could seat only ninety people, if they were all thin.

"You can't afford Mel in a club that size," said Dale.

"Yes, I can," argued Marty.

"Impossible," said Dale.

"How much?" Marty pressed.

Dale told him.

"Okay," Marty agreed.

"You're crazy," said Dale.

Marty was crazy like a fox. He knew the Apple better than we did. The engagement at Marty's was one of my real triumphs. We were jam-packed nightly. My trio, with Donny on drums, a bassist named Rufus Reed (soon to be replaced by a magnificent bass-playing composer/singer named Jay Leonhart), and a gifted pianist from Providence, Rhode Island, Mike Renzi, was beyond compare, supplying the kind of collaborative inspiration necessary to keep things fresh and exciting night after night.

Singing the popular song can be a grind. To try to make each performance sound like the first, to convince a demanding, sometimes jaded New York audience that this time, this very performance, is the one during which you, the singer, finally understand the lyric perfectly and have total command of the melodic structure of the tune, is no mean feat. The trio helped make that happen on a nightly basis.

Those were great evenings. I had never felt more welcome in the Big Town. I used to joke about the "high rate of recidivism" at Marty's. People would come to hear me three, four, five times during a single three-week engagement. Incredible! Marty would come up to my dressing room, harried as hell.

"Holy Christ!" he would say, wiping his brow. "I just nearly got creamed by a guy down there. He offers me five hundred dollars if I can get him a table for the first show. I tell him I can't; there isn't a single seat to be had. Bastard takes a swing at me. Shit, Tormé, what are you doing to my life?"

I reminded him the engagements were his idea.

"Oh, yeah." He would grin and go down to face the mob at the entrance. My booking agency, Regency Artists, was virtually the first I had actually bragged about during my long and checkered career. A conscientious, conscienceful group of men led by a prince named Rich Rosenberg and an old friend, former dancer Frank Rio, they were taking advantage of my later-in-life "heat" and booking me into places I had never been offered before.

Most exciting for me among my newer opportunities were the long string of symphony dates the office had secured for me. Those concerts represented hard work on the part of Regency and Dale Sheets. Within the course of eighteen months, I experienced the musical pleasure of appearing with the Atlanta, Pittsburgh, Dallas, Denver, San Francisco, Hartford, Tulsa, Indianapolis, Kansas City, and Philly Pops symphony orchestras, to name a few. I had labored long at my piano, prior to these dates, writing new symphonic arrangements for myself. Every time a symphony musician complimented me on them, I felt like I could leap out of a twentieth-story window and fly.

George Wein of the Newport Jazz Festival had become a kind

of mentor. On March 28, 29, and 30 of 1980, he produced a trio of Carnegie Hall concerts under my aegis. The weekend was called *Mel Tormé and Friends*. What friends!

Shearing and Mulligan. Teddy Wilson and Bill Evans. Anita O'Day. Woody Herman and his Herd. A long interview in the *New York Times* accompanied these concerts. That was enormously pleasing to me, since I had, in recent months, written three major articles for the *Times*.

Whitney Balliett called. He wanted to do a profile on me in *The New Yorker* magazine. I would walk past a mirror, stop, grin stupidly at myself, and say, "It's happening. Took a long time, Melvie, but, I'm a son of a bitch, it is happening!"

It was. Things got better and better. I thought about my kids. I thought about Jan and what had happened. Terrible stuff, unquestionably, but now, I told myself, look at all the good stuff.

I had won new respect in my profession and the heart of a truly fine lady. I had more friends than ever before. My fortunes were increasing. My health was holding.

There was a balance in the universe.

41.

WYNNER

I HAD worked on my novel for nearly seven years. What I had set out to do was to create something about a pop singer that was not simply a crassly commercial page-turner indistinguishable from the spate of books churned out in recent years whose heroes were nothing more than thinly disguised Sinatra clones.

My literary agent, the prestigious Sterling Lord, called me on my birthday, 1977, to advise me that a small company called Stein & Day was interested in publishing my book and was offering a substantial advance against royalties.

I was smack dab in the middle of my personal troubles at the time, and the offer was another of those morale boosters I sorely needed.

I flew to New York in early October to meet with the publisher, Sol Stein. He was a charming man, but I could see right away there was going to be a problem. Stein was, in addition to being a publisher, a talented novelist in his own right. The first thing he hit me with was the length of my book.

"It's too long," he pronounced. "I want it shortened, considerably. I want to be able to sell it for nine ninety-five."

Sort of puts you in mind of the emperor's pontification to Mozart: "Yes, yes, it's very good. Very good, but . . . too many notes."

The manuscript ran 879 pages. On purpose. The story, which began in 1916 in Poland and ended present day, was constructed to chart the lives of many characters, not merely the progress of the career of "Marty Wynner," the central character of the piece. I explained that to Sol.

He would have none of it. "Cut it. Radically," he commanded. "And," he added, "I don't like your chapters on World War Two. But then, no one—*no* one has ever really written the definitive World War Two novel."

"Sol," I said, unbelieving, "Shaw's *Young Lions*? Uris's *Battle Cry*? *From Here to Eternity*?"

"No good, any of them. They don't ring true. I know. I was an officer during the war."

I was disturbed and a little angry. I had meticulously researched the World War Two portion of my book. I had taken advantage of my recent friendship with Paddy Chayevsky and got him to read passages from that part of my novel. He praised the hell out of them. Now here came Sol Stein, shooting that whole segment down in flames.

In fairness, I have only myself to blame for acceding to Stein's editorial demands. I felt it might be possible to walk both sides of the line and still maintain the book's integrity. Certainly nothing one writes is engraved in granite.

I began cutting *Wynner* with the help of an intelligent, likable young woman named Michaela Hamilton. She was a Stein & Day senior editor at the time. She sensed my concern about slashing the novel, but she was also under orders to cut, cut, cut. She and I worked well together, but I could see where the work was heading. *Wynner* was going to wind up being precisely what I had not wanted it to be: a quick-read page-turner.

Stein & Day seemed to have great faith in the final draft. They spent a lot of money on advertising and sent me on a multicity tour, during which I appeared on the predictable talk shows and did the standard newspaper interviews. Everyone welcomed me, including the "Today" show, "Good Morning America" and my constant friend and booster, Merv Griffin. Two who refrained from granting me time on their respective shows were Johnny Carson and Phil Donahue.

In 1974, I had appeared for the umpteenth time on the "Tonight" show with Carson. He was in one of his feisty moods that night. "What's going on, Mel?" he asked in front of insomniac America. "Where are you playing next?"

"John, I'm excited about my upcoming engagement in Tasmania."

"Tasmania? Where's that?"

"It's actually part of Australia. It's the island where Errol Flynn was born, by the way."

Carson grunted and tapped his pencil on the desk like a drummer keeping time. "Haw!" he guffawed. "Your agents are booking you in all the big-time spots these days, huh?"

I was capable of playing his game, tit for tat.

I smiled sweetly at him. "Thanks, Merv," I said.

The audience went "oooooooohhhh."

I never appeared on the "Tonight" show again with him. Too bad. I like the guy and admire him as a talent. I guess nothing is forever.

In Donahue's case, I had come to his rescue in an emergency situation at channel seven in Miami, several years ago. I was appearing at one of the hotels. In those pre-VCR days, I took my movie entertainment where I could find it, in this instance at the aforementioned television station, thanks to a sympathetic film department director, a well-used RCA projector, and a fine library of old MGM classics. As I sat in a cubicle, dressed in casual, comfortable clothes, unshaven, watching an old Spencer Tracy movie, a young man burst into the tiny room and cried, "My God! It _is_ you! You're really here. Listen, I'm with the Phil Donahue show. We're downstairs, all set up to do an interview with Sammy Davis. He's—he got sick, all of a sudden. An ambulance just took him to the hospital. There are over three hundred people down there, waiting to see him, and no Sammy. Phil is tearing his hair. Please, _please_, would you come down and fill in for Sammy?"

I went down, did the show, and count it as one of the best I have ever done. Donahue and his producer came over to me afterward, dousing me with praise and thanks and the assurance that if I ever needed a favor, I had but to pick up the phone. When _Wynner_ came out, I did pick up the phone to call in their marker. Donahue ignored me and refused to honor his word to "repay" me for the spot I had gotten him out of; and once again I looked heavenward and shouted to an amused God, "Show biz is my life!"

At any rate, I wasn't too disturbed about being bypassed by Donahue and Carson, since I did have the pleasure of appearing on Larry King's program. King, a great old friend, is also unequivocably the finest interviewer in our country.

The book tour was fascinating, not to mention illuminating. I suspect that Sol Stein had bought *Wynner* because he saw the possibilities for promotion, since he knew that I was a welcome guest in all forms of the media.

Most of the interviewers I encountered were kind and seemingly interested. Some had previously read and liked the Garland book. A few sneered openly. It was that same attitude I had encountered during the early publication days of *The Other Side of the Rainbow*, that is, "What the hell is a singer doing writing a book?" Apparently, most news/media people think all singers are airheads. That's unfortunate and unfair. Most singers I know are bright, articulate individuals. Many are actually literate. The prevailing attitude during that book tour, nonetheless, was that I was a pretender in the world of the literati.

Unlike *Rainbow*, which got about 96 percent super reviews, *Wynner* did not fare well with many of the critics. I didn't blame them, really, since the book they reviewed was not really the book I had originally intended.

Anyway, I keep at it.

Paddy Chayevsky once told me, at the Brasserie restaurant in New York, "You're going to have to write at least five books before the public and the critics take you seriously."

This is my fourth. We'll see.

42.

PROFILES

*N*ORMAN SCHWARTZ was a superb producer of records. The live album recorded at Marty's, *Mel Tormé and Friends*, featuring "friends" Gerry Mulligan, Janis Ian, Cy Coleman, and Jonathan Schwartz, was Norman's brainchild. It is an album of which I am proud. After making the album, however, I reluctantly parted professional company with Norman. Though I still have the highest regard for his capabilities, his acumen as a businessman left something to be desired.

While I was appearing at Marty's, during the early eighties, Harry Reasoner walked in one night with Dorothy Rodgers, the widow of Richard Rodgers. At the time, I was doing my set piece on all those early lyrics to "Blue Moon." Remembering the go-round I had had with Mr. Rodgers during the filming of *Words and Music*, I was wary of doing that "Blue Moon" trilogy in front of his widow. In addition, I couldn't help remembering yet another embarrassing incident involving Richard Rodgers.

≡

A few years earlier, the David Frost show called to ask if I had seen their tribute to Richard Rodgers.

"Saw it and loved every minute. An absolutely great show."

"Well, Mel, we're preparing to do 'Part Two,' and the first people David mentioned for the show were Shirley Jones and you."

"Really?"

"Well, after all, you are totally identified with two of Rodgers's biggest songs, 'Mountain Greenery' and 'Blue Moon.' So, if you're available, we would certainly like—"

"I'm available, I'm available. And if I'm not, I'll see to it that I am. Seriously, I'm thrilled you thought of me."

"Right. Well. We'll be in touch in the next few days with details and such. Delighted to have you on board. So will David be."

Four days later.

"Hello, is that you, Mel?"

"Yes. Happy to hear from you. I've been expecting—"

"Yes. Well, I'm afraid I have some unhappy news."

"Oh? You're not going ahead with the show?"

"Ummm—yes. I believe we are. I don't know how to tell you this but . . . Richard Rodgers has turned you down."

Silence. Then, "I see. I didn't know he had casting approval."

"Well, the thing is, you see, he is going to be on the show and, naturally, we want him to be comfortable. . . ."

"Look, say no more. I can tell this is embarrassing for you. I can't say I'm not disappointed, but, what the hell—"

"Don't hang up just yet. I want you to hear the rest."

"There's more?"

"Indeed, yes. Mr. Rodgers okayed Shirley Jones but not you. So, we suggested several other male singers. He turned them down as well. Now we began to wonder what was running around in his head. I said to him: 'Mr. Rodgers, what if we could get Frank Sinatra to do this?' "

"And?"

"He bloody well said 'no.' Sillier and sillier. Then, for a lark, I suggested Peggy Lee. 'No' again. Can you believe it? Finally, I pushed for Ella Fitzgerald and, damn me, if he didn't reject her! Ella Fitzgerald! Can you imagine?"

"There has to be a punch line to this story."

"Oh, there is, to be sure. When I asked him what singer or singers he would like to have on the show, he pulled a list out of his pocket and began to read from it. I can't remember the names but they all sounded like Mary Lou Witherspoon, Tom McMillan, Linda Forbush, James Thompson—this endless parade of people no one ever heard of. I asked him candidly just who the hell these people were. He explained they were all Broadway chorus singers who had appeared in some of his shows and—here's the telling part—who sang his songs exactly—no, he said 'precisely' the way he had written them."

I smiled to myself, remembering the "Blue Moon" incident years before at MGM. David's producer sighed and tendered another apology. I thanked him once again and that, I assumed, was that.

Not quite.

The very next day, he called again. "The hell with Richard Rodgers. We've decided to cancel part two. We still want you to come east and do the show with us. David would love to have you sit at the piano and talk about music and sing and play what you like."

I accepted that invitation (particularly gracious in light of David's history with Jan) and ended up doing the first extended guest shot ever on the David Frost show. I sat at the piano, talking informally with David about Richard Rodgers.

"David," I said, at the beginning of my "spot." "I think the tribute you did recently, honoring Mr. Rodgers, was one of the finest programs I have ever seen. Tonight, I would like to pay tribute to his equally talented collaborator, Lorenz Hart." I then proceeded, for the next fifty minutes, to sing and play Richard Rodgers melodies and the attendant witty, sophisticated, poetic lyrics of Larry Hart, pausing from time to time to extol the virtues of that brilliant lyricist.

Standing behind the camera, David's producer grinned knowingly.

≡

Okay. Back to Marty's.

I took a deep breath and sang my "Blue Moon" trilogy. Afterward, Dorothy Rodgers and Reasoner came up to my dressing room and were quite complimentary about the performance, in general, and the "Blue Moon" medley, in particular.

Reasoner must have admired my work because, then and there, he said he wanted to do a "60 Minutes" piece on me. That thrilled me no end. I rarely failed to watch the show, and, certainly, exposure on the number one–rated program in America could be nothing short of sensational for my reputation.

Morley Safer got into the act. He came into Marty's, saw me work, and made my heart beat a little faster by stating he was going to suggest to Phillip Scheffler, the senior "60 Minutes" producer, that both he and Harry conduct the interview, a first for the show. Clouds formed under my feet.

A luncheon was set up in the Palm Court at the Plaza: Scheffler, Reasoner, and I. We sat down, ordered drinks, and exchanged small talk. Finally, we got to the business at hand. Harry squinted sideways at me and the ball commenced. "You used to have a drug problem, didn't you?" he thrusted.

My jaw dropped. I parried with: "Harry, this may come as a blow to you, but I have never even smoked pot. Nor a single cigarette. Not once. Not ever. I don't even take aspirin when I have a headache."

"Hmmm. I thought I had read that you ... Well, you know, being a jazz singer and all, I thought—"

"No, Harry. Not once. Not ever."

A pregnant pause.

Scheffler cleared his throat. "Maybe it was booze. Did you used to drink a lot?"

I picked up my Perrier water and took a swig. " 'Fraid not, Phil. Unless you consider my one great addiction excessive drinking."

Scheffler brightened. "Oh, yeah? What's that?"

I managed to look grim. "It's—it's milkshakes, Phil. I'm a chocolate junkie. Always have been. Since I was a kid. Hard-to-kick habit." I saw where this interview was going. I smiled and said, "No, Phil, I don't drink and never have. I simply don't like the taste of hard liquor. An occasional glass of good wine with dinner is about the extent of my drinking."

Reasoner jumped in. "Well, Mel, wasn't there a scandal of some kind that you were involved in? Seems to me I remember ..."

In that microsecond, I knew "60 Minutes" would never do a profile on me.

I remembered the one they had produced on Anita O'Day a few months prior to this luncheon. It centered on her drug addiction and comeback after having kicked the habit. I was disturbed and disappointed to realize that one of my favorite TV magazine shows considered sensationalism—scandal, drug and alcohol use—good reason to do pieces on show people.

I have been in the business since the age of four. I have been a child radio actor, a singer at a tender age in vaudeville, a drummer, composer, lyricist, arranger, writer, author, pilot, gun collector, and talk-show host. Overcoming the sobriquet "Velvet Fog" and making the transition into the jazz world from the "pop" genre would have, I thought, been fairly decent fodder upon which to build a "60 Minutes" segment. I was wrong.

A few months went by. I was invited to a dinner party in New York. Ed Bradley, the most recent addition to the "60 Minutes" staff, sat next to me at supper.

"I came here tonight specifically to meet you," he announced. A grin split my face. He was a charming guy and a damned good interviewer. I was flattered by his remark. He continued, "You know, I'm new at '60 Minutes,' so I don't really have much clout yet. But I want to do pieces on two people, you and Fred Astaire."

"Well, Ed, I don't think you'll have any trouble selling your second choice to Phil Scheffler—"

"Oh, you know Phil?"

"Uh . . . yes. In a way." I filled Bradley in on my brief moment in the sun with Reasoner, Safer, and Scheffler. He seemed bemused and disturbed.

"I have never heard any of this, Mel. I didn't even know you had been considered for the show prior to our meeting tonight. Listen, would you mind if I approached them again? From my standpoint?"

"I'd be delighted, if you don't mind kicking what I feel is a terminally ill horse."

Word got back to me a few days later. Tormé is a no-go on "60 Minutes." "Too dull," was the pronouncement from on high.

I had been called a lot of things over the years. "Dull" certainly wasn't one of them. Still, I accepted the verdict with as much equanimity as I could muster. Harry Reasoner stopped me in a restaurant days later, shook my hand warmly, and said, "Hey, we'll get around to doing you on our show one of these days."

I smiled just as warmly and answered, "Whatever."

I will admit that I was let down by the affair. So much good was happening for and to me. I suspected that was why Reasoner and "60 Minutes" had been interested in the first place. I was enjoying the highest visibility of my career since the early "Fog" days at the Copa, back in 1947. It bothered me to be rejected by the CBS magazine show.

Just when I had finally resigned myself to the fact that I was not going to be presented to America in the form of a national TV profile, I got a call, out of the blue, from ABC's "20/20." "There is one hell of a lot of stuff going on with you right now. We'd like to profile you on '20/20.' "

I laughed. "Well, first I'd better tell you a few things." I filled the "20/20" rep in on the "60 Minutes" fiasco. "If you're looking to do a standard 'star-to-skid-row, back-to-star' kind of piece, I am definitely not your man."

"Hey," came the reply, "we want to do a piece on you. Period. What you do, what you like, where you're going as a singer and a musician. If you watch our show, you know we won't deal in muckraking or sensationalism for sensationalism's sake. Are you interested?"

"Hell, yes!"

The "20/20" crew, with producer Joe Pffiferling, interviewer Bob Brown, plus camera and sound people followed me around for weeks, filming me on the road, with George Shearing in Toronto and, ultimately, at home in Beverly Hills with three of my kids and Ali. The piece aired in August 1983 and was warmly received by friends and critics alike.

Almost simultaneously, the distinguished CBS program, "Sunday Morning" with Charles Kuralt, decided to examine my career. The fact that ABC's "20/20" had just done their thing with me made no difference to CBS. Once again, I was filmed in various locations, including a stint with the Sioux Falls, South Dakota, Symphony Orchestra. (No cracks, Mr. Carson!)

What really knocked me out was a call I received from Boyd Matson of NBC's "Today" show. "We want to come to your Monterey Jazz Festival concert, film you 'live' there, and then turn it into an interview/profile for the 'Today' show." Now I had to tell Boyd about both the "20/20" piece and the Kuralt "Sunday Morning" segment.

"I know all about them," Boyd explained. "I saw you on '20/ 20' a couple of weeks ago. They did a hell of a job. Now we want our turn with you, okay?"

And so it came to pass, in the years of our Lord, 1983–84, that three of the four major newsmagazine programs in America did career/profile segments on me within the course of fourteen months. I'm told that's some kind of record. An executive with one of the networks was genuinely surprised.

"You know, Mel, it's almost unbelievable that all three major networks did those pieces so close together. Usually, when one of them decides to explore your life and work, the other two avoid doing the same thing like they'd avoid a broken leg. You're lucky."

Lucky is right. And I hope you enjoy irony.

Almost one year after the "20/20" episode aired, I got a call from Dale Sheets. "Are you sitting down?"

"No, should I?"

"Very definitely. Sit down and fasten your seat belt."

"What's going on?"

"Mel, hold on to your hat. Your '20/20' segment won the Emmy for Best Documentary Profile."

"Good God, you're kidding!"

"Joe Pffiferling just called me from New York to tell me the good news. How do you feel about that?"

"Well, Dale, in view of the brush-off from '60 Minutes'..."

"Exactly."

43.

MUSICIANS

*M*ORE and more I found myself working in collaboration with George Shearing. Each year we did Carnegie Hall. Then came pairings at the various Fairmont hotels and Charlie's in Georgetown, D.C., and a gang of symphony dates shared. To try explaining Shearing's enormous talent is tantamount to pursuing fireflies with an eyecup. George is quicksilver and mercurial, with the most delicate pianistic touch on this planet. He can swing mightily, enmesh you with sensitive, lovely chord patterns during a ballad performance, and, as an accompanist, he possesses the kind of omniscient radar that the Nazis wished they had during the Battle of Britain.

Shot through with whimsy, a puckish penchant for puns, a squeaky singing voice (I am not his favorite pianist; he is not my favorite singer!) and married to his Ellie who, herself, is a fine musician and singer, George Shearing is, quite simply, one of my best friends.

Carl Jefferson, owner of Concord Jazz Records, nodded yes when George suggested that a Shearing/Tormé recording might be worthwhile. We decided on a "live" effort scheduled for April of 1982, said performance to be given at the Mark Hopkins in San Francisco in aid of Guide Dogs International.

Shearing, Mulligan, and I appeared on April 3 of that year in concert at the Music Center in downtown Los Angeles. The next day I went into the hospital out at Long Beach for an operation. I had been born with a congenital hernia that had been giving me more and more pain as time went on. Singing and, particularly, playing drums seemed to exacerbate the problem weekly. A great specialist, Dr. Carroll Bellis, chief of surgery at St. Mary's Hospital in Long Beach, took me into his care and performed the operation on the morning of April 5. On April 15, foolhardy though it may seem, I flew up to San Francisco and sang with Shearing at the Mark in front of a blue ribbon northern California audience.

The result of that evening was an album called _An Evening with George Shearing and Mel Tormé_. I was worried that I might not be at my best physically or vocally that evening, so soon after the operation. Consequently, I was more than a little surprised when, less than a year later, I won a Grammy as Best Male Jazz Vocalist for that album.

Surprised and, I might add, disturbed. George Shearing was not even nominated. That George should be bypassed when, clearly, the album was a total collaboration, seemed insupportable to me. I got very vocal about it on TV and in radio and newsprint interviews. I am sure I sounded like the biggest ingrate on earth, and for that I am sorry. Certainly, being honored by one's peers is gratifying. I had been nominated ten or eleven times before and had just about given up believing I would ever win one of those little trophies. On the other hand, NARAS's snubbing of the Shear rankled me.

History repeated itself the following year. Our second album together, _Top Drawer_, won me my thirteenth nomination in the same "Best Male Jazz Singer" category. The night of the Grammy Awards I was otherwise engaged, singing at a State dinner at the White House for President and Mrs. Reagan, assorted notables, and the guests of honor—the president of Austria and his wife.

Peter Nero, another splendidly gifted pianist, and I performed the Gershwin medley I had put together years before. My concentration was strictly on the business at hand. So help me, I had almost completely forgotten about the Grammy Awards that evening. Peter and I rose to this special occasion, and it was a performance that made us both proud. Nancy Reagan, an old friend from our days together at MGM, led the standing ovation. Then she walked up to the small performance platform and asked, "Is this all there is? We want more." Peter and I moved out into the foyer of the White House and, while the President and his lady and their guests danced, we played and sang an impromptu medley of Kern, Berlin, and Rodgers and Hart.

On the way back to our hotel, Ali (no way would I have left her in L.A. on an evening such as this) and I agreed it was one of our finer experiences.

As I put the key into the door, the phone rang. I picked up the receiver to hear Dale say, "Well, Pappy, you've done it again!"

"The Grammy?"

"That's right. Number Two."

I was genuinely surprised. I never believed I would or could win two in a row. I experienced a strange, ambivalent flash of joy and anger; joy for the obvious reason, anger over the omission of Shearing once again by NARAS. Still, it was one hell of a night to remember.

Peter Nero and I had recently appeared together with the Philly Pops orchestra at the Academy of Music in Philadelphia and in Carnegie Hall, where we performed an all-Gershwin concert. Peter was (and is) the Philly Pops' conductor and a marvelous one. While you're at it, Nero is, to my mind, one of the finest musicians in the world and an underrated jazz artist. His mind works similarly to Shearing's when it comes to what are called "substitutions": chords to a given song that are different from the composer's originals, which, in the hands of a Shearing or a Nero, are often an improvement. He is also a gadget-lover, an electronics whiz, and an all-around good guy.

The Philly Pops is an eighty-plus body of some of Philadelphia's finest players. A man named Leonard Tessler serves as president of the orchestra. If kindness, gentleness, and thoughtfulness were prerequisites for immortality, Tessler would live forever. A non-musician, albeit a great music lover, he is the head of a thriving business in Philadelphia. He and his charming wife, Mildred, have become two of my closest friends. I have appeared with the Philly Pops several times at this writing, and the experience of being aided and abetted by a symphony orchestra of this caliber is indescribable.

Hearing my arrangements played by a large, supercompetent ensemble such as the P.P. is an incredible "high" for me.

When I began doing a raft of symphony dates, I sat down for weeks beforehand and wrote several arrangements for myself and the orchestras with which I would appear. This phase of my music-writing career was the toughest, since the process was new ground for me to break. I asked dozens of questions and got lots of help from my arranging heroes once again, and particularly from Howard Drew, my longtime friend and copyist.

"Howard," I would pester him on the phone, "what's the effective range of the French horn? Top and bottom?"

"Howard, when I write for the double bass, do I place the note in the bass clef where I want the instrument to sound or an octave higher? Or lower? Or what?"

"Howard, I'm having trouble understanding how to write for the harp. Now, if I want a gliss from a low G-minor seventh up to a resolving C-ninth, how do I indicate that on the score?"

Unfailingly, and with superhuman patience, Howard Drew took the time to answer my questions and correct my notations once they were in his educated hands.

And educated is what I am getting at. I sorely regret not having formally studied music. All my arranging and composing is strictly instinctive and untutored. The orchestration process I go through is time-consuming and sometimes laborious. When I think of the arrangers I admire who can scribble beautiful patterns of music without even referring to a piano, I grow green with envy. Even though I have written over 250 arrangements, I still suffer from a kind of musical dyslexia, thanks to my lack of music instruction at an earlier age. I sit at the piano and painstakingly write the notes down for the various instruments. Then I hand my score over to Howard, who copies those notes onto individual parts for the trumpets, woodwinds, strings, *et al.* He delivers the completed work back to me. I take that new baby of mine to rehearsal to have the orchestra christen it with a first reading. Now here's where the "dyslexia" sets in.

When an orchestra is rehearsing a new chart of mine and an offending wrong note is sounded, I have to refer to my score to find the answer. Now, suddenly, that score I have written is a huge jumble of notes. The individual quarters and halves and eighth-notes I originally penned, one at a time, are now a mass of black-penciled scribblings, and I am slow in finding the problem and correcting it. My one consolation is that I have learned the same problem exists with other, better arrangers than I. Cold comfort.

The symphony dates are great fun and musically very rewarding, not only during my portion of the evening's entertainment, but during the first half as well. I stand in the wings of each auditorium and listen as the house conductor or a guest baton wielder takes the orchestra through the paces of some of the greatest classical and light popular music.

Many jazz musicians have held down chairs in symphony organizations. They function quite well, wearing both the classical and jazz hats. Conversely, symphony brass players find it difficult to convert mentally to the jazz idiom. Almost always, they play eighth-notes too rigidly, in far too staccato a manner to "swing" the figures placed in front of them. They are almost always, however, wonderfully cooperative, and, usually, symphony players seem to enjoy performing popular/jazz music. I think the greatest compliments I have ever received have come from various philharmonic musicians who have praised my arranging abilities and commented on how much they enjoyed playing my scores.

Predictably, there have also been a few who turned their noses up at my kind of music. But, as in every other walk of life, the grousing usually came from not-very-good practitioners whose grumbling and bad manners sprang from insecurities of their own. Generally, the symphony experience has been exhilarating.

My first love as an arranger is writing for the Big Band. My early role models cling to me with a kind of musical static electricity: Jimmie Lunceford's Billy Moore, Jr.; Goodman's Fletcher Henderson and Eddie Sauter; Shaw's Jerry Gray; Duke's Duke. And the latter-day saints: Mulligan and Gil Evans, Paich and Rogers, Neal Hefti and Ralph Burns, and so many more.

The Big Bands have been in decline since 1946. What a shame. Personally, I think we reached the highest level of musicality, taste, and inventiveness during the era of the Big Bands. Many of those leaders are gone now: Basie, Lunceford, Duke, Harry James, Benny Goodman, the Dorseys, and my close friends Woody Herman and Buddy Rich. Thank God, Les Brown is still here to remind us of former glory days.

Still, just when you think you have heard it all, along comes a Torontonian named Rob McConnell with an all-Canadian band to knock your feet out from under you. McConnell, hands down, is, for my money, the greatest arranging talent and the best valve trombone player I have come across in donkey's years.

Jazz is most definitely alive and kicking out there. And despite the recession of Big Bands as the dominant force in music, new ones keep springing up and thrilling us with their spirit and drive and downright swingability.

The admirable drummer/composer/arranger Louis Bellson has such an ensemble. Bob Florence, as well. Frankie Capp, Bill Berry, and a Rob McConnell/Boss Brass sound-alike called "Silverware," are West Coast entries in the newer Big Band sweepstakes, and of course, the aforementioned Artie Shaw orchestra usually fronted by Dick Johnson. The Basie, Tommy Dorsey, and Glenn Miller mastheads also adorn new, young troupes of musicians led by hardy perennials like Buddy Morrow and Tommy Pederson.

Most of those current touring bands are staffed by young players from North Texas State College, Berkeley School of Music, or similar universities with gifted teachers and a curriculum that sidesteps simpler forms of popular music and prepares their students for a professional future based on theory, harmony, tutoring on all the major instruments, and perhaps most importantly, attitude.

The young people I have worked with, from the jazz experience of the Buddy Rich band to the classical/light pop music of the Tulsa Symphony, are far better equipped musicians than their antecedents of the thirties, forties, and even the 1950s. Funny. I used to think I had been born ten years too late. I had, from my early teen years, yearned to be a bandleader. Now, I'm glad I became known for my singing. I live and work in the best of both possible worlds.

It is difficult to write about new songs with any degree of specificity. It is tempting to dismiss rock and roll tunes as inconsequential, mindless twaddle, serving a restless, shallow young public. It is equally self-serving to defend the "golden era" of popular music—the decades from 1925 to 1945—as the most fruitful, attractive, romantic period, when our youthful spirits were buoyed

by the sounds of Glenn Miller, Artie Shaw, the Duke and the
Count and the Earl and the King—Benny Goodman—royal cats
all.

Obviously, every musical age has its geniuses, its hacks, its
mediocrities, its good tunes and lousy tunes, its "originals" and
their imitators. In the midst of the Swing Era's great songs ("All
the Things You Are," "That Old Black Magic," "Serenade in
Blue"), and their exciting instrumental counterparts ("Benny Rides
Again," "Every Tub," "Cherokee," "Take the 'A' Train"), we
suffered the deadly banalities of "Three Little Fishies," "Oh Johnny,
Oh Johnny, Oh!" and "Mairzy Doats." Even those latter trivialities
served a purpose: millions loved them, bought the records, played
them to death in jukeboxes and on home phonographs. If I have
learned anything at all in the years I have plied my various musical
trades, it is simply that we all march to an endless parade of
"different drummers."

The careful, inoffensive lyrics of the '30s and '40s have given
way to the explicit, topical, uninhibited words we now hear on a
daily basis. I cannot, in all honesty, say I like much of what passes
for popular music these days, but, in a sense, the new crop of tunes
represents the current mores of our society more honestly and
realistically than did the suffocated songs of pre–World War Two
America. The current songs are cruder, far less intelligent, and the
craftsmanlike lyrics of bygone days have gone out the window—
but more than ever before on the music scene, art is imitating life.
Is that good? *Quien sabe?*

44.

ONWARD

ONE day, in May of 1984, Ali and I sat down over breakfast and decided it was time to get married. We had kept company for over eight years, and I felt it was time she made an honest man out of me.

My desire to tie the knot again astounded me. After the debacle with Jan and the attendant pain, I thought I had sworn off marriage for good. I think I fell in "like" with Ali on that first night we dated, back in October 1976. Her patience and understanding were not only admirable, but far beyond the call of duty where a girl friend was concerned. As I have mentioned before, I was a royal pain during my "Jan-has-left-me-whatever-shall-I-do?" phase.

Most women, upon hearing those tired mewlings and pukings once too often, would have told me to take a walk. Not Ali. She hung in there, carefully walking the line between concern and sympathy, holding patronization at arm's length all the while. There were nights, during my phase-out-of-Jan agony, when I simply could not believe I had found a woman of Ali's caliber to ease the pain, shoo the blues, listen to my tirades, proffer tender, loving care and, in general, become my best friend.

So ... we flew down to Miami, boarded the S.S. *Norway* (on which I was to perform as part of a "jazz" cruise of the Caribbean) and, on Tuesday, October 30, 1984, exactly eight years and one day after we had first met, we exchanged vows in a judge's chambers on the island of St. Thomas. Shearing and his Ellie stood up for us. Donny, Paul Langosh, a fine bassist from Washington, D.C., and Mike Renzi were in attendance, along with Shelley Shire and

Hank O'Neill, two nifty people/producers who had conceived the
Norway jazz cruise to begin with.

The judge turned out to be a nice Jewish boy from my old
hometown of Chicago. A sweet-faced gent in his late thirties or
early forties, with a head of curly hair, he looked like a cross
between Gene Wilder and Mr. Pickwick. As we entered his sanc-
tum, we heard "The Christmas Song" being played on his ghetto-
blaster. Then I saw a poster of me hung on the far wall. Gee,
that's nice, I thought. This guy's gone to a lot of trouble to make
me and Ali and our wedding party feel welcome annd comfortable.

Wrong. Turns out, he had many tapes of mine and the poster
for a long time. Fate can be kind.

And now, we stood before him, waiting for the traditional
marriage vows to be read and spoken and taken.

Wrong again. The judge had prepared a very special ceremony,
some of which was biblical, some of it original, and still another
portion taken from Kahlil Gibran's *The Prophet*. I know, I know.
Sounds contrived and even a little corny. I assure you, it was not.
The judge's words were touching, meaningful, and, most important, personal. We all got a little misty, standing there and listening
to this kind man's words about hope and love and the acknowl-
edgment of each other's right to personal "space."

Then it was over and there were congratulations and kissing
and thank-you's to His Honor and picture taking across the street
in the little park, then back to the *Norway* and a small wedding
party on board.

I looked at Ali, sitting beside me. She was glowing, and I
realized at that precise moment that I loved her far more deeply
than I had loved anyone else before. I thought about a lyric I had
written to a Gerry Mulligan melody, just after I had met Ali, and
it occurred to me how fitting those words had been then and how
much more they meant on our wedding night:

VERSE: You'd think, by now, I would have learned my lesson,
You'd think, by now, I would have grown more wise.
What I once thought could never re-occur
Is taking place

Before my eyes.
I can't believe what's happening is true,
I've got this awful sense of déjà vu.

CHORUS: This couldn't be the real thing;
Ask me, I've been in love before.
I've known the pain and heartache and tears.

This couldn't be the real thing;
Not now, not knowing what I know.
I've fought against these feelings for years.

And yet, this sudden weakness of knees,
The absolute conviction that she's
The very one
To conquer all my foolish fears.

How could this be the real thing?
I thought I'd left that all behind;
Much better safe than sorry, I swore,
Yet here I stand before her
Saying I adore her
I guess I'll try the real thing
Once more.

All in all, things have never been better. Jan remarried (not to
Kevin Francis) and moved back to England, where Daisy and
James go to a pair of great schools. Both kids come home to Beverly
Hills every Christmas and Easter as well as five or six weeks during
their summer vacation. In the fall of 1988, Daisy, eighteen and
lovely, will be going to UCLA in West Los Angeles.

Ali did a brilliant job of decorating the house as well as mas-
terminding the remodeling. The result is the most livable home I
have ever enjoyed.

Tracy has sold his screenplays, _Elixir_ and _The Witching Hour_,
and is well on his way to realizing his dream of becoming a
producer/writer. He recently joined the writing staff of "Star Trek:
The Next Generation," and has written three of that program's
most praised episodes, one of which recently won the coveted

Peabody Award. Steven now hosts a new TV show called "Ci-
nemattractions." He is constantly writing songs and singing in several Los Angeles clubs.

Melissa manages several talented young actors and actresses.

Dale Sheets is still my manager after eighteen years. As excellent
a manager as Dale is, his greatest value to me is his friendship.
Someone once described his personal manager to me in these terms:
"We don't have to be pals. He gets me the jobs, that's all I give a
damn about. I don't socialize with the crumb. He does his thing
and I do mine. I like it that way!"

I don't. My great affection for Dale is inextricably tied to our
professional relationship. I simply could not function any other
way. I have had good relationships with all of my managers. The
one I have with Dale is the best, hands down.

In early 1985, I was once again nominated for a Grammy for
a third album I made with George Shearing, "An Evening at
Charlie's." I lost to Joe Williams, who was long overdue to win
that award.

One of the great thrills for me was appearing on *Night of 100
Stars* at Radio City Music Hall in New York. I sang in a ten-
minute jazz segment that included Lena Horne, Sarah Vaughan,
Al Jarreau, Joe Williams, Wynton Marsalis, and Woody Herman.
That it was the highest-rated ten minutes of the entire three-hour
extravaganza was gratifying. What knocked me out even more
was the once-in-a-lifetime experience in the "green room," where
all the stars gathered to watch the show on a monitor before (or
after) appearing themselves.

Standing in that star-packed room after having done my bit
on the show, I was blessed with kind words from Dinah Shore,
John Updike, Ed Asner, Dabney Coleman, Anne Baxter, John
Forsythe, Richard Dreyfuss, Linda Evans, and Robert De Niro. I
hung out with Betty Thomas, Bruce Weitz, and Joe Spano and
his wife ("Hill Street Blues" was my longtime TV obsession).

I saw a man I have admired for years make his way through
the room, moving in my general direction. I flushed with joy when
(the late) Yul Brynner walked right up to me, extended his hand,
and said, "I've always wanted to meet you."

As I have said, there is nothing quite so wonderful as being admired by someone you admire.

I went away from that evening feeling more a respected member of the entertainment community than I ever had before. Being on the road as much as I am is tantamount to living on a space station, where socializing is confined to the narrow circle of acquaintances, friends, and coperformers within your immediate purview. Don't laugh: I was surprised that Yul Brynner even knew who I was. Or that Anne Baxter had ever seen or heard me prior to that evening. If you think I am spouting phony modesty, you are mistaken. I am always delightfully surprised when someone, other than a fellow musical artist, expresses admiration for my work.

I think the scales have evened out pretty well in my personal as well as professional life. I am on the road for short periods of time, followed by equal periods of time at home. Ali and I love the house and seldom go to parties. Her daughter, Carrie, graduated from Harvard and works for the Walt Disney Company. Her son, Kurt, lives in the cottage where I spent my eighteen months prior to divorcing Jan. He is going to college.

I have what I feel is an overabundance of friends. In addition to all those I've mentioned throughout this book, people like Bill Hooper, Chuck and Betty McCann, the Dick Stewarts, Ted and Rhonda Fleming Mann, Jonathan Schwartz, Maureen McGovern, Jack Jones, Rex Reed, Hugh Hefner, Henry and Ginny Mancini, Mr. & Mrs. Donald O'Connor, and more recent friendships with Burt Reynolds and Loni Anderson, Lydia and Charlton Heston, the Holly Hollenbecks, P. J. Montrone, Ron McClure, the Graham Pratts (Leslie Uggams), Mary Prappas, Tom Buckley, Ron Ogan, Mel Guy . . . Wow, the list is happily almost endless . . . and Harry Anderson of "Night Court" fame—all of the above (and more) grace my life, sweeten my thoughts, bolster my belief in lasting friendships. Incidentally, about Harry Anderson and "Night Court." . . . The "Night Court" experience has been one of the most amazing things to happen to me in years. Almost daily, someone tells me how much he enjoys "Judge Harry Stone's" references to me. In the past few years I have made four or five appearances on the show, and the subsequent reaction to those guest shots has once again been prime evidence of just how potent the medium of television is.

The running gag, of course, is Judge Stone's obsession with my singing. I am literally his idol (can you believe it!) and his one desire is to meet me personally. The cleverest ingredient of the guest shots I have done on "Night Court," is the number of ways the writers have devised to keep that meeting from taking place.

On the first episode I did, Harry walked out of one door, as I entered another, missing me by a hair's breadth. Then, as I bent over a drinking fountain with my back to him, he complained to his prosecuting attorney, played by John Larroquette, about this "geek," monopolizing the fountain, slobbering over it, and so forth. Finally, as I attempted to enter his courtroom, he walked over to the door without seeing me, and slammed it unwittingly in my face. All this was accomplished in the best tradition of French farce and it worked wonderfully.

On another occasion, Larroquette spots me in the corridor of the courtroom, and having accidentally just ruined Harry's collection of my records, kidnaps and manacles me in the judge's chambers, thinking that if he can bring the judge in to meet me, it will soften the blow of the wrecked recordings.

The "gag" continues on an almost weekly basis. What a bonus for me. Young people who never had heard of me now attend my concerts, curious to get a look at this guy Harry Anderson is always talking about. The biggest kick of all, though, is working with the cast and crew of that show, some of the nicest, most professional people I have ever had the pleasure of meeting.

I'm sure it won't surprise you to learn that Harry Anderson and creator/producer Reinhold Weege have become great friends of mine. In fact, Harry and I spent a joyous New Year's Eve, 1987, together cohosting PBS's "Happy New Year U.S.A." extravaganza.

I continue to perform for George Wein in his series of concerts, currently known as the JVC Jazz Festival at Carnegie Hall, the Playboy Jazz Festival at the Hollywood Bowl, as well as those evenings called "Jazz at the Bowl," produced by the Los Angeles Philharmonic Association.

Certain stands have become almost ritual: the Fairmont hotels, the Paul Masson Winery Music Festival prior to Labor Day each September. I have recently hosted a TV special at the Hollywood Palladium for public broadcasting. My recorded effort with Rob McConnell's Boss Brass actually made "the charts."

A few Christmas Eves ago, along with my kids, Ali's kids, my mom and dad, Rudy Behlmer and Betty White, and Gene Hackman and his lovely Betsy came to dinner. We sat around and talked careers and their attendant vagaries.

I explained how I had called someone at a record company a few weeks back.

"May I ask who's calling, please?"

"Yes. Tell him it's Mel Tormé."

"Would you spell that, please?"

I cleared my throat. "That's T-o-r-m-e."

"May I ask what this is about, sir?"

"Er . . . just tell him 'Mel Tormé.' I think he'll understand."

"Excuse me, Mr. Tormé, does Mr. ——— know you? May I ask what firm you're with?"

I laughed. "May I ask an impertinent question, young lady?"

"Uh . . . I guess so."

"How old are you?"

"Nineteen."

"I see."

There was a time, when, in a youthful burst of self-importance, bruised ego, and the absolute conviction that every man, woman, and child in America should have known who I was, I would have been insulted, embarrassed, and, ultimately, hostile toward that young lady. At this time of my life, however, I am sensibly aware of the fact that a whole new generation of music consumers is out there—young, enamored of their own youthful idols, and inundated on an hourly basis with rock via the overwhelming majority of radio stations from which that music blares forth.

There is no reason on earth why a nineteen-year-old receptionist should know who Mel Tormé is, and that is a fact I have learned to live with quite comfortably. Yet, some of those late-teen, early-twenties people I mentioned earlier show up at my concerts and are interested and intrigued by the jazz sound. Most gratifying are the young, upwardly mobile Americans who have literally flooded my shows and concerts with their attendance.

I still play drums during my performances. I am free to arrange what I like. Shearing, Peter Nero, Jay Leonhart, and a new young pianist, John Campbell, plus a few super West Coast musicians named Carl Schroeder, Bob Maize, and John Leitham brighten my musical life.

Donny Osborne has worked out far beyond my expectations. The timorous lad of thirteen years ago is now a seasoned musician and a good friend.

I sing what and where I wish to sing. I am more than generously compensated for my services. I am in reasonable health. I have come to a place in the road where I am no longer scrambling for work; thanks to a kind God, I have all I can use.

Early on, it certainly wasn't *all* velvet. Now the fog has lifted.

AFTERTHOUGHTS

SELF-CRITICISM. The vagaries of written criticism can be maddening. In my case, the cruelest, toughest, most relentless critic of my work is...me. I ascribe to an old George Bernard Shaw quote: "We are all amateurs: no one lives long enough to become a professional."

To seek a perfect performance every time out is to search vainly for a kind of musical Holy Grail. On many evenings, my inadequacies as a singer have sent me into a rage against myself, and on those occasions, no critic born of woman's womb could ever describe in print what I know is true about me.

≡

Friends: During your lifetime, if you can count real friends on the fingers of your hand, even if you have to bypass your thumb and pinkie, consider yourself lucky. There's a saying that goes: a friend in need is a pain in the ass. True enough, I suppose, but what are friends for? It's in times of stress, despair, tragedy that you find out who your friends—your real friends—are. The itinerant ones, the kind who move in and out of your life, who can tolerate you only during the good times, fall away like melting Jell-O. The strong ones, the real ones, hang in there, even when it is inconvenient and uncomfortable.

≡

Singing: I have lost track, in the past few years, of the number of times reviewers have commented on my increased strength in the vocal department. I recall the numerous TV, radio, and newsprint interviewers who have asked me why, when middle-age—and beyond—normally ushers in diminishing strength, wobbly vibrato, and increasing hoarseness in certain singers, I seem to have reversed the process.

The answer is spectacularly simple. I have never smoked. Anything. I don't drink hard liquor. And when I know I have to sing on a given occasion, I make sure I rejuvenate my vocal cords with at least seven hours of sleep. Eight is better, but seven—no less— is sufficient. I am told the vocal cords are like any muscle in the body: they need to be exercised, then regenerated. I follow that line of reasoning and it seems to work for me.

I think the most important—and the toughest—aspect of singing/performing is consistency. It is difficult to maintain a level of quality performances over a period of, say, six months, when you are singing the same material night after night. To me, being consistent is the real challenge for any singer. What always concerns me is playing a venue like Michael's Pub in Manhattan for a month and having my work compared by someone who sees me on a Tuesday night, then returns to catch me again on the following Friday evening. God help me if I don't strive to make the second and third hearing as enjoyable as the first. It's not easy to invest fresh meaning and emotion into lyrics that have become as painfully familiar through repetition as the back of your hand, but I try. So does virtually every singer I admire. As Frank Sinatra once told me, the key is concentration, and when it works and you "touch" an audience, there's no feeling in the world like it.

Choice of musical material is, obviously, an important factor, particularly when a piece of music is eminently "performable." Some tunes are better left on record: others are worthy of exposure in one's personal appearance repertoire. Lyrical content, obviously, is the key. Finding a proper vocal "tour de force" takes a great amount of research. When one does come up with such a gem (Sinatra's version of the "Soliloquy" from *Carousel* by Rodgers and Hammerstein is a case in point), it can become a vital centerpiece for any given performance.

I also think that perception of a singer in the collective mind of the public can sometimes make or break a career. Image is what

I am talking about. Crosby and Sinatra and Como and Dick Haymes and Englebert Humperdinck are guys who have enjoyed a romantic image with their audiences. While Frank's early nickname ("The Voice") was almost generic, Bing's sobriquet ("The Groaner") was hardly flattering, yet it never impeded his romantic persona.

At the inception of my solo vocal career, the bobby-sox brigade viewed my nickname, "The Velvet Fog," as a sexy-sounding appellation, and for twenty minutes there, I was part of that sex-image clutch of singers peculiar to the early post-war years. When I switched gears in 1955 and made inroads into the jazz area of singing, my fans, old and new, took an entirely different view of my work and my image as a singing performer. The "Velvet Fog" label was no longer valid; my actual style of singing had changed.

As I have said before, I initially hated that nickname. I now look back on it with equal amounts of tolerance, amusement, and even nostalgia. Two of my automobiles have license plates that read, consecutively, EL FOG and LE PHOG. Considering my long-standing intolerance for that nickname, I think I've come a long way, baby.

≡

Judges: Hang 'em high.

≡

Lawyers: Hang 'em higher.

≡

Heroes and heroines: Winston Churchill, F.D.R. and Eleanor Roosevelt, Anwar Sadat, Orson Welles, Ayn Rand, Spencer Tracy, Vivien Leigh, Jerry Lewis, Laurence Olivier, Nevil Shute, John Gardner (author of *Excellence*), Gerald Seymour, Airline Pilots, Teachers, Mario Andretti, George S. Patton, John F. Kennedy, Every Single Astronaut, Leonardo DaVinci, Edward R. Murrow, Toulouse-Lautrec.

≡

Musical heroes and heroines: Frederick Delius, J. S. Bach, George Frederick Handel, Frank Sinatra, Ella Fitzgerald, Martha Raye,

Helen Forrest, Erich Wolfgang Korngold, Max Steiner, Miklós Rozsa, Dimitri Tiomkin, Buddy Rich, Duke Ellington, Artie Shaw, George Shearing, Gerry Mulligan, Richard Rodney Bennett, Sir Thomas Beecham, Deanna Durbin, Bernard Herrmann, Fred Astaire, Percy Grainger, Igor Stravinsky, Edvard Grieg, Mabel Mercer, Rob McConnell, Bing Crosby, Benny Goodman, Maureen McGovern, Judy Garland, Gene Krupa . . . and so many more.

≡

Marriage: It is either, as mentioned previously, a) the greatest invasion of privacy known to mankind, or b) the sweetest state of shared pleasures, secrets, interests, philosophies, sexual compatibility, and goals imaginable. Take your pick.

≡

Children: Mainly, they are a blessing requiring large amounts of patience and understanding along the way. My kids have their "up" and "down" sides, with the positive far outweighing the negative. I'd hate to think how pointless my life would have been without my children to grace it, strengthen it, and generally light it up.

≡

Movies: Say what you will about the naïve, narrow films of the thirties and forties, it is difficult to recall any of them that exhibited the questionable taste on display in certain more recent films. Was it necessary to watch Jane Fonda, in *Fun with Dick and Jane*, while she sat in the bathroom, urinating, then matter-of-factly wiped herself with a piece of toilet paper?

We have seen the pendulum swing far over to one side where movies are concerned. In the name of "realism," we have watched graphic examples of maiming, rapes, gunshot wounds, gruesome murders, and the like. Obviously, if young, impressionable people are going to be exposed to this kind of fare, the least damaging is sexual explicitness. Yet time and again, a sexually explicit film will get an "X" rating, while violent, frightening, foul-language entries are rewarded with "R" and "PG" categories.

Are the old movies better than the new ones? Since the overwhelming majority of today's movies are aimed at the teen-age market, films that are comparable in intelligence, wit, setting, and acting, to the films of the Golden Era of the thirties and forties are few and far between. But when those few films are peopled by the likes of Robert De Niro, Meryl Streep, Robert Redford, and Gene Hackman, to name a few, the acting is as convincing and true to life as the work done by the likes of Spencer Tracy, Ingrid Bergman, and Paul Muni in the old black-and-white classics I love and watch again and again.

≡

About guns: Relax. I am not about to enrage you with bumper-sticker slogans ("Guns don't kill people—people kill people"; "If they want my guns, they'll have to pry 'em outta my cold, dead hands," et cetera). Guns obviously *do* kill people. That aspect of weapons, particularly in the commission of crimes, sickens me. By the same token, a gun used in self-defense and/or for the protection of a loved one being threatened, say, in one's home, is literally the only chance a citizen may have to save himself (or herself) and his family.

I wish there was far more gun "education" in this country. Statistics don't lie: many deaths are caused by ignorance in the handling of firearms and the accidental discharge of a pistol in the hands of an innocent child. Obviously, placing guns in an absolutely safe, child-proof place is mandatory if you are going to keep such weapons in the house. Some people find this out too late, and that is tragic.

More and more, however, I am meeting people who were antigun, who have experienced the trauma of armed robbery, rape, and assault or even a murder in the family, and who have done a 180 where having a defense weapon in the house is concerned.

My love of guns is purely and simply historic. My penchant for the old Colt "Peacemaker," the six-shooter that Won the West, is based on what I read and the westerns I saw as a kid growing up in big-city Chicago. The mechanical innards, the external blued and ivory-stocked beauty of some of these artifacts of the Old West, strike a responsive chord within me.

When I find an old cavalry Colt, or a six-gun some sheriff used back in the 1880s to keep the peace, I am no less intrigued by these pieces than are the most rabid stamp collectors or dedicated connoisseurs of old, rare coins.

≡

Finally, a few words about those near and dear to me.

My mother and father are amazing. Dad is ninety, Mom is eighty-seven. Both are in good health, considering their time of life.

Aunt Faye, the erstwhile "Wonder Frisco Dancer," clings to her Chicago roots. We see her every now and then, either on the West Coast or in our old hometown by the lake.

Uncle Art never really recovered from the death of his only son, Ira. He lives in Tucson, Arizona, with his stepdaughter and her son.

My beloved Uncle Al passed away several years ago. He was the baby of the three brothers. You can imagine how my dad felt.

Aunt Ruth, my mother's younger sister, died in late 1986.

Robert Ginter, my friend and business manager for over two decades, died painfully five years ago of cancer. He was a lovable bear of a man who possessed the ability to laugh at himself, an attribute we all should develop.

Jan Bloom, who took over my bookkeeping chores when Bob Ginter passed away, died suddenly of a heart attack on the day after New Year's, 1987.

*B*UDDY RICH, my longtime friend and drumming idol, died on April 2, 1987. He was sixty-nine years old, far too young, too vital a guy to pass on. Still, it was his time, his Appointment in Samarra, as John O'Hara would have put it.

The day before Buddy died, we spent three hours talking and taping his reminiscences in preparation for his eventual biography. He had been after me since 1975 to write it, and we had tentatively begun work on it back then.

On April 1, scant hours before he passed away, he commanded: "Write it, Tormé. Nobody knows me as well as you."

"B," I said, as gently as possible, "how do I write this—warts and all?"

He smiled his first and only smile that day and said: "Absolutely. Warts and all. Just be accurate. Tell the truth."

I am currently at work on that biography.

DISCOGRAPHY

JEWEL
1944

Singles:

WHITE CHRISTMAS, Mel Tormé and His Mel-Tones   Jewel G-400

WHERE OR WHEN, Mel Tormé and His Mel-Tones

DECCA
1945

Singles:

NIGHT MUST FALL, Mel Tormé and His Mel-Tones   ——

I'M DOWN TO MY LAST DREAM, Mel Tormé and His Mel-Tones   ——

A STRANGER IN TOWN, Mel Tormé and His Mel-Tones   ——

YOU'VE LAUGHED AT ME FOR THE LAST TIME, Mel Tormé and His Mel-Tones   18653

AM I BLUE?, Mel Tormé and His Mel-Tones   ——

I FALL IN LOVE TOO EASILY, Mel Tormé and His Mel-Tones with Eugenie Baird   Decca 18707

DAY BY DAY, Bing Crosby with Mel Tormé and His Mel-Tones   ——

PROVE IT BY THE THINGS YOU DO, Bing Crosby with Mel Tormé and His Mel-Tones   Decca 18746

MUSICRAFT
1946–48

Singles:

THERE'S NO ONE BUT YOU, Mel Tormé and the Mel-Tones with Sonny Burke Orchestra	363
WILLOW ROAD, Mel Tormé and the Mel-Tones with Sonny Burke Orchestra	363
SOUTH AMERICA, TAKE IT AWAY, Mel Tormé and the Mel-Tones with Sonny Burke Orchestra	381
TRY A LITTLE TENDERNESS, Mel Tormé and the Mel-Tones with Sonny Burke Orchestra	381
IT HAPPENED IN MONTEREY, Mel Tormé and the Mel-Tones with Sonny Burke Orchestra	397
BORN TO BE BLUE, Mel Tormé with Sonny Burke Orchestra	397
THEY CAN'T CONVINCE ME, Mel Tormé with Artie Shaw Orchestra	441
I GOT THE SUN IN THE MORNING, Mel Tormé and the Mel-Tones with Artie Shaw Orchestra	365-T
ALONG WITH ME, Mel Tormé with Artie Shaw Orchestra	365-L
GET OUT OF TOWN, Mel Tormé with Artie Shaw Orchestra	390
WHAT IS THIS THING CALLED LOVE? Mel Tormé and the Mel-Tones with Artie Shaw Orchestra	390
FOR YOU, FOR ME, FOREVER MORE, Mel Tormé and the Mel-Tones with Artie Shaw Orchestra	412-T
CHANGING MY TUNE, Mel Tormé and the Mel-Tones with Artie Shaw Orchestra	412-L
THEY CAN'T CONVINCE ME, Mel Tormé and the Mel-Tones with Artie Shaw Orchestra	441-T
AND SO TO BED, Mel Tormé and the Mel-Tones with Artie Shaw Orchestra	441-L

DON'T BELIEVE IT DEAR, Mel Tormé and the   445
Mel-Tones with Artie Shaw Orchestra

IT'S THE SAME OLD DREAM, Mel Tormé and the   492
Mel-Tones with Artie Shaw Orchestra
I BELIEVE, Mel Tormé and the Mel-Tones   492
with Artie Shaw Orchestra

ONE FOR MY BABY, Mel Tormé with Ray Linn   15107
Orchestra
A LITTLE KISS EACH MORNING, Mel Tormé with   15107
Ray Linn Orchestra

DREAM AWHILE, Mel Tormé and the Mel-   15099
Tones with Ray Linn Orchestra
THERE'S NO BUSINESS LIKE SHOW BUSINESS, Mel   15099
Tormé and the Mel-Tones with Ray Linn
Orchestra

IT'S DREAMTIME, Mel Tormé with Sonny   15102
Burke Orchestra
YOU'RE DRIVING ME CRAZY!, Mel Tormé with   15102
Sonny Burke Orchestra

WHO CARES WHAT PEOPLE SAY?, Mel Tormé   15104
with Sonny Burke Orchestra
EASY TO REMEMBER, Mel Tormé with Walter   ———
Gross Orchestra

KOKOMO, INDIANA, Mel Tormé with Walter   15109
Gross Orchestra
HOW LONG HAS THIS BEEN GOING ON?, Mel   15109
Tormé with Walter Gross Orchestra

THAT'S WHERE I CAME IN, Mel Tormé and the   15111
Mel-Tones with Sonny Burke Orchestra

BOULEVARD OF MEMORIES, Mel Tormé with   15114
Walter Gross Orchestra
AND MIMI, Mel Tormé with Page Cavanaugh   15114
Trio

I CAN'T GIVE YOU ANYTHING BUT LOVE, Mel   528
Tormé with Page Cavanaugh Trio
THREE LITTLE WORDS, Mel Tormé with Page   528
Cavanaugh Trio

MY BABY JUST CARES FOR ME, Mel Tormé with   589
Page Cavanaugh Trio

A FOGGY DAY, Mel Tormé with Hal Mooney   589
Orchestra

I'LL ALWAYS BE IN LOVE WITH YOU, Mel Tormé   529
with Page Cavanaugh Trio

LOVE, YOU FUNNY THING, Mel Tormé with   529
Page Cavanaugh Trio

THE DAY YOU CAME ALONG, Mel Tormé with   530
Page Cavanaugh Trio

THE BEST THINGS IN LIFE ARE FREE, Mel Tormé   15118
with Page Cavanaugh Trio

MAGIC TOWN, Mel Tormé with Page   15118
Cavanaugh Trio

WHAT ARE YOU DOING NEW YEAR'S EVE, Mel   15116
Tormé with Page Cavanaugh Trio

BALLERINA, Mel Tormé with Page Cavanaugh   15116
Trio

IF I HAD A GIRL LIKE YOU, Mel Tormé with   573
Page Cavanaugh Trio

FINE AND DANDY, Mel Tormé with Page   573
Cavanaugh Trio

UNTIL THE REAL THING COMES ALONG, Mel   MGM10874
Tormé with Hal Mooney Orchestra

BUT BEAUTIFUL, Mel Tormé with Hal Mooney   538
Orchestra

NIGHT AND DAY, Mel Tormé with Hal Mooney   538
Orchestra

COTTAGE FOR SALE, Mel Tormé with Hal   573
Mooney Orchestra

LOVE IS THE SWEETEST THING, Mel Tormé with   ———
Hal Mooney Orchrestra

WHEN IS SOMETIME?, Mel Tormé with Hal   ———
Mooney Orchestra

"GONE WITH THE WIND," Mel Tormé with Hal   558
Mooney Orchestra

LITTLE WHITE LIES, Mel Tormé with Hal   558
Mooney Orchestra

WITH YOU, Mel Tormé with Hal Mooney   ———
Orchestra

I COVER THE WATERFRONT, Mel Tormé with   5009
Hal Mooney Orchestra

COUNTY FAIR, Mel Tormé with Hal Mooney   5009
Orchestra

MAKIN' WHOOPEE!, Mel Tormé with Hal   534
Mooney Orchestra

DO IT AGAIN, Mel Tormé with Hal Mooney   ———
Orchestra

DO-DO-DO, Mel Tormé with Sonny Burke   1177
Orchestra

GOOD-BYE, Mel Tormé with Sonny Burke   ———
Orchestra

SHE'S A HOME GIRL, Mel Tormé with Sonny   15379
Burke Orchestra

THERE ISN'T ANY SPECIAL PERSON, Mel Tormé   54-583
with Sonny Burke Orchestra

CAPITOL
1949–53

Singles:

CARELESS HANDS, Mel Tormé with Sonny   15379
Burke Orchestra

STOMPIN' AT THE SAVOY, Mel Tormé with   ———
Sonny Burke Orchestra

YOU'E GETTING TO BE A HABIT WITH ME, Mel   57-591
Tormé with Sonny Burke Orchestra

BLUE MOON, Mel Tormé with Peter Rugolo   15428
Orchestra

AGAIN, Mel Tormé with Peter Rugolo   ———
Orchestra

THE FOUR WINDS AND THE SEVEN SEAS, Mel   57-671
Tormé with Frank DeVol Orchestra

IT'S TOO LATE NOW, Mel Tormé with Frank   57-671
DeVol Orchestra

THE MEADOWS OF HEAVEN, Mel Tormé with Frank DeVol Orchestra	57-743
SONNY BOY, Mel Tormé with Frank DeVol Orchestra	57-743
OH YOU BEAUTIFUL DOLL, Mel Tormé with Frank DeVol Orchestra	57-751
THERE'S A BROKEN HEART FOR EVERY LIGHT ON BROADWAY, Mel Tormé with Frank DeVol Orchestra	57-751
THE BLOSSOMS ON THE BOUGH, Mel Tormé with Frank DeVol Orchestra	57-775
DON'T DO SOMETHING TO SOMEONE ELSE, Mel Tormé with Frank DeVol Orchestra	57-775
BLESS YOU (FOR THE GOOD THAT'S IN YOU), Mel Tormé with Peggy Lee and Lou Busch Orchestra	791
I HADN'T ANYONE TILL YOU, Mel Tormé with Peggy Lee and Lou Busch Orchestra	880
CROSS YOUR HEART, Mel Tormé with orchestra conducted by Harold Mooney	880
THE QUEEN OF HEARTS IS MISSING, Mel Tormé with orchestra conducted by Harold Mooney	825
THERE'S AN "X" IN THE MIDDLE OF TEXAS, Mel Tormé with Harold Mooney Orchestra	825
GEORDIE, Mel Tormé with orchestra conducted by Harold Mooney	880
SKYLARK, Mel Tormé with Pete Rugolo	1291
LULLABY OF THE LEAVES, Mel Tormé with Pete Rugolo	1291
THE PICCOLINO, Mel Tormé with Pete Rugolo	1000
BEWITCHED, Mel Tormé with Pete Rugolo	1000
RECIPE FOR ROMANCE, Mel Tormé with Pete Rugolo	1177
JUST IN CASE WE HAVE TO SAY GOODBYE, Mel Tormé with Pete Rugolo	———

I OWE A KISS TO A GIRL IN IOWA, Mel Tormé with Pete Rugolo	1237
SAY NO MORE, Mel Tormé with Pete Rugolo	1237
AROUND THE WORLD, Mel Tormé with Pete Rugolo	1383
THE SIDEWALK SHUFFLERS, Mel Tormé with Pete Rugolo	1383
A LONESOME CUP OF COFFEE, Mel Tormé with Pete Rugolo	————
SAILIN' AWAY ON THE HENRY CLAY, Mel Tormé with Pete Rugolo	1402
COME OUT SINGIN', Mel Tormé with orchestra conducted by Pete Rugolo	————
WHO SENDS YOU ORCHIDS, Mel Tormé with orchestra conducted by Joe Lipman	1598
YOU LOCKED MY HEART, Mel Tormé with orchestra conducted by Sid Feller	1598
BUNDLE OF LOVE, Mel Tormé with orchestra conducted by Joe Lipman	1524
THE WORLD IS YOUR BALLOON, Mel Tormé with orchestra conducted by Sid Feller	1524
THE ONE FOR ME, Mel Tormé with orchestra	————
LOVE IS SUCH A CHEAT, Mel Tormé with orchestra	1712
MY BUDDY, Mel Tormé with orchestra	5-1761
TAKE MY HEART, Mel Tormé with orchestra	5-1761
DON'T FAN THE FLAME, Mel Tormé with Peggy Lee and orchestra conducted by Sid Feller	5-1738
TELLING ME YES, TELLING ME NO, Mel Tormé with Peggy Lee and Sid Feller Orchestra	5-1738
YOU'RE A HEAVENLY THING, Mel Tormé with orchestra	5-1864
FOOLISH LITTLE RUMORS, Mel Tormé with orchestra	————
HEART AND SOUL, Mel Tormé with orchestra	————
I LOVE EACH MOVE YOU MAKE, Mel Tormé with orchestra	————

CALIFORNIA SUITE, Mel Tormé with the Mel-   P-200
Tones and chorus, and Hal Mooney
Orchestra

CORAL
October 1953–August 1954

Singles:
JUST ONE MORE CHANCE, with Neal Hefti and   CRL 9-61136
his Orchestra
ANYTHING CAN HAPPEN-MAMBO, with Neal
Hefti and his Orchestra

BLUE SKIES, with Neal Hefti and his   CRL 9-61089
Orchestra
OO YA YA, with Neal Hefti and his Orchestra
YES INDEED, with Sy Oliver Orchestra

Musical Sounds Are the Best Songs, with or-   CRL 57044
chestra conducted by George Cates and
Sonny Burke (LP)
Gene Norman Presents Mel Tormé "Live" at   CRL 57012
the Crescendo, with combo directed by Al
Pellegrini (LP)
Spellbound/All of You, with George Cates   CRL 9-61294
Orchestra (LP)
My Rosemarie/How, with the Mel-Tones and   CRL 9-61588
George Cates Orchestra (LP)

BETHLEHEM
August 1955–March 1957

It's a Blue World with orchestra conducted by   BCP 34
Al Pellegrini (LP)

Mel Tormé with the Marty Paich Dektette (LP)   BCP 52

AN INTERLUDE OF
BRITISH RECORDINGS ON DECCA
September 1956

Singles:
WALKIN' SHOES, with Ted Heath Orchestra   DFE 6384

CUCKOO IN THE CLOCK, with Ted Heath Orchestra	DFE 6384
WALTZ FOR YOUNG LOVERS, with Roland Shaw Orchestra	DEC 6384 /F 10809
I DON'T WANT TO WALK WITHOUT YOU, with Roland Shaw Orchestra	DEC 6384 /F 10809
THE SHENANDOAH VALLEY with Cyril Stapleton Orchestra	DEC 10809
HOORAY FOR LOVE, with Cyril Stapelton Orchestra	DEC 10809

BETHLEHEM
(cont'd)

Mel Tormé Sings Fred Astaire with the Marty Paich Dektette (LP)	BCP 6013
Porgy and Bess, with Mel Tormé, Frances Faye, Duke Ellington Orchestra, George Kirby, Frank Rossolino, and Others (3-record LP boxed set)	EXLP-1
Live at the Crescendo, with small group led by Marty Paich (LP)	BCP 6020
Mel Tormé's California Suite, Marty Paich arranger/conductor with the Bethlehem orchestra and chorus (LP)	BCP 6016
Songs for Any Taste (remainder of songs unused in *Live at the Crescendo)* (LP)	BCP 6031

PHILLIPS
Summer 1957

Singles:

EVERY WHICH WAY	PHILLIPS PB 728
TIME WAS	
Tormé Meets the British, with Wally Stott and His Orchestra (LP)	PHILLIPS BBL 7205

TOPS
November 1957

Prelude to a Kiss, with Marty Paich and His   TOPS L-1615
   Orchestra (LP)

VERVE
June 1958

Singles:

WALK LIKE A DRAGON   VER 10211

POOR WAYFARING STRANGER

                                           VER 2105

Tormé, with orchestra conducted by Marty
   Paich (LP)

Ole Tormé, with Billy May and His Orchestra   VER 6-2117
   (LP)

Back in Town, Mel Tormé with the Mel-   VER 2120
   Tones, Marty Paich, Conductor (LP)

Mel Tormé Swings Shubert Alley, with the   VER 8505
   Marty Paich Dektette (LP)

Swingin' on the Moon, with Russ Garcia   VER 2144
   Orchestra (LP)

Broadway, Right Now!, Mel Tormé and Mar-   VER 62146
   garet Whiting with Russ Garcia Orchestra
   (LP)

My Kind of Music, recorded in England with   VER 8440
   orchestra conducted by Geoff Love, Tony
   Osborne and Wally Stott (LP)

I Dig the Duke! I Dig the Count!, Mel Tormé   VER 2153
   with orchestra conducted by Johnny Man-
   del (LP)

ATLANTIC
1962–63

Singles:

COMIN' HOME BABY

RIGHT NOW   ATL SD-8069

CAST YOUR FATE TO THE WIND

THE GIFT   ATL 2183

MY GAL'S BACK IN TOWN

GRAVY WALTZ   ATL 2187

YOU CAN'T LOVE 'EM ALL

YOU BELONG TO ME   ATL 2202

Mel Tormé at the Red Hill Inn, with the   ATL 8066
  Jimmy Wisner Trio (LP)

Comin' Home Baby, with Shorty Rogers   ATL 8069
  Orchestra (LP)

Sunday in New York, with orchestra con-   ATL 8091
  ducted by Dick Hazard (LP)

COLUMBIA
1964–66

Singles (arranged by Ernie Freeman):

I KNOW YOUR HEART   4-43022

YOU'D BETTER LOVE ME   4-43022

ONE LITTLE SNOWFLAKE   4-43167

EVERYDAY'S A HOLIDAY   4-43167

THE POWER OF LOVE   4-43550

DOMINIQUE'S DISCOTHEQUE   4-43550

HANG ON TO ME   4-43677

ALL THAT JAZZ   4-43677

I REMEMBER SUZANNE   4-44180

LOVER'S ROULETTE   4-44180

LIMA LADY   4-44399

WAIT UNTIL DARK   4-44399

THE CHRISTMAS SONG, Mel Tormé with Pat   4-45283
  Williams Orchestra

That's All, A Lush Romantic Album, arranged,   CL-2318 (mono)
  conducted, and produced by Robert Mersey   CL-9118 (stereo)
  (LP)

Mel Tormé: Right Now (LP), arranged and   CS 9335
  conducted by Mort Garson

CAPITOL
1969–70

A Time for Us, with Jimmy Jones Orchestra
(LP)

SCO 52-80379

Raindrops Keep Fallin' on My Head, with
Jimmy Jones Orchestra (LP)

CAP ST-430

LIBERTY
1969–70

A Day in the Life of Bonnie and Clyde, with
Lincoln Mayorga Orchestra (LP)

LST-7560

Singles:
DIDN'T WE, with Shorty Rogers Orchestra
FIVE FOUR, with Shorty Rogers Orchestra

LIBERTY 56066

LONDON
early 1970s

Singles:
WHOSE GARDEN WAS THIS
MORNING STAR

LONDON 45-171

I CRIED FOR YOU
PHONE CALL TO THE PAST (arranged by Mel
Tormé)

LONDON 45-180

ATLANTIC
1974

Live at the Maisonette, with Al Porcino Orchestra (LP)

ATLANTIC SD-
18129

GRYPHON
1977–78

Tormé—A New Album, recorded in London
with Chris Gunning Orchestra (LP)

GRYPHON G-796

*Mel Tormé and Buddy Rich—Together Again
for the First Time,* with Buddy Rich Orchestra (LP)

GRYPHON G-784

(Also released on direct-to-disc CENTURY
CRDD-1100)

FINESSE
1981

Mel Tormé and Friends, with Gerry Mulligan,   FINESSE WX2
Janis Ian, Cy Coleman, and Jonathan   37484
Schwartz (double LP)

MISCELLANEOUS RECORDINGS
1981–88

Mel Tormé and Della Reese: Live in Concert,   MCA Laservision
with Edmonton Symphony, 1981 (Video-   No. 74-009
disc *only*)

Was (Not Was): Born to Laugh at Tornadoes,   Geffen GHS-4016
Mel Tormé sings one track, "Zaz Turned
Blue," 1982 (LP)

The Glenn Miller Orchestra: In the Digital   GRP-A-1002
Mood, Mel Tormé sings (for a lark) in the
vocal group, 1983 (LP)

Mel Tormé: Encore at Marty's, 1988 (LP)   FLAIR PG-8200

Barry Manilow: 2 A.M. Paradise Cafe, Mel   ARISTA AL-8-
Tormé sings one duet with Manilow, "Big   8254
City Blues, 1984" (LP)

CONCORD JAZZ
1982–

An Evening with George Shearing and Mel   CJ-190
Tormé, recorded live in April 1982, at
Mark Hopkins Hotel, San Francisco (LP)

Top Drawer: George Shearing/Mel Tormé (LP)   CJ-219

An Evening at Charlie's: Mel Tormé/George   CJ-248
Shearing (LP)

An Elegant Evening: George Shearing/Mel   CJ-294
Tormé (LP)

Mel Tormé, Rob McConnell and The Boss Brass   CJ-306
(LP)

A Vintage Year: Mel Tormé and George Shearing (LP)	CJ-341
In Preparation:	
Mel Tormé with the Marty Paich Dektette: Reunion (LP)	
Untitled Christmas LP by Mel Tormé and Full Orchestra	

RECENT RELEASES OF
OLDER MEL TORMÉ RECORDINGS,
AIR CHECKS, AND <u>TRANSCRIPTIONS</u> ON LPs

Mel Tormé Live with the Mel-Tones, air checks from the Mel Tormé radio show, circa 1948, Dean Elliott Orchestra (LP)	SOUNDS GREAT SG-5006
Mel Tormé Live with the Mel-Tones, same as above also featuring Sidney Miller and Janet Waldo or Barbara Eiler (LP)	SOUNDS GREAT SG-5012
Round Midnight: Mel Tormé, from a 1962 National Guard Show, with Shorty Rogers and His Giants (LP)	STASH-ST 252
Mel Tormé, MacGregor transcriptions released on Glendale Records, 1978 (LP)	GL 6007
Easy to Remember: Mel Tormé, MacGregor transcriptions released on Glendale Records, 1979 (LP)	GL 6018
Mel Tormé Sings About Love, World Broadcasting transcriptions, 1958; released on Audiophile, 1982 (LP)	AP-67
Mel Tormé: Legendary Singers collection, Time-Life, (4 LP boxed set)	————
The Mel Tormé Collection, recorded in Italy (LP)	DEJA VU DVLP 2046

INDEX

Abie's Irish Rose, 83
"Abraham," 50
Acosta, Rodolfo, 190
Adams, Don, 212
Adams, Franklin, Jr., 10–11
"Again," 152
Ah, Wilderness (O'Neill), 106
Air Corps band, 74, 76
Allen, Duane, 205
Allen, Steve, 23
"All the Things You Are," 344
Allyson, June, 104, 132
Anderson, Cat, 234
Anderson, Harry, 349–50
Andrews, Dana, 184, 213
Andrews, Nancy, 127
Anka, Paul, 189
Ankers, Evelyn, 68, 69
Archerd, Army, 251
Aristocrats, 23, 24
Arkin, Alan, 264
Arlen, Harold, 43, 188
Armed Forces Radio Service, 71
Armstrong, Louis, 24
Arnow, Max, 78
Artie Shaw Orchestra, 267
Artie Shaw Plays Cole Porter, 88
Ash, Paul, 11
Asner, Ed, 348
Astaire, Fred, 335
Atlanta Symphony Orchestra, 17, 325
Atlantic Records, 192–96, 214, 275
autobiographies, vii
Aylesworth, John, 199
Ayres, Mitch, 149

Baby (eagle), 270–71
Bacon, James, 257
Baer, Ben, 22
Baer, Ruth Sopkin, 22, 31–32
Ballard, Kaye, 149, 150
Balliett, Whitney, 326
Barnet, Charlie, 19, 24, 36, 48, 53
Bartlett, Sy, 2

Barzi, Tino, 131
Basehart, Diana, 302
Basehart, Gala, 302
Basehart, Richard, 302
Basie, Count, 18, 19, 36, 342
Basin Street East, 229, 230–35
Bateman, Kent, 266, 268, 269, 270
Bauduc, Ray, 17
Baxter, Anne, 348, 349
Baxter, Les, 70, 81
"Be a Ladies Man," 104
bebop, 179–80
Beckett, Scotty, 68
Behlmer, Rudy, 276, 303–305, 351
Behlmer, Sandy, 304
Bellis, Carroll, 339
Bellson, Louis, 139, 231, 343
Bennett, Tony, 65, 214, 215
Benny, Jack, 182–83
"Benny Rides Again," 344
Berg, George, 150
Berghof, Gary, 200
Bergman, Ingrid, 357
Berlin, Irving, 129, 188
Berlin, Larry, 22, 32
Berry, Bill, 343
"Best Things in Life Are Free, The," 104
Bethlehem Records, 167, 169, 179, 185,
   192
Beveridge, Betty, 70, 81, 142
"Beverly Hillbillies, The," 169
Biano, Solly, 78
Biberman, Abner, 249, 250
Big John (bodyguard), 206
"Big Noise from Winnetka," 19
Big Operator, The, 189
billing, 233–34
Billingsley, Glen, 103
Billingsley, Sherman, 103
"Black, Brown and Beige," 20
Blackhawk Restaurant, 3–5, 53
Blair, Sally, 185
Blane, Paul, 169–70
Blane, Ralph, 106

Block, Sandy, 89
Bloom, Jan, 358
blue laws, 57
"Blue Moon," 132, 133–35, 136, 140, 145, 331, 333
Blyden, Larry, 251
Bob Crosby band, 17, 19, 68
Bocage, 103, 120
Bogart, Humphrey, 79, 137
"Bonanza," 197
Borge, Victor, 63, 64
"Born to Be Blue," 83
Boston Globe, 121
Boston Strangler, The (Frank), 261
Bradford, John, 256
Bradley, Ed, 335
"Breaking Up Is Hard To Do," 299
Break It Up, 115, 127–28
Brennan, Walter, 251
Brewer, Teresa, 151
Britton, Barbara, 97
Brown, Bob, 336
Brown, John, 142
Brown, Les, 35, 93–94, 342
Bruce, Lenny, 186–87
Brynner, Yul, 348, 349
Buddy's Place, 275–77, 280–82, 324
Burke, Johnny, 83, 84, 103, 107, 124
Burke, Sonny, 113
Burke and Van Heusen, 83, 123
Burnett, Carol, 244, 253
Burns, David, 127
Buschhausen, Doug, 251–52
Busse, Ted, 278
Byner, John, 244

California Suite, 142
Call Me Mister, 152–53
"Camel Caravan," 44
Cameron, Rod, 109
Campbell, John, 352
Caniff, Milton, 109
Cantor, Eddie, 79
Capitol Records, 140, 142, 167, 254–55
Capp, Frankie, 343
"Captain Midnight," 10
"Careless Hands," 140
"Caribbean Clipper," 44
"Carioca," 37
Car Life, 149, 154
Carney, Harry, 234
"Carol Burnett Show, The," 247
Carousel, 354
Carroll, John, 82, 103
Carson, Johnny, 235, 319, 328–29, 330
Casino Gardens Ballroom, 87
Catlett, Sid, 268
Catlett, Walter, 68
Caught in the Draft, 75
Cavanaugh, Dave, 254–55
Challenge to Survive, 269–72
Champion, John, 109

Chan, Darlene, 267
Chaplin, Charlie, Jr., 189
Chapman, Mark, 188
Charisse, Cyd, 59
Chayevsky, Paddy, 255, 328, 330
"Cherokee," 344
Cherokee Arrows, 247–48
"Chicago," 89
Chicago *Daily News,* 53
Chicago *Herald,* 53
Chicago Tribune, 34, 53, 226
Chicago World's Fair (1933), 9–10
Chico Marx Orchestra, 46–62, 82, 94
"Christmas Song, The," 84, 97, 122, 298, 346
"Christmas Was Made for Children," 286
Cilento, Diane, 209
"Clarinet à la King," 268
Clark, Bobby, 49, 56, 57, 60, 61
Clark, Buddy, 35
Clavell, James, 190
Clemmons, Walter, 262
Cleopatra, 239–40
Cleveland Press, 143
Clinton, Larry, 35
Club De Lisa, 36, 60
Clyde, Red, 167, 185
Cochran, Steve, 189
Cohn, Harry, 78–79
  Toxton pursued by, 137, 138
Cole, Marie, 206
Cole, Nat, 84, 97, 100, 103, 123, 129, 205–206
Coleman, Cy, 331
Coleman, Dabney, 348
College Inn, 5
Collier, Ralph, 268
Collins, Cora Sue, 66
Columbia Records, 214–17, 255
"Comedian, The," 181–83, 184
"Comin' Home Baby," 193–94
Como, Perry, 23, 132, 149, 355
Concord Jazz Records, 196, 338
Conkling, Jim, 142
Connery, Sean, 209
Conniff, Ray, 216–17
Conroy, Cynthia, 205–208
Cookies, 193
Cool Elephant, The, 208–11, 229
Cooley, Lee, 149
Coon, Carlton, 4
Coon-Sanders Orchestra, 3–4
Cooper, Elise, 48, 49, 55, 57
Cooper, Gary, 120
Cooper, Jackie, 150
Cooper, Rocky, 120
Copacabana, 96, 105, 114
  Tormé's stint at, 115–21, 242
Copa Club, 124, 170–71
Corridor of Mirrors, 141
"County Fair, The," 83, 116, 117, 120
Courage, Sandy, 167

Courtney, Bob, 278
Cowan, Warren, 91
Coward, Noel, 188
Cox, Wally, 151
Crack in the World, 213
Crosby, Bing, 35, 39, 82, 83, 285–87, 355
Crosby, Bob, 17, 19, 68
Crosby, Harry, 286
"Cross and Cockade," 16, 203, 245
Crowd Roars, The, 113
Cummings, Jack, 141

Dailey, Dan, 152
Daley, William, 150
D'Amico, Johnny, 110
Dancing Lady, 162
Daniels, Billy, 130
Dankworth, John, 209
Darnell, Linda, 103
Davis, Miles, 169, 180, 323
Davis, Sammy, Jr., 165, 242, 254, 329
    Tormé's show with, 250–53
Dean, James, 168, 169
De Carlo, Yvonne, 103
Decca, 82–83
Dee, Mary, 59
Deegan, Vince, 70
De Haven, Gloria, 107
De Niro, Robert, 348, 357
Depression, Great, 5–6, 16–17
    movies and musicals during, 7
Derek, John, 137
Devil's Disciple, The, 210
Devine, Andy, 88
Dillinger, John, 121, 134
DiMaggio, Joe, 161, 164, 165
Disney, Walt, 83
Disruhd, Sheldon, 70
Dodds, Baby, 46
Dollarhide (Tormé), 248
Donahue, Phil, 328, 329–30
Dorothy (waitress), 55–57
Dorsey, Jimmy, 24, 42, 342
Dorsey, Pat Dane, 90, 91, 132
Dorsey, Tommy, 19, 20, 24, 38, 39, 42, 85, 86, 87, 89–91, 131–32, 141, 342
Douglas, Kirk, 210
Down Beat, 115, 120, 149, 192, 196, 323
Downs, Cathy, 113, 114
Downs, Orme, 23
Drew, Howard, 341
Dreyfuss, Richard, 348
Driscoll, Bobby, 68
"Drum Fantasy," 22
Drury, James, 248
Duchess of Idaho, The, 141–42
Dunham, Sonny, 35
Durante, Jimmy, 133
Durgom, Bullets, 141

Earp, Virgil, 249
"East Meets West," 61
Eberle, Ray, 50
Ebony Club, 130
Edgewater Beach Motel, 23
Edison Award, 289, 317, 323
Edwards, Blake, 108–13
Eiler, Barbara, 142
Eklund, Britt, 210
Eldridge, Roy, 26
Elixir (Tormé), 347
Ellington, Duke, 18, 19, 20, 21, 53, 88, 124, 150, 185, 191, 230–36, 323, 342, 344
Elliott, Dean, 100, 101, 142
Elman, Ziggy, 26, 38, 39, 85
Emmy Award, 337
England, Tormé in, 171, 172–76, 184–85, 203–204, 208–14, 241–42, 272, 290–94
Entertainer, The, 241
Entratter, Jack, 242–43
Erdman, Dick, 79
Errol, Leon, 63, 64
Ertegun, Ahmed, 192–94, 195
Ertegun, Nesuhi, 192–96
Evans, Bill, 326
Evans, Gil, 342
Evans, Linda, 348
"Evening at Charlie's, An," 348
Evening with George Shearing and Mel Tormé, An, 339
"Every Tub," 19, 344
Eythe, William, 127

Fagen, Donald, 188
Fain, Harry, 170
Fairseas, 294, 295, 300
Farentino, James, 244
Farlow, Tal, 150
Farrell, Frank, 235
Faye, Frances, 185
Fearmakers, The, 183–84, 190
Feist, Felix, 67
Ferrer, José, 124–25
Field, Shirley Anne, 241
Films of Errol Flynn, The, 304
Fine Arts String Quartet, 17
Finian's Rainbow, 122
Fink, Max, 298–99, 300, 304, 307
Fisher, Larry, 237
"Fitch Bandwagon," 88, 89
Fitzgerald, Ella, 149, 191–92, 289, 332
Florence, Bob, 343
"Fogettes," 126
Foley, Marie Agnes, 10, 11
Fonda, Jane, 356
Ford, Art, 95, 96, 116, 117, 125
Ford, Connie, 182
Ford, Glenn, 200, 262

Forsythe, John, 348
Fort MacArthur, 73–75
Forty-Second Street, 7, 162
Foster, Bill, 244
Francis, Freddie, 291, 292
Francis, Kevin, 291–92, 293, 294, 295, 309,
  310–14, 318, 320, 347
Frank, Gerold, 261
Frankenheimer, John, 181, 182
Franz, Pat, 252
Frazier, George, 120, 121
Freed, Arthur, 103–104, 105–106, 129,
  141
French, Winsor, 143–45
Freund, Fritzy, 24
Frigo, John, 49
Froman, Jane, 151
Frost, David, 210, 212, 213, 214, 219, 331–
  33
"Frozen Image, The," 243
"Funny Clothes," 251
Fun with Dick and Jane, 356

Gabbe, Lutz, Heller and Loeb, 185
Gable, Clark, 104
Garcia, Russ, 167
Gardner, Ava, 88, 89, 97–102, 103, 104–
  108, 120, 138, 165, 166
Gardner, Jimmy, 115, 127
Garland, Judy, vii, 66, 165, 197, 198–201,
  250, 256–62, 264, 288, 297, 330
Gastel, Carlos, 83, 84, 93–96, 100, 103,
  114, 117, 118–19, 121, 124, 126, 129,
  140, 149
Gazzara, Ben, 243
Gelinas, Gabe, 55
Gene Krupa Orchestra, 22, 71
General Artists Corporation Talent
  Agency, 95
Gershwin, Ira, 188
"Get Out of Town," 89
Getz, Stan, 125
Ghosts in English Houses, 172
Gillespie, Dizzy, 88, 179
Gillis, Ann, 66
Gilman, Lucy, 10
Gilmore Stadium, 104
Ginter, Bob, 322, 358
Girls' Town, 189
Glaser, Joe, 232–33, 234
"Goin' to Heaven on a Mule," 10
Gold Diggers, The, 7
Golden Gate Theatre, 94
Goodman, Benny, 17, 19, 42, 88, 125, 179,
  229, 266–69, 342
Good News, 103–106, 129
Gould, Lucille, 20–21
Goulet, Robert, 283
Grable, Betty, 152–54
Graham, Virginia, 259–61
Grainger, Gerry, 244
Grammy Awards, 289, 339–40, 348

Grant, Cary, 79, 160
Granz, Norman, 192
Gray, Jerry, 20, 342
Great Waldo Pepper, The, 241
Green, Buddy, 32
Green, Johnny, 124
Green, Mitzi, 96, 115, 116, 117, 119, 120
Greene, Milton, 165
Greer, Sonny, 20
Grenrock, Vic, 18, 21–22
Griffin, Chris, 267
Griffin, George, 185
Griffin, Merv, 159, 328
Griffres, Ethel, 64
Gross, Nate, 10
Gross, Walter, 125, 127
Gryphon Records, 289
Guest, Edgar A., 10
Guion, King, 71
Gunning, Chris, 317
Guns, 149, 245

Haas, Chuck, 189
Hackman, Betsy, 351
Hackman, Gene, 351, 357
Haines, Connie, 141
Hale, Barbara, 63, 64
Haley, Jack, 63, 64
Hall, Jon, 90
"Hallelujah!," 38
Hamilton, Jimmy, 234
Hamilton, John, 121
Hamilton, Lorry, 121
Hamilton, Michaela, 328
"Handy Man, The," 248–50
Hanks, Sam, 154–55
"Happy New Year U.S.A.," 350
Harburg, E. Y. (Yip), 122–24
Harlow, Jean, 133
Harrah's, 250, 251–53, 272
Harris, Bill, 150
Harris, Phil, 79
Hart, Lorenz, 132, 134, 333
Hart, Schaffner & Marx, 5, 8
Hartman, Grace, 63
Hartman, Paul, 63
Hartman, Johnny, 185
Hartman Theatre, 290
Harvey's, 242
"Have Yourself a Merry Little Christ-
  mas," 97
"Hawaiian War Chant," 38, 85
Hawks, Howard, 103
Haymer, Herbie, 71
Haymes, Dick, 25, 26, 29, 50, 355
Hayton, Lennie, 133
Heflin, Van, 97
Hefti, Neal, 142
Heindorf, Ray, 247
Heller, Betty Hope, 32
Hell's Angels, 255
Henderson, Fletcher, 20, 268–69, 342

Hendrix, Wanda, 79
Hepburn, Katharine, 251
Herman, Woody, 93, 94, 140, 141, 236,
    289, 326, 342, 348
Herman Herd, 140, 326
Hershey, Dale, 24, 28, 31, 32, 36
Higher and Higher, 60, 62–66
Hinckley, John, 188
Hird, Thora, 241–42, 278–79, 290,
    291
Hires Root Beer radio show, 82
Hollywood, Calif., 48
Hollywood Canteen, 77–79
Hollywood Hotel, 17
Hollywood Party, 133
Hollywood Reporter, 257
Holt, David, 66
Hope, Bob, 22, 39, 75
Horne, Lena, 289, 348
Horton, Bob, 215, 216
"How Long Has This Been Going On,"
    268
Hucksters, The, 104, 106, 108
Huggins, Roy, 243–44
Hughes, Howard, 102, 255
Hulman, Tony, 221
Hunter, Kim, 182
"Hut, The," 35
Hyde Park High School, 21, 22, 27–29,
    36, 45–46, 89

Ian, Janis, 188, 331
"In Chicago Tonight," 10
"Indiana," 125
Indiana Roof, 54
Inside Nazi Germany, 91–92
Inside Warner Bros. (Behlmer), 304
"I Saw You First," 63
"It Can Be Done," 10
It's a Blue World, 167–68
It's a Mad, Mad, Mad, Mad World, 240,
    241
"It Was a Very Good Year," 264–65

"Jack and Jill Players, The," 10
"Jack Armstrong," 10
Jagger, Dean, 180
"Jamboree Jones," 103, 116
James, Harry, 25–27, 29, 34, 153, 342
Janie Gets Married, 80
Japan, 237–39
Jarreau, Al, 348
jazz, 179, 324, 342–44
Jean, Gloria, 66, 67, 68
Jefferson, Carl, 196, 338
Jenkins, Gordon, 142
Jennings, Al, 132
Jessel, George, 119–20
Johnson, Van, 141
Jolson, Al, 10
Jones, Dick, 142
Jones, Jack, 244

Jones, Marcia Mae, 66
Jones, Shirley, 331, 332
Jones, Tommy, 73
"Judy Garland Show, The," 197–201, 247,
    256, 257, 283*n,* 293
"Just Imagine," 104

Kalcheim, Harry, 25, 39
Kalcheim, Henry, 25–26, 30, 39–40
Kalcheim, Nat, 25, 39
Kallen, Kitty, 88
Kaufman, Dave, 244
Kay, Hershey, 62
Kay, Stanley, 276, 280, 281
Kaye, Sammy, 35
Kelly, Gene, 68–69
Kelman, Fred, 159
Kennedy, George, 255
Kennedy, Revel, 255
Kenton, Stan, 71, 103
Kern, Jerome, 188
Kessel, Barney, 52
Keyes, Paul, 283–84
Kilgallen, Dorothy, 120, 121, 150
Killer McCoy, 113
Kimberly, Kim, 57
King, Dennis, 174
King, Larry, 330
King, Peggy, 149
Kirby, George, 185
Kleinfelter, Gil, 32
Knock on Any Door, 137
Knowles, Patric, 68
Koplin, Mert, 249
Korman, Harvey, 247
Kostak, Sophie, 23
Krupa, Gene, 17, 22, 35, 60, 71, 268
Kuralt, Charles, 336, 337

Ladd, Alan, 180
"Lady Be Good," 269, 289
"Lady's in Love with You, The," 22
Laine, Cleo, 209
Laine, Frankie, 123, 244
Lakeside Park Ballroom, 50, 61
Lamb, John, 231
"Lament for May," 19
"Lament to Love," 23, 26, 34–36, 40, 42
Lancaster, Burt, 210
Lancer, Martin, 183–84, 190
Landsburg, Alan, 264
Langosh, Paul, 345
Lanza, Mario, 45
Larroquette, John, 350
"Laugh-In," 282–85
Lawford, Peter, 98, 100, 101, 104, 137–138
Lawrence, Steve, 283, 284
Lawrence, Vicki, 247
Lee, Michele, 244
Lee, Peggy, 103, 142, 149, 332
Legrand, Michel, 289
Leitham, John, 352

Lemmon, Jack, 264
Leo Burnett Agency, 304
Leonard, Fat Jack, 229
Leonhart, Jay, 324, 352
Leslie, Joan, 79
"Let's Face the Music," 45
Let's Go Steady, 71, 77–78
Le Vien, Jack, 175
Levin, Mike, 115, 120
Lewis, Jerry, 272–73
Lewis, Joe E., 96, 118
Lewis, Sandy, 273
Lieberson, Goddard, 215–16
"Lightning Jim Whipple," 10
"Lights Out," 10
Lilley, Joe, 39
Lilley, Pauline, 290
Linder, Leslie, 209–10
Lishness, Niles, 23
Little, Jeannie, 303
Little, Rich, 199–200, 303
"Little Orphan Annie," 10
Littman, Lenny, 124, 170
Loeb, Bill, 185, 191
Loesser, Frank, 124
Logan, Ella, 122
London, Jimmy, 222–24
Lopez, John, 11
Lord, Del, 68
Lord, Jack, 190, 191
Lord, Sterling, 258, 327
Los Angeles City College, 66–67
Los Angeles Herald-Examiner, 257
Los Angeles High, 72
"Loveless Love," 45
Loy, Myrna, 5
"Lucky in Love," 104
Luft, Lorna, 259–61
Luft, Sid, 259
"Lulu's Back in Town," 169
Lunceford, Jimmie, 342
Lyon, Ben, 255–56
lyrics, reading of, 135

McBride, Raven (Evelyn), 109
McClure, Doug, 248
McConnell, Rob, 343
McCracken, Joan, 104
McDonald, Ray, 68, 104, 106
MacDonnell, Norman, 248
McGarity, Lou, 269
McGuire, Marcy, 63
McKusick, Hal, 150
McMickle, Mickey, 150
MacPhail, Doug, 68
Magic Town, 83
Mailer, Norman, 159
"Mairzy Doats," 344
Maize, Bob, 352
Maley, Peggy, 104–105
Manhattan Melodrama, 134
Manhattan Tower, 142

Mankewicz, Tom, 255
Mann, Herbie, 193
Mantee, Paul, 249
Mantz, Paul, 240
Manulis, Martin, 181–82, 183
March, Hal, 157–58
Margaret, Princess, 210
Margolis, Marvin, 31
marijuana, 49–50
Marilyn (Mailer), 159
Marsala, Marty, 49, 60–61
Marsalis, Wynton, 348
Marshall, Patricia, 104
Marshall, William, 64
Martin, David, 169
Martin, Dick, 253, 255, 282–85
Martin, Dolly, 253, 255, 282–83, 284
Marty's, 324–25, 331, 333–34
Marvin, Lee, 155–56
Marx, Albert, 88, 96
Marx, Chico, 46, 48, 49, 59–62
Marx, Groucho, 48
Marx, Harpo, 61
Masters, Frankie, 5
Maté, Rudy, 180
Matson, Boyd, 336–37
Matthews, Shirley, 23–24, 28, 31, 32, 36, 52, 53, 55, 60
Mattola, Tony, 127
Maxwell, Marilyn (Marvel), 23, 96–97, 98, 100, 101, 103, 104, 106–8
May, Billy, 20, 142
Mayehoff, Eddie, 151
Mellowlarks, 150
"Mel's Angels," 126
"Mel's Belles," 126
Mel-Tones, 54, 67, 70–72, 73, 78, 79, 93, 142
    armed services shows played by, 77
    dissolution of, 93–94, 96
    naming of, 71
    recordings of, 82–83, 88–89, 91
    on Yosemite trip, 80–82
Mel Tormé and Friends, 326, 331
Mel Tormé: Live at the "Maisonette," 275
"Mel Tormé Show" (television program), 149–51
"Mel Tormé Show, The" (radio program), 142
Memo from David O. Selznick, 304
Mercer, Johnny, 43, 44, 103, 124, 188
    "newsie-bluesies" written by, 45
    Tormé's friendship with, 82
Metronome, 53, 149, 192
MGM, 103, 104, 129–30, 132, 133, 189
M.G.-TC, 128–30, 149
Michaels, Marilyn, 244
Mickey Mouse Waddle Book, 15–16, 62
midget auto races, 104
Miles, Arlene (second wife), 170–78, 200, 219–20, 237, 316

Miles, Arlene (*cont.*)
  Tormé's divorce from, 201–203, 204,
    207–208, 224–28, 310
  Tormé's marriage to, 177–78, 186, 189,
    191, 194, 196, 197
  Tormé's parents and, 176–77
"Milkman's Matinee," 95
Miller, Glenn, 20, 42, 49, 82, 344
  Tormé's audition for, 42–44
Miller, Sidney, 66, 91, 92, 100, 142
Mills, Donna, 313
Mills, Jack, 127
Mills, Marty, 127
Milner, Martin, 190
Minelli, Liza, 259, 261, 262
Mitchelson, Marvin, 305, 307–10, 313,
  314, 315, 318–21
Mitchum, Robert, 97
Mocambo, 151–52
Modernaires, 49, 67, 70
Moe's Main Street, 143–46
Monkey Business, 160
Monroe, Marilyn, 159–66
Montalban, Georgiana, 255, 302
Montalban, Ricardo, 244, 255, 302
Moone, Billy, Jr., 20, 342
Mooney, Hal, 142
Moore, Dudley, 209, 210
Moore, Garry, 244
Moreno, Rita, 280
Morgan, Michele, 63, 64
Morgan, Russ, 35
Morrow, Buddy, 343
Moseley, Roy, 291–92, 317
motorcycles, 196, 247
"Mountain Greenery," 132, 171, 172, 174,
  331
"Movie Game Show, The," 251
Movieland Magic, 80
movies, 7, 8, 48, 356–57
Mulligan, Gerry, 323, 326, 331, 338
Mundy, Jimmy, 20
Muni, Paul, 357
Munnell, William, 224–25, 226
Musicraft, 88, 96, 113, 115, 125–26
muscular dystrophy telethon, 272–
  173
My Darling Clementine, 113

Napoleon, Marty, 49, 55, 56
Nathan, Anna Lee, 301–302
Nathan, Robert, 301–302
Nelson, Skip, 50, 53, 55, 57
Nero, Peter, 196, 339–40, 352
New York, N.Y., 39–41, 325
  Chico Marx Orchestra's appearance in,
    59–61
New Yorker, 326
New York Post, 235
New York Times, 229, 257, 326
Niesen, Gertrude, 115
Night and Day, 79, 80

"Night Court," 349–50
Night Light, 190
Night of 100 Stars, 348
Nijinsky, Vaslav Fomich, 2
Nixon, Marion, 255
Noalls, Jim, 191, 192
No Highway in the Sky, 211, 256
Noone, Jimmie, 46
Norman, Freddy, 49, 50
Norman, Gene, 186
Norvo, Red, 150
Norway, S.S., 345–46

O'Brien, Edmond, 180–81, 182, 183
O'Connor, Carroll, 283
O'Connor, Donald, 65, 66, 91–92, 100
O'Connor, Ginny, 70, 81
O'Day, Anita, 326, 334
"Official Mel Tormé Fan Club," 126
Ohio Theatre, 54
"Oh Johnny, Oh Johnny, Oh!," 344
Okinawa, 237, 238, 239–40
O'Neill, Eugene, 106
O'Neill, Hank, 346
open-voiced harmonies, 70
"Opus No. 1," 89
orgies, 130
Oriental Theatre, 60
Osborne, Don, Jr., 273–74, 299, 300, 324,
  345
Osborne, Gail, 299, 300
Other Side of the Rainbow, The (Tormé),
  256–62, 264, 288, 330
"Over the Rainbow," 122
Owens, Gary, 284

Pacelli, Frankie, 11
Page Cavanaugh Trio, 103
Paich, Marty, 167, 169, 229
Palace, 54
Paley, William, 150
Palladium, 71
Panhandle, 109
Panico, Louis, 5
Paramount Theatre, 124, 125, 139–40, 149
Pardon My Rhythm, 66–69, 71
Parke, Bernie, 70, 71, 81
Parker, Charlie, 180
Parker, Lew, 127
Pasternak, Joe, 141
Paul Masson Winery Music Festival, 351
Peabody Award, 348
Pearl Harbor, Hawaii, Japanese attack on,
  40–41
Peck, Charlie, Jr., 115
Peck, Gregory, 264
Pederson, Tommy, 343
Pellegrini, Al, 143, 146–48, 150, 151, 154,
  155, 167, 169
Pellegrini, Norma, 143
People, 196

Peppiatt, Frank, 199
Perelman, S. J., 126, 144
Petrie, Julius, 145–46
Pettigrew, Arch, 22, 23
Pevney, Joe, 115
Pffaf, Alton, 204
Pffiferling, Joe, 336, 337
Phi Alpha Phi, 29, 31, 36
Pied Pipers, 67
Piper Aircraft Corporation, 205, 248
Pittsburgh Press, 125
"Playhouse 90," 181, 183
Plimpton, George, 255
Plimpton, Jean, 23
Podell, Jules, 115, 117, 120
Poister, John, 24, 28, 31, 46, 53, 60
   "Let's Face the Music" and, 45
   on Tormé's Chico Marx Orchestra
      days, 53–54
   Tormé's fame announced by, 27–28,
      30, 32–33
Pollack, Ben, 42, 45, 46, 47, 48–49, 52, 57,
   60–61, 62, 66–67, 77–78, 82, 94
pop-up books, 15–16, 62
Porcino, Al, 275
Porgy and Bess, 185
Porter, Cole, 79
Porter, Jean, 80, 82
Powell, Dick, 88, 89
Powell, Mel, 269
Preisser, June, 71
Presley, Elvis, 187
Presnell, Harvey, 244
Previn, André, 167
Prince of Wales Theatre, 174
Pringle, Norm, 270
Private Lives, 188
Private Lives of Adam and Eve, The, 190
Prophet, The (Gibran), 346
Proser, Monte, 96, 115, 117
"Prosschai," 37
Pulagi, Danny, 18
Purdom, Edmund, 209

radio:
   Tormé's career on, 10–11
   Tormé's early love of, 3–4
   Tormé's New York exposure on, 95–
      96, 116, 117
   Tormé's program on, 142
"Radio Auditions Finals," 9–10
Rae, Jackie, 221
Rand, Jess, 254
Randall, Tony, 237, 238
Raskin, Milt, 71
Rawlinson, Peter, 309
Raye, Martha, 71
Reagan, Nancy, 339–40
Reagan, Ronald, 339–40
Reasoner, Harry, 331, 333, 334, 335–
   336
record rooms, 143, 146, 149

Redford, Robert, 357
Red Hill Inn, 193
Redlich, Heidi, 225, 228
Redlich, Howard, 225–28, 299
Redwing, Rod, 190–91
Reed, Rex, 290
Reed, Rufus, 324
Reid, Don, 26, 27, 29, 30, 32
Reilly, Charles Nelson, 244
"Reminiscing in Tempo," 19
Renfro, Brian, 270, 272
Renzi, Mike, 324, 345
Revellis, 49, 67
"Revelli's Serenade," 51
Rich, Buddy, 36–39, 65, 86, 89, 129, 187,
   290, 342
   death of, 359
   Dorsey Orchestra quit by, 89–90
   jokes played on Tormé by, 275–76,
      280–82, 290
   Tormé's first encounter with, 85–87
   Tormé's Paramount stint with, 139–40
Rich, Marie, 280
Rickey, Bobby, 85
Rio, Frank, 325
Risdon, Elizabeth, 64
Ritz, Betty, 153
Ritz, Harry, 153
Ritz, The, 280
Rivers, Joan, 232
Robbins, Fred, 95, 96, 116, 117, 125
"Robbins' Nest," 95
Robertson, Cliff, 203–204, 244, 245
Robinson, Edward G., 244, 253–54
Robinson, Jane, 253
Robison, Willard, 44
rock and roll, 179, 180, 324
"Rockin' in Rhythm," 230
Rockwell, Tom, 95, 126
Rodgers, Dorothy, 331, 333
Rodgers, Richard, 124, 133, 134–35, 331–
   33
Rogers, Buddy, 5
Rogers, Shorty, 229
Rogosin, Joel, 248
"Roll 'Em," 19
Romney, Edana, 305
Rooney, Mickey, 66, 107, 112–13, 120,
   132–33, 135–136, 181–83, 189, 190
Rose, Glenn, 91–92
Rosenberg, Rich, 325
Rosenbloom, Larry, 278, 303
Rosenbloom, Stephanie, 279, 303
Rosenstein, Sophie, 79
Ross, Lanny, 35
Ross, Marty, 277, 280, 281, 324, 325
Ross, Shirley, 22, 134
Rowan, Dan, 283
Roxy, 59–61, 159
Run for Your Life series, 243–44, 248
Ryan, Irene, 169
Ryan, Peggy, 66

Saeta, Judge, 314, 323
Safer, Morley, 334, 335
Sahl, Mort, vii
Sanders, Joe, 4
Sands, 242–43, 250
San Juan, Olga, 180
Sarris, Andrew, 257
Saunders, Red, 60, 61
Sauter, Eddie, 269, 342
Savini, Bob, 255
Scheffler, Phillip, 334, 335
Schlatter, George, 197, 282–83
Schoolkids, The, *see* Mel-Tones
Schroeder, Carl, 352
Schwartz, Jonathan, 273, 331
Schwartz, Norman, 289, 317, 331
Scott, James, 241, 278–79, 290
Scott, Janette (third wife), 210–14, 218–
    222, 227, 231, 234–35, 252, 255–56,
    263, 264, 271, 272, 273, 284, 285, 290,
    347
  in custody battle, 309–12, 313–14
  pregnancies of, 247, 253–54, 265–66
  Tormé left by, 295–305
  Tormé's divorce from, 318–21, 326
  Tormé's marriage to, 236, 237–40
Scrima, Mickey, 25, 26, 27, 37, 79
Segal, John, 32
Sellers, Peter, 210
Senior, John, 146–48
"September Song," 151
"Serenade in Blue," 344
"Sergeant Was Shy, The," 19
Serling, Rod, 181
Severson, Ali (fourth wife), 65, 314–17,
    320, 322–23, 336, 340
  Tormé's marriage to, 345–47, 349
Seymour, Jane, 313
Shakespeare Grammar School, 11
  Drum and Bugle Corps of, 17
Shatner, William, 270
Shaw, Artie, 36, 88–89, 91, 93, 120, 266–
    67, 276, 344
Shaw, George Bernard, 353
Shearing, Ellie, 338, 345
Shearing, George, 323, 326, 336, 338–339,
    340, 345, 348, 352
Sheets, Dale, 250, 252, 254, 300, 322, 325,
    337, 340, 348
Sheets, Joan, 300, 322
Shelbyville, Ind., 35–36
Sherock, Shorty, 71
Shevelove, Bert, 231
Shigeta, James, 190
Shire, Shelley, 345
Shore, Dinah, 35, 79, 348
"Show Band Show," 172
Shribman, Joe, 201, 214, 215, 216, 230–
    231, 232–33, 234, 242, 254
Shute, Nevil, 256
sight-reading, 181–82

Simms, Ginny, 79
Sinatra, Frank, 25, 38–39, 60, 62–65, 86,
    87, 115, 125, 243, 331, 354,
    355
  on *Higher and Higher* set, 63–64
Sinatra, Nancy, 65
"Sing, Sing, Sing," 17, 143, 269
singers, 306–307
"Singers, The," 244–45
"Sing Me a Swing Song and Let Me
    Dance," 39
Six Hits and a Miss, 49, 70
"$64,000 Challenge, The," 249
"60 Minutes," 333–36
Skar, Manny, 220, 225–26
Skelton, Red, 220
Sklar, Dan, 202, 224–25, 226
Slatkin, Bert, 303
Slatkin, Muriel, 303
Smeck, Roy, 35
"Snowman," 269–72
"So Dear to My Heart," 83
"Soliloquy," 354
Solley, Fern, 300
Solley, John, 277, 278–80, 300
Some Like It Hot, 22
"Some Like It Hot," 22
"Song of India," 19, 45
"Song of the City," 10
Sopkin, Ben, 7
Sopkin, Dora, 8, 9, 17, 19
Sopkin, George, 17
Sopkin, Harry, 8, 19
Sopkin, Henry, 17
Spano, Joe, 348
Speed Age, 149
Spivak, Charlie, 53, 71, 85, 126
Spooky (dog), 156–57
SS-100 Jaguar, 174–75, 176
Stack, Bob, 83
Stanley Theatre, 55
Stapelton, Cyril, 172
Star Is Born, A, 200
"Star Trek: The Next Generation," 347–
    48
Stein, Sol, 327–28, 330
Stein & Day, 327–28
Stephens, Phil, 71
Steubenville, Ohio, 57
Stevens, Stella, 313
Stewart, James, 256
Stineway Drugstore, 10
"Story of Mary Marlin, The," 10
Stott, Wally, 212, 229, 242
"Stranger in Town, A," 54, 82
Streep, Meryl, 357
Streisand, Barbra, 198
Stromberg-Carlson Cathedral radio, 3, 4
Summer Holiday, 106–107
Sunday in New York, 196
"Sunday Morning," 336, 337

"Sunny Side of the Street," 89
"Swingtime," 71

Tainan, 238–39
Taiwan, 237, 238
"Take the 'A' Train," 344
Talk of the Town, 241, 242, 290, 291
Tallman, Frank, 240–41
Taurog, Norman, 132, 133, 136
"Tenderly," 125
Tessler, Leonard, 340
"That Old Black Magic," 344
"This Love of Mine," 38
Thomas, Betty, 348
Thomas, Danny, 153
Thompson, Kay, 70
"Thompson Man, The," *see Wynner*
"Three Little Fishies," 344
Tilton, Martha, 54
Times (London), 257
Tivoli Theatre, 7, 22, 168
"Today" show, 336–37
Together Again for the First Time, 129
Tommy Dorsey Band, 25, 37, 38, 87, 89
"Tonight" show, 235
Top Drawer, 339
Tormé, Albert (uncle), 2, 3, 8–9, 11, 13–14, 358
Tormé, Arthur (uncle), 2, 8, 11–12, 15–18, 25, 26, 30, 226, 358
Tormé, Betty Sopkin (mother), 2, 3, 8, 358
Tormé, Daisy (daughter), 254, 265, 266, 271, 285, 294, 298, 302, 305, 310, 311, 318, 319, 347
Tormé, Faye (aunt), 2, 358
Tormé, Grandma, 9
Tormé, Ira (cousin), 226, 358
Tormé, James Scott (son), 266, 273, 294, 298, 305, 310, 311, 318, 319
Tormé, Melissa (daughter), 157, 158, 172, 186, 241, 297, 348
Tormé, Melvin Howard:
  army induction of, 72–77
  articles written by, 147, 154, 229, 245, 326
  books written by, 256–62
  as child performer, 4–5, 9
  Copacabana stint of, 115–21
  Davis's performing style compared with, 253
  drums played by, 4, 17, 19, 61–62, 71, 89–90, 150, 168, 352
  in earthquake, 263–64
  in family singalongs, 3
  fan clubs of, 126
  first movie appearance of, 11
  first professional experiences of, 4–5, 11
  first song sung by, 3
  flat feet of, 72–73, 76–77

flying enjoyed by, 203–204, 205, 221–224, 245, 247–48
  in grammar school, 11
  gun collecting of, 73–74, 148, 156–157, 245, 277–80, 319, 357–58
  heroes of, 355–56
  innocence lost by, 55–57
  Judy Garland show and, 197–201, 247, 258, 293
  model building as hobby of, 16, 186
  movies loved by, 7, 8, 48, 159–60, 283, 356
  piano lessons of, 20–21
  as radio actor, 10–11
  record collecting of, 17, 18
  school violence and, 11–13
  screen tests of, 60, 67, 78
  solo debut of, 103
  songwriting of, 19, 20–21, 23, 34–36, 43, 54, 82–84, 106
  teleplays written by, 243–45, 248
  as "velvet fog," 95, 167, 179, 335, 355
Tormé, Myrna (sister), 5, 11, 66, 93, 100, 138
Tormé, Steven Michael (son), 154, 156, 158, 172, 186, 241, 297, 347, 348
Tormé, Tracy (son), 186, 191, 194, 196, 202, 204–205, 208, 214–15, 216, 219, 220, 224, 225–28, 237, 246, 253, 263, 265, 297, 298–300, 311
  television career of, 347–48
Tormé, William (father), 2, 7, 8, 9, 11, 12, 13, 15–16, 42, 66, 358
Tormé: A New Album, 317
"Touch of Your Hand, The," 87
Tough, Davey, 268
Tourneur, Jacques, 184
Towne, Cleveland, 11
Toxton, Candy (first wife), 64, 137–38, 152, 170, 172, 191, 206, 241, 316
  Tormé's first encounters with, 131–132, 133
  Tormé's marriage to, 138–39, 140–141, 150–51, 153, 155, 157–58, 165, 167
Tracy, Spencer, 357
"Traffic Jam," 37
"Trouble Is a Girl," 103, 116
Tucker, Sophie, 116, 121
Tunnell, George "Bon Bon," 38
"TV's Top Tunes," 149
Twelve O'Clock High, 2
"20/20," 336–37
"Two O'Clock Jump," 25

Updike, John, 348

Van, Bobby, 244
Van Doren, Mamie, 189, 190
Van Heusen, Jimmy, 64–65, 83, 103, 107, 124
Vannerson, Leonard, 267

Variety, 244
Vaughan, Sarah, 88, 348
Vaundry, Gordon, 23
Verve Records, 192
Villipigue, Paul, 142
"Virginian, The," 248, 249

Waggoner, Lyle, 247
Wagner, Ron, 278
Waldo, Janet, 142
Walk Like a Dragon, 190–91
Wallop, Douglass, 190
Walters, Teddy, 88
Waring, Fred, 35
Warner Brothers, 78–79, 80
Warren, Harry, 107
Wasserman, Lew, 250
Waters, Ethel, 1, 6
Watson, Nancy, 300, 305
Wayne, John, 151–52
Weaver, Marjorie, 68
Webb, Chick, 17, 192
Weege, Reinhold, 350
Weems, Ted, 23, 97
Weill, Kurt, 151
Wein, George, 323, 325–26, 350
Weitz, Bruce, 348
Wells, Bob, 82–84, 91, 100, 104, 106, 107–
    108, 109–10, 113, 114, 115, 117, 119,
    121, 122, 127–28, 130, 167, 256, 298
"We're in the Money," 7
Weston, Paul, *see* Wetstein, Paul
Wet Parade, The, 283
Wetstein, Paul (Paul Weston), 49
Wettling, George, 46, 49, 55, 61
Wexler, Jerry, 196
"What Is This Thing Called Love?," 89
What Price Glory, 160
Whelan, Tim, 63
White, Betty, 351
Whiting, Margaret, 97

Whitman, Stu, 203
Whitman Publishing Company, 15–16
"Whose Sweet Patootie Are You?," 11
Wicker, Ireene, 10
Wicker, Walter, 10
Wickes, Mary, 64
Widmark, Richard, 264
Wilder, Alec, 103
Willi, Arthur, 59–60, 62
William Morrow and Company, 258, 259
William Penn Hotel, 55
Williams, Andy, 104, 214, 215, 217
Williams, Esther, 97, 141
Williams, Joe, 348
Williams, Paul, 188
"Willow Road," 83, 123
Wilson, Earl, 120, 121
Wilson, Larry, 277, 278, 279
Wilson, Teddy, 326
Winters, Eileen, 255
Winters, Jonathan, 255
"Wire Brush Stomp," 22
Wisner, Jimmy, 231
Witching Hour, The (Tormé), 347
Wolper, David, 264
Wonder, Stevie, 188
Wonder Bar, 10
Words and Music, 132–36, 141, 331
Wright, O. K., 248–49
Wynn, Keenan, 154, 155, 156–57, 196
Wynn, Sharley, 154
Wynner (Tormé), vii–viii, 288–89, 327–
    328, 329, 330

Yankee Inn, 146–48
Young, Lester "Pres," 19
"You're Driving Me Crazy," 3–4, 113–
    114
"You're the Top," 79

Zugsmith, Albert, 189, 190
Zumbach, Mr., 128, 129, 174–75